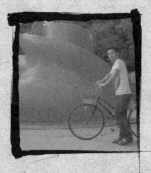

It's evening, and getting darker. I look around and notice the area is deserted. "I have to hurry to the station," I think to myself, and just then, from the other direction, I hear the *kriik kriik* sound of a bicycle. An old man with a huge head is slowly coming toward me. (By the way, this scene was the inspiration for the Ungaikyo episode.) I sprint away as fast as I can, but I still wonder what that was all about.

—HIROSHI SHIIBASHI, 2009

HIROSHI SHIIBASHI debuted in BUSINESS JUMP magazine with *Aratama*. NURA: **RISE OF THE YOKAI CLAN** is his breakout hit. He was an assistant to manga artist Hirohiko Araki, the creator of *Jojo's Bizarre Adventure*. *Steel Ball Run* by Araki is one of his favorite manga.

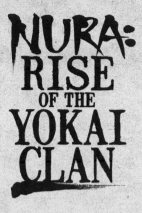

NURA: RISE OF THE YOKAI CLAN

NURA: RISE OF THE YOKAI CLAN
VOLUME 3
SHONEN JUMP Manga Edition

Story and Art by HIROSHI SHIIBASHI

Translation – Yumi Okamoto
Adaptation – Mark Giambruno
Touch-up Art and Lettering – Gia Cam Luc
Graphics and Cover Design – Fawn Lau
Editor – Daniel Gillespie

Printed in the U.S.A.

Published by VIZ Media, LLC
P.O. Box 77010
San Francisco, CA 94107

10 9 8 7 6 5 4 3 2 1
First printing, June 2011

www.viz.com www.shonenjump.com

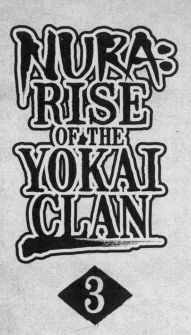

NURA: RISE OF THE YOKAI CLAN

3

THE NURA CLAN ASSEMBLY

STORY AND ART BY
HIROSHI SHIIBASHI

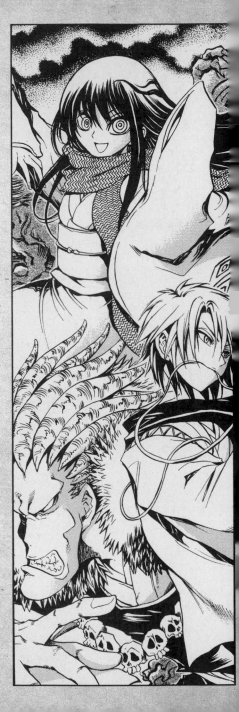

CHARACTERS

NURARIHYON

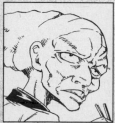

Rikuo's grandfather and the Lord of Pandemonium. He intends to pass leadership of the Nura clan—leaders of the yokai world—to Rikuo.

RIKUO NURA

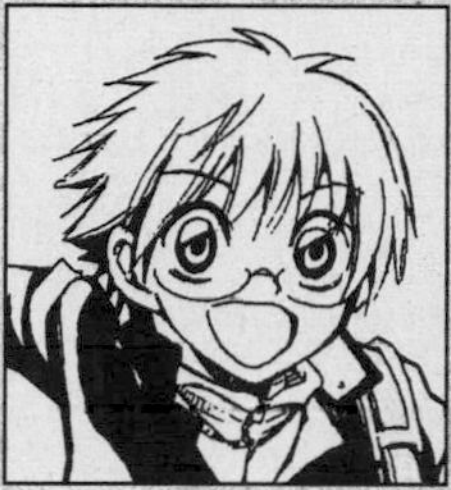

Though he appears to be a human boy, he's actually the grandson of Nurarihyon, a yokai. His grandfather's blood makes him one-quarter yokai, and he transforms into a yokai at times.

KIYOTSUGU

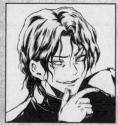

Rikuo's classmate. He has adored yokai ever since he was saved by Rikuo in his yokai form, leading him to form the "Kiyojuji Paranormal Patrol."

KANA IENAGA

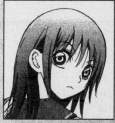

Rikuo's classmate and a childhood friend. Even though she hates scary things, she's a member of the Kiyojuji Paranormal Patrol for some reason.

YUKI-ONNA

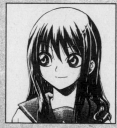

A yokai of the Nura clan who is in charge of looking after Rikuo. She disguises herself as a human and attends the same school as Rikuo to protect him from danger. When in human form, she goes by the name Tsurara Oikawa.

YURA KEIKAIN

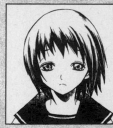

Rikuo's classmate and a descendant of the Keikain family of onmyoji. She transferred into Ukiyoe Middle School to do field training in yokai exorcism. She has the power to control her shikigami and uses them to destroy yokai.

AOTABO

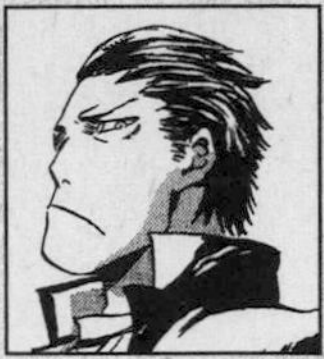

Another Nura clan yokai who, along with Yuki-Onna, looks after and protects Rikuo when he attends school. He uses the name Kurata when disguised as a human.

ZEN

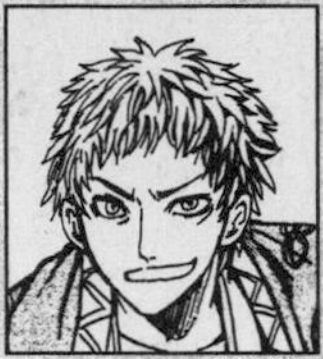

The leader of Zen Group, a branch of the Nura clan. He's a bird yokai who can produce medicine and poisons, and is physically fragile due to that special quality. He has undergone the "brotherhood" rite with Night Rikuo, in which they interlocked arms and drank sake together.

GYUKI

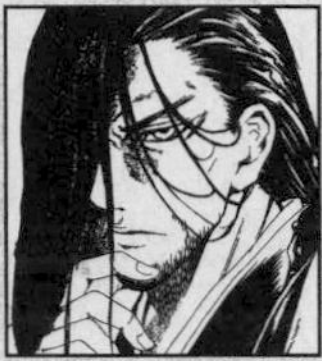

Leader of the Gyuki Clan (part of the Nura Syndicate), he also holds an executive position in the Nura Clan, but is trying to kill Rikuo. What could be his motivation for such an act?!

SHIMA

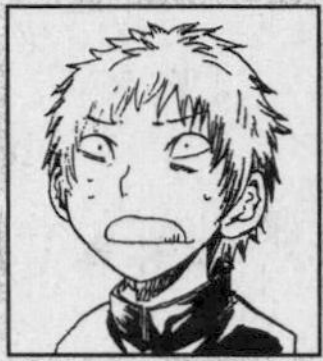

Rikuo's classmate, an acquaintance he's known since grade school. He's part of Kiyotsugu's circle and a member of the Kiyojuji Paranormal Patrol.

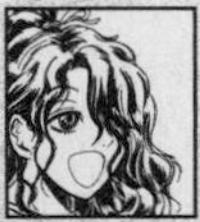

KEJORO

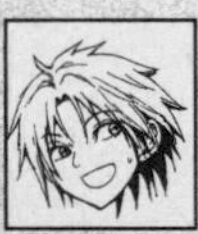

KUBINASHI

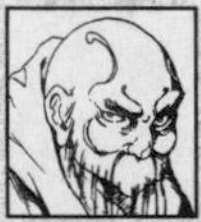

MOKUGYO-DARUMA

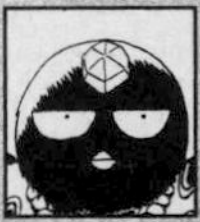

KARASU-TENGU

STORY SO FAR

Rikuo Nura, a student at Ukiyoe Middle School, appears to be a normal boy. In actuality, he is the grandson of Nurarihyon—the Lord of Pandemonium—and is the young heir apparent to the leadership of the Nura clan, the yokai headquarters. He is expected to become a great Supreme Commander like his grandfather, but in the meantime lives his days as a human being.

As part of his plans to destroy the Nura clan, the rat yokai Kyuso kidnaps Yura and Kana. Rikuo transforms into his yokai form and successfully defeats Kyuso, saving the girls and his clan from a life-or-death predicament. However, the one pulling Kyuso's strings from the shadows is none other than Nura clan executive Gyuki! Unaware of this, Rikuo embarks on a trip with Kiyotsugu and the members of the Kiyojuji Paranormal Patrol. Their destination is Mt. Nejireme, where many yokai legends persist even to this day. Coincidentally, it's also the mountain where Gyuki's residence is located...

After the Kiyojuji Paranormal Patrol members arrive at Mt. Nejireme, Rikuo gets uneasy and suggests leaving the mountain, but is overruled. Later, Gyuki's henchmen—who are successful at making their prey remain on the mountain—ferociously attack the Kiyojuji Paranormal Patrol! In this moment of crisis, Rikuo transforms and fights back. Then, he marches alone into the residence at the summit and confronts Gyuki. Finally, the curtains open to reveal this life-or-death battle!

TABLE OF CONTENTS

NURA:RISE OF THE YOKAI CLAN

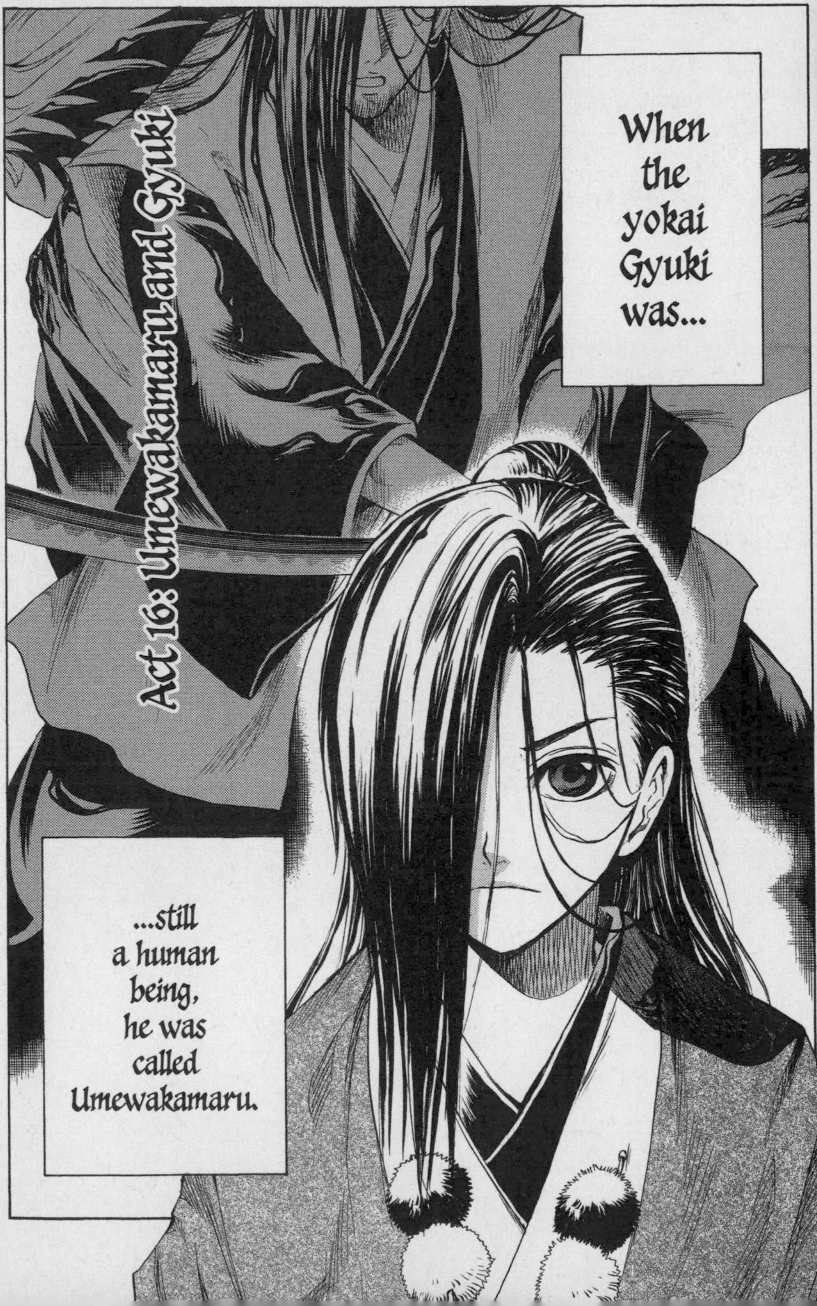
When the yokai Gyuki was...
Act 16: Umewakamaru and Gyuki
...still a human being, he was called Umewakamaru.

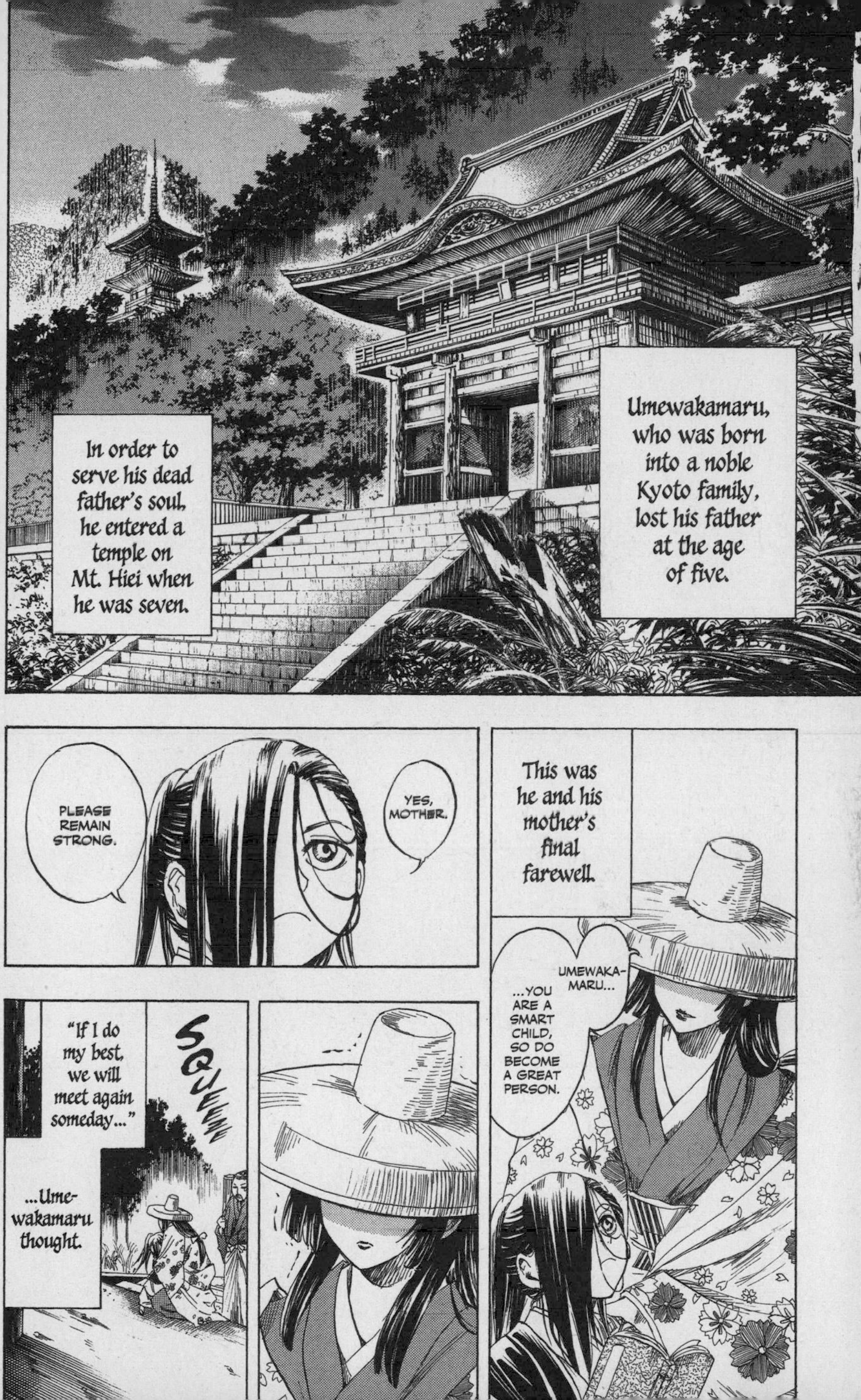
Umewakamaru, who was born into a noble Kyoto family, lost his father at the age of five.
In order to serve his dead father's soul, he entered a temple on Mt. Hiei when he was seven.
This was he and his mother's final farewell.
UMEWAKA-MARU...
...YOU ARE A SMART CHILD, SO DO BECOME A GREAT PERSON.
PLEASE REMAIN STRONG.
YES, MOTHER.
"If I do my best, we will meet again someday..."
SQUEEE
...Ume-wakamaru thought.

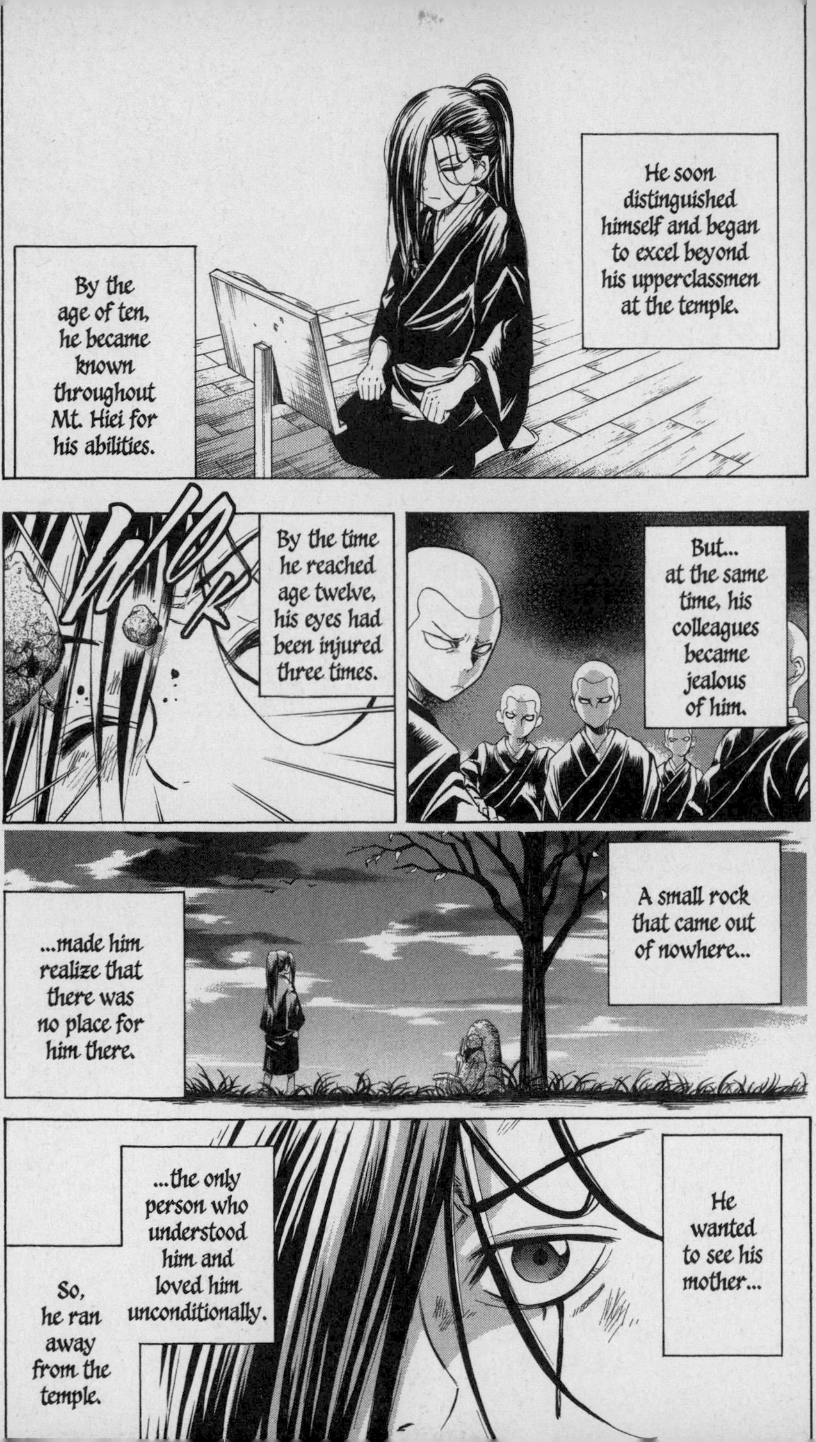
He soon distinguished himself and began to excel beyond his upperclassmen at the temple.
By the age of ten, he became known throughout Mt. Hiei for his abilities.
But... at the same time, his colleagues became jealous of him.
By the time he reached age twelve, his eyes had been injured three times.
A small rock that came out of nowhere...
...made him realize that there was no place for him there.
He wanted to see his mother...
...the only person who understood him and loved him unconditionally.
So, he ran away from the temple.

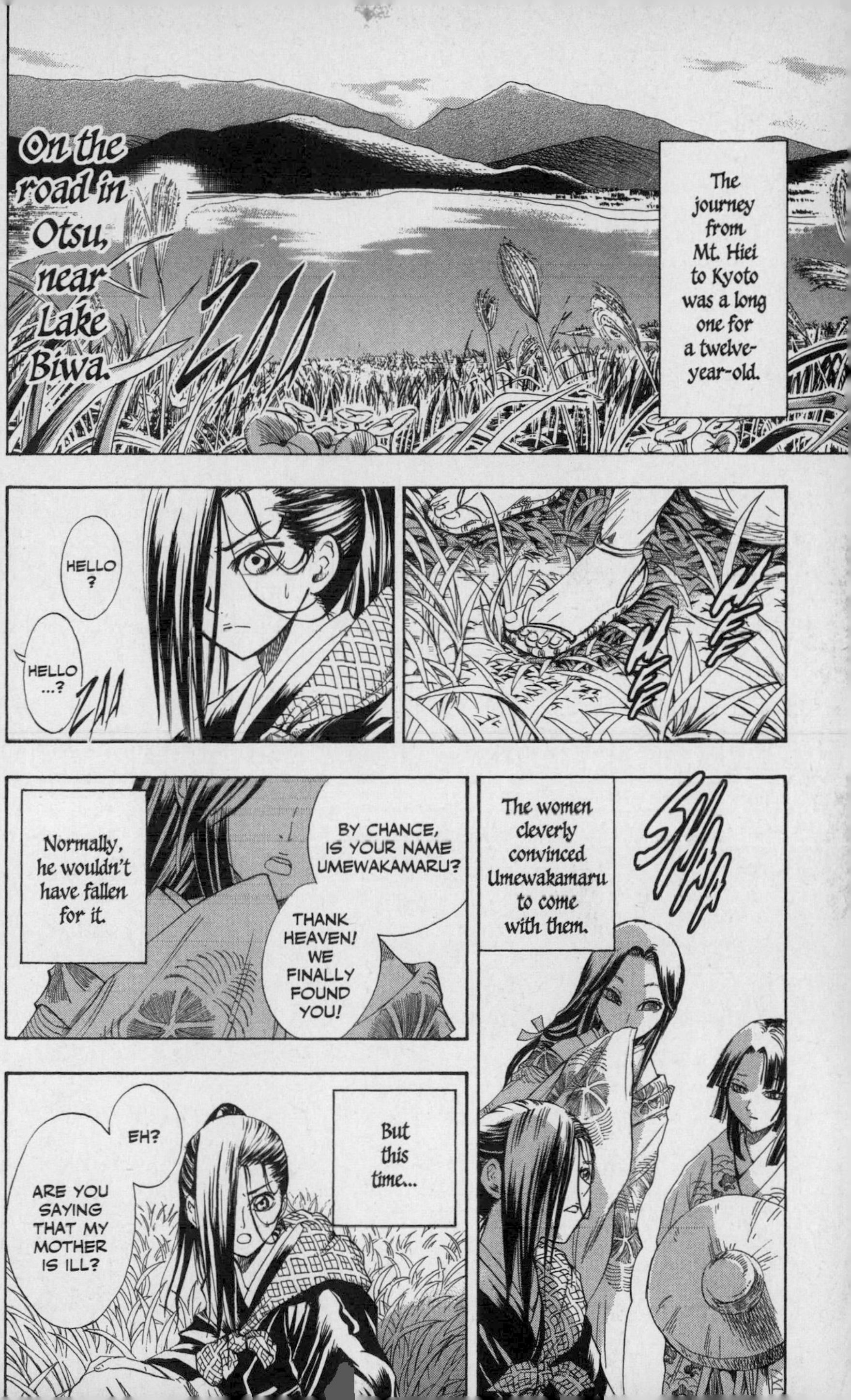
The journey from Mt. Hiei to Kyoto was a long one for a twelve-year-old.
On the road in Otsu, near Lake Biwa.
ZAA
HELLO?
HELLO...?
ZAA
The women cleverly convinced Umewakamaru to come with them.
BY CHANCE, IS YOUR NAME UMEWAKAMARU?
THANK HEAVEN! WE FINALLY FOUND YOU!
Normally, he wouldn't have fallen for it.
But this time...
EH?
ARE YOU SAYING THAT MY MOTHER IS ILL?

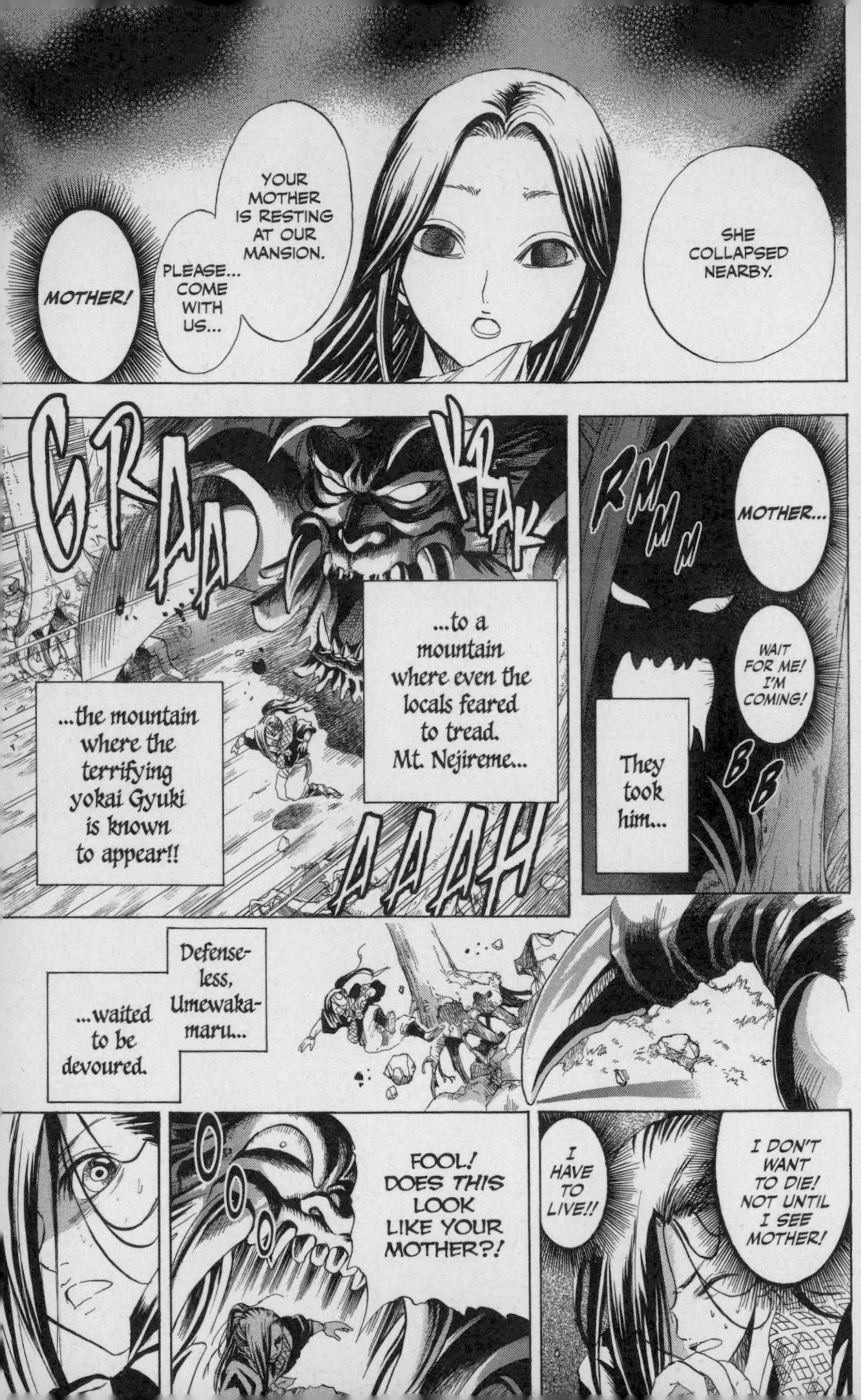
SHE COLLAPSED NEARBY.
YOUR MOTHER IS RESTING AT OUR MANSION.
PLEASE... COME WITH US...
MOTHER!
MOTHER...
WAIT FOR ME! I'M COMING!
RMMMM
They took him...
BB
KRAK
...to a mountain where even the locals feared to tread. Mt. Nejireme...
GRAA
...the mountain where the terrifying yokai Gyuki is known to appear!!
AAAAH
Defense-less, Umewaka-maru...
...waited to be devoured.
I DON'T WANT TO DIE! NOT UNTIL I SEE MOTHER!
I HAVE TO LIVE!!
FOOL! DOES THIS LOOK LIKE YOUR MOTHER?!

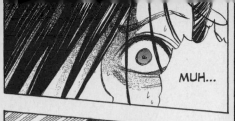

MUH...

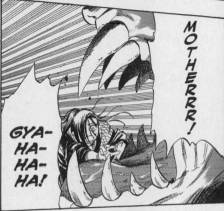

MOTHERRR!

GYA-HA-HA-HA!

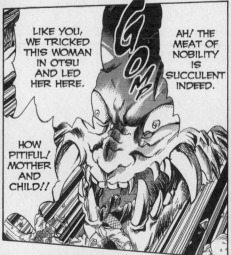

AH! THE MEAT OF NOBILITY IS SUCCULENT INDEED.

LIKE YOU, WE TRICKED THIS WOMAN IN OTSU AND LED HER HERE.

HOW PITIFUL! MOTHER AND CHILD!!

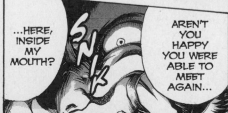

AREN'T YOU HAPPY YOU WERE ABLE TO MEET AGAIN...

...HERE, INSIDE MY MOUTH?

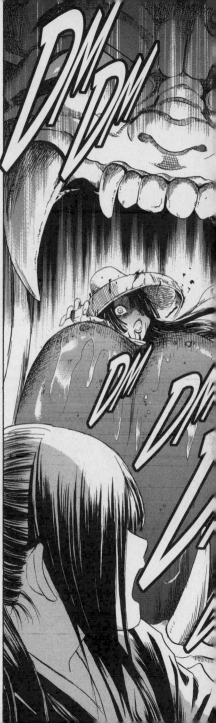

DM DM

DM

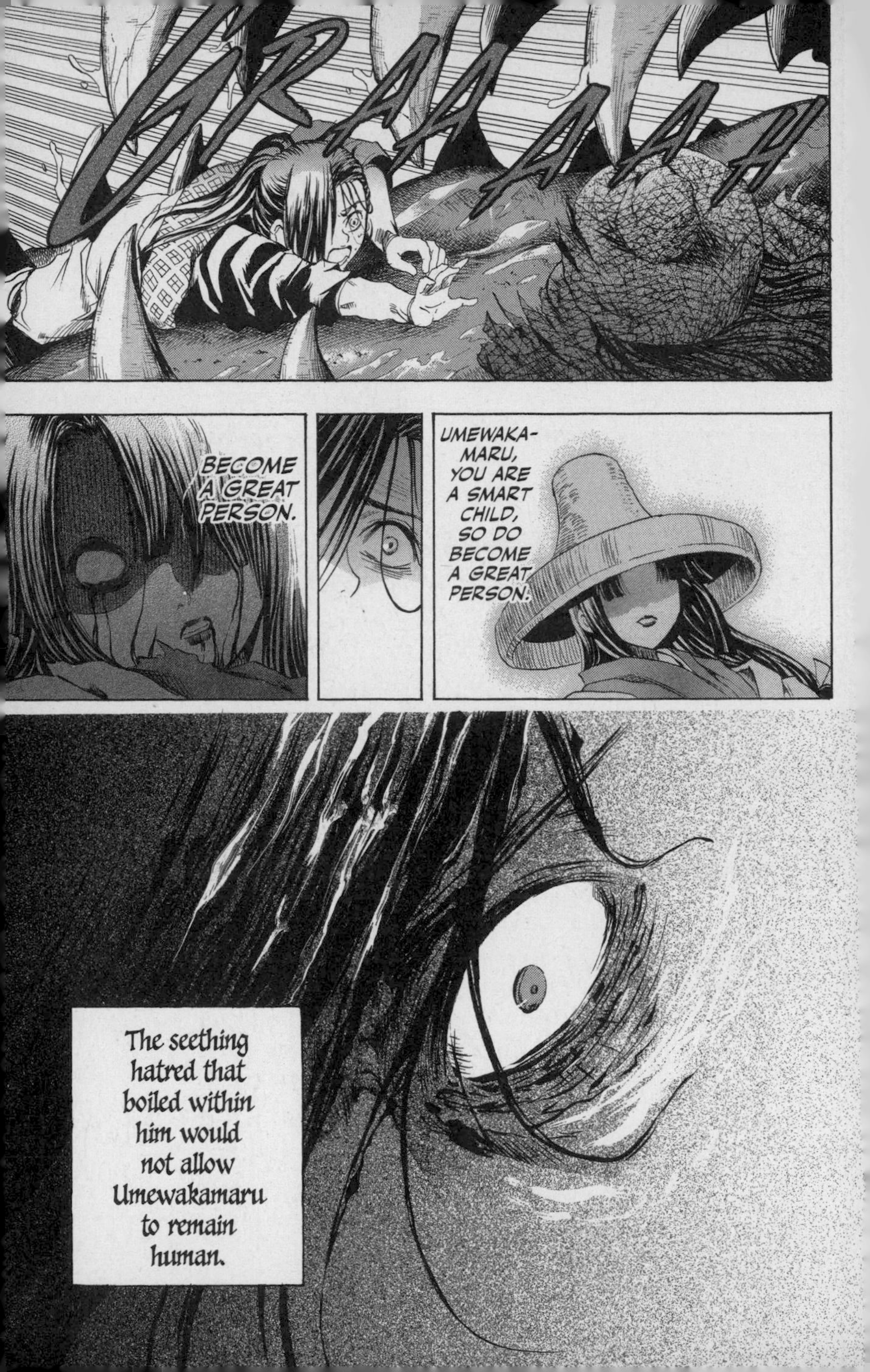
URAAAAAAH
UMEWAKA-MARU, YOU ARE A SMART CHILD, SO DO BECOME A GREAT PERSON.
BECOME A GREAT PERSON.
The seething hatred that boiled within him would not allow Umewakamaru to remain human.

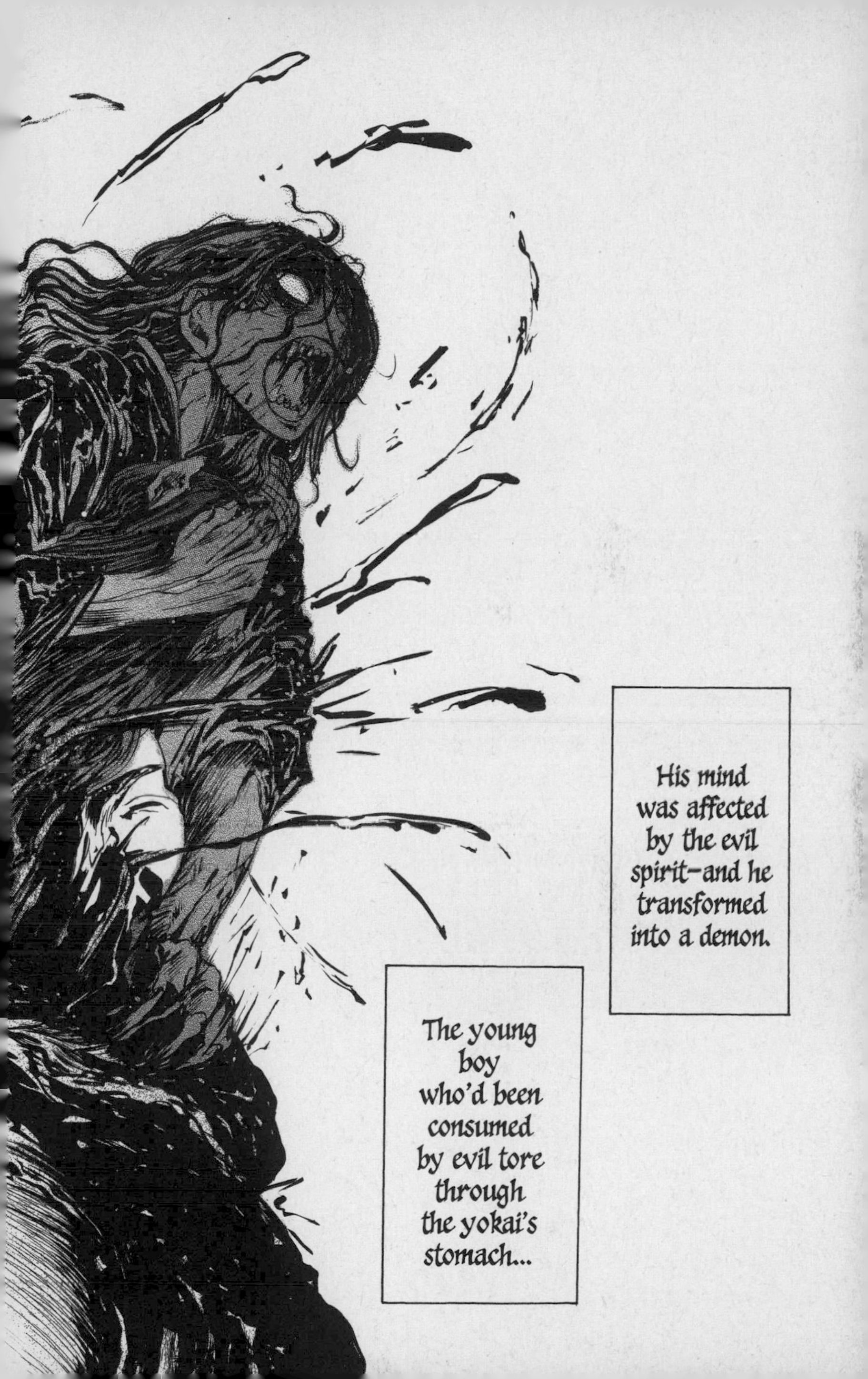
His mind was affected by the evil spirit—and he transformed into a demon.
The young boy who'd been consumed by evil tore through the yokai's stomach...

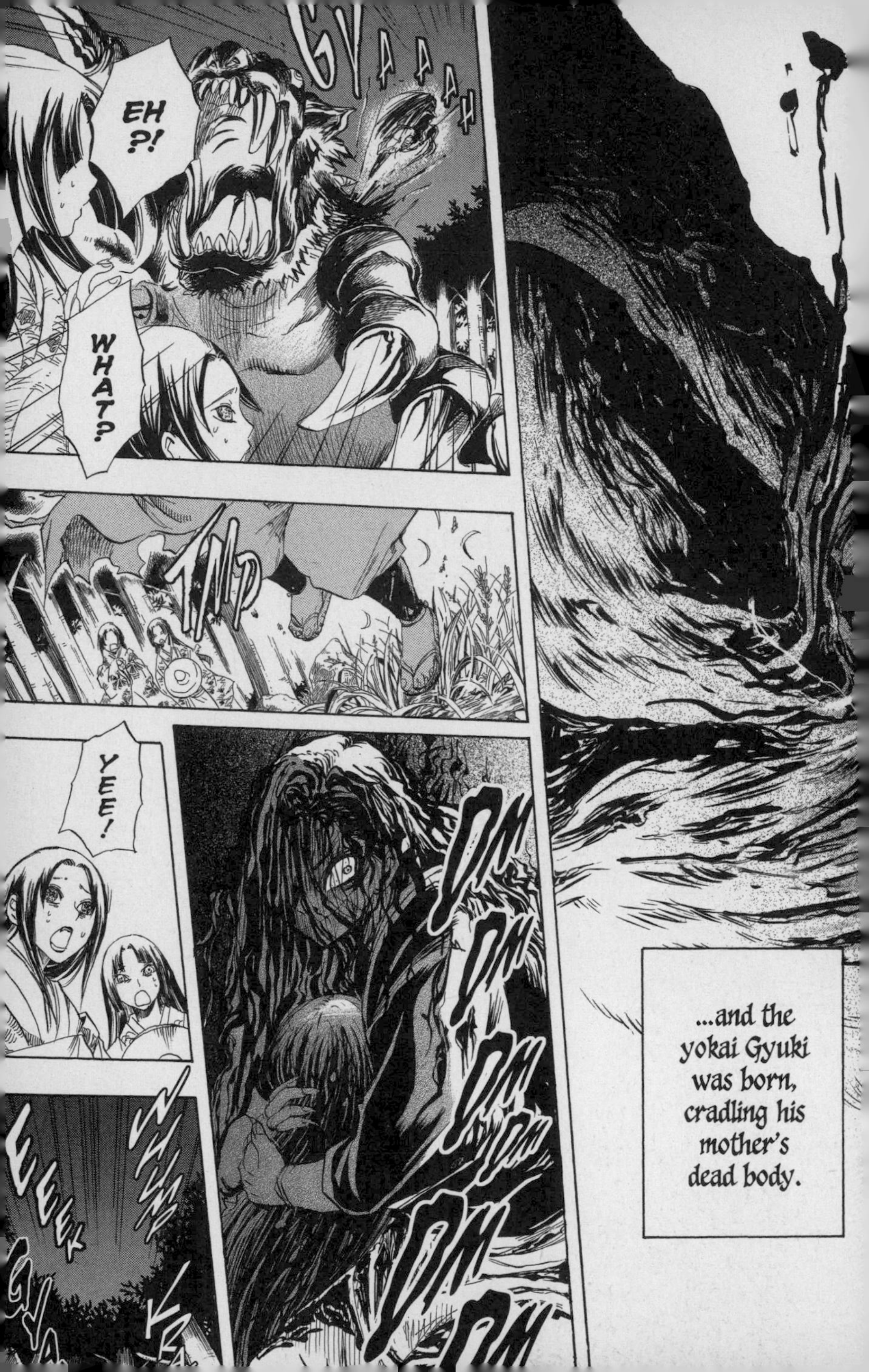
...and the yokai Gyuki was born, cradling his mother's dead body.
GYAAAAH
EH?!
WHAT?
YEE!
EEEK

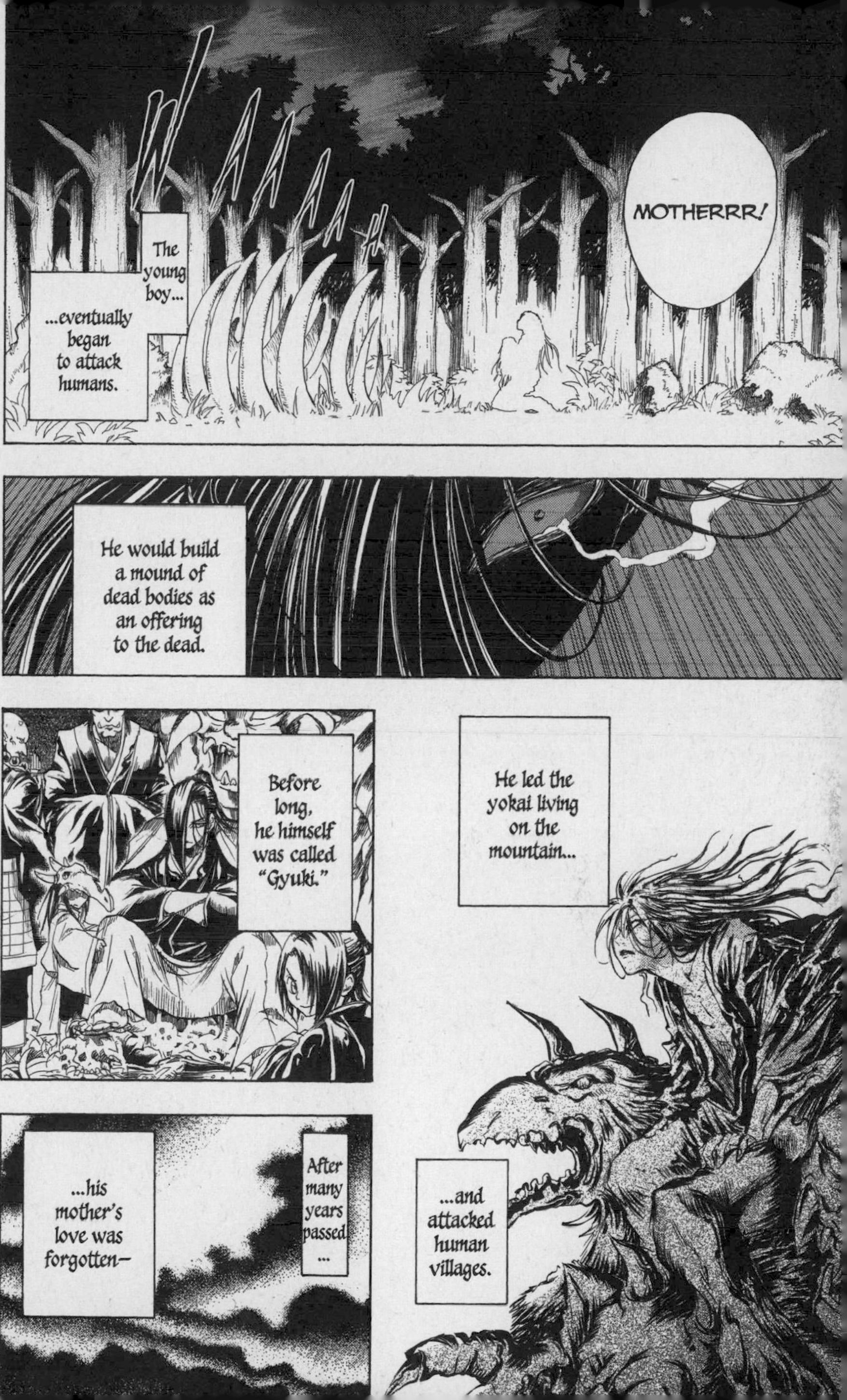
MOTHERRR!
WAAAAAH
The young boy...
...eventually began to attack humans.
He would build a mound of dead bodies as an offering to the dead.
He led the yokai living on the mountain...
...and attacked human villages.
Before long, he himself was called "Gyuki."
After many years passed...
...his mother's love was forgotten—

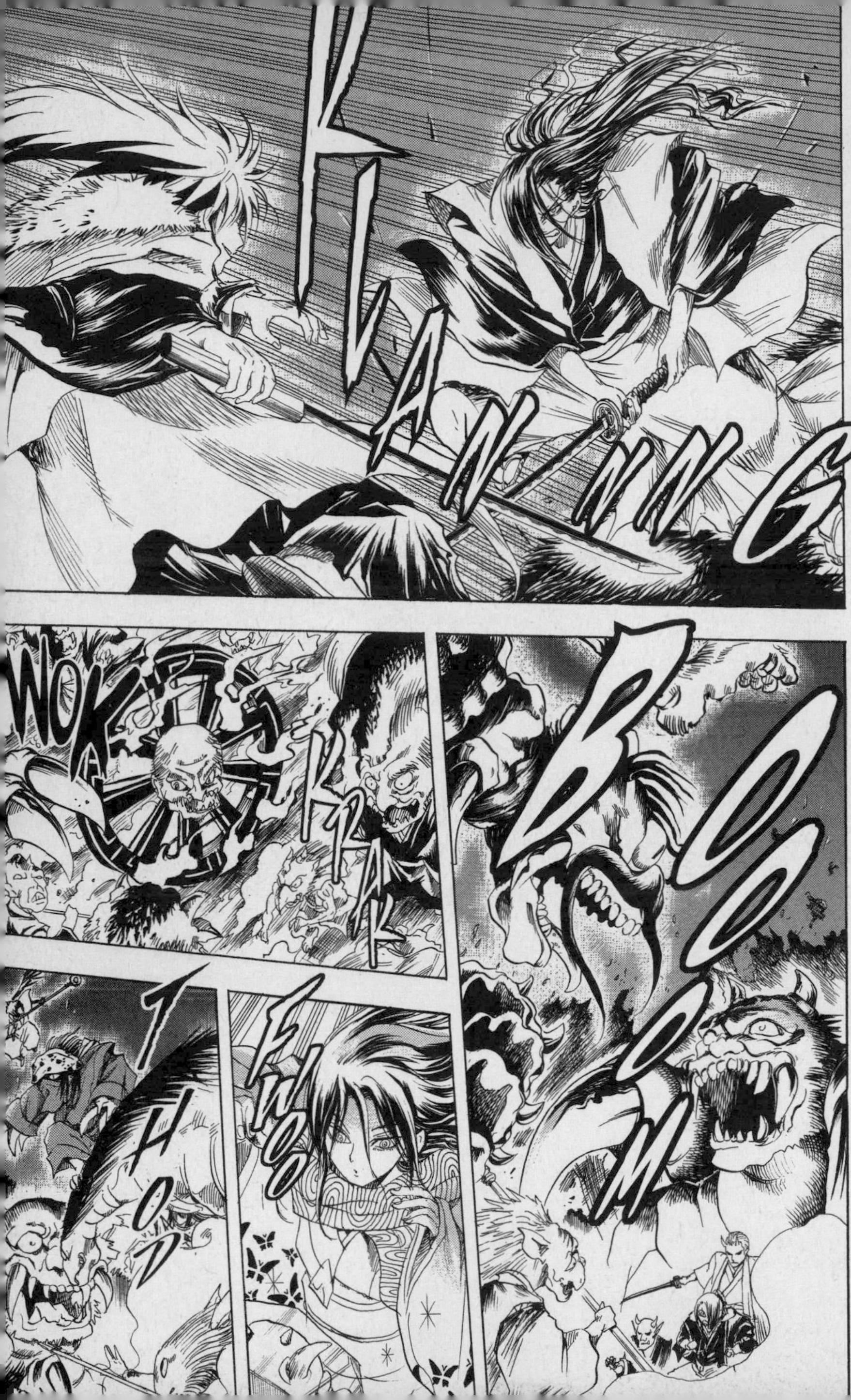

KLANNNG
BOOOOM
KRAK
WOK
FWOOO
THOO

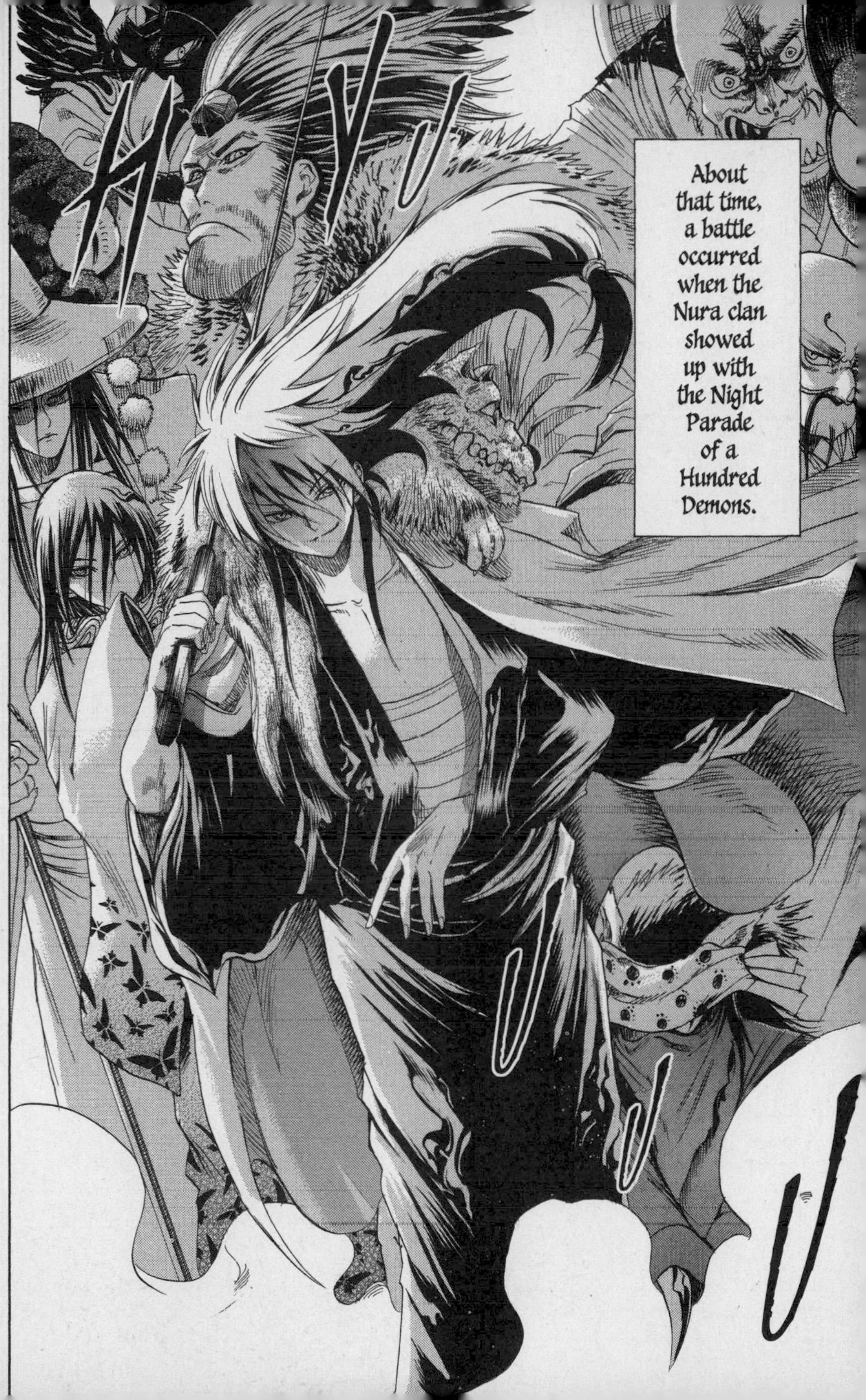
About that time, a battle occurred when the Nura clan showed up with the Night Parade of a Hundred Demons.
HYU

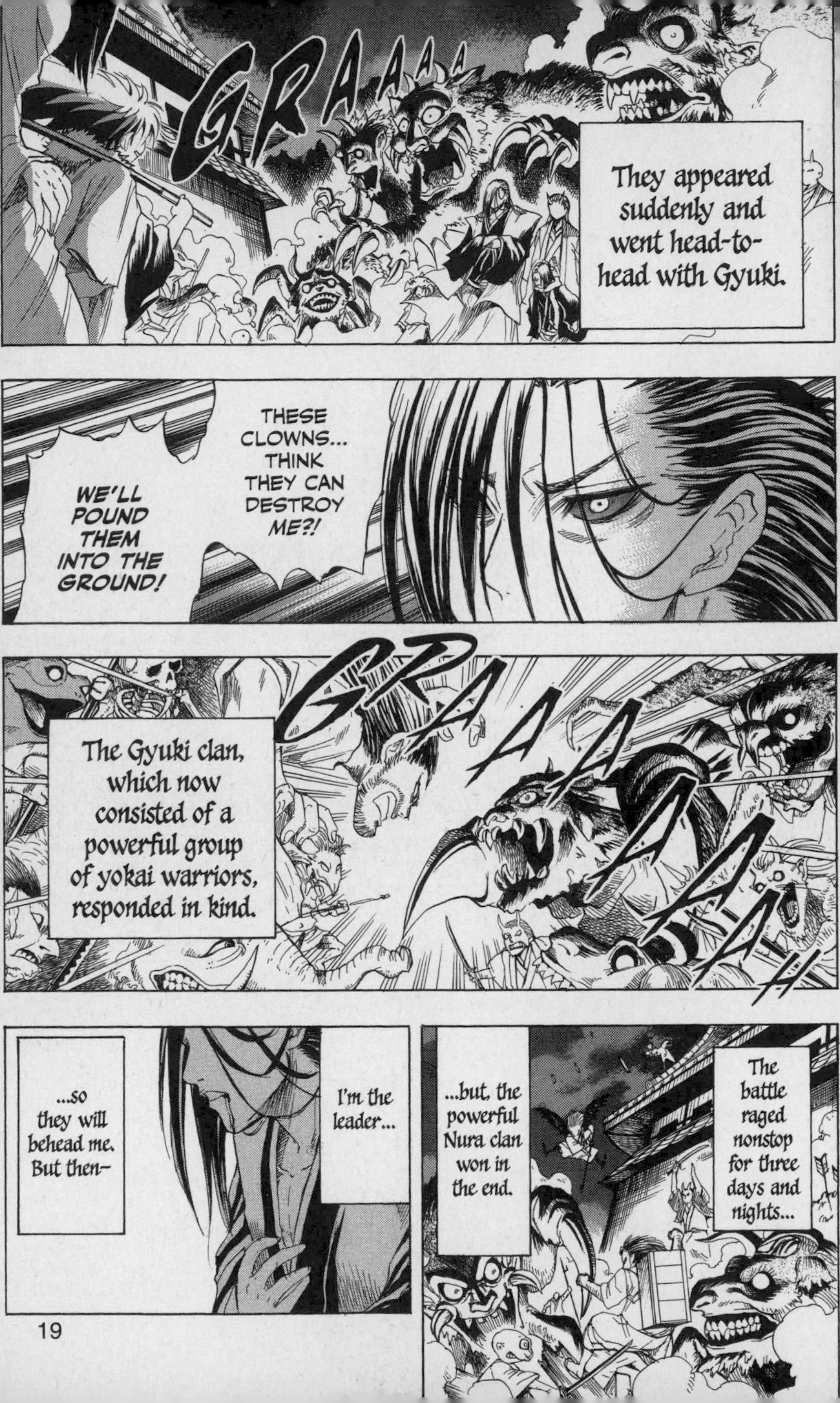
GRAAAAA
They appeared suddenly and went head-to-head with Gyuki.
THESE CLOWNS... THINK THEY CAN DESTROY ME?!
WE'LL POUND THEM INTO THE GROUND!
GRAAAAAAAAH
The Gyuki clan, which now consisted of a powerful group of yokai warriors, responded in kind.
The battle raged nonstop for three days and nights...
...but, the powerful Nura clan won in the end.
I'm the leader...
...so they will behead me. But then–

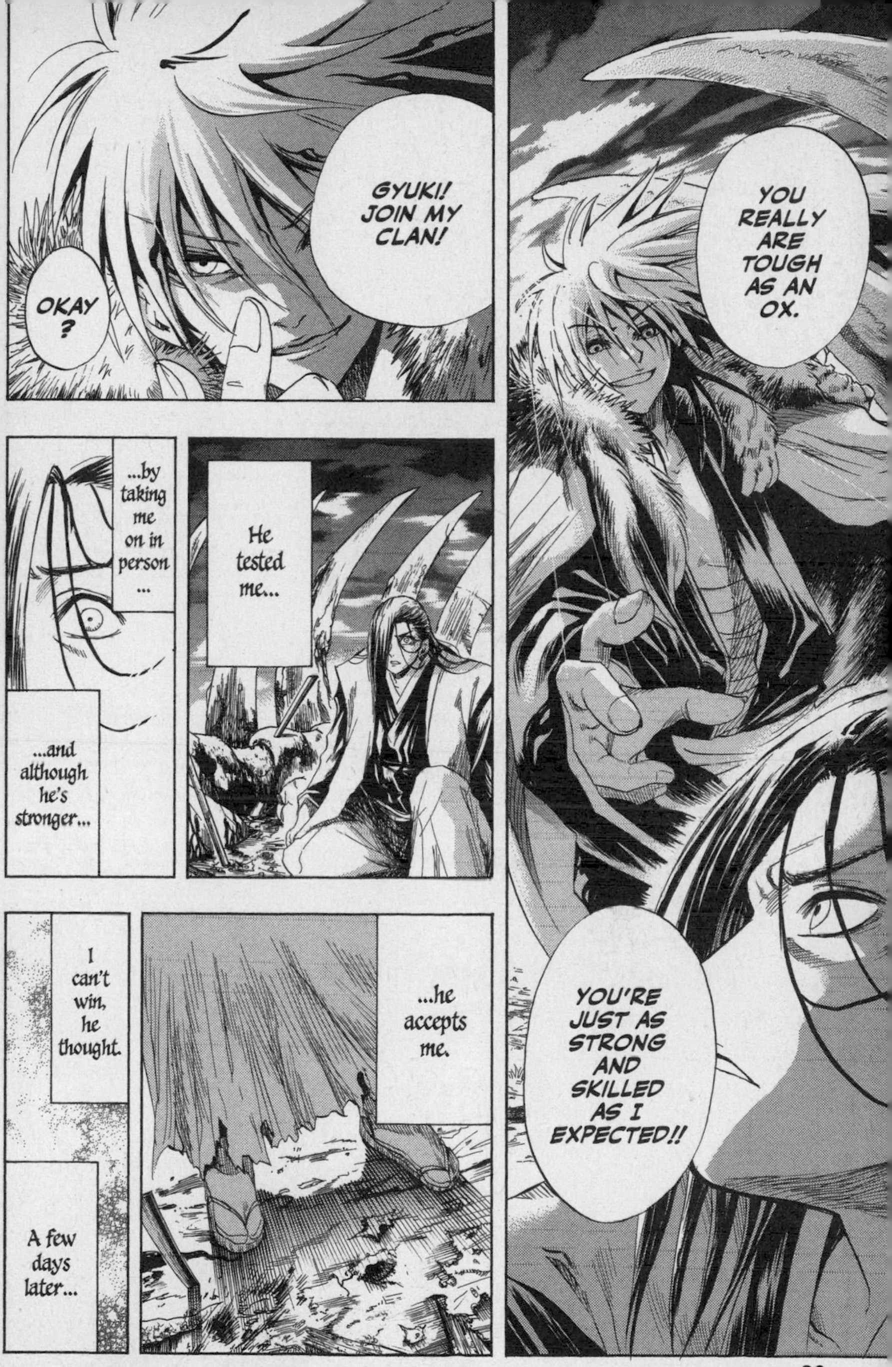
YOU REALLY ARE TOUGH AS AN OX.
YOU'RE JUST AS STRONG AND SKILLED AS I EXPECTED!!
GYUKI! JOIN MY CLAN!
OKAY?
He tested me...
...by taking me on in person...
...and although he's stronger...
...he accepts me.
I can't win, he thought.
A few days later...

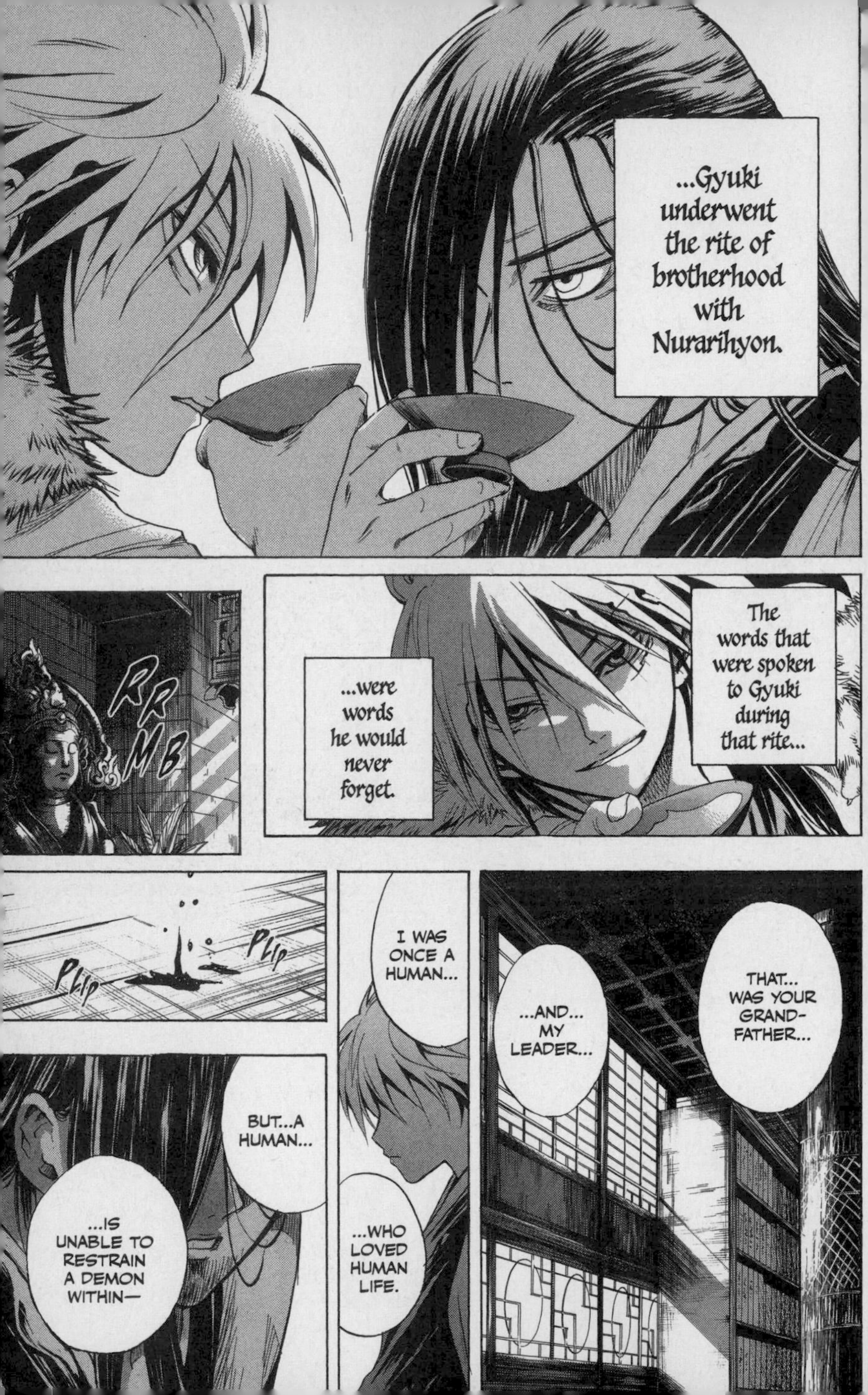

...Gyuki underwent the rite of brotherhood with Nurarihyon.
The words that were spoken to Gyuki during that rite...
...were words he would never forget.
RRRMB
THAT... WAS YOUR GRAND-FATHER...
...AND... MY LEADER...
I WAS ONCE A HUMAN...
...WHO LOVED HUMAN LIFE.
PLIP
PLIP
BUT...A HUMAN...
...IS UNABLE TO RESTRAIN A DEMON WITHIN—

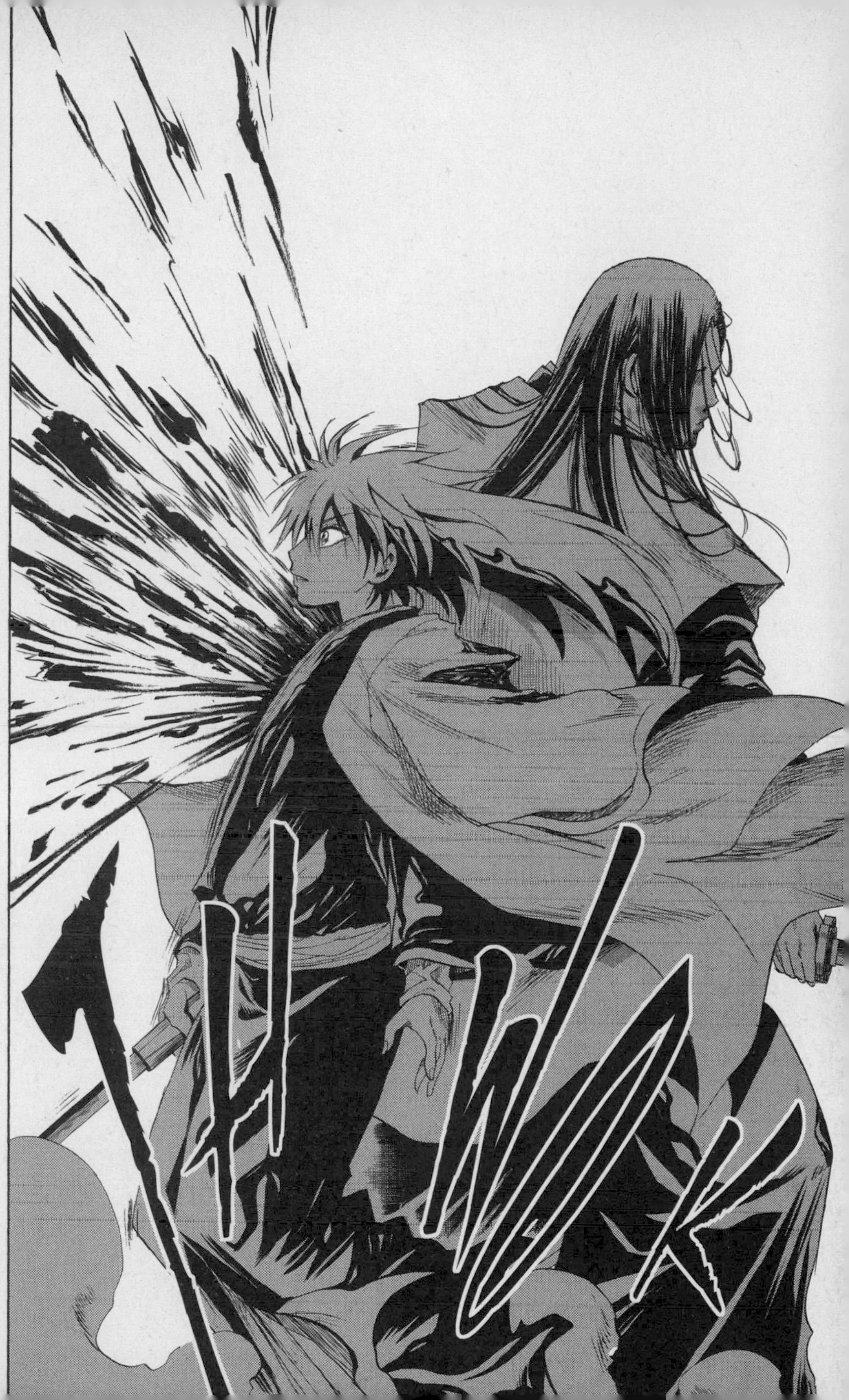
THWACK

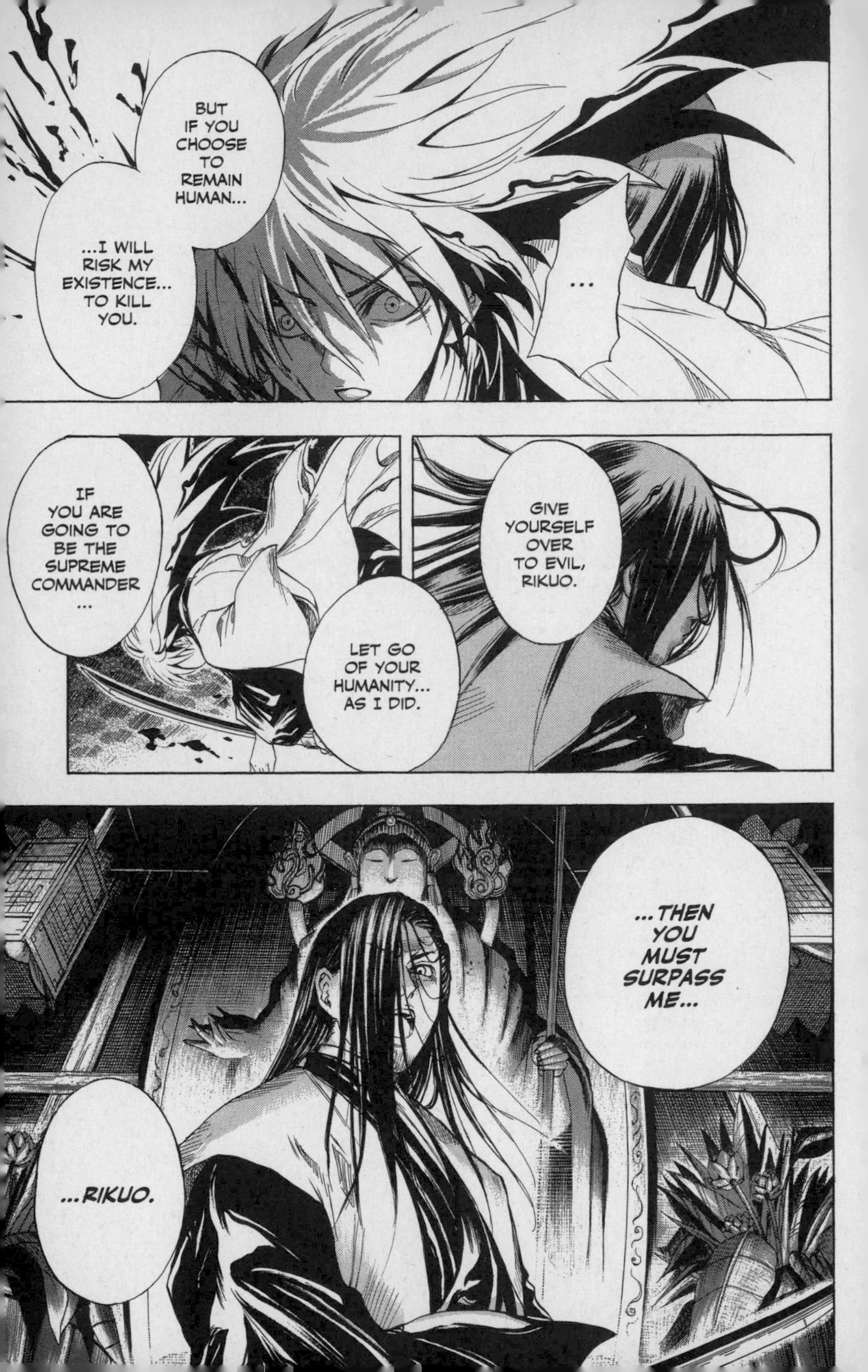
...
BUT IF YOU CHOOSE TO REMAIN HUMAN...
...I WILL RISK MY EXISTENCE... TO KILL YOU.
GIVE YOURSELF OVER TO EVIL, RIKUO.
LET GO OF YOUR HUMANITY... AS I DID.
IF YOU ARE GOING TO BE THE SUPREME COMMANDER ...
...THEN YOU MUST SURPASS ME...
...RIKUO.

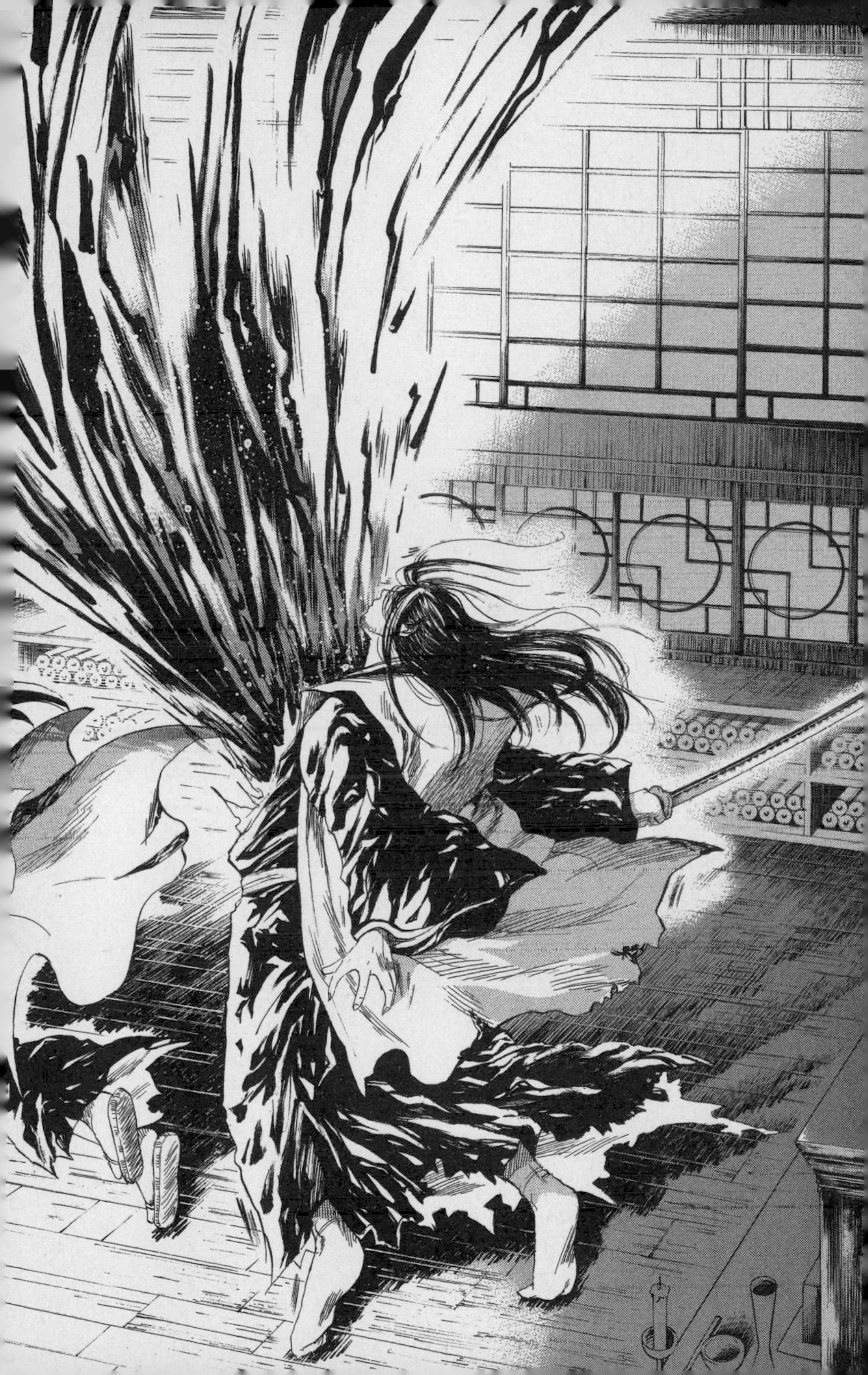

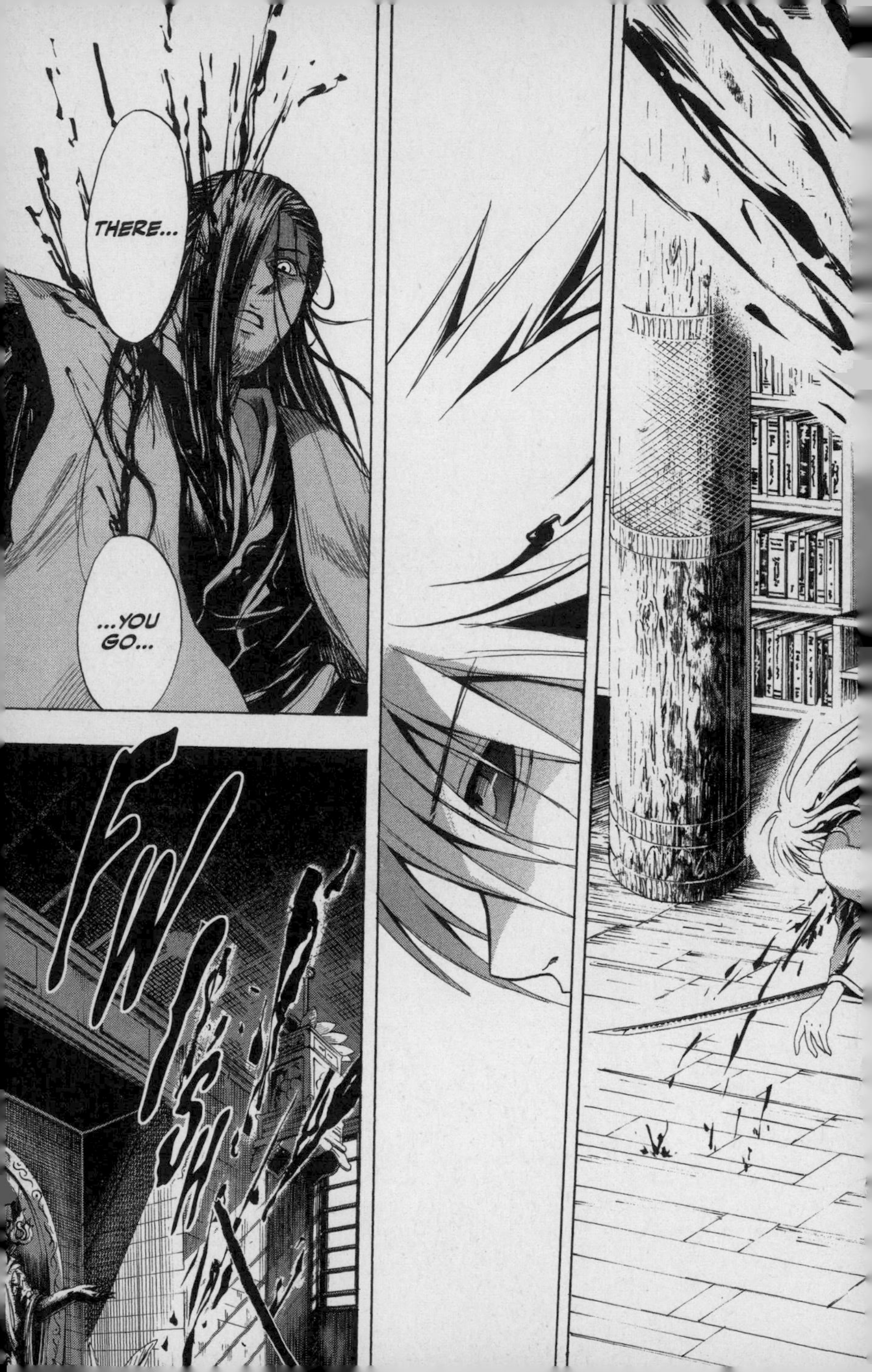
THERE...
...YOU GO...

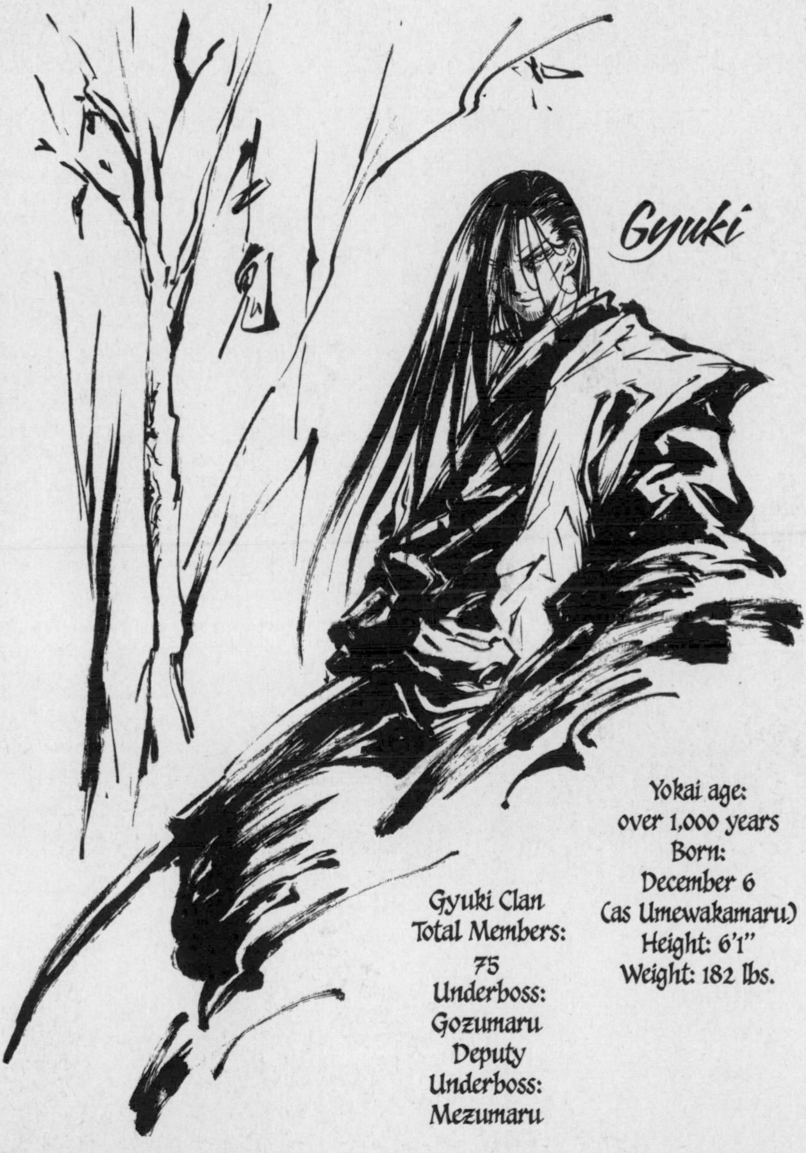
牛鬼

Gyuki

Gyuki Clan
Total Members:
75
Underboss:
Gozumaru
Deputy
Underboss:
Mezumaru

Yokai age:
over 1,000 years
Born:
December 6
(as Umewakamaru)
Height: 6'1"
Weight: 182 lbs.

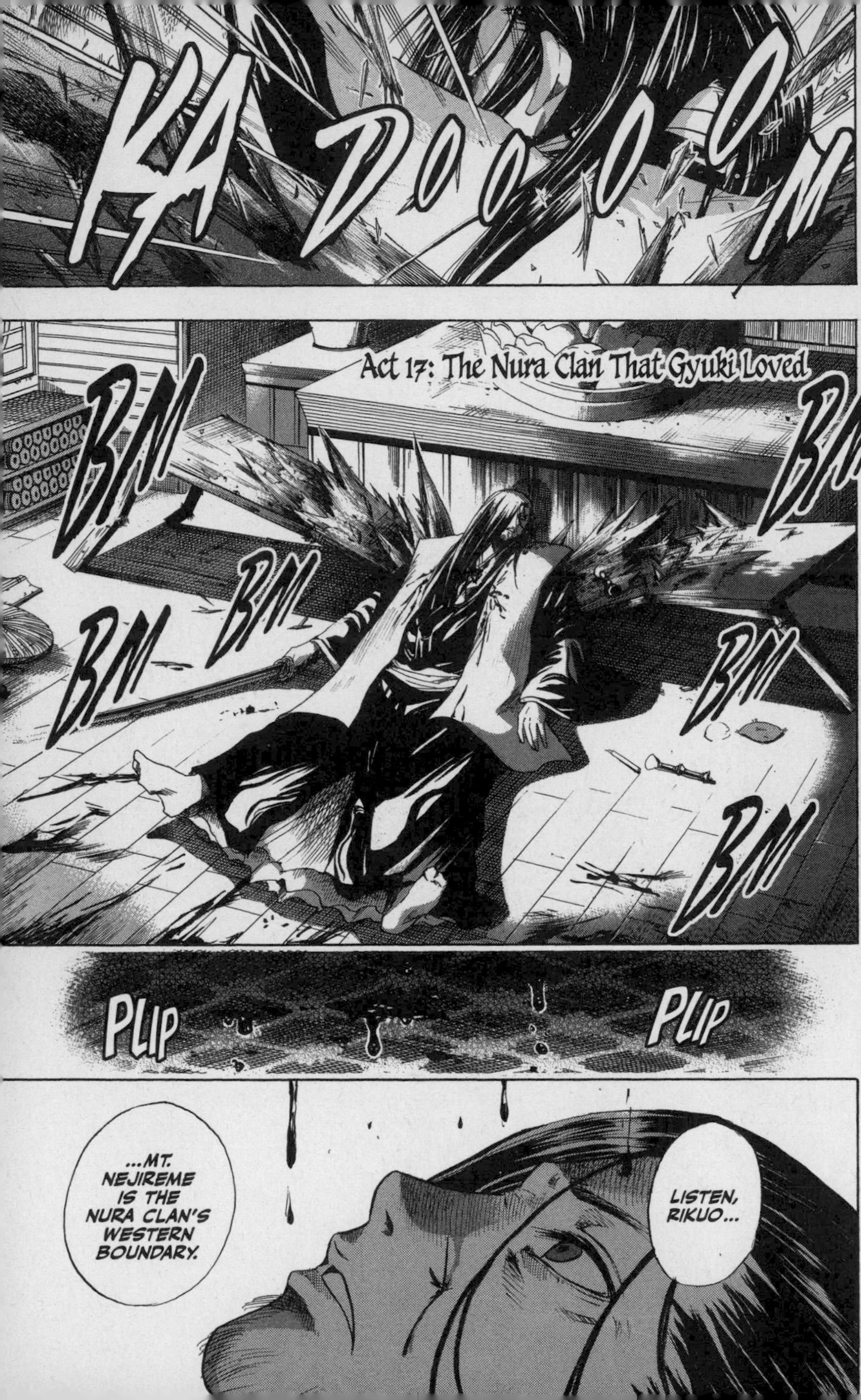
KA-DOOOOOM
Act 17: The Nura Clan That Gyuki Loved
BM
BM
BM
BM
BM
BM
BM
PLIP
PLIP
LISTEN, RIKUO...
...MT. NEJIREME IS THE NURA CLAN'S WESTERN BOUNDARY.

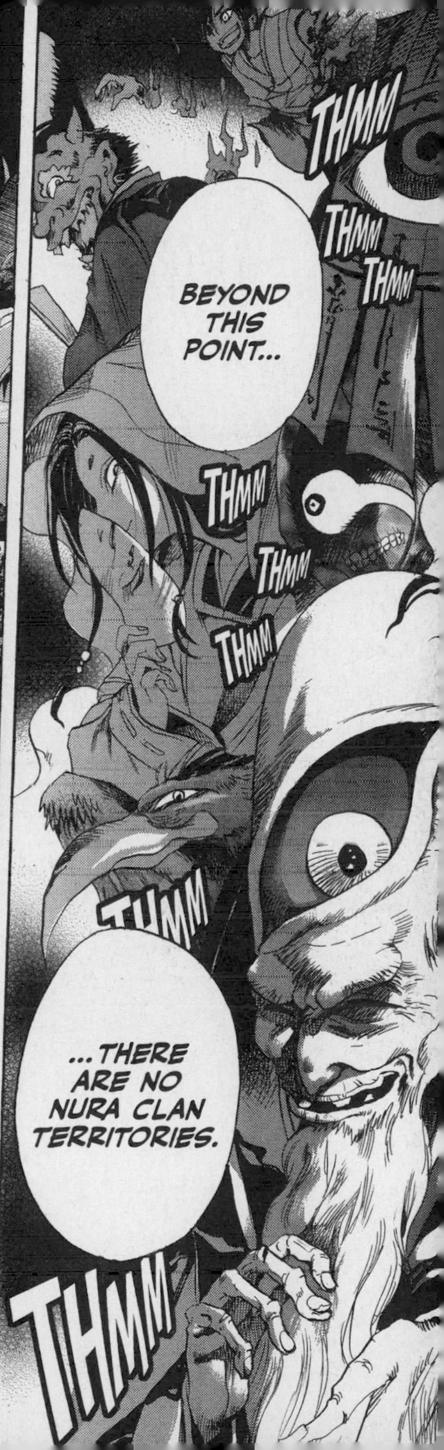
THMM
THMM
THMM
BEYOND THIS POINT...
THMM
THMM
THMM
THMM
...THERE ARE NO NURA CLAN TERRITORIES.
THMM

Act 17: The Nura Clan That Gyuki Loved

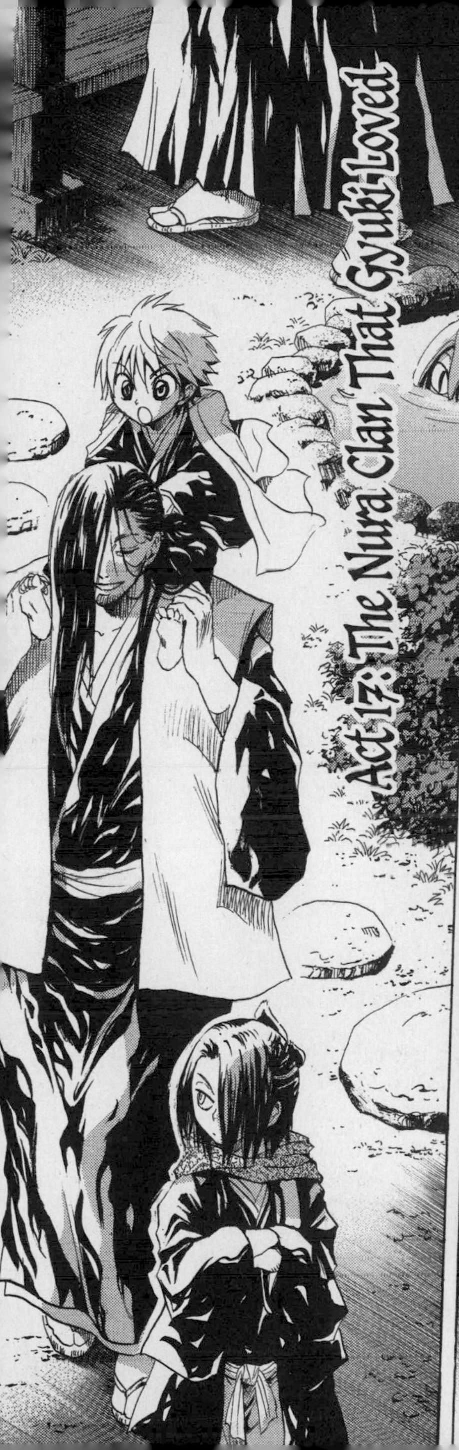

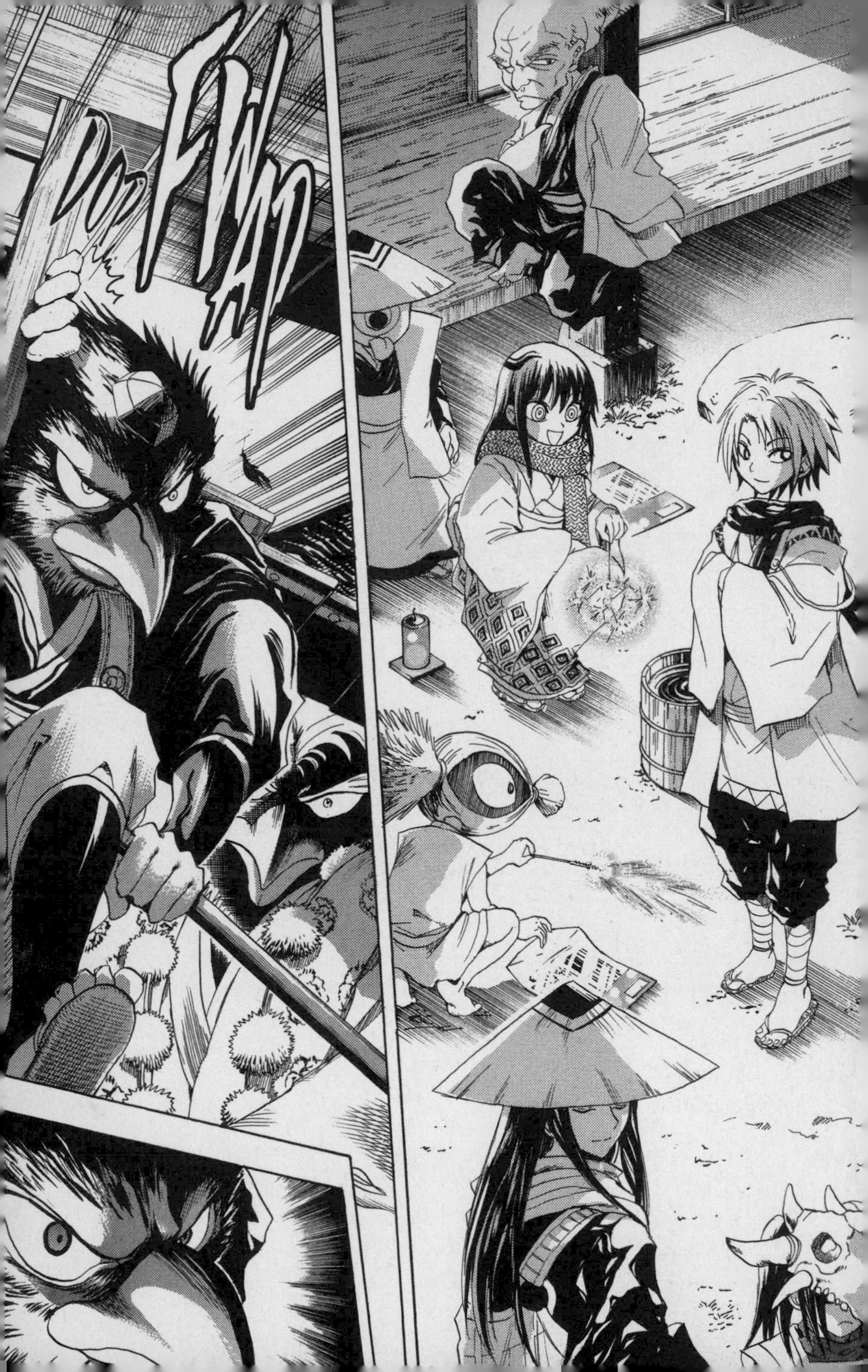

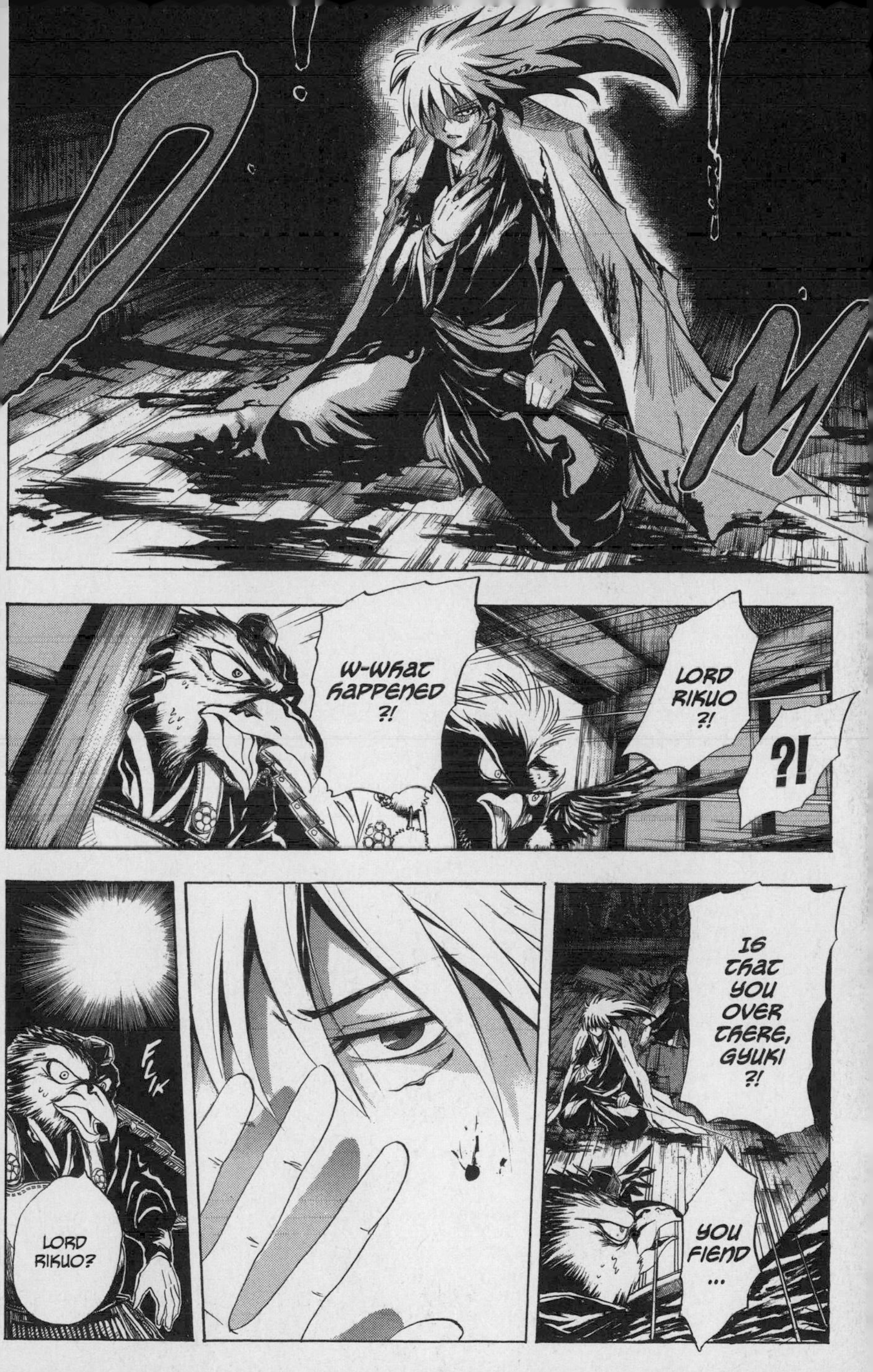
?!
LORD RIKUO ?!
W-WHAT HAPPENED ?!
IS THAT YOU OVER THERE, GYUKI ?!
YOU FIEND ...
FLIK
LORD RIKUO?

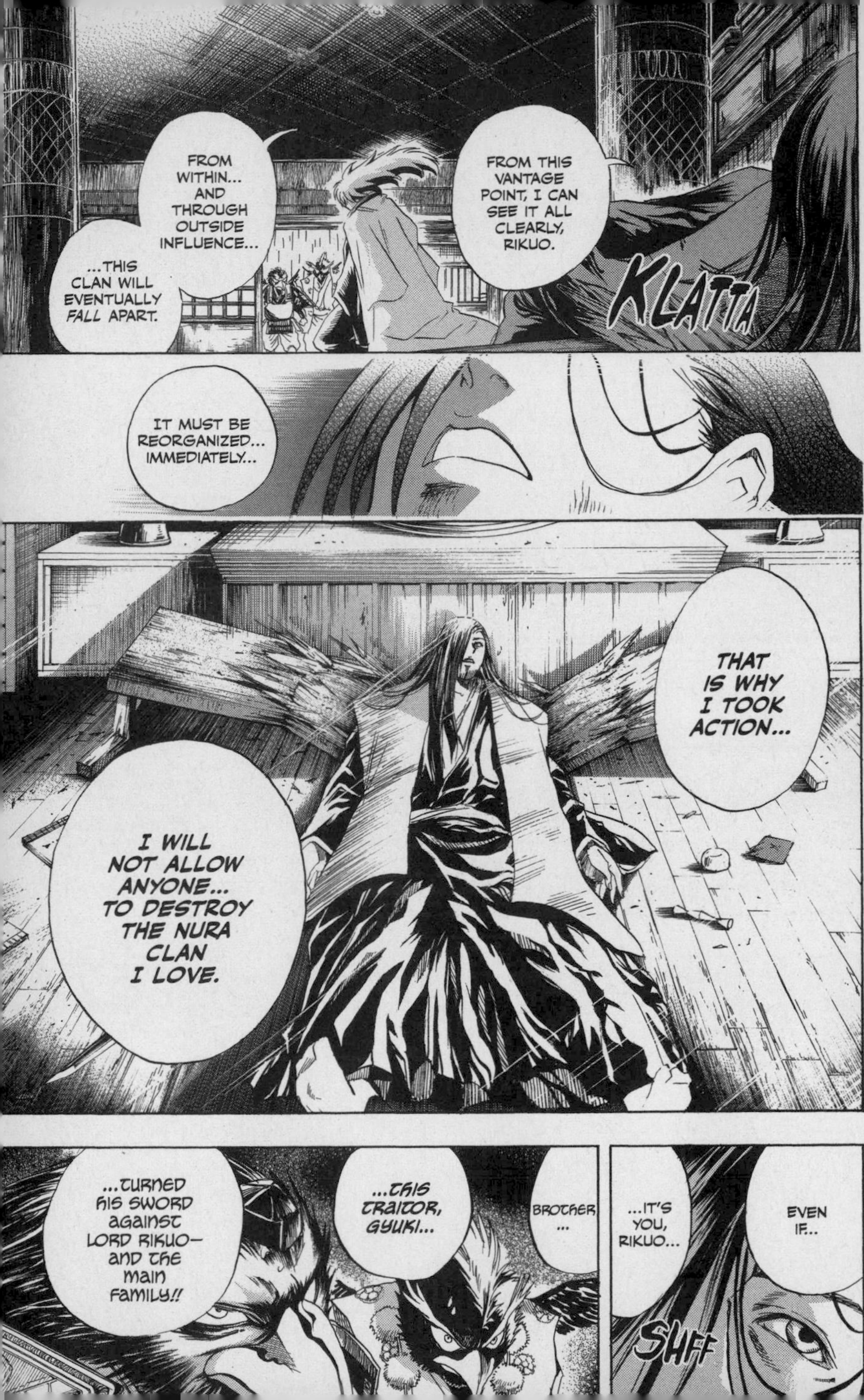
FROM THIS VANTAGE POINT, I CAN SEE IT ALL CLEARLY, RIKUO.
KLATTA
FROM WITHIN... AND THROUGH OUTSIDE INFLUENCE...
...THIS CLAN WILL EVENTUALLY FALL APART.
IT MUST BE REORGANIZED... IMMEDIATELY...
THAT IS WHY I TOOK ACTION...
I WILL NOT ALLOW ANYONE... TO DESTROY THE NURA CLAN I LOVE.
EVEN IF...
...IT'S YOU, RIKUO...
SHFF
BROTHER...
...THIS TRAITOR, GYUKI...
...TURNED HIS SWORD AGAINST LORD RIKUO— AND THE MAIN FAMILY!!

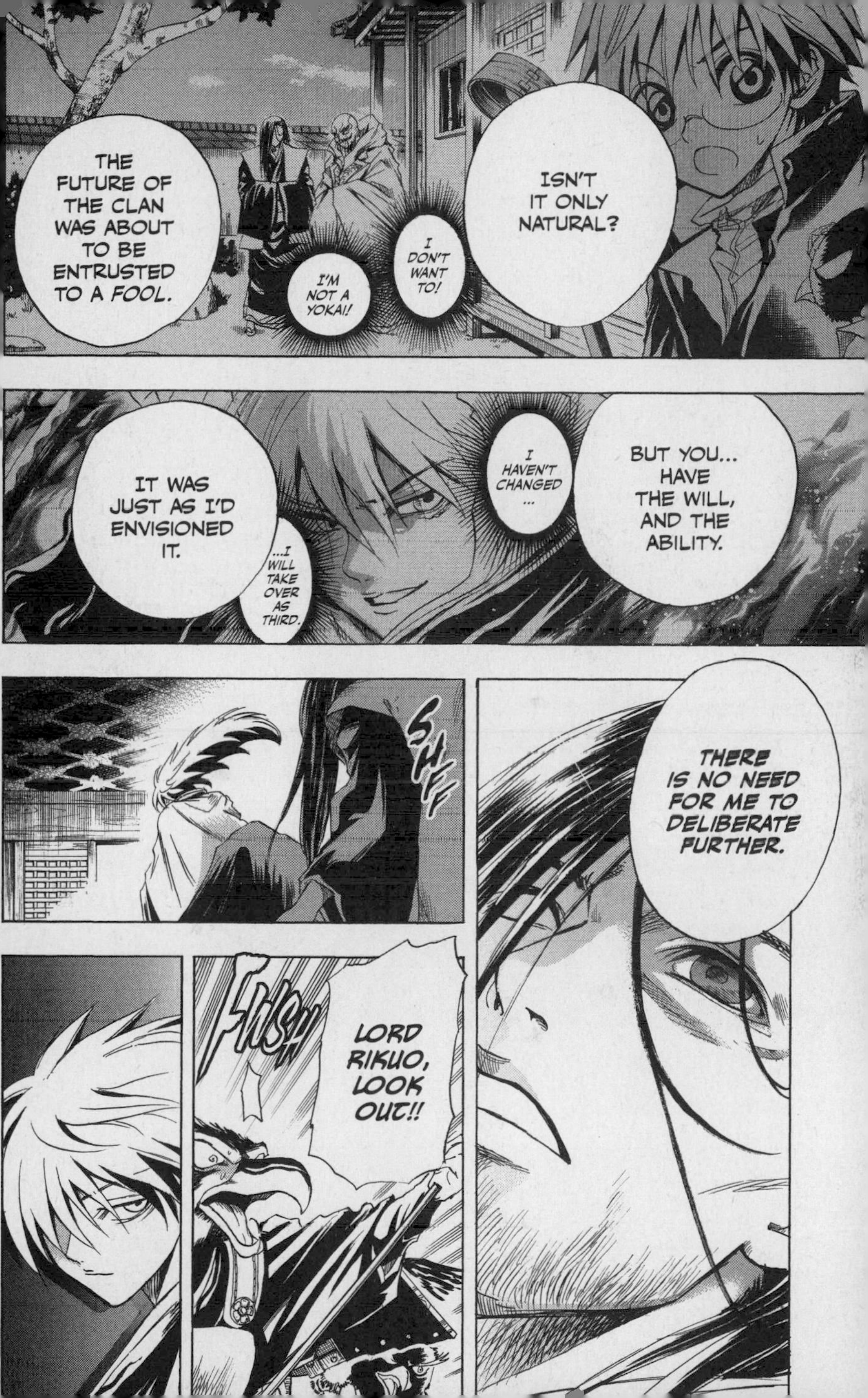
ISN'T IT ONLY NATURAL?
I DON'T WANT TO!
I'M NOT A YOKAI!
THE FUTURE OF THE CLAN WAS ABOUT TO BE ENTRUSTED TO A FOOL.
BUT YOU... HAVE THE WILL, AND THE ABILITY.
I HAVEN'T CHANGED...
...I WILL TAKE OVER AS THIRD.
IT WAS JUST AS I'D ENVISIONED IT.
THERE IS NO NEED FOR ME TO DELIBERATE FURTHER.
SHFF
LORD RIKUO, LOOK OUT!!
FWSH

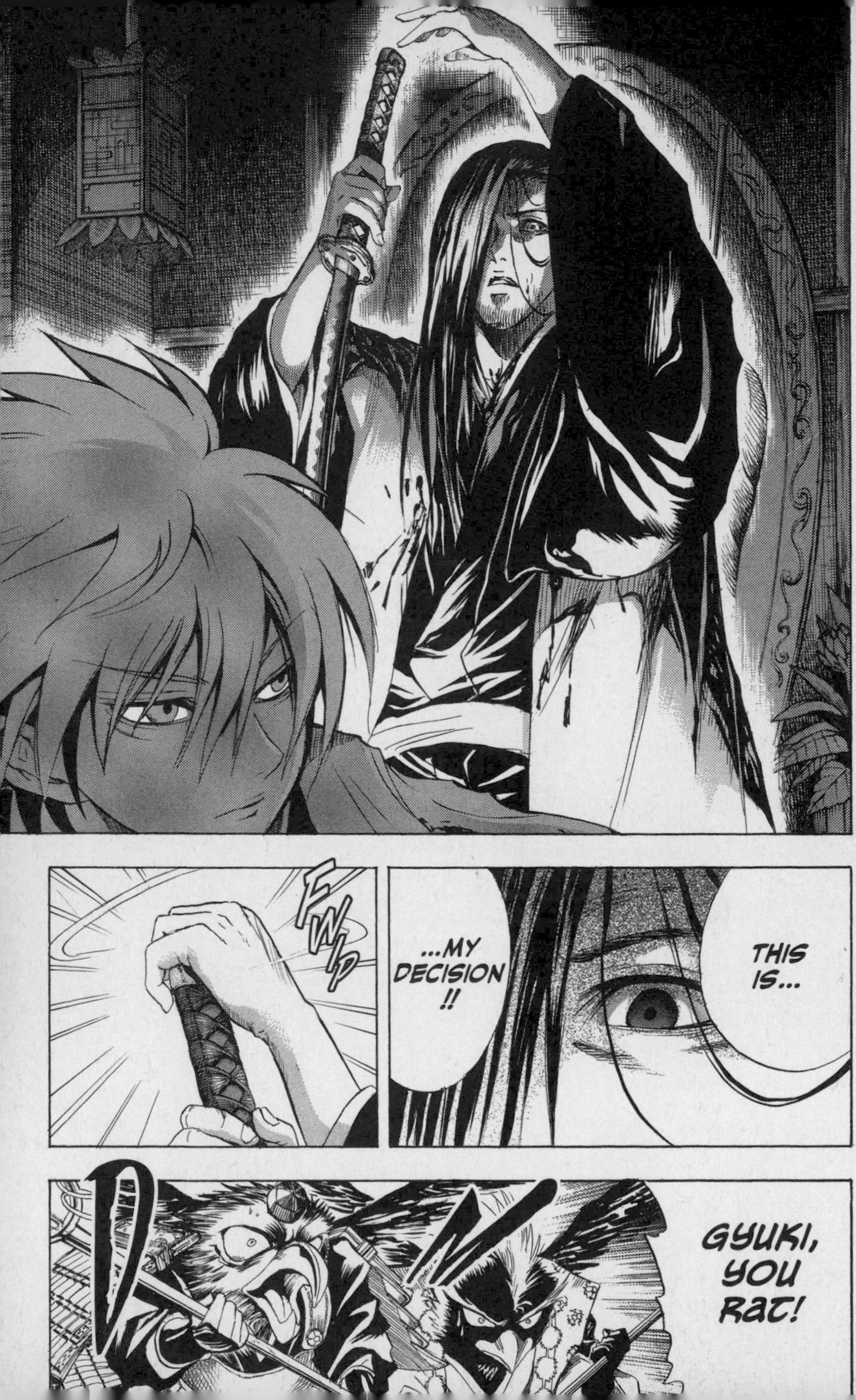
THIS IS...
...MY DECISION!!
FWIP
GYUKI, YOU RAT!

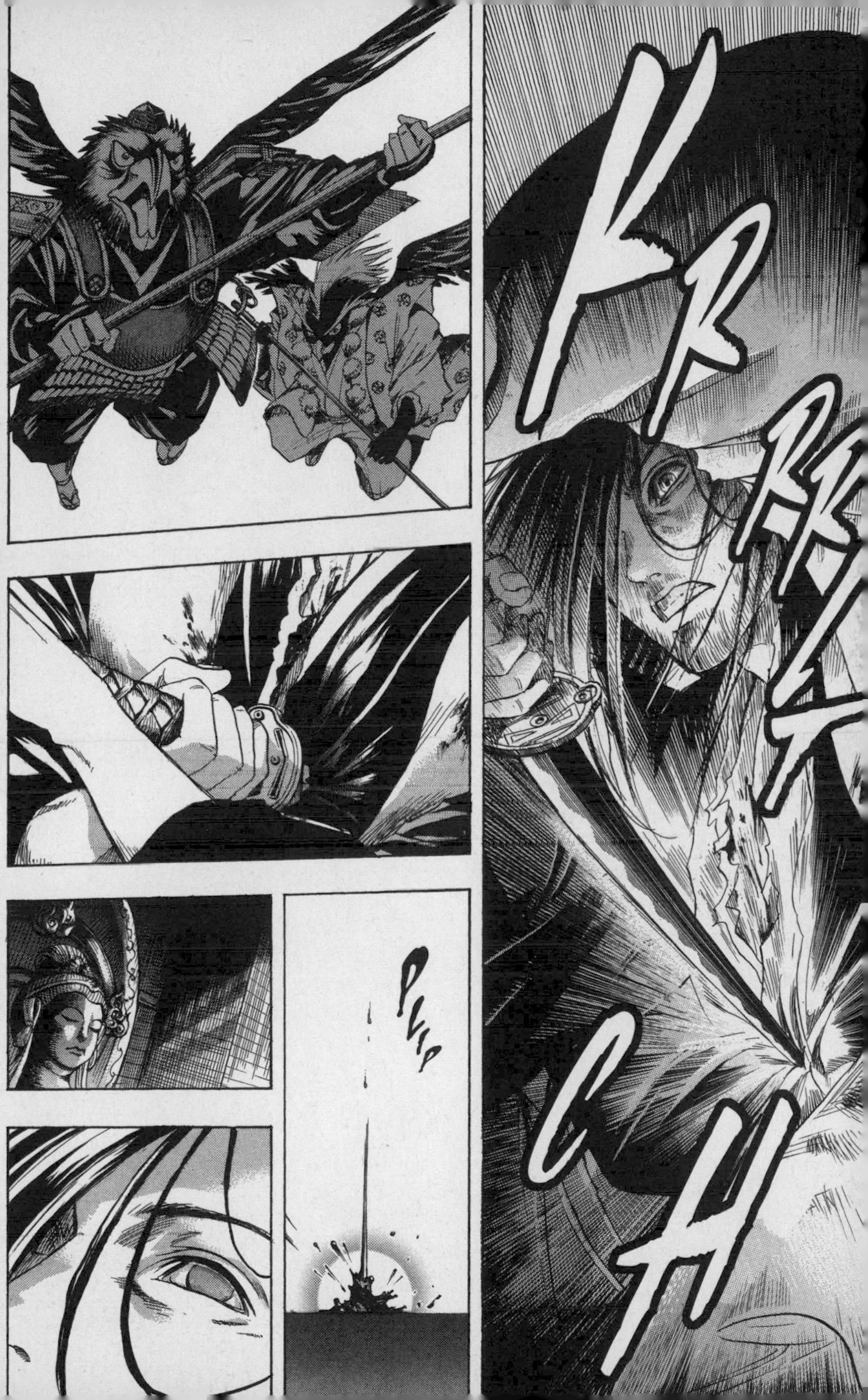
KRRAACH
PLIP

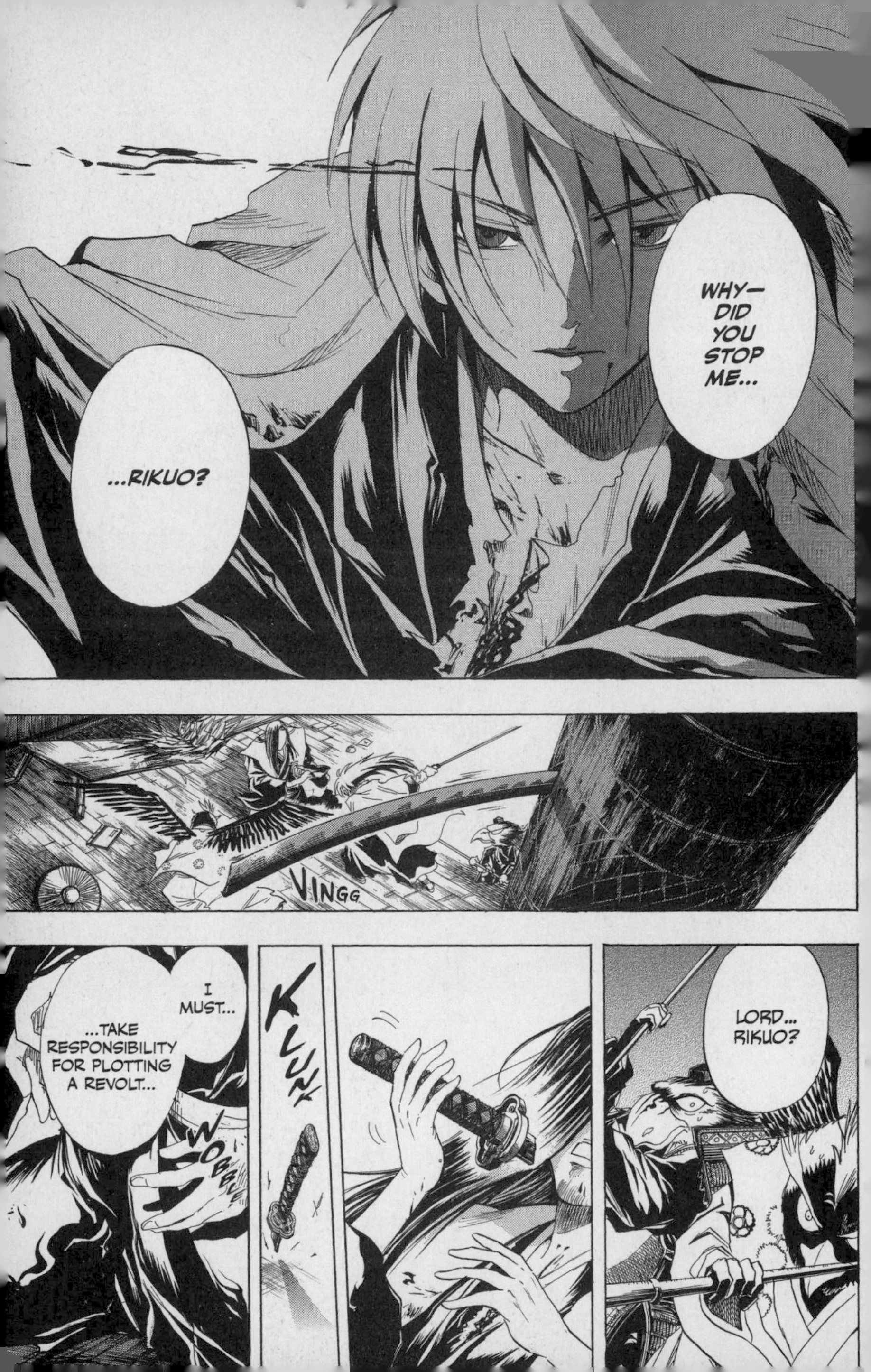
WHY—DID YOU STOP ME...
...RIKUO?
VINGG
LORD... RIKUO?
KLUNK
I MUST...
...TAKE RESPONSIBILITY FOR PLOTTING A REVOLT...
WOBBLE

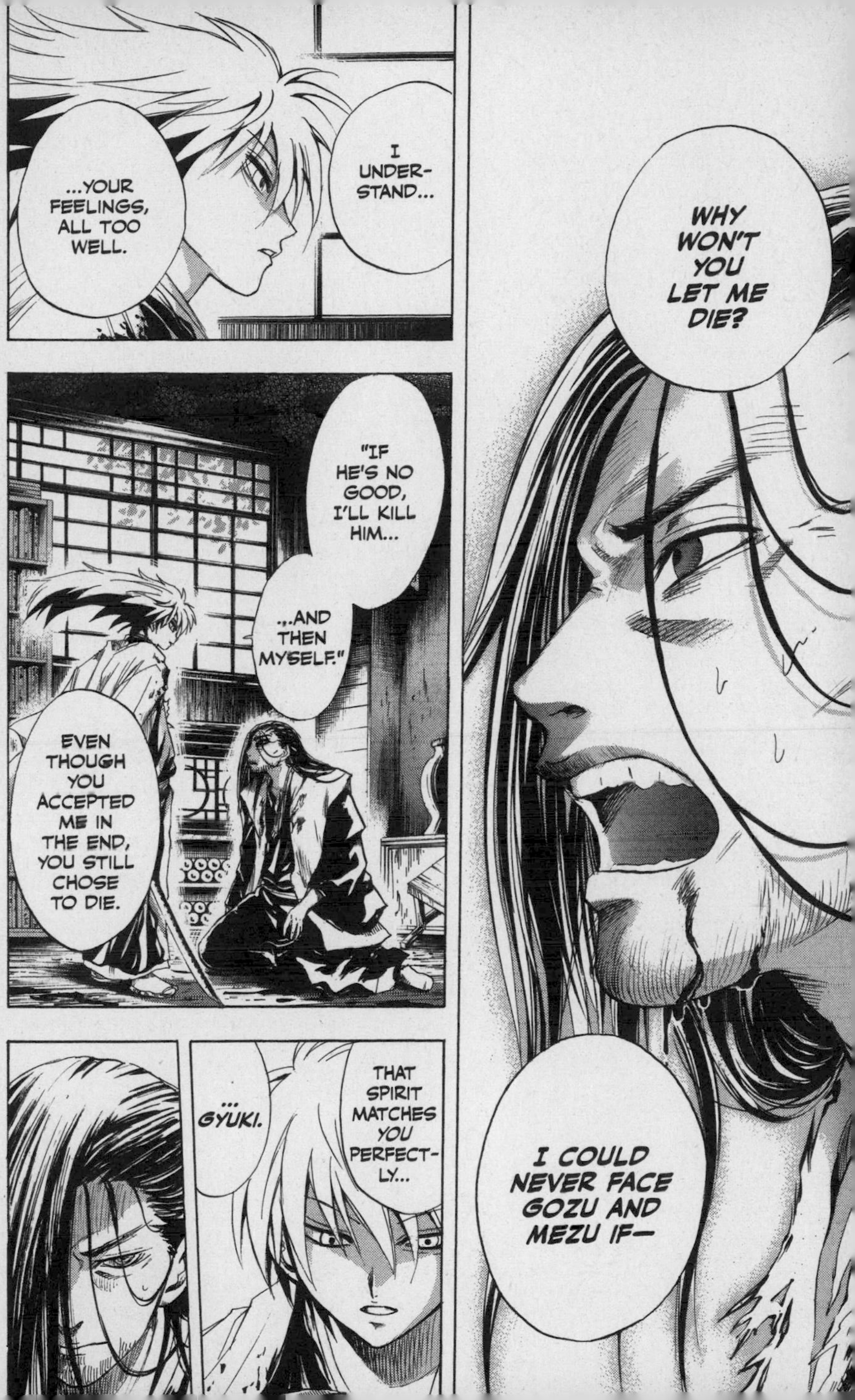
WHY WON'T YOU LET ME DIE?
I COULD NEVER FACE GOZU AND MEZU IF—
I UNDER-STAND...
...YOUR FEELINGS, ALL TOO WELL.
"IF HE'S NO GOOD, I'LL KILL HIM...
...AND THEN MYSELF."
EVEN THOUGH YOU ACCEPTED ME IN THE END, YOU STILL CHOSE TO DIE.
THAT SPIRIT MATCHES YOU PERFECT-LY...
...GYUKI.

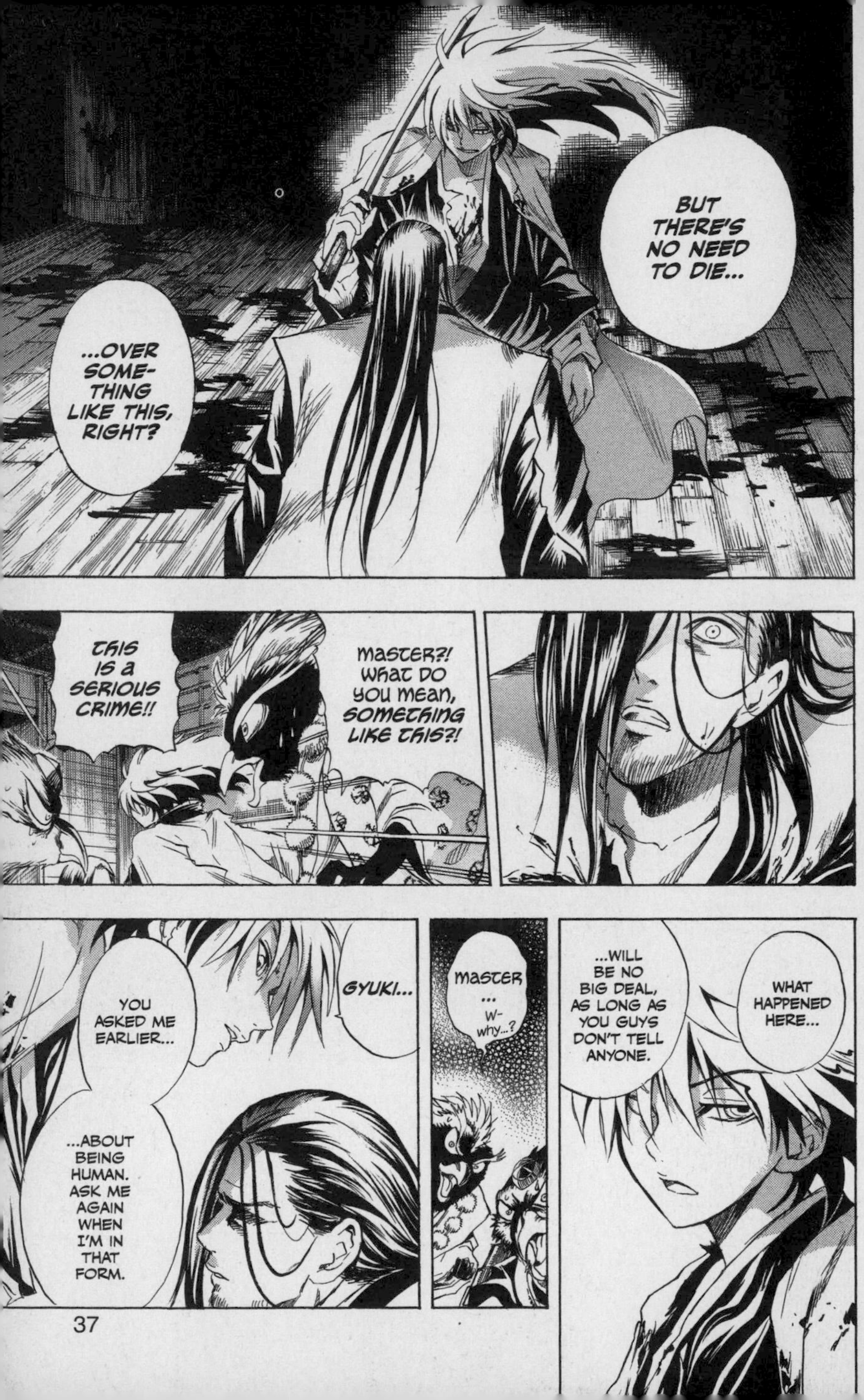
BUT THERE'S NO NEED TO DIE...
...OVER SOME-THING LIKE THIS, RIGHT?
MASTER?! WHAT DO YOU MEAN, SOMETHING LIKE THIS?!
THIS IS A SERIOUS CRIME!!
WHAT HAPPENED HERE...
...WILL BE NO BIG DEAL, AS LONG AS YOU GUYS DON'T TELL ANYONE.
MASTER...
W-why...?
GYUKI...
YOU ASKED ME EARLIER...
...ABOUT BEING HUMAN. ASK ME AGAIN WHEN I'M IN THAT FORM.

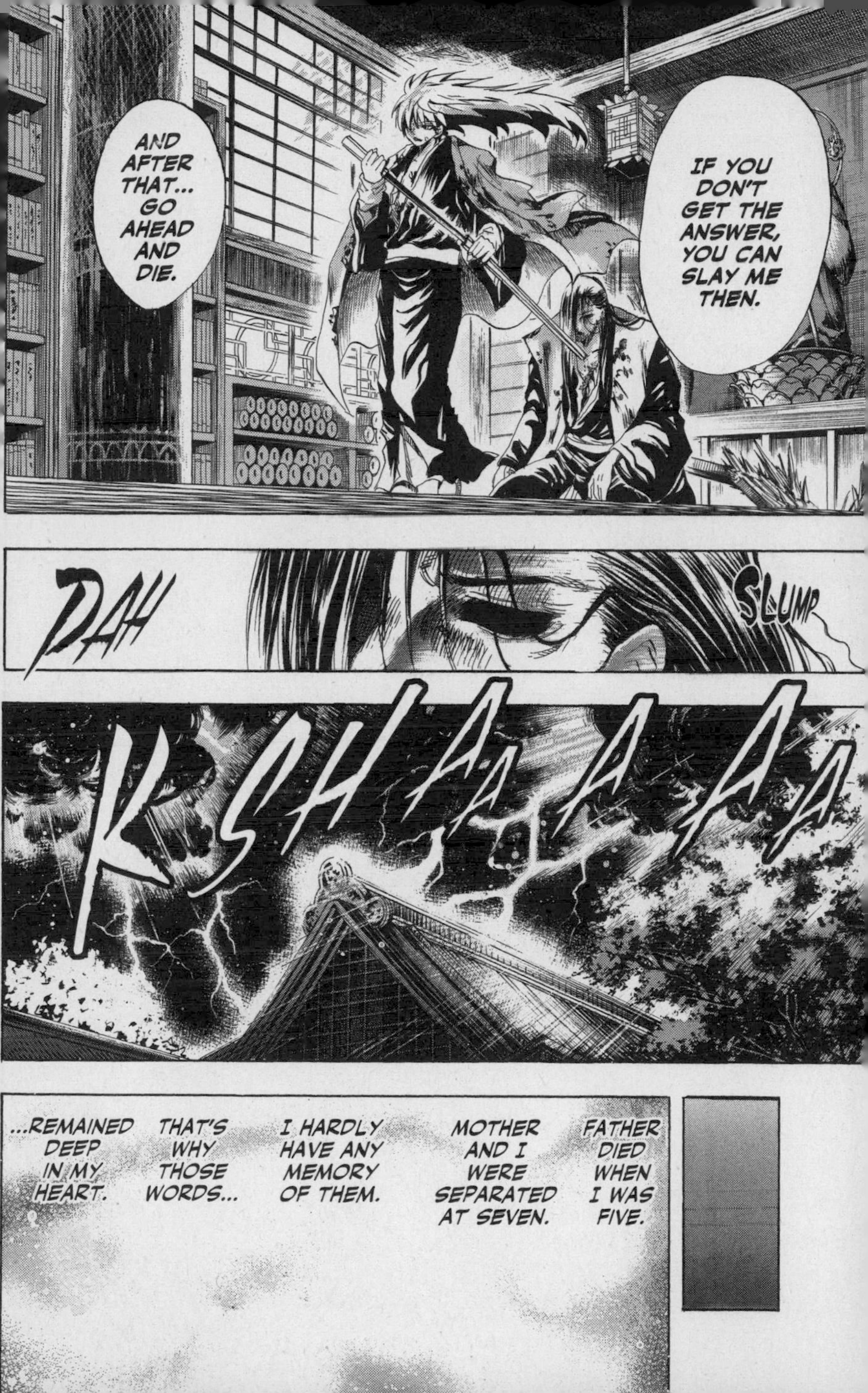
IF YOU DON'T GET THE ANSWER, YOU CAN SLAY ME THEN.
AND AFTER THAT... GO AHEAD AND DIE.
SLUMP
DAH
KSHAAAA
FATHER DIED WHEN I WAS FIVE.
MOTHER AND I WERE SEPARATED AT SEVEN.
I HARDLY HAVE ANY MEMORY OF THEM.
THAT'S WHY THOSE WORDS...
...REMAINED DEEP IN MY HEART.

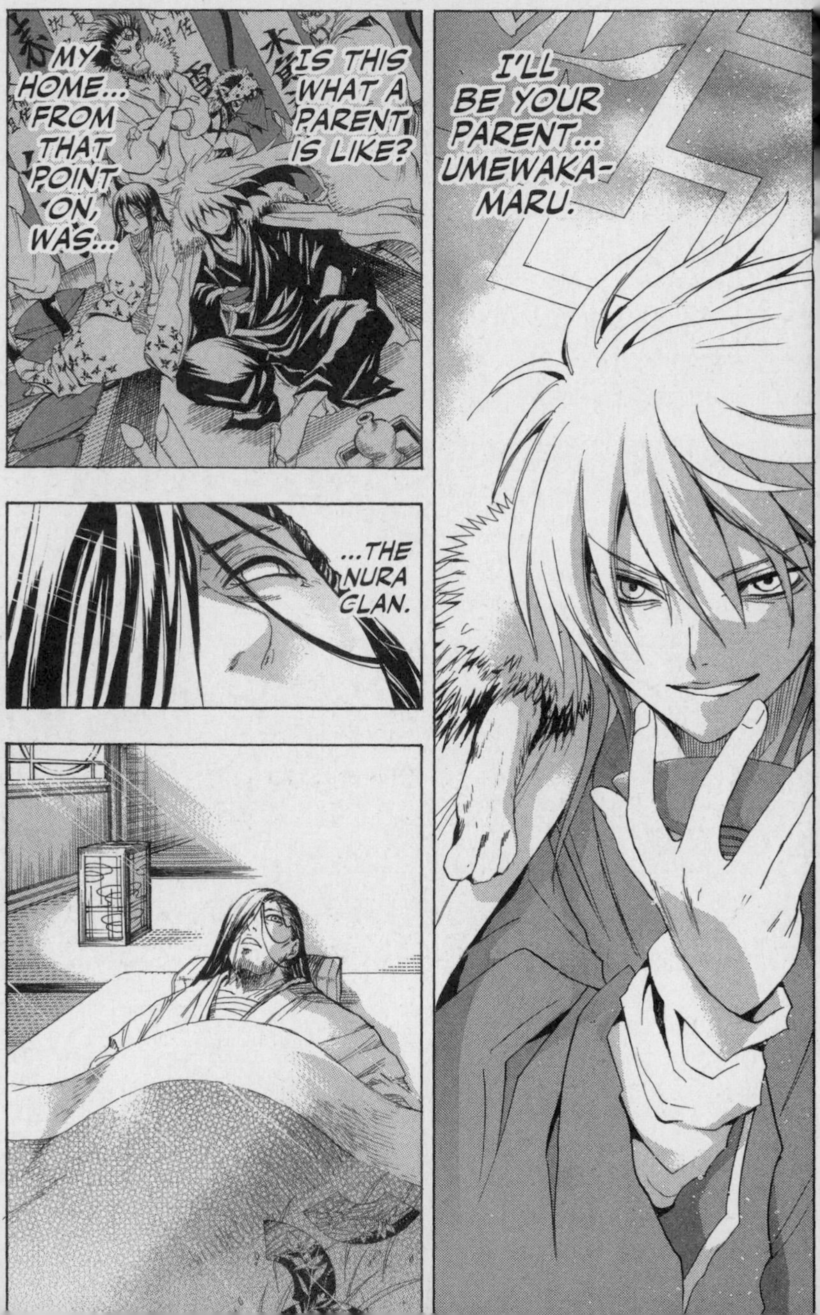
I'LL BE YOUR PARENT... UMEWAKA-MARU.
IS THIS WHAT A PARENT IS LIKE?
MY HOME... FROM THAT POINT ON, WAS...
...THE NURA CLAN.

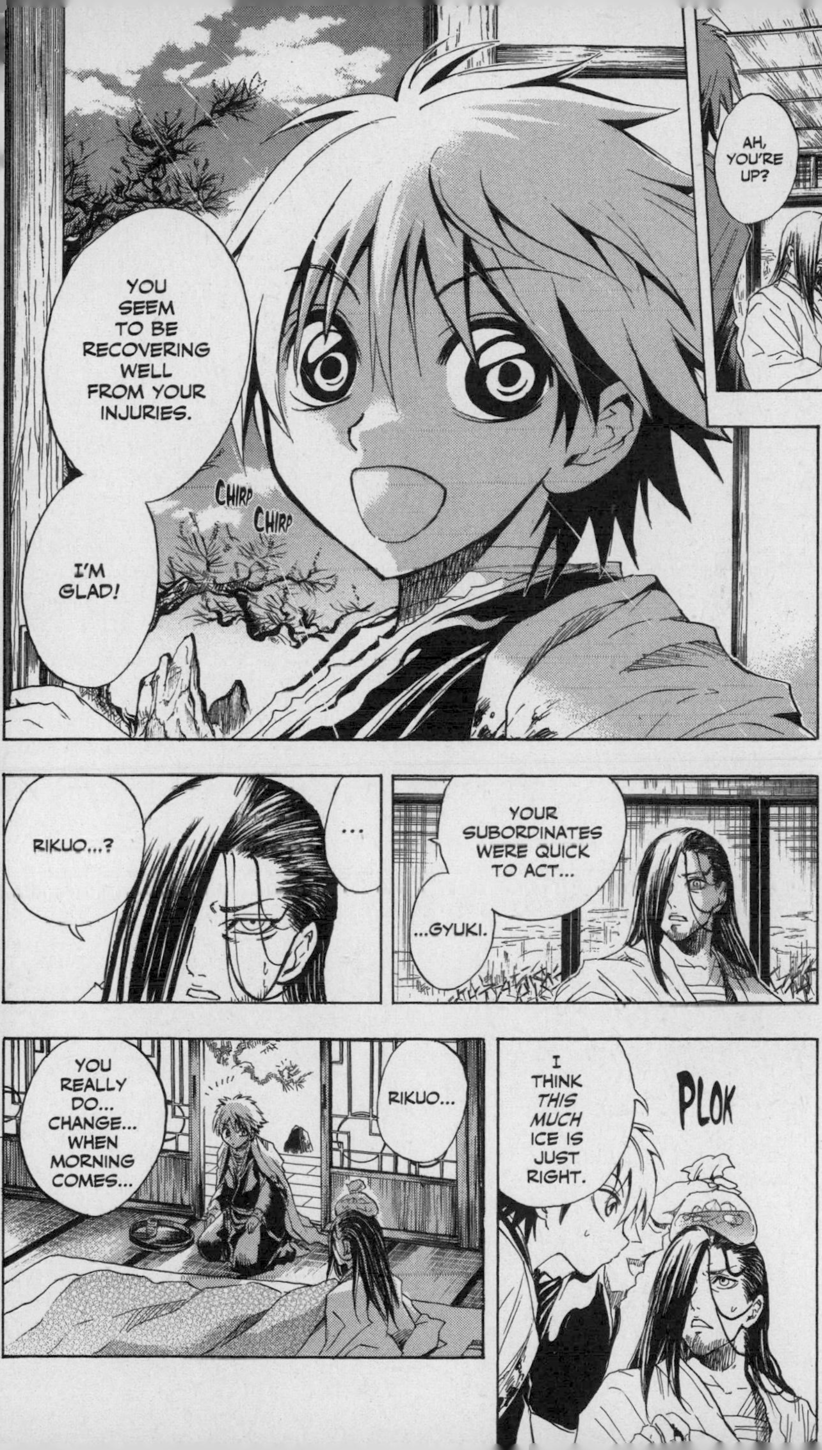
AH, YOU'RE UP?
YOU SEEM TO BE RECOVERING WELL FROM YOUR INJURIES.
CHIRP CHIRP
I'M GLAD!
YOUR SUBORDINATES WERE QUICK TO ACT...
...GYUKI.
...
RIKUO...?
PLOK
I THINK *THIS MUCH* ICE IS JUST RIGHT.
RIKUO...
YOU REALLY DO... CHANGE... WHEN MORNING COMES...

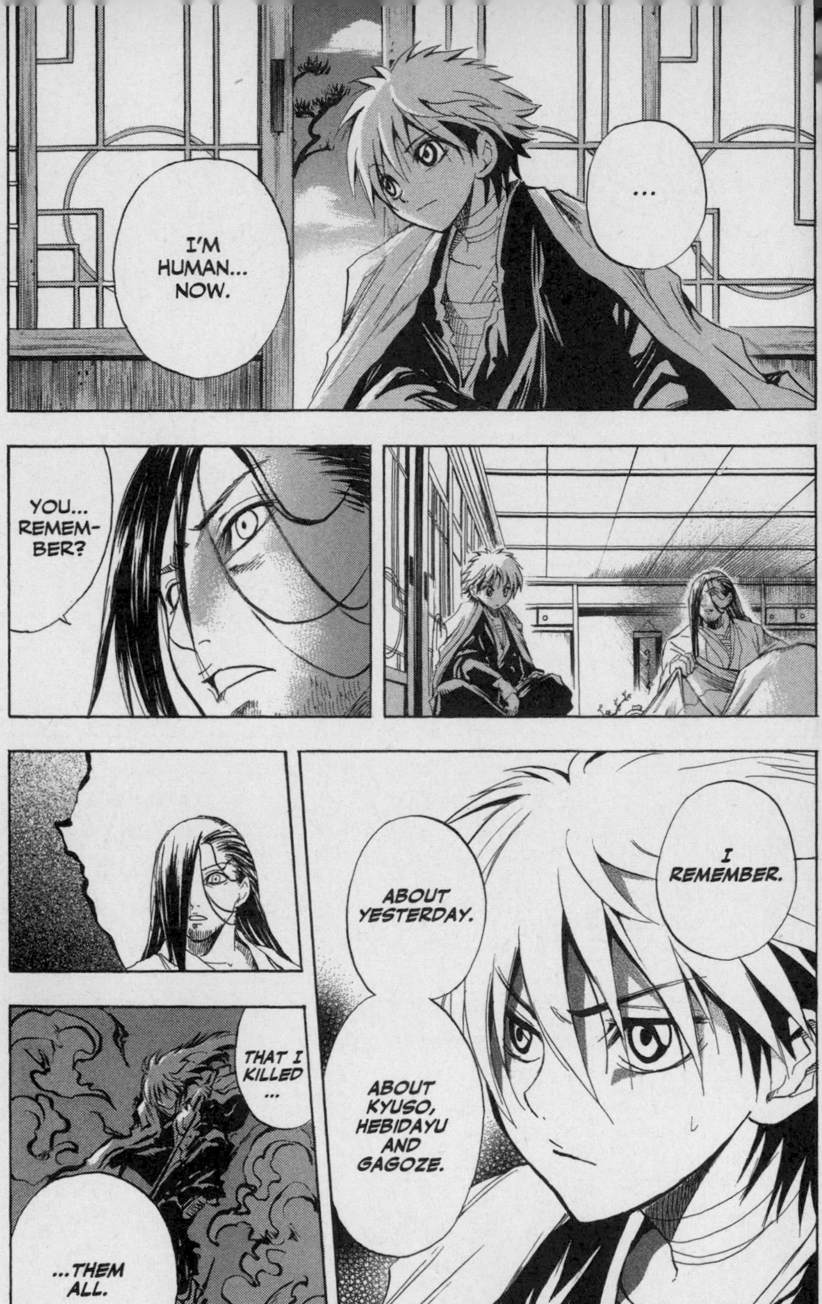
...
I'M HUMAN... NOW.
YOU... REMEMBER?
I REMEMBER.
ABOUT YESTERDAY.
ABOUT KYUSO, HEBIDAYU AND GAGOZE.
THAT I KILLED ...
...THEM ALL.

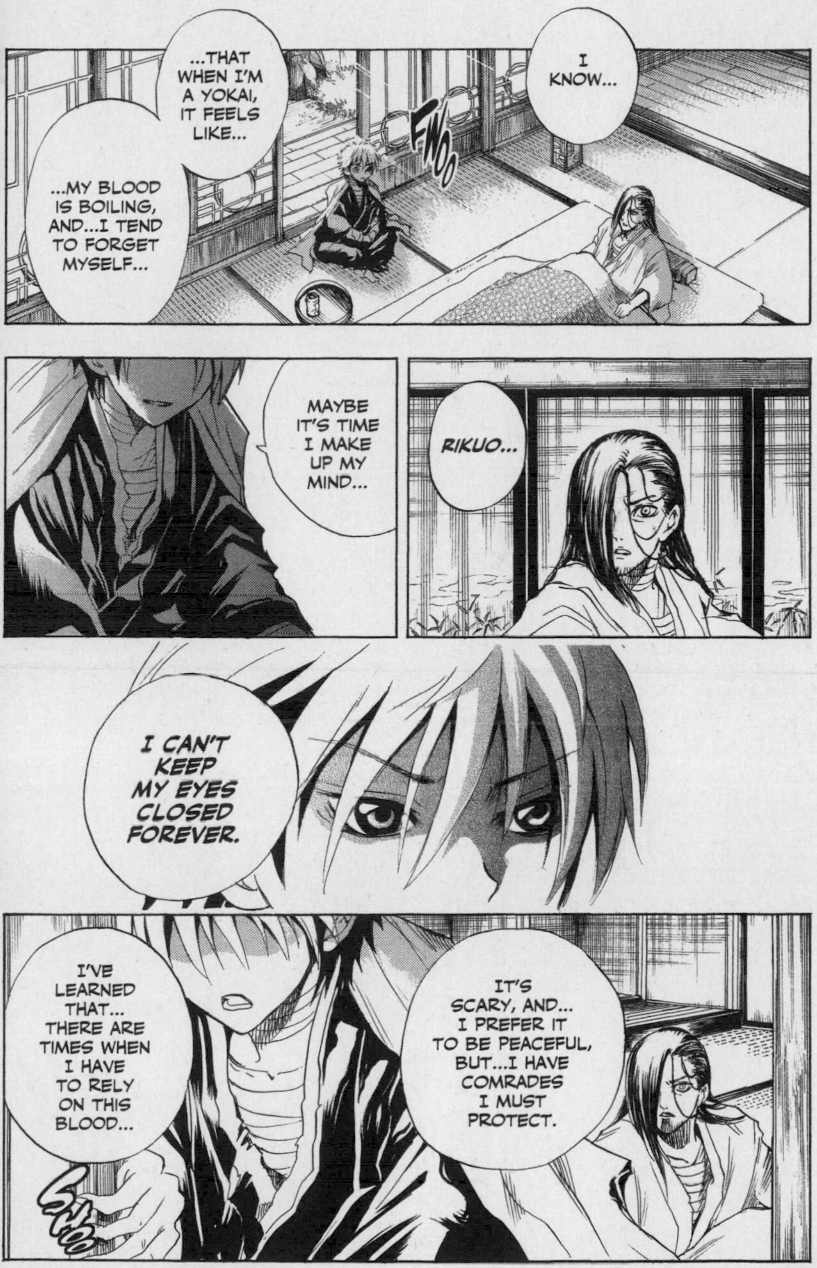
I KNOW...
...THAT WHEN I'M A YOKAI, IT FEELS LIKE...
FWOO
...MY BLOOD IS BOILING, AND...I TEND TO FORGET MYSELF...
RIKUO...
MAYBE IT'S TIME I MAKE UP MY MIND...
I CAN'T KEEP MY EYES CLOSED FOREVER.
IT'S SCARY, AND... I PREFER IT TO BE PEACEFUL, BUT...I HAVE COMRADES I MUST PROTECT.
I'VE LEARNED THAT... THERE ARE TIMES WHEN I HAVE TO RELY ON THIS BLOOD...
SHOO

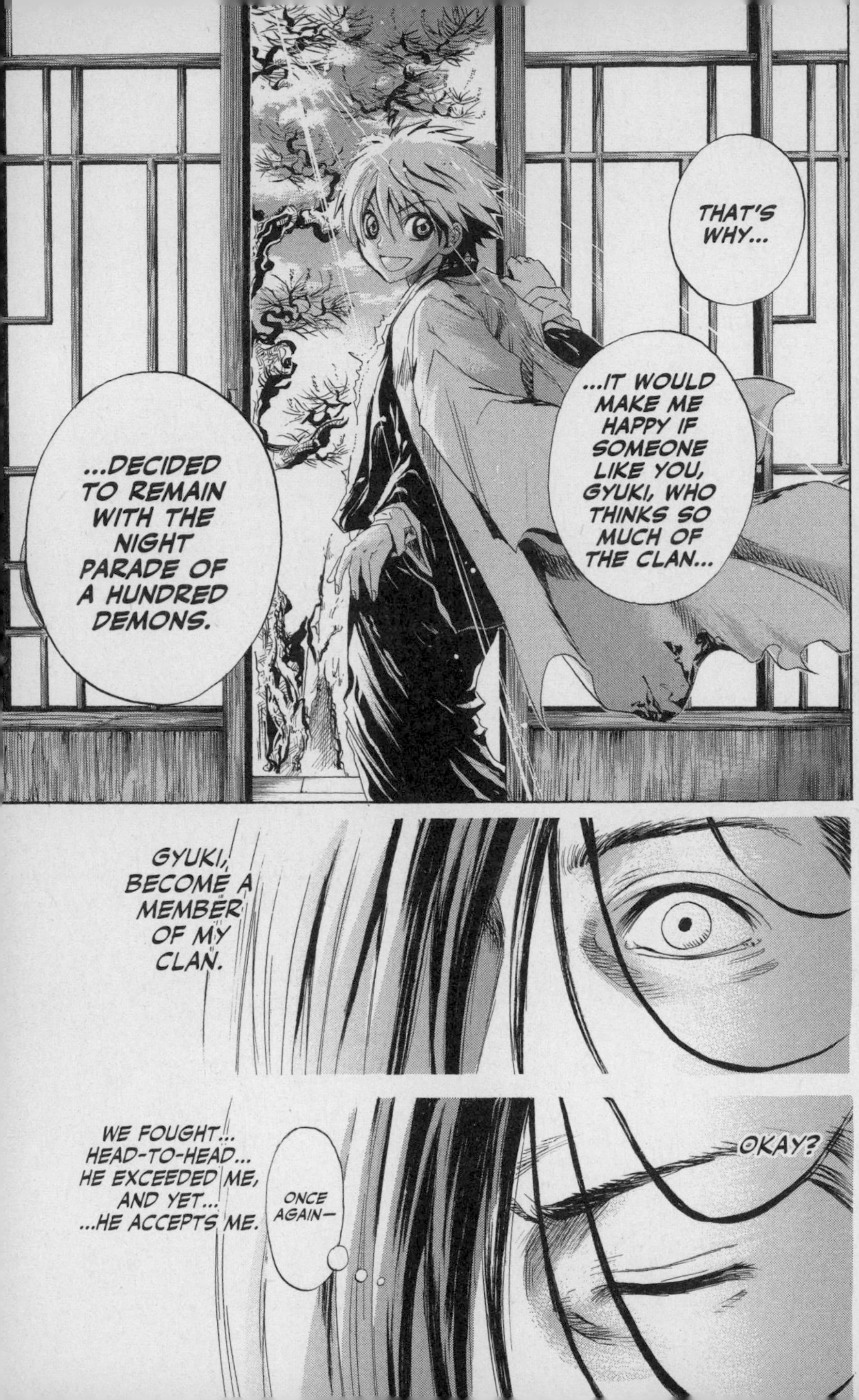
THAT'S WHY...
...IT WOULD MAKE ME HAPPY IF SOMEONE LIKE YOU, GYUKI, WHO THINKS SO MUCH OF THE CLAN...
...DECIDED TO REMAIN WITH THE NIGHT PARADE OF A HUNDRED DEMONS.
GYUKI, BECOME A MEMBER OF MY CLAN.
OKAY?
ONCE AGAIN—
WE FOUGHT... HEAD-TO-HEAD... HE EXCEEDED ME, AND YET... ...HE ACCEPTS ME.

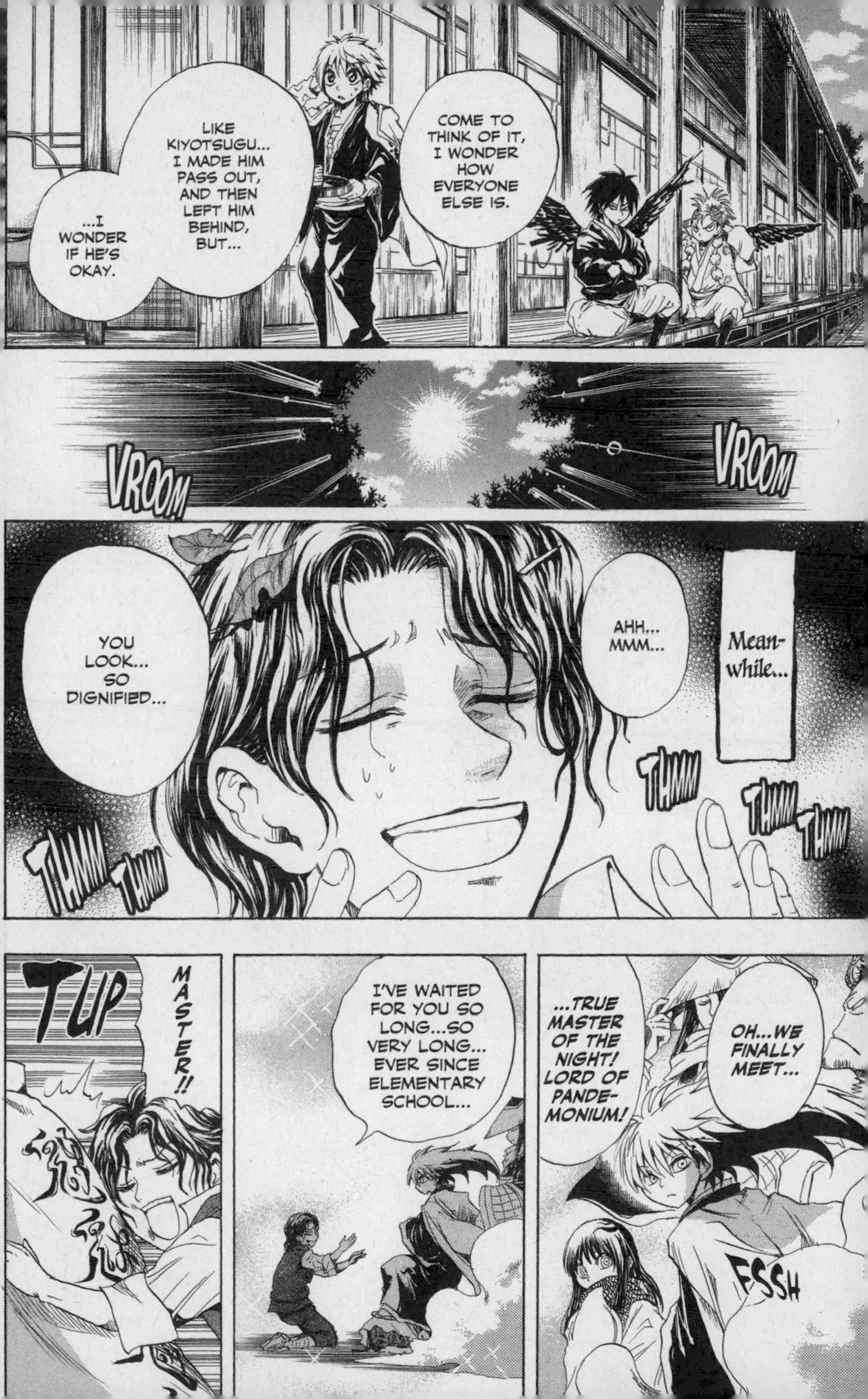
COME TO THINK OF IT, I WONDER HOW EVERYONE ELSE IS.
LIKE KIYOTSUGU... I MADE HIM PASS OUT, AND THEN LEFT HIM BEHIND, BUT...
...I WONDER IF HE'S OKAY.
VROOM
VROOM
Mean-while...
AHH... MMM...
THMM
THMM THMM
YOU LOOK... SO DIGNIFIED...
THMM THMM
OH...WE FINALLY MEET...
...TRUE MASTER OF THE NIGHT! LORD OF PANDE-MONIUM!
FSSH
I'VE WAITED FOR YOU SO LONG...SO VERY LONG... EVER SINCE ELEMENTARY SCHOOL...
MASTER!!
TUP

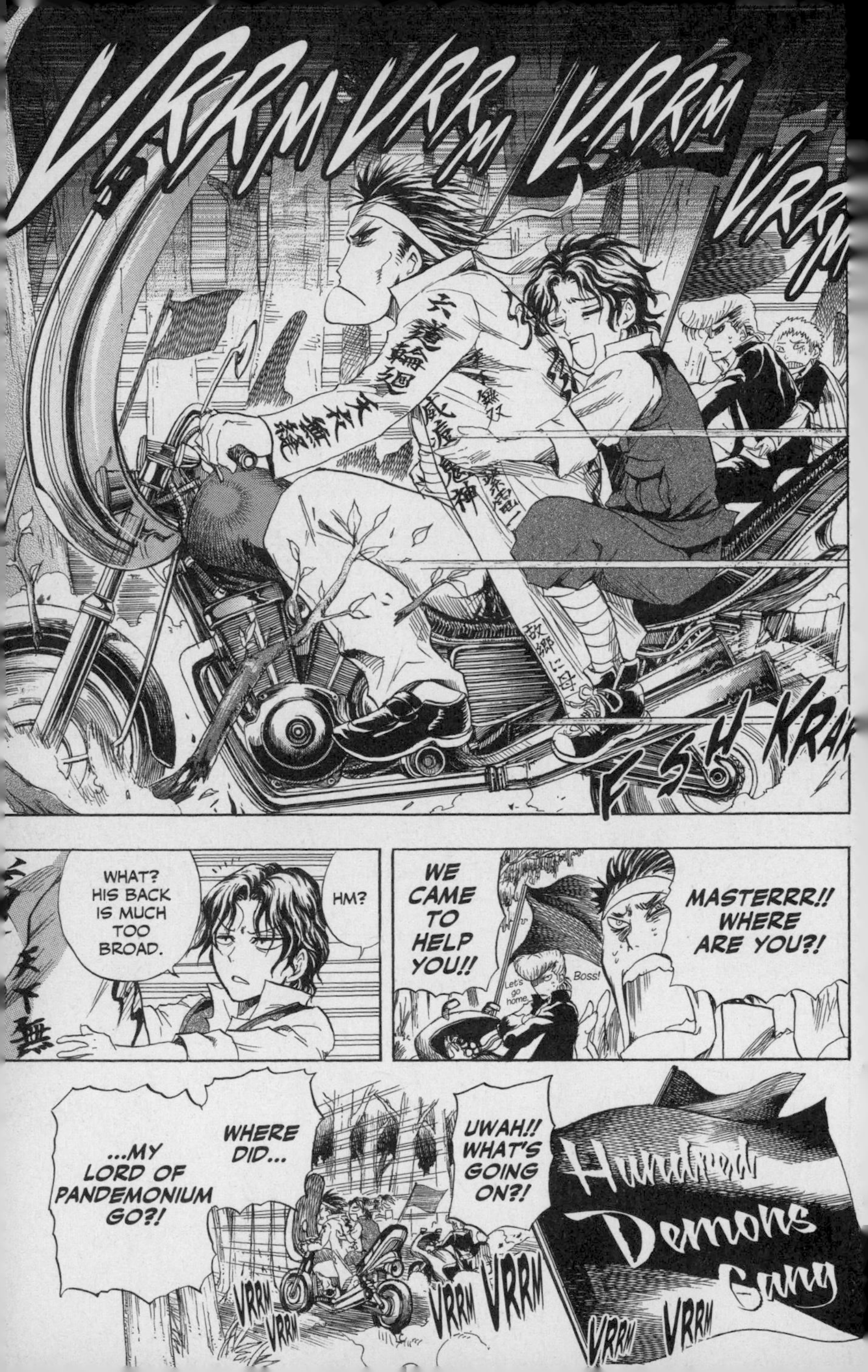
VRRM VRRM VRRM VRRM
FSH KRAK
MASTERRR!! WHERE ARE YOU?!
WE CAME TO HELP YOU!!
Boss!
Let's go home.
HM?
WHAT? HIS BACK IS MUCH TOO BROAD.
Hundred Demons Gang
UWAH!! WHAT'S GOING ON?!
WHERE DID...
...MY LORD OF PANDEMONIUM GO?!
VRRM VRRM VRRM VRRM VRRM VRRM

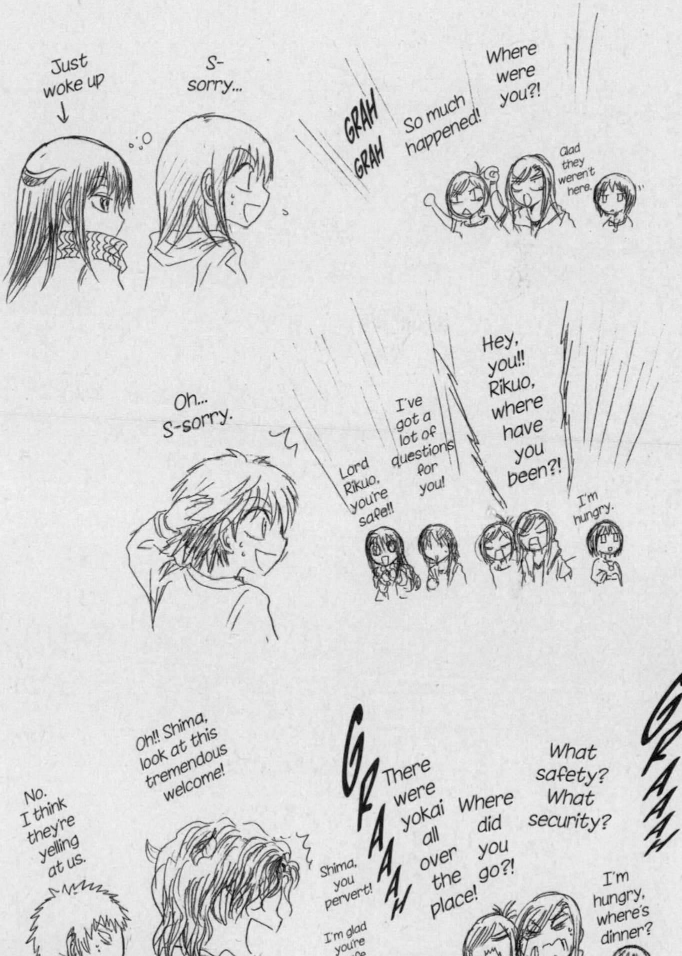
Where were you?!
GRAH
GRAH
So much happened!
Glad they weren't here.
S-sorry...
Just woke up
Hey, you!! Rikuo, where have you been?!
I'm hungry.
I've got a lot of questions for you!
Lord Rikuo, you're safe!!
Oh... S-sorry.
GRAAAAH
What safety? What security?
I'm hungry, where's dinner?
Where did you go?!
There were yokai all over the place!
GRAAAAH
Shima, you pervert!
I'm glad you're safe
Oh!! Shima, look at this tremendous welcome!
No. I think they're yelling at us.

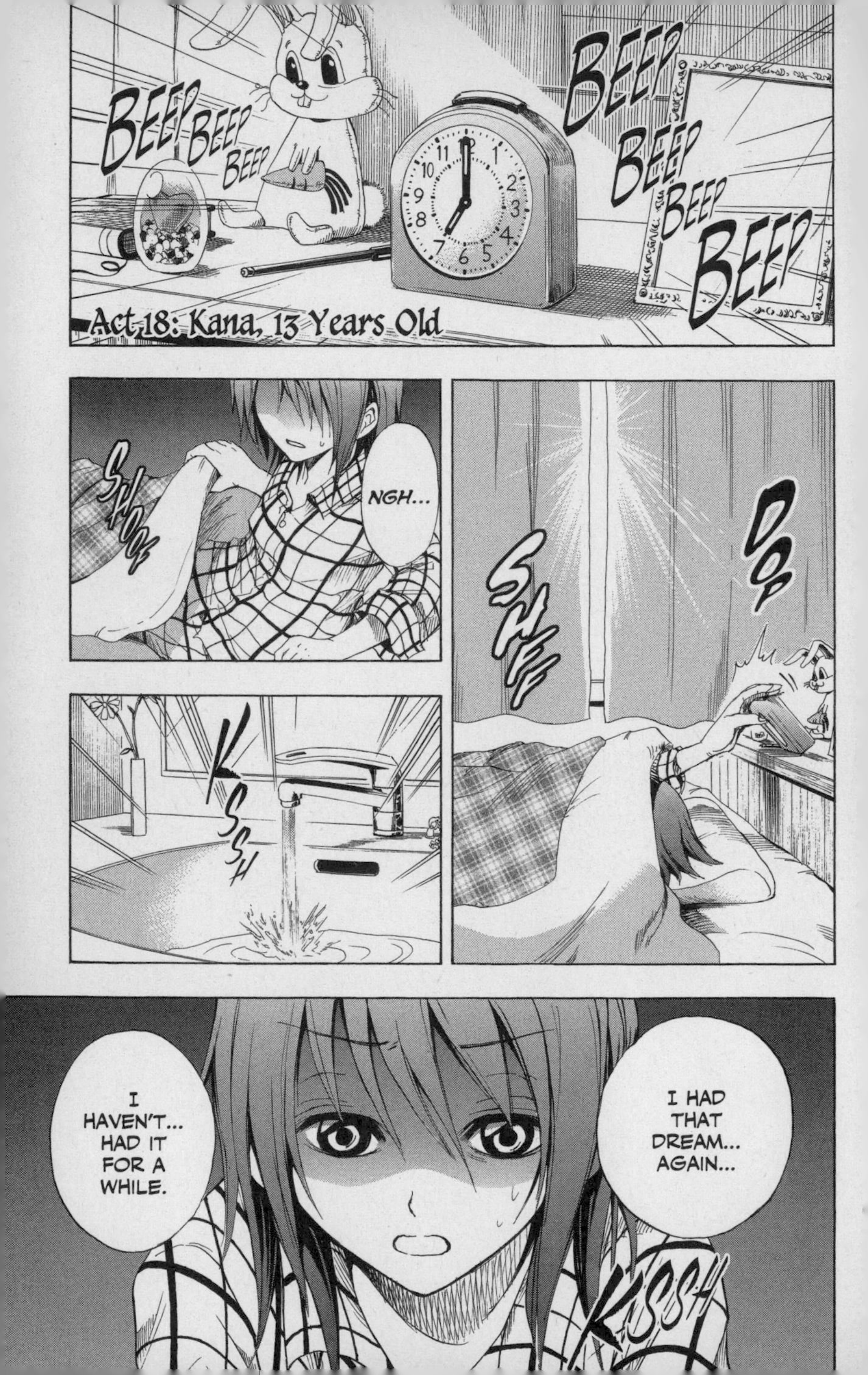
BEEP BEEP BEEP BEEP
BEEP BEEP BEEP
Act 18: Kana, 13 Years Old
DOP
SHFF
NGH...
SHOOF
KSSH
I HAD THAT DREAM... AGAIN...
I HAVEN'T... HAD IT FOR A WHILE.
KSSH

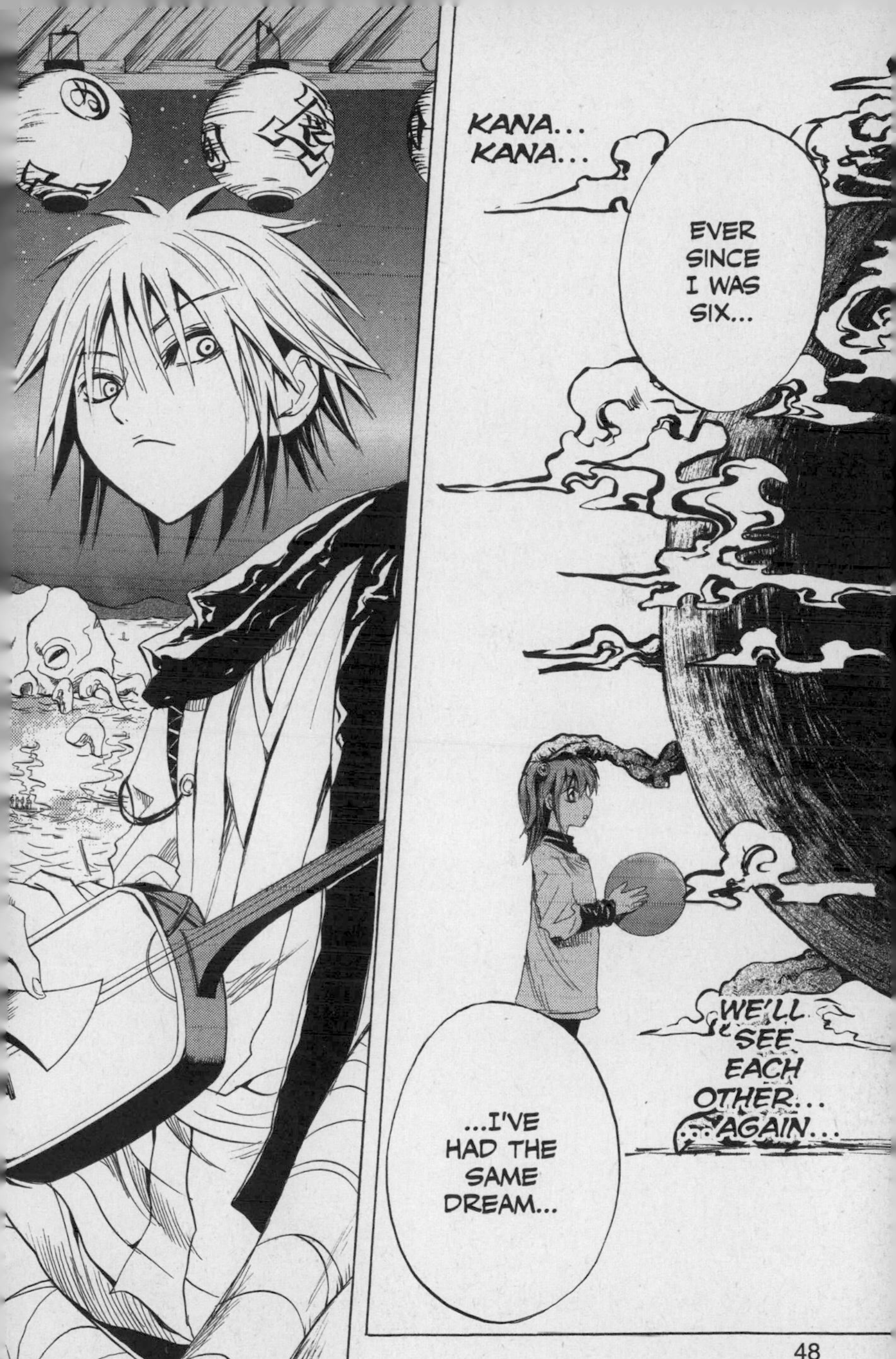
KANA... KANA...
EVER SINCE I WAS SIX...
WE'LL SEE EACH OTHER... ...AGAIN...
...I'VE HAD THE SAME DREAM...

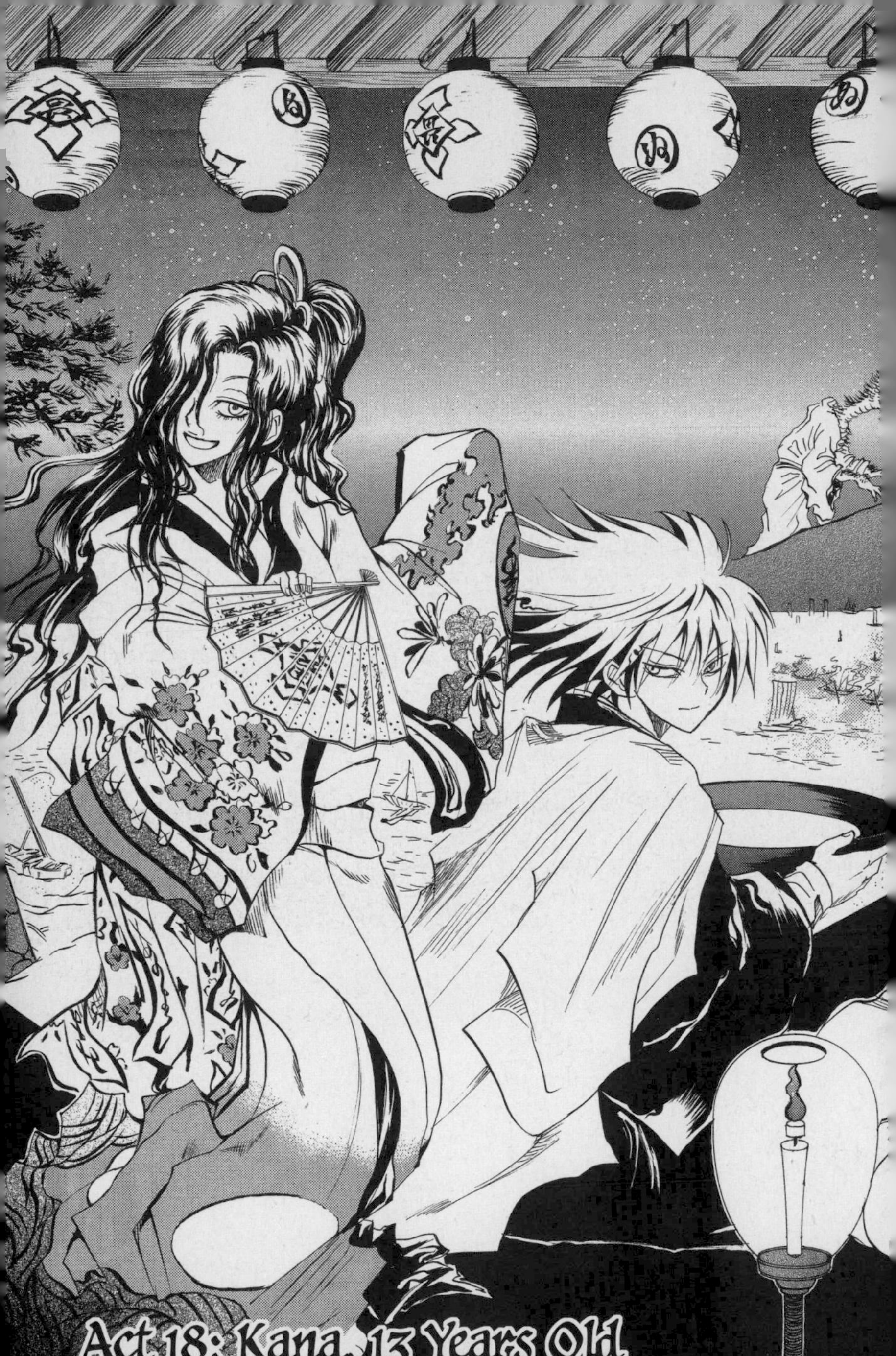

Act 18: Kana, 13 Years Old

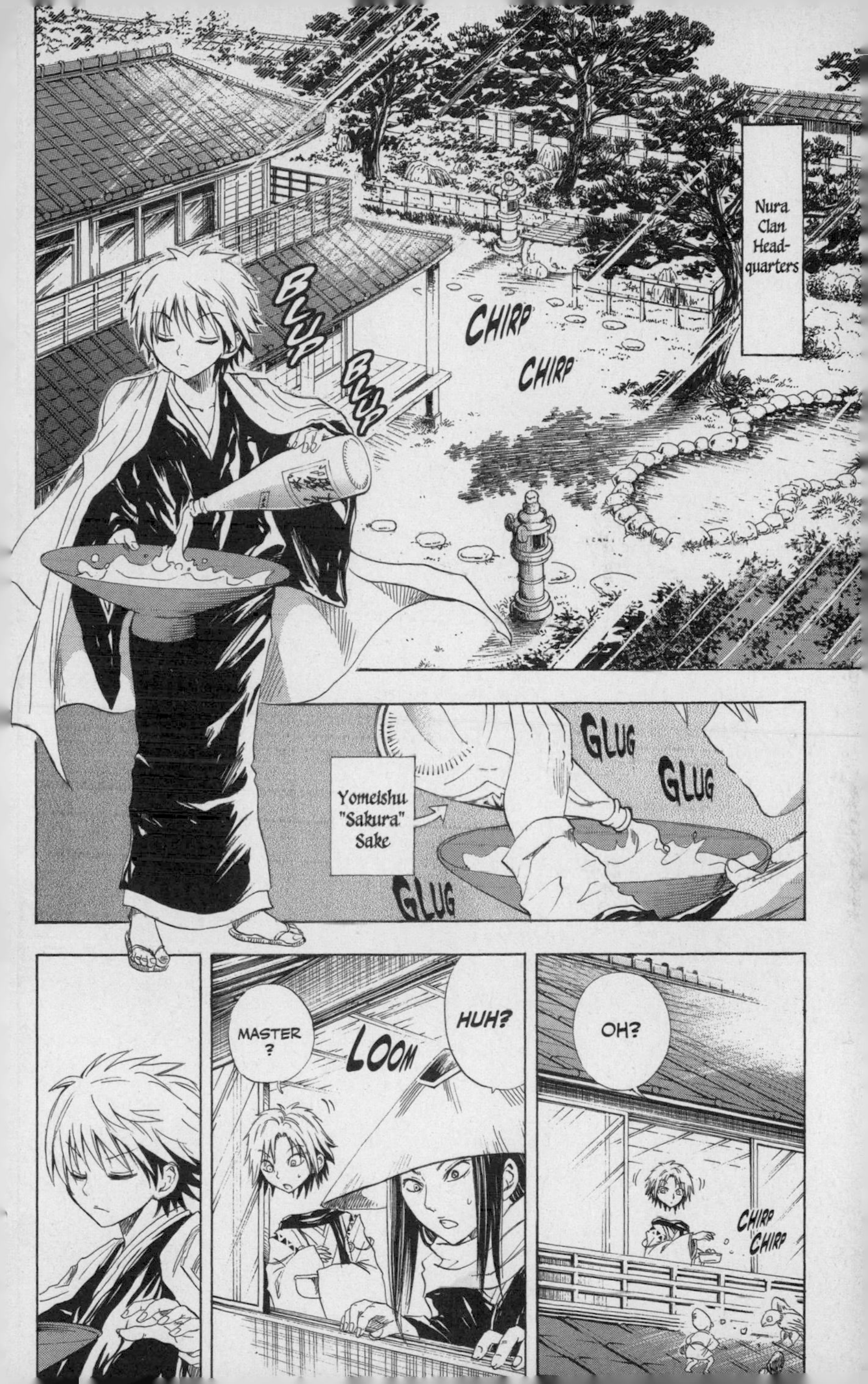
Nura Clan Head-quarters
CHIRP
CHIRP
BLUP
BLUP
GLUG
GLUG
Yomeishu "Sakura" Sake
GLUG
OH?
CHIRP
CHIRP
HUH?
LOOM
MASTER?

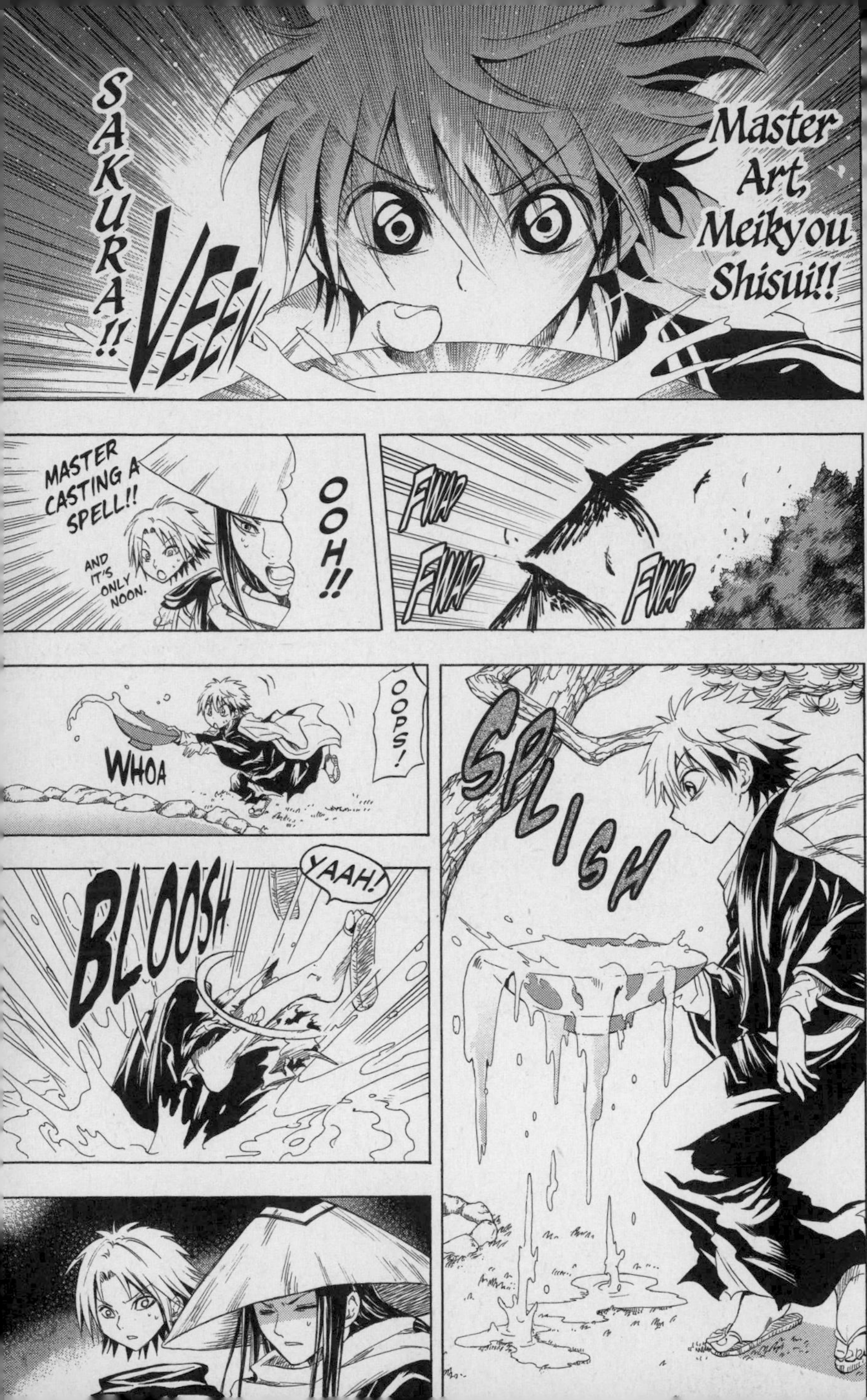
Master Art, Meikyou Shisui!!
SAKURA!!
VEEN
FWAP
FWAP
FWAP
OOH!!
MASTER CASTING A SPELL!!
AND IT'S ONLY NOON.
SPLISH
OOPS!
WHOA
YAAH!
BLOOSH

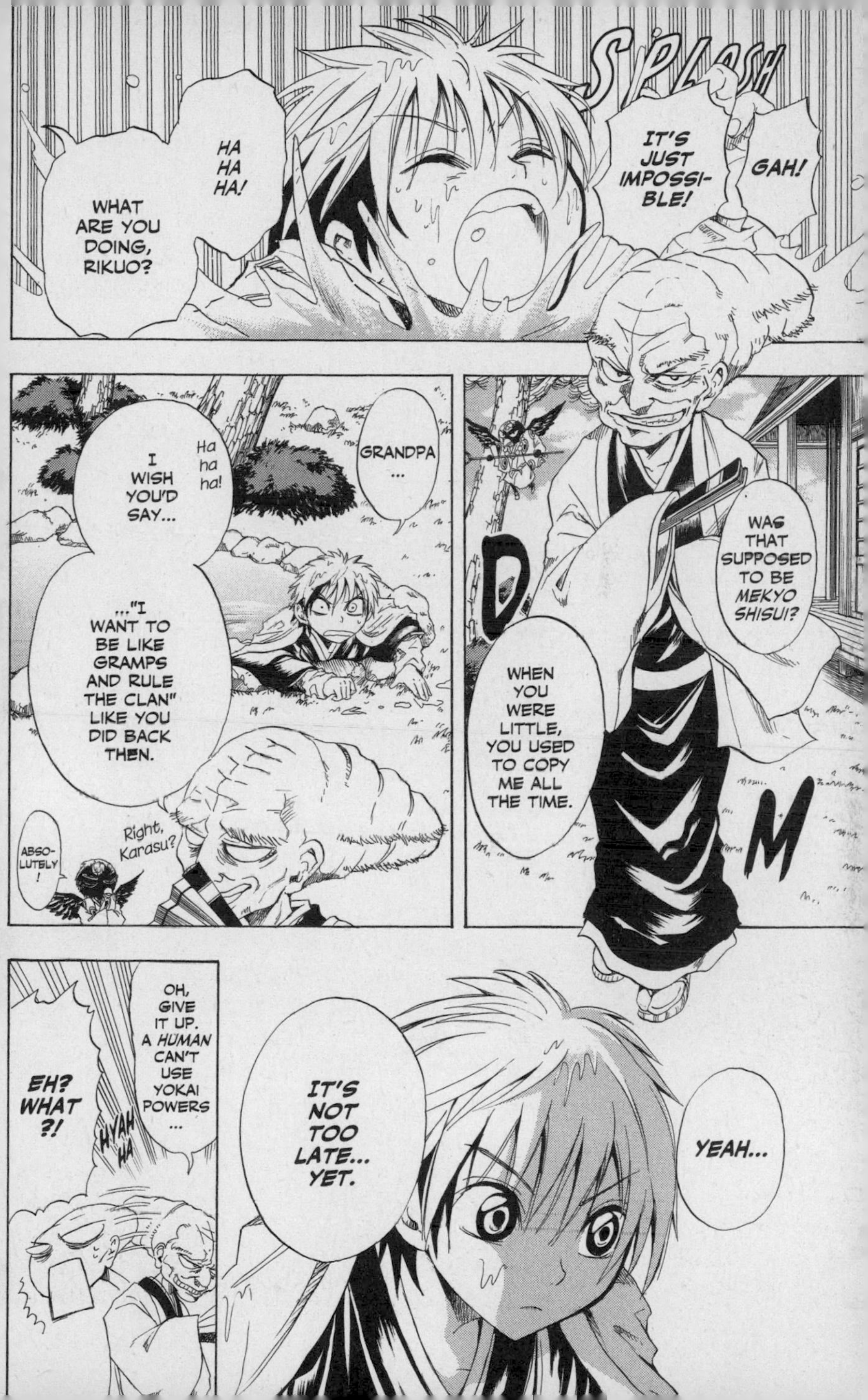
SPLASH
GAH!
IT'S JUST IMPOSSIBLE!
HA HA HA!
WHAT ARE YOU DOING, RIKUO?
WAS THAT SUPPOSED TO BE *MEKYO SHISUI*?
D
WHEN YOU WERE LITTLE, YOU USED TO COPY ME ALL THE TIME.
M
GRANDPA...
Ha ha ha!
I WISH YOU'D SAY...
..."I WANT TO BE LIKE GRAMPS AND RULE THE CLAN" LIKE YOU DID BACK THEN.
Right, Karasu?
ABSOLUTELY!
YEAH...
IT'S NOT TOO LATE... YET.
OH, GIVE IT UP. A *HUMAN* CAN'T USE YOKAI POWERS...
HYAH HA
EH? WHAT?!

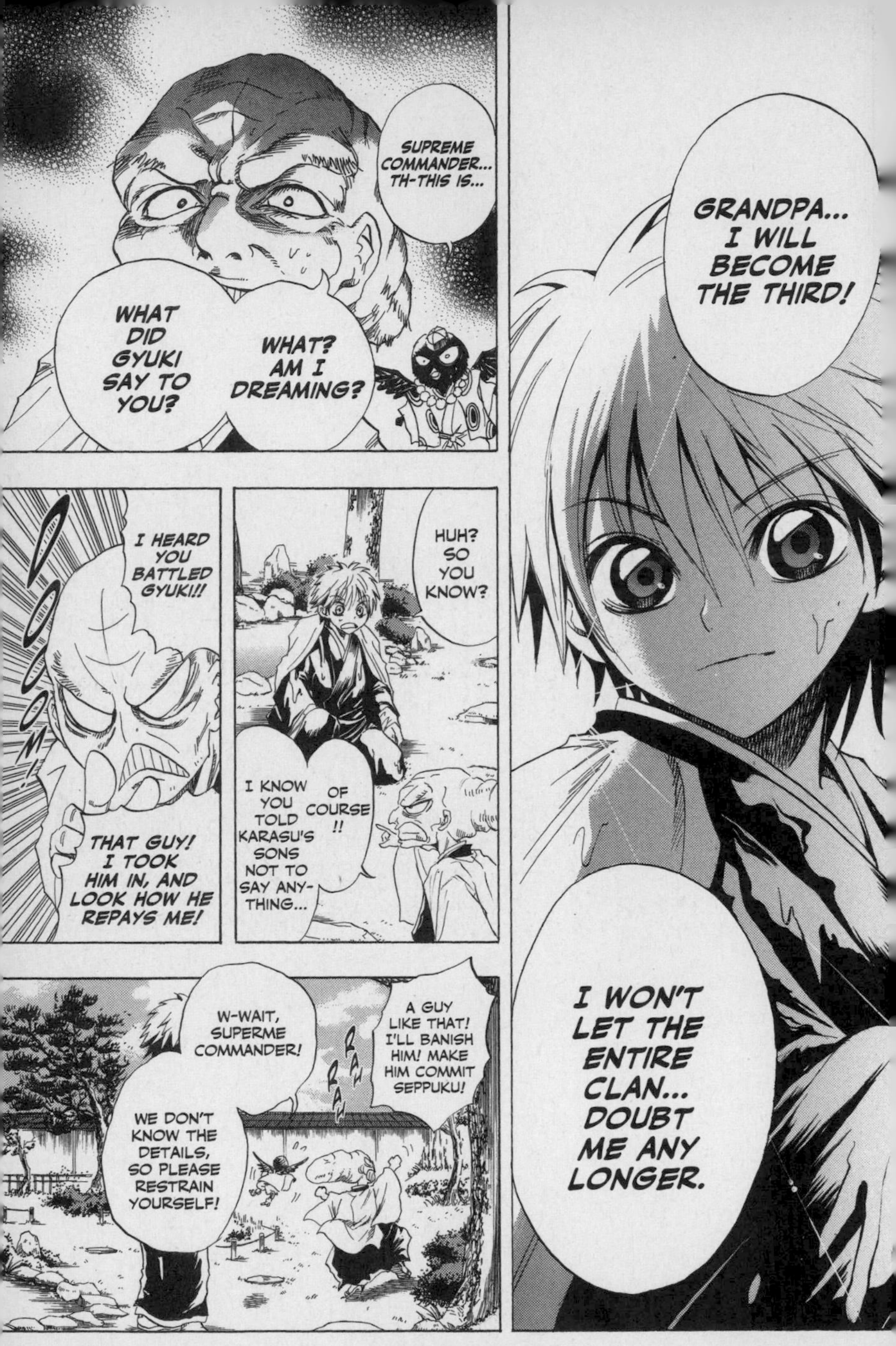
GRANDPA... I WILL BECOME THE THIRD!
I WON'T LET THE ENTIRE CLAN... DOUBT ME ANY LONGER.
SUPREME COMMANDER... TH-THIS IS...
WHAT? AM I DREAMING?
WHAT DID GYUKI SAY TO YOU?
HUH? SO YOU KNOW?
OF COURSE!!
I KNOW YOU TOLD KARASU'S SONS NOT TO SAY ANY-THING...
I HEARD YOU BATTLED GYUKI!!
THAT GUY! I TOOK HIM IN, AND LOOK HOW HE REPAYS ME!
A GUY LIKE THAT! I'LL BANISH HIM! MAKE HIM COMMIT SEPPUKU!
W-WAIT, SUPERME COMMANDER!
WE DON'T KNOW THE DETAILS, SO PLEASE RESTRAIN YOURSELF!

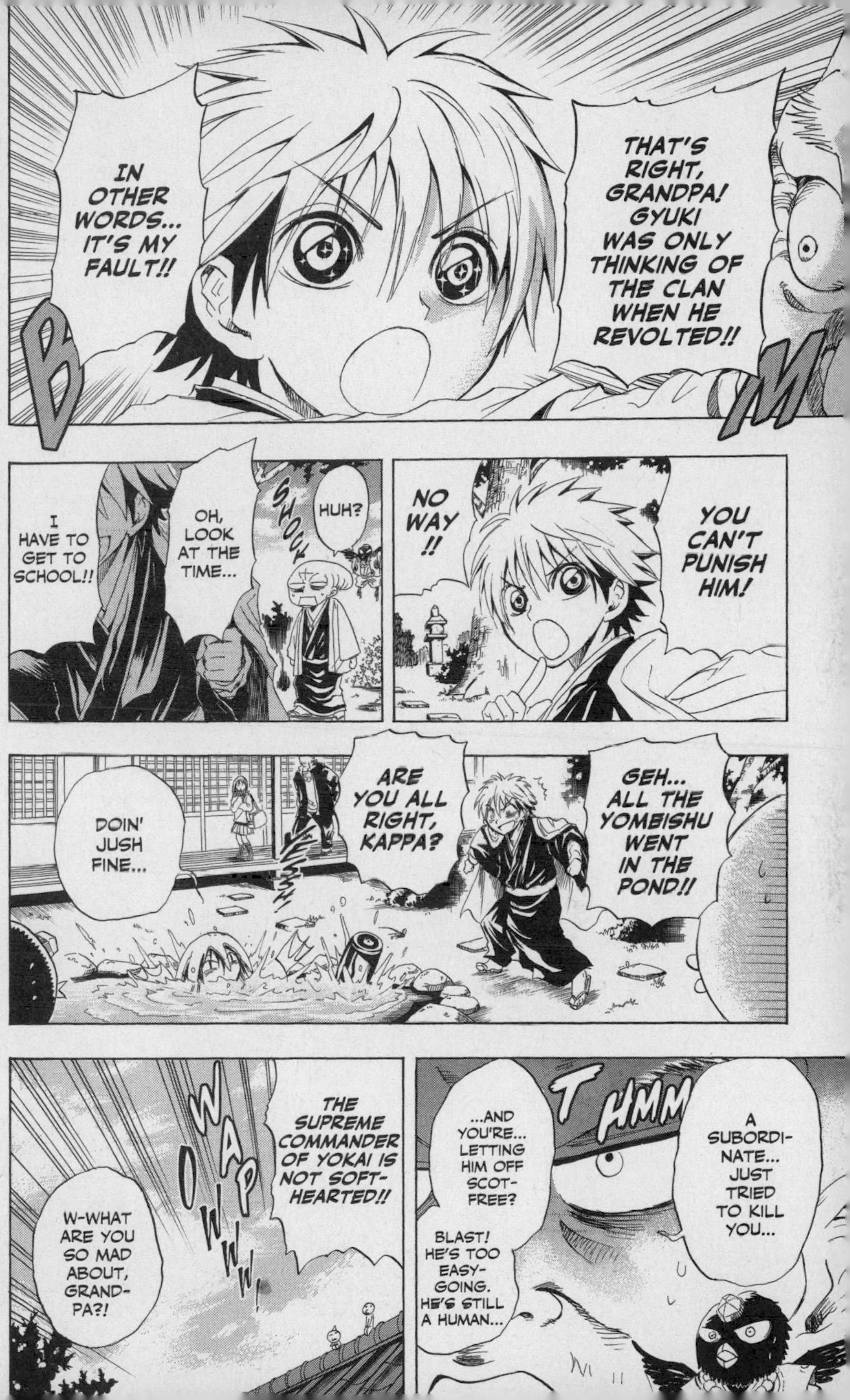
THAT'S RIGHT, GRANDPA! GYUKI WAS ONLY THINKING OF THE CLAN WHEN HE REVOLTED!!
IN OTHER WORDS... IT'S MY FAULT!!
YOU CAN'T PUNISH HIM!
NO WAY!!
HUH?
OH, LOOK AT THE TIME...
I HAVE TO GET TO SCHOOL!!
GEH... ALL THE YOMBISHU WENT IN THE POND!!
ARE YOU ALL RIGHT, KAPPA?
DOIN' JUSH FINE...
THMM
A SUBORDINATE... JUST TRIED TO KILL YOU...
...AND YOU'RE... LETTING HIM OFF SCOT-FREE?
BLAST! HE'S TOO EASY-GOING. HE'S STILL A HUMAN...
THE SUPREME COMMANDER OF YOKAI IS NOT SOFT-HEARTED!!
WAP
OWWW!
W-WHAT ARE YOU SO MAD ABOUT, GRANDPA?!

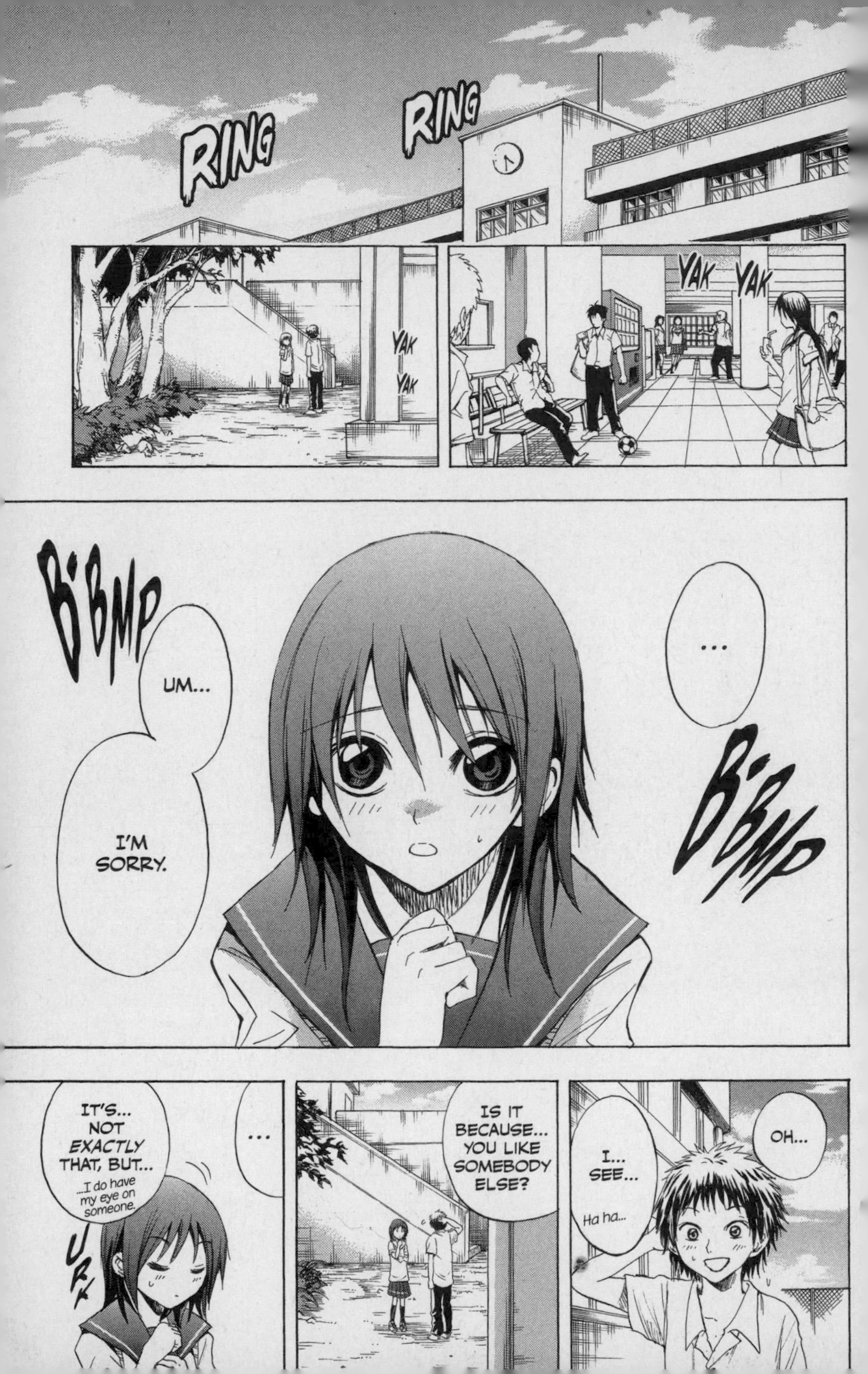
RING
RING
YAK YAK
YAK YAK
...
B'BMP
UM...
I'M SORRY.
B'BMP
OH...
I... SEE...
Ha ha...
IS IT BECAUSE... YOU LIKE SOMEBODY ELSE?
...
IT'S... NOT *EXACTLY* THAT, BUT...
...I do have my eye on someone.
URK

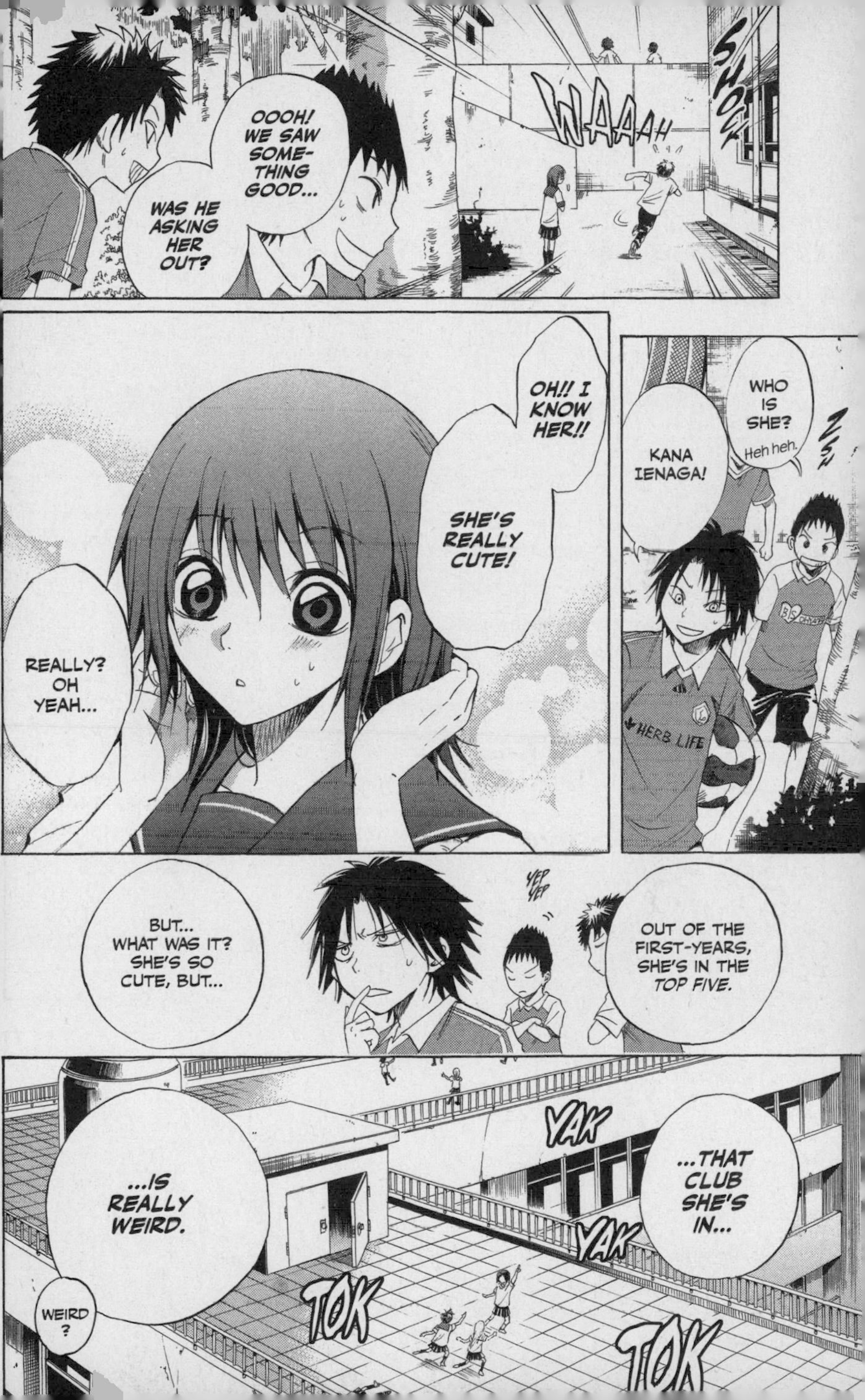
SHOCK
WAAAH
OOOH! WE SAW SOME-THING GOOD...
WAS HE ASKING HER OUT?
WHO IS SHE? Heh heh.
KANA IENAGA!
HERB LIFE
OH!! I KNOW HER!!
SHE'S REALLY CUTE!
REALLY? OH YEAH...
OUT OF THE FIRST-YEARS, SHE'S IN THE *TOP FIVE*.
YEP YEP
BUT... WHAT WAS IT? SHE'S SO CUTE, BUT...
...THAT CLUB SHE'S IN...
YAK
YAK
...IS REALLY WEIRD.
WEIRD?
TOK
TOK

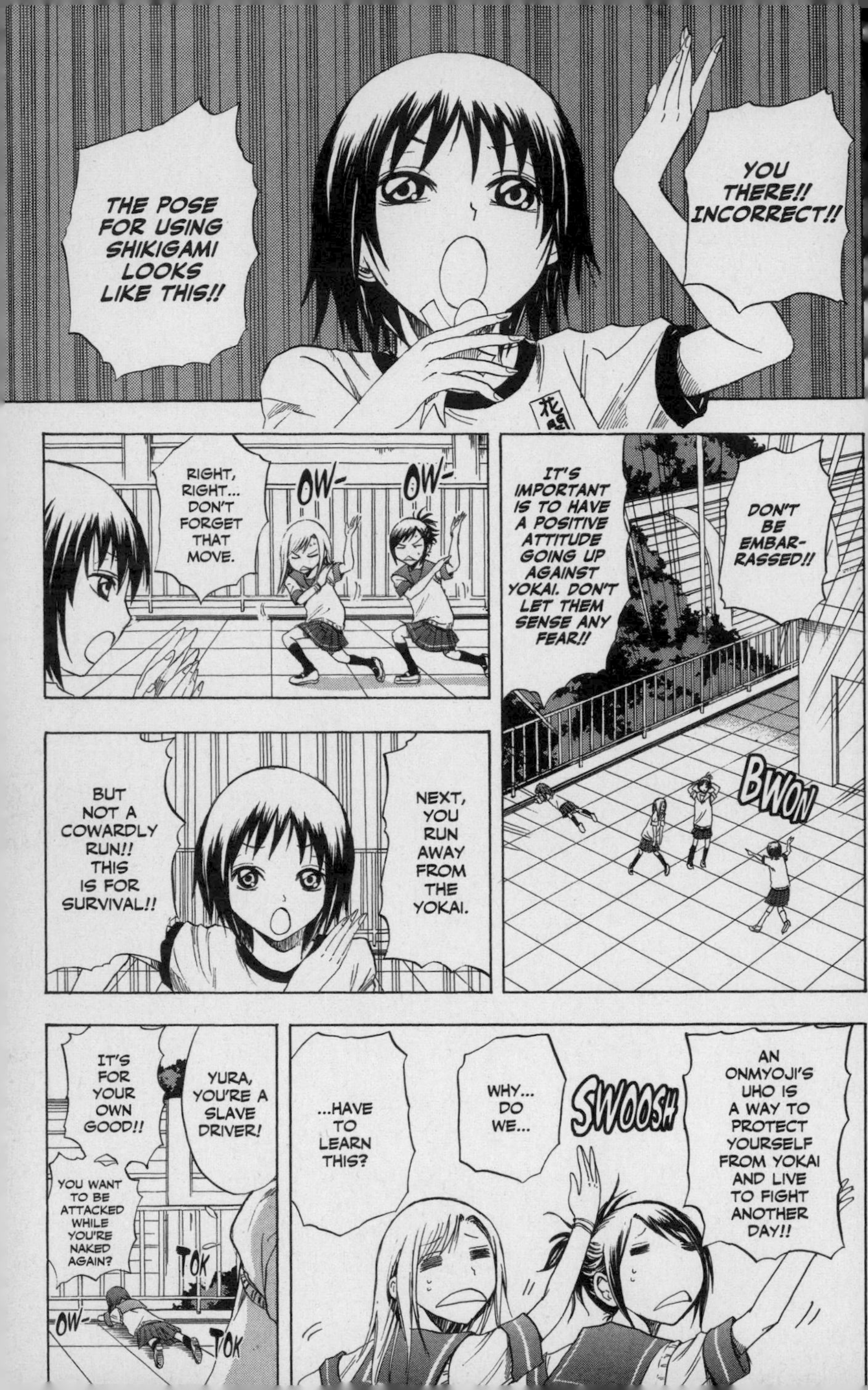
YOU THERE!! INCORRECT!!
THE POSE FOR USING SHIKIGAMI LOOKS LIKE THIS!!
DON'T BE EMBARRASSED!!
IT'S IMPORTANT IS TO HAVE A POSITIVE ATTITUDE GOING UP AGAINST YOKAI. DON'T LET THEM SENSE ANY FEAR!!
BWON
OW- OW-
RIGHT, RIGHT... DON'T FORGET THAT MOVE.
NEXT, YOU RUN AWAY FROM THE YOKAI.
BUT NOT A COWARDLY RUN!! THIS IS FOR SURVIVAL!!
AN ONMYOJI'S UHO IS A WAY TO PROTECT YOURSELF FROM YOKAI AND LIVE TO FIGHT ANOTHER DAY!!
SWOOSH
WHY... DO WE...
...HAVE TO LEARN THIS?
YURA, YOU'RE A SLAVE DRIVER!
IT'S FOR YOUR OWN GOOD!!
YOU WANT TO BE ATTACKED WHILE YOU'RE NAKED AGAIN?
TOK
TOK
OW-

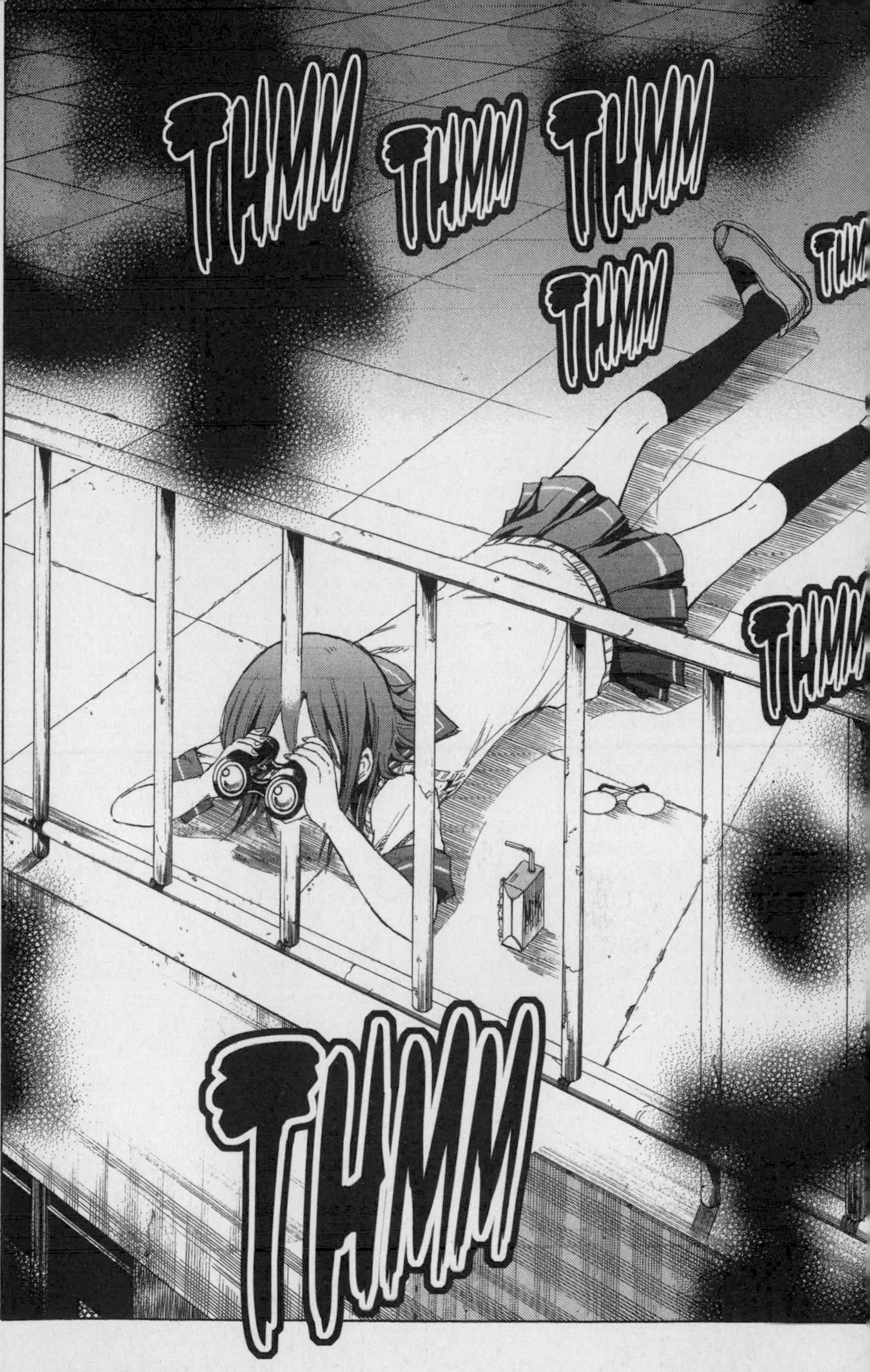
THMM
THMM
THMM
THMM
THMM

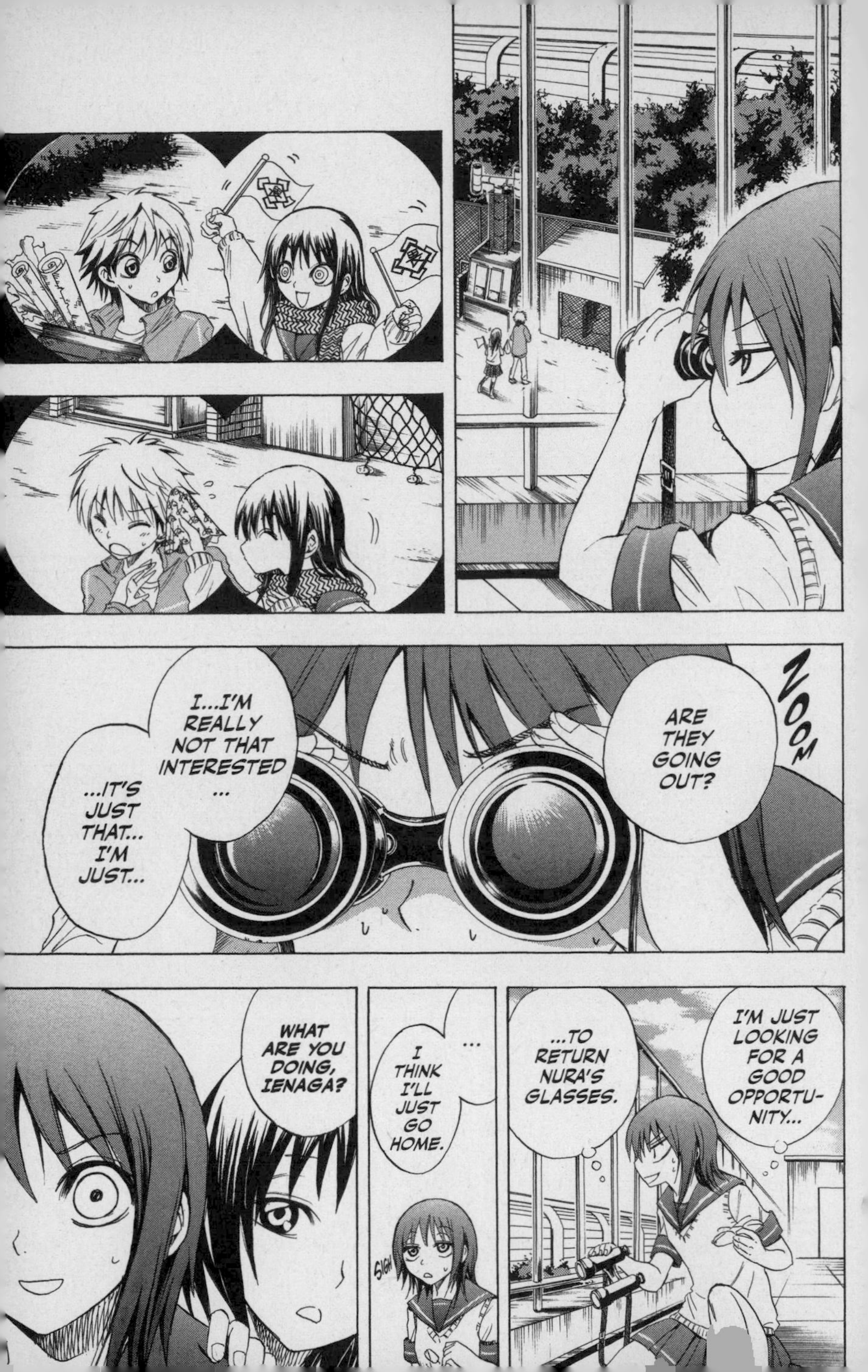
ZOOM
ARE THEY GOING OUT?
I...I'M REALLY NOT THAT INTERESTED ...
...IT'S JUST THAT... I'M JUST...
I'M JUST LOOKING FOR A GOOD OPPORTU-NITY...
...TO RETURN NURA'S GLASSES.
...
I THINK I'LL JUST GO HOME.
SIGH
WHAT ARE YOU DOING, IENAGA?

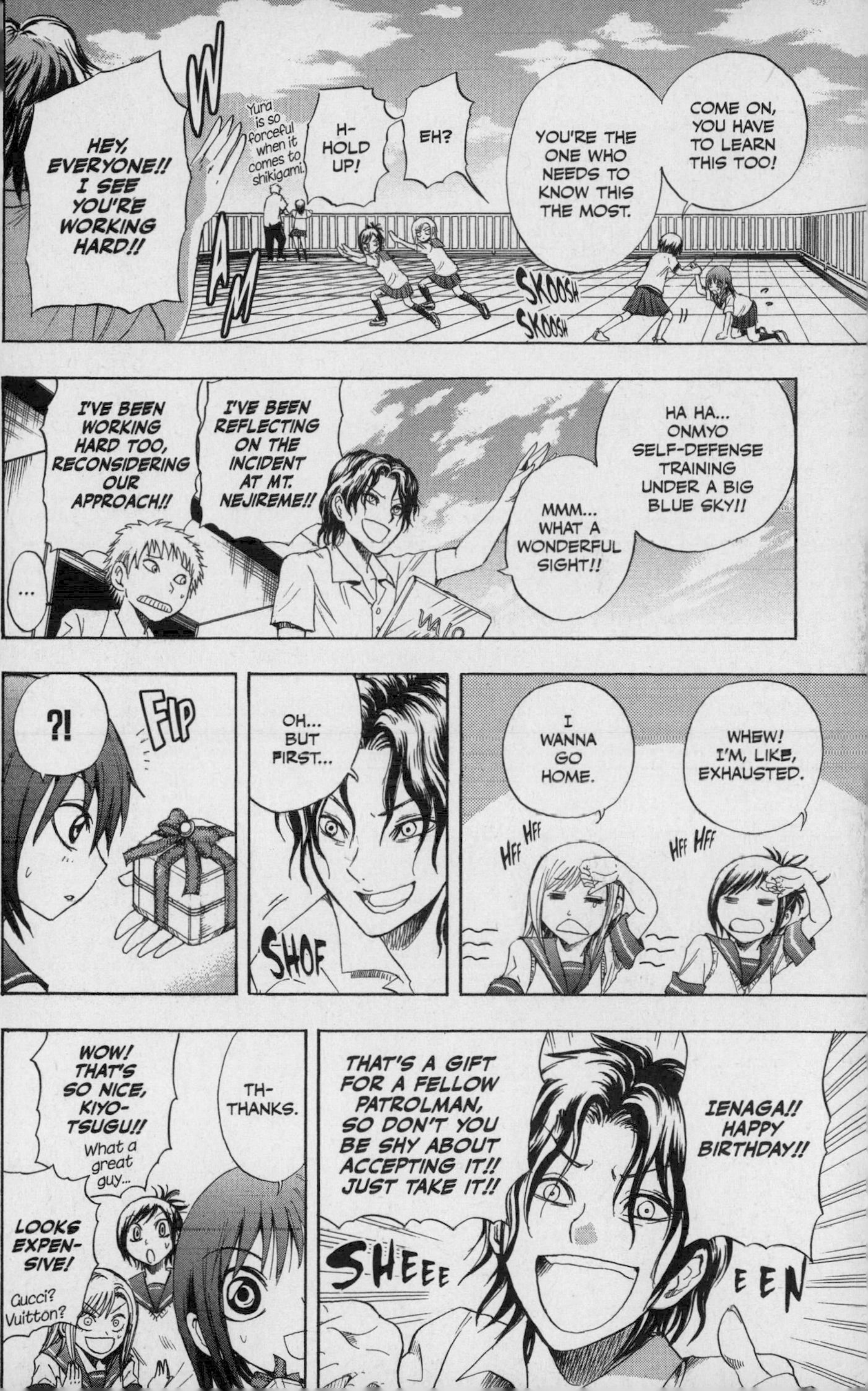
COME ON, YOU HAVE TO LEARN THIS TOO!
YOU'RE THE ONE WHO NEEDS TO KNOW THIS THE MOST.
SKOOSH
SKOOSH
EH?
H- HOLD UP!
Yura is so forceful when it comes to shikigami.
WAM
HEY, EVERYONE!! I SEE YOU'RE WORKING HARD!!
HA HA... ONMYO SELF-DEFENSE TRAINING UNDER A BIG BLUE SKY!!
MMM... WHAT A WONDERFUL SIGHT!!
I'VE BEEN REFLECTING ON THE INCIDENT AT MT. NEJIREME!!
I'VE BEEN WORKING HARD TOO, RECONSIDERING OUR APPROACH!!
...
WHEW! I'M, LIKE, EXHAUSTED.
I WANNA GO HOME.
HFF HFF
HFF HFF
OH... BUT FIRST...
SHOF
FIP
?!
IENAGA!! HAPPY BIRTHDAY!!
THAT'S A GIFT FOR A FELLOW PATROLMAN, SO DON'T YOU BE SHY ABOUT ACCEPTING IT!! JUST TAKE IT!!
SHEEEEEN
TH- THANKS.
WOW! THAT'S SO NICE, KIYO-TSUGU!!
What a great guy...
LOOKS EXPENSIVE!
Gucci? Vuitton?

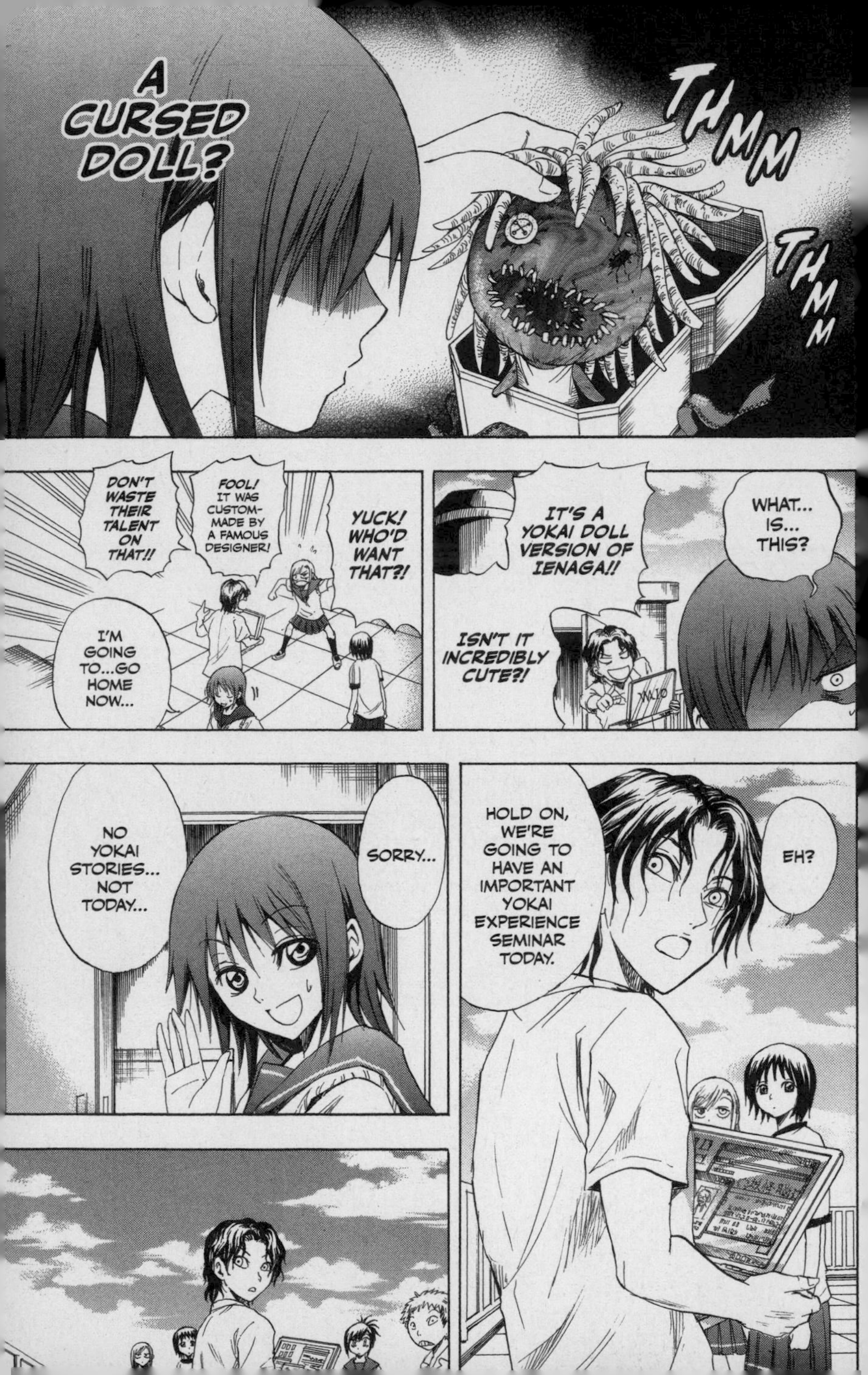
THMM
THMM
A CURSED DOLL?
WHAT... IS... THIS?
IT'S A YOKAI DOLL VERSION OF IENAGA!!
ISN'T IT INCREDIBLY CUTE?!
YUCK! WHO'D WANT THAT?!
FOOL! IT WAS CUSTOM-MADE BY A FAMOUS DESIGNER!
DON'T WASTE THEIR TALENT ON THAT!!
I'M GOING TO...GO HOME NOW...
EH?
HOLD ON, WE'RE GOING TO HAVE AN IMPORTANT YOKAI EXPERIENCE SEMINAR TODAY.
SORRY...
NO YOKAI STORIES... NOT TODAY...

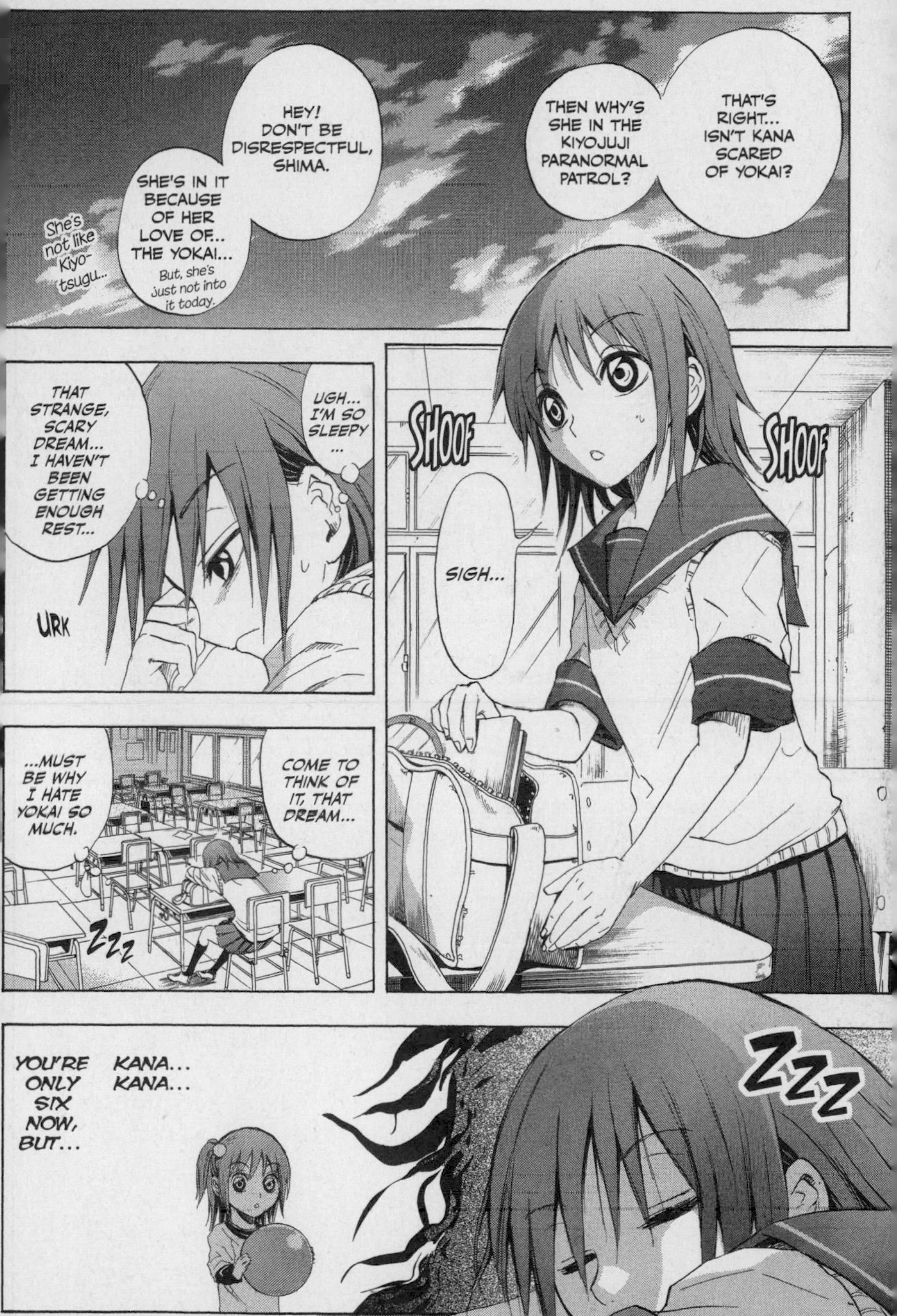
THAT'S RIGHT... ISN'T KANA SCARED OF YOKAI?
THEN WHY'S SHE IN THE KIYOJUJI PARANORMAL PATROL?
HEY! DON'T BE DISRESPECTFUL, SHIMA.
SHE'S IN IT BECAUSE OF HER LOVE OF... THE YOKAI...
But, she's just not into it today.
She's not like Kiyo-tsugu...
SHOOF
SHOOF
SIGH...
UGH... I'M SO SLEEPY...
THAT STRANGE, SCARY DREAM... I HAVEN'T BEEN GETTING ENOUGH REST...
URK
COME TO THINK OF IT, THAT DREAM...
...MUST BE WHY I HATE YOKAI SO MUCH.
ZZZ
ZZZ
KANA... KANA...
YOU'RE ONLY SIX NOW, BUT...

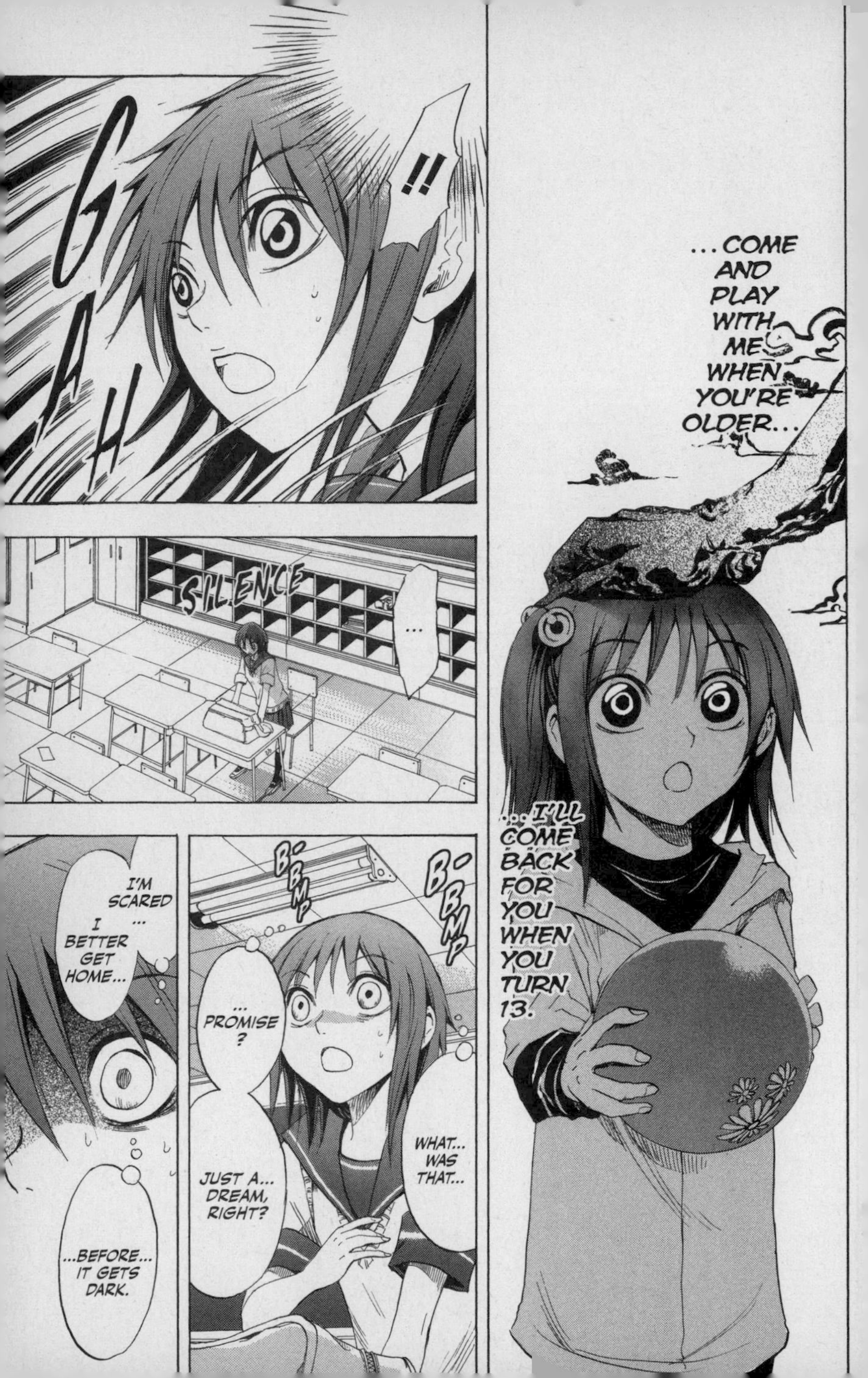
...COME AND PLAY WITH ME WHEN YOU'RE OLDER...
...I'LL COME BACK FOR YOU WHEN YOU TURN 13.
GAH
!!
SILENCE
...
B-BMP
B-BMP
...PROMISE?
WHAT... WAS THAT...
JUST A... DREAM, RIGHT?
I'M SCARED... I BETTER GET HOME...
...BEFORE... IT GETS DARK.

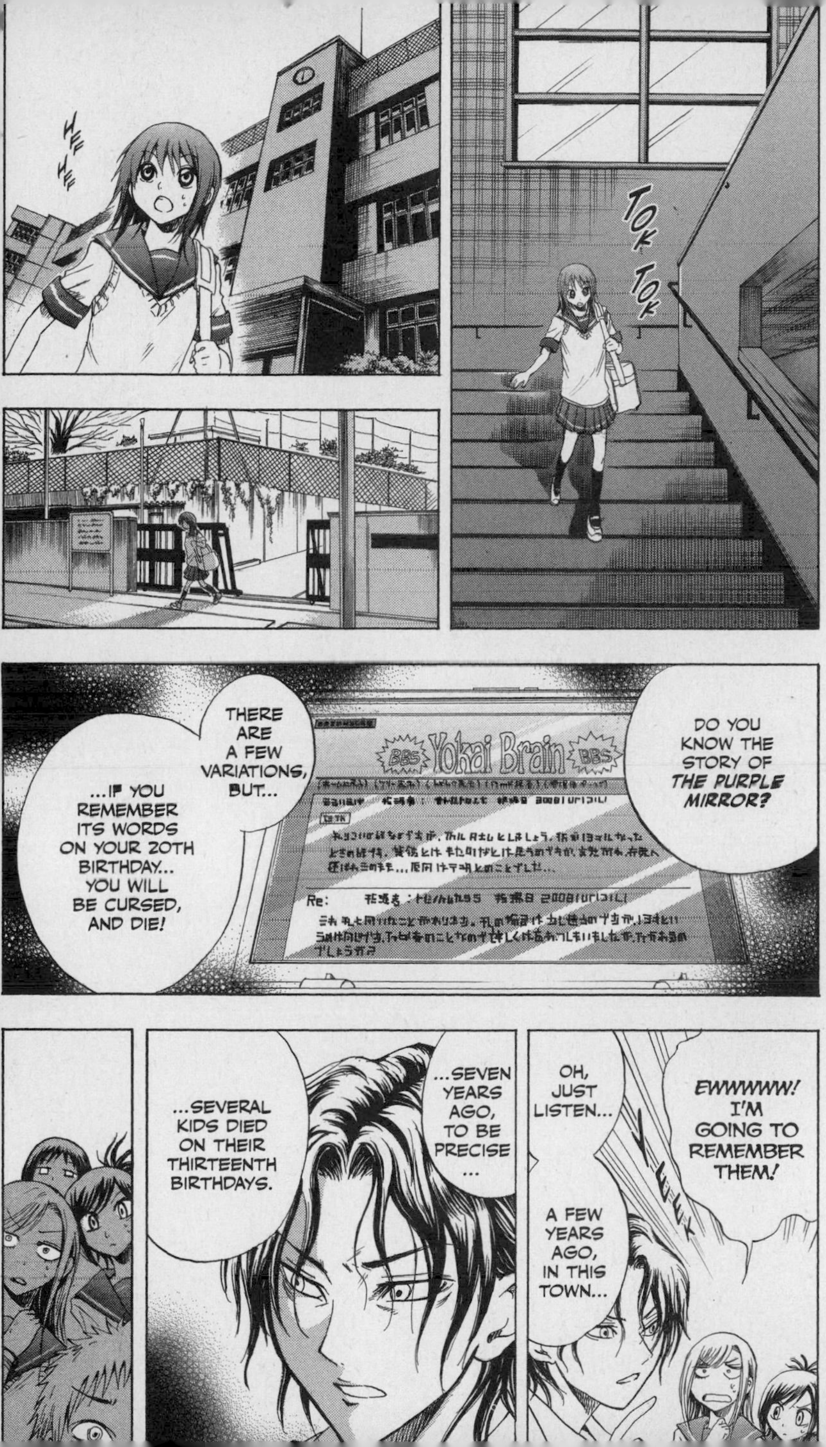
TOK TOK
HEF HEF
BBS
Yokai Brain
BBS
DO YOU KNOW THE STORY OF THE PURPLE MIRROR?
THERE ARE A FEW VARIATIONS, BUT...
...IF YOU REMEMBER ITS WORDS ON YOUR 20TH BIRTHDAY... YOU WILL BE CURSED, AND DIE!
Re:
EWWWWWW! I'M GOING TO REMEMBER THEM!
OH, JUST LISTEN...
A FEW YEARS AGO, IN THIS TOWN...
...SEVEN YEARS AGO, TO BE PRECISE...
...SEVERAL KIDS DIED ON THEIR THIRTEENTH BIRTHDAYS.

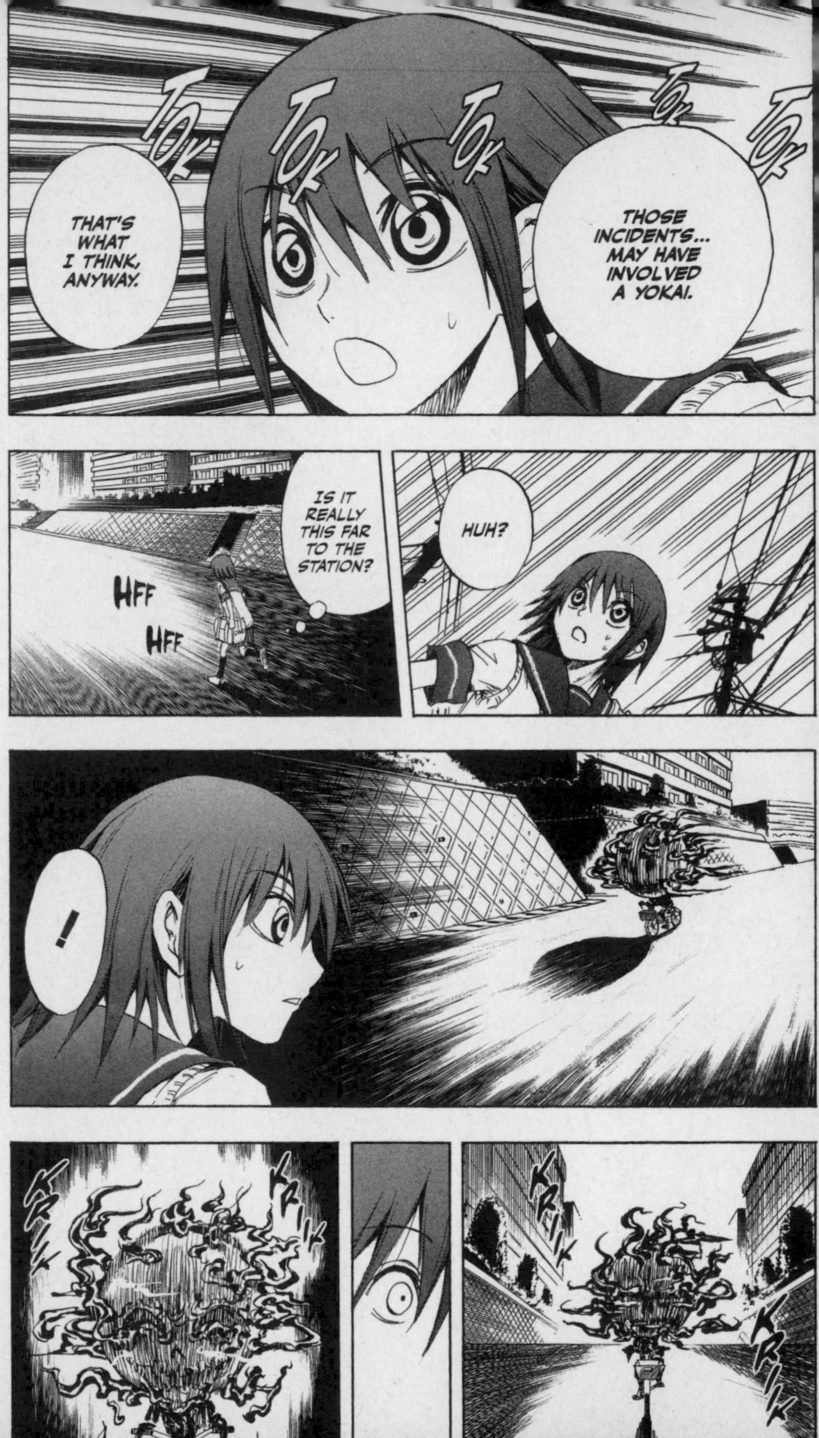
TOK
TOK
TOK
TOK
TOK
THOSE INCIDENTS... MAY HAVE INVOLVED A YOKAI.
THAT'S WHAT I THINK, ANYWAY.
HUH?
IS IT REALLY THIS FAR TO THE STATION?
HFF
HFF
!
KRIK
KRIK
KRIK
KRIK

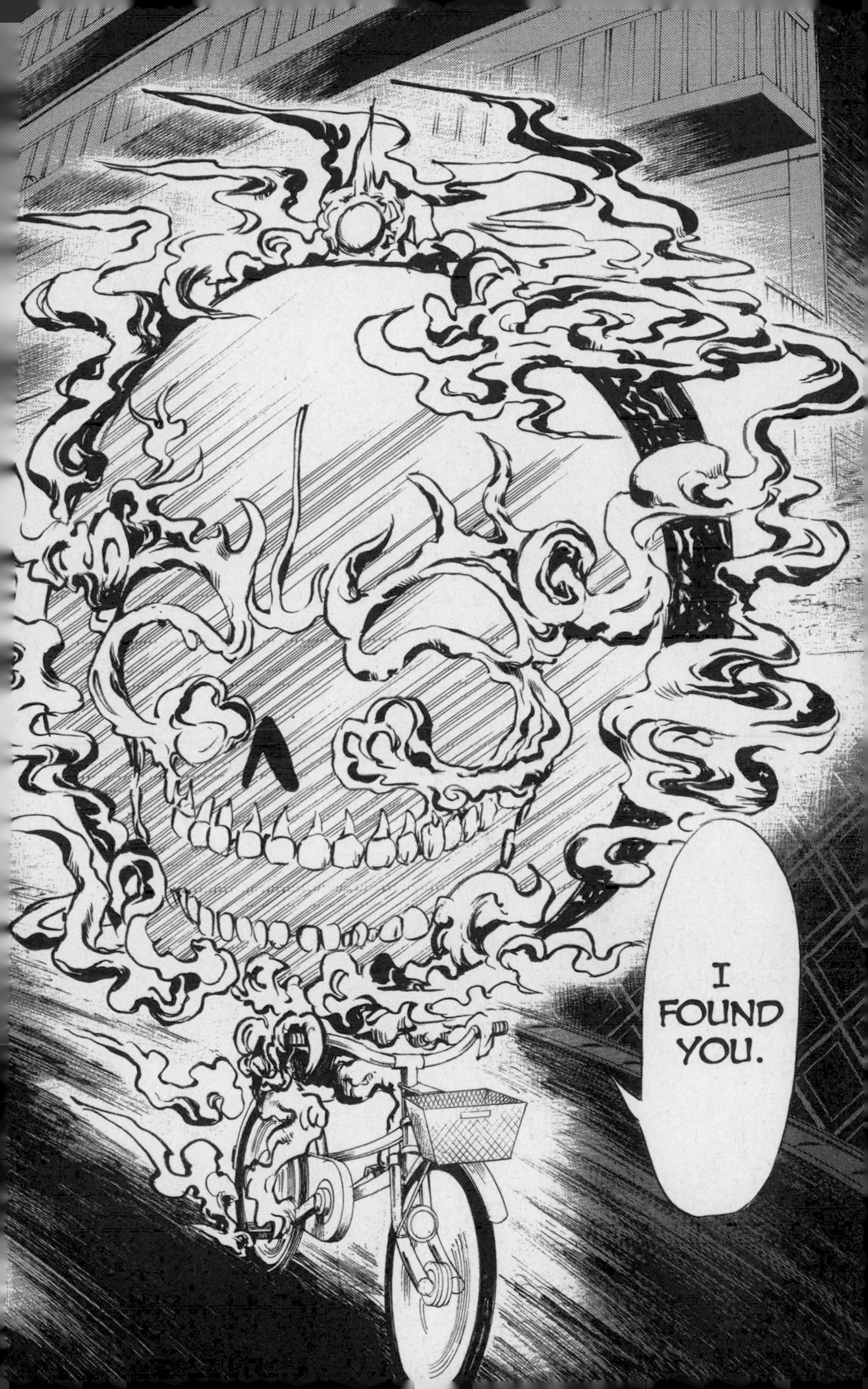
I FOUND YOU.

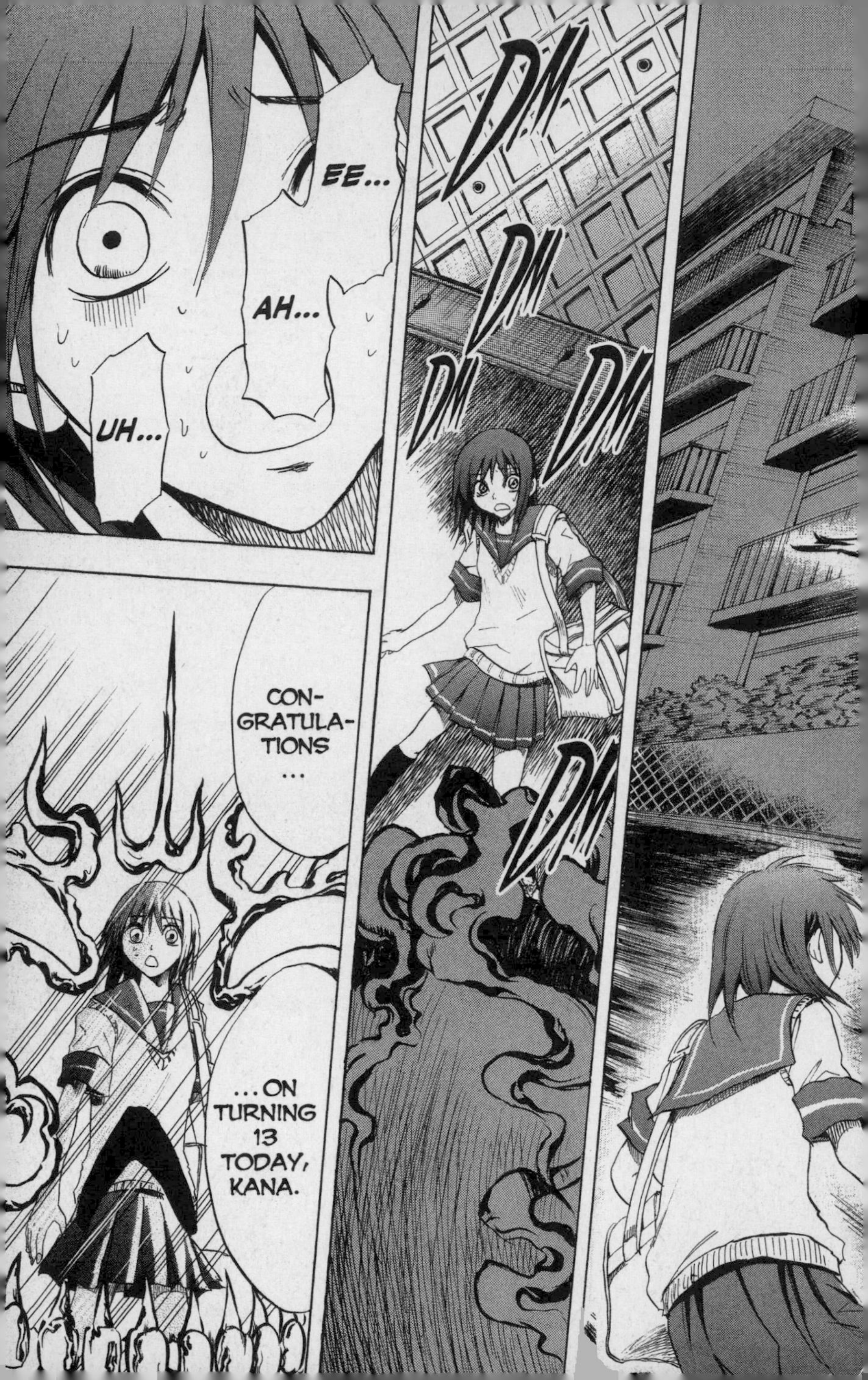
DM
DM
DM
DM
DM
EE...
AH...
UH...
CON-GRATULA-TIONS...
...ON TURNING 13 TODAY, KANA.

KIYOTSUGU'S YOKAI BRAIN

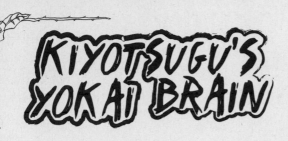

FIELD TRIP EDITION #2
by Kiyo

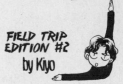

Kiyo: Hey, everyone!! Your leader, Kiyotsugu, here!! How are you!? Are you doing anything yokai-related today?

Auuugh!!

Sorry, Shima!! I didn't mean to alarm you, but no need to be so scared. Right, Rikuo? From now on, my site, "Yokai Brain" is going to be published in the comics. Therefore, I plan to answer all of the questions you send!! First up is this: "Illness begins in the mind!!" Deep!! Very Deep!!

Question 1: How many yokai are there? Are you able to separate them by type? —*Yokai Daimao, Aichi Prefecture*

Kiyo: Oooo?! Right off the bat, I get a question from someone who calls himself "King of the Yokai"?! If you're the Daimao, I would think that you'd know everything already!! Well, never mind that. According to my research, there are over 2,500 yokai, but some could have different names, and some are ones that no one has seen, so we can't be absolutely certain. By the way, have you ever seen a yokai? I have, but just once, when I was in elementary school!! Type? Hmm, I wonder. Oh, there's a user comment already...

Re: There are many different types of yokai...they also have clans. —*Karasu-Tengu, Tokyo*

Kiyo: What? What's with this comment? Is it true? It's not entirely believable, but...that's okay!! Alright, next question!!

Question 2: What happens to people who have seen or are assaulted by yokai? —*Okka, Hyodo Prefecture*

Kiyo: Well!! That makes me think back to that time when I actually saw a yokai, and...oh, I said that already. Speaking from personal experience, I idolize them!! I want to meet *him* again, I want to talk to him, that's how I feel!! I wonder what this feeling is...? Huh? You think it's scary? Shima, that varies from person to person!!

Question 3: Please tell us about the members of the Kiyojuji Paranormal Patrol! —*Meketa, Niigata Prefecture, and Shirayuki, ?? Prefecture*

Kiyo: Oh!! It looks like our Kiyojuji Patrol has some fans already!! Okay! Let's ask everyone to share something about themselves!! Huh? Where did everyone go...? Oh! Perfect timing, Ienaga!!

Kana: Huh...?

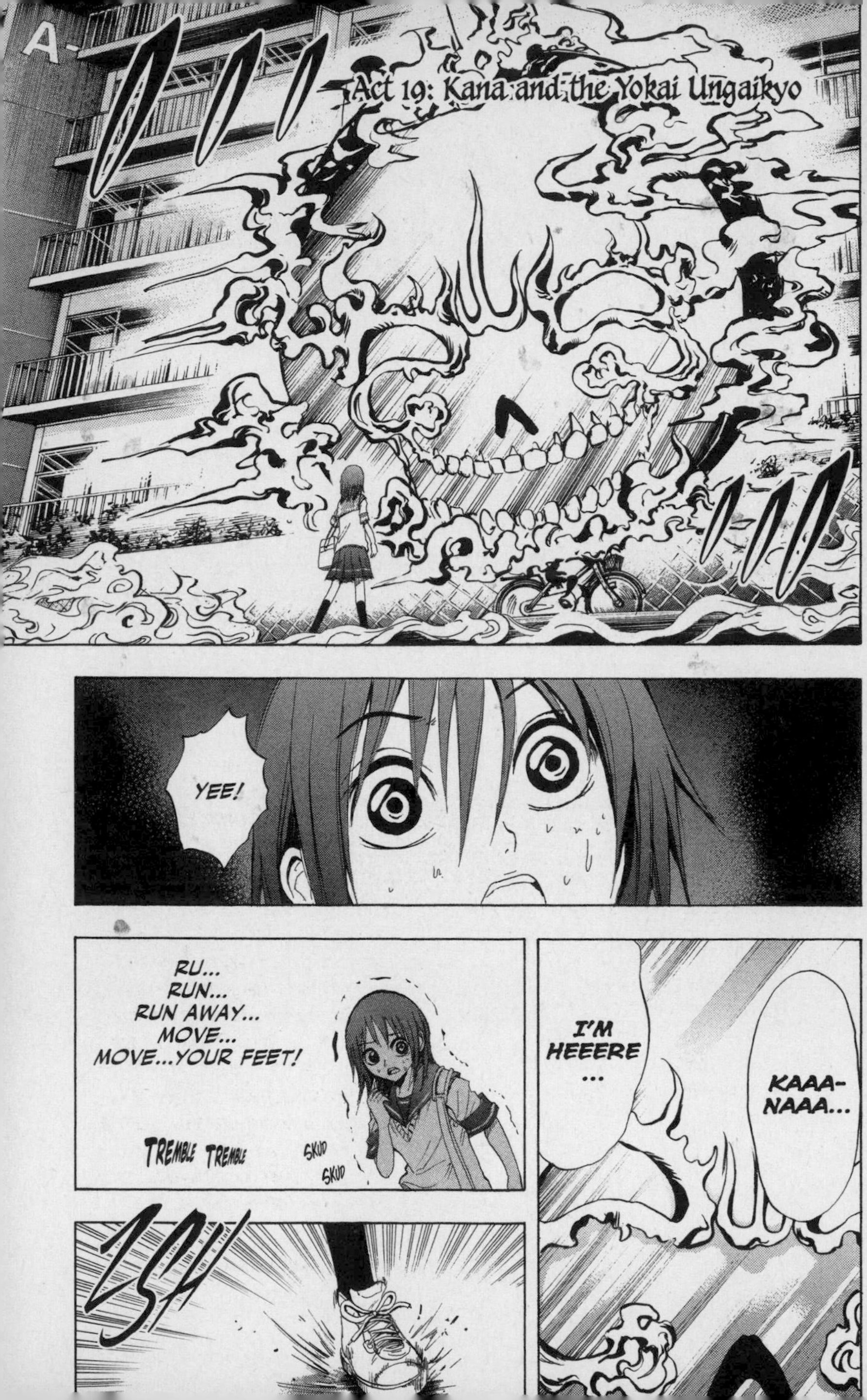
Act 19: Kana and the Yokai Ungaikyo
A-
YEE!
KAAA-NAAA...
I'M HEEERE...
RU... RUN... RUN AWAY... MOVE... MOVE...YOUR FEET!
SKUD SKUD
TREMBLE TREMBLE
ZSH

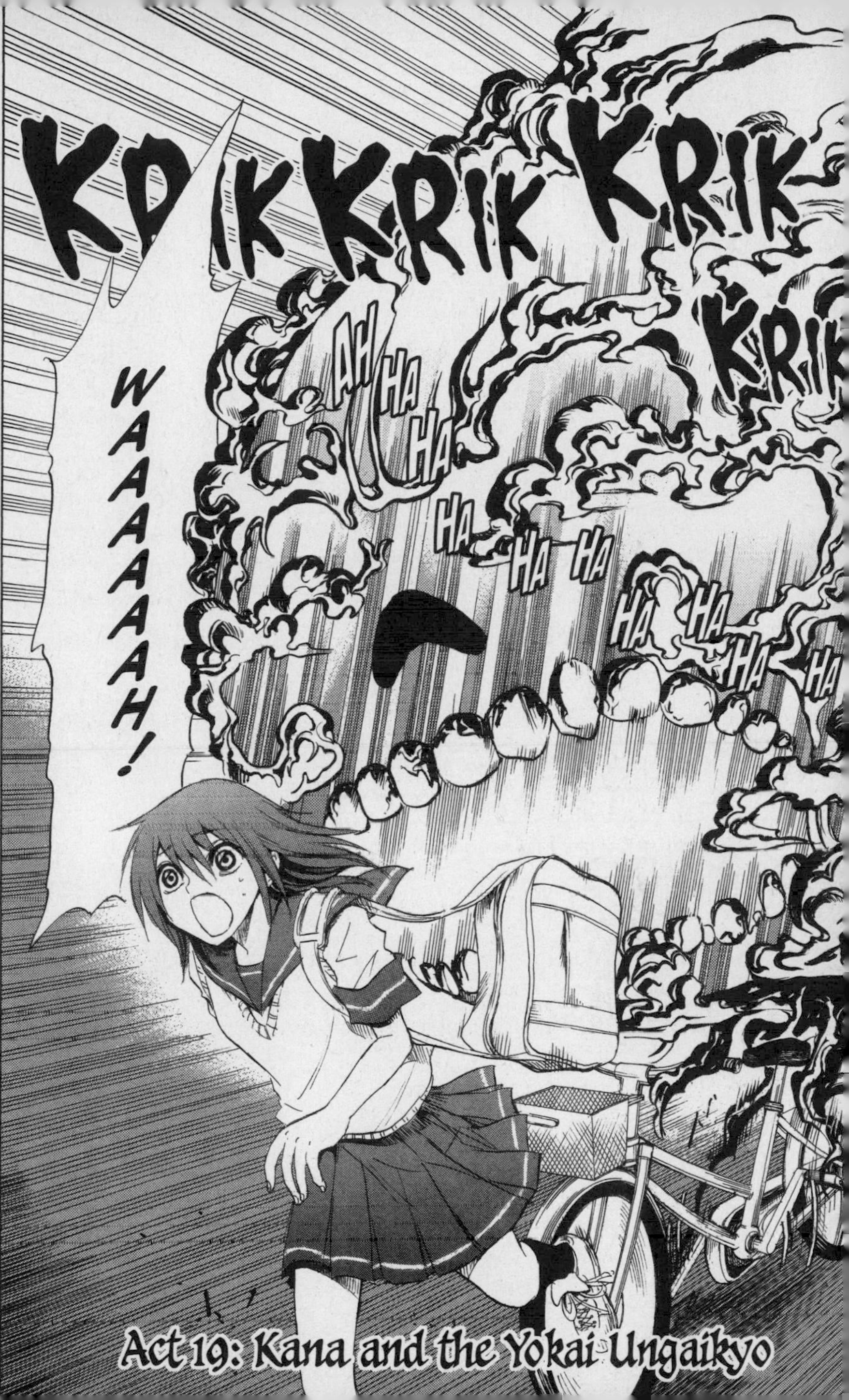
KRIK
KRIK KRIK KRIK KRIK
AH HA HA HA HA HA HA HA HA HA HA
WAAAAAAH!
Act 19: Kana and the Yokai Ungaikyo

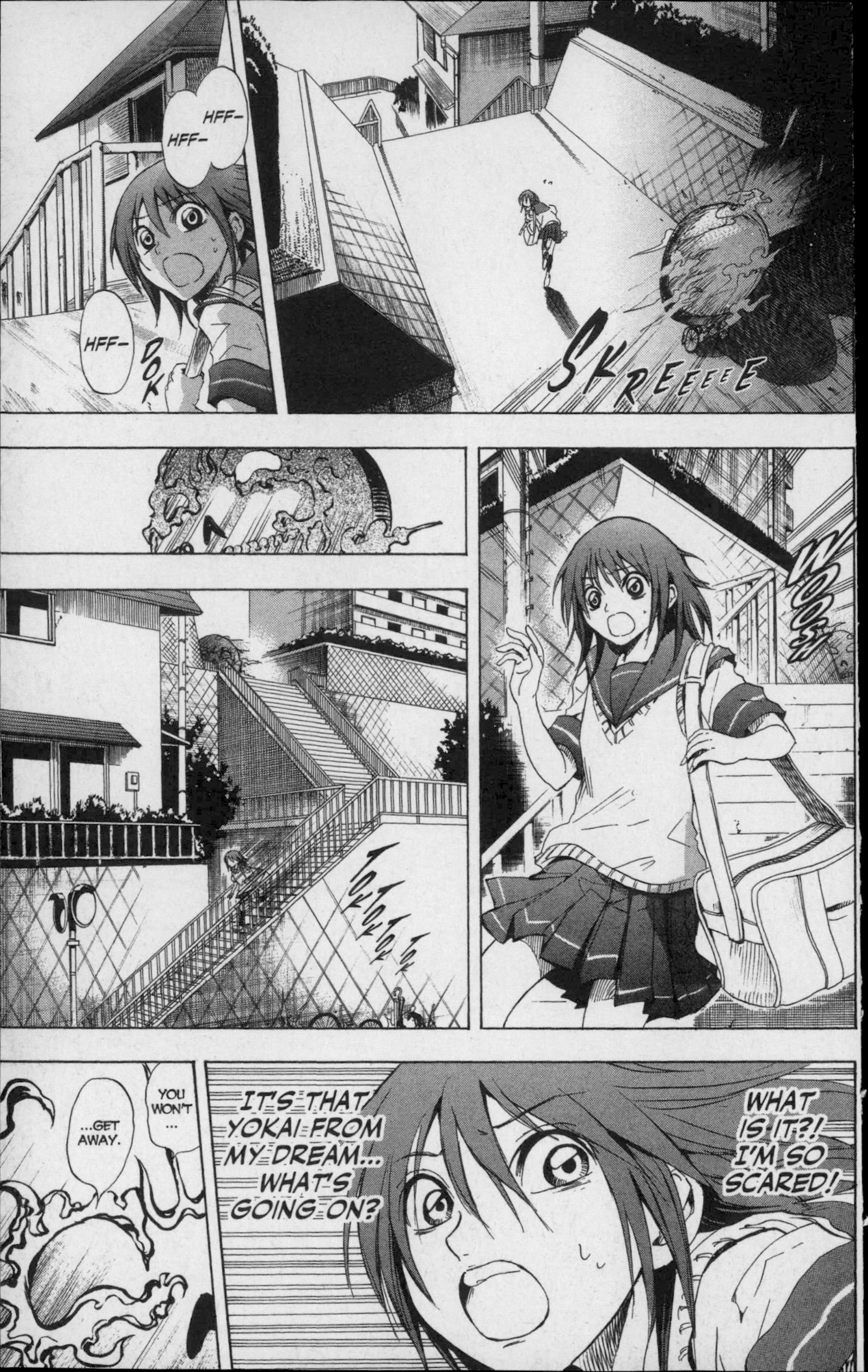
HFF– HFF–
SKREEEEE
HFF–
DOK
WOOSH
TOK TOK TOK TOK
WHAT IS IT?! I'M SO SCARED!
IT'S THAT YOKAI FROM MY DREAM... WHAT'S GOING ON?
YOU WON'T ...
...GET AWAY.

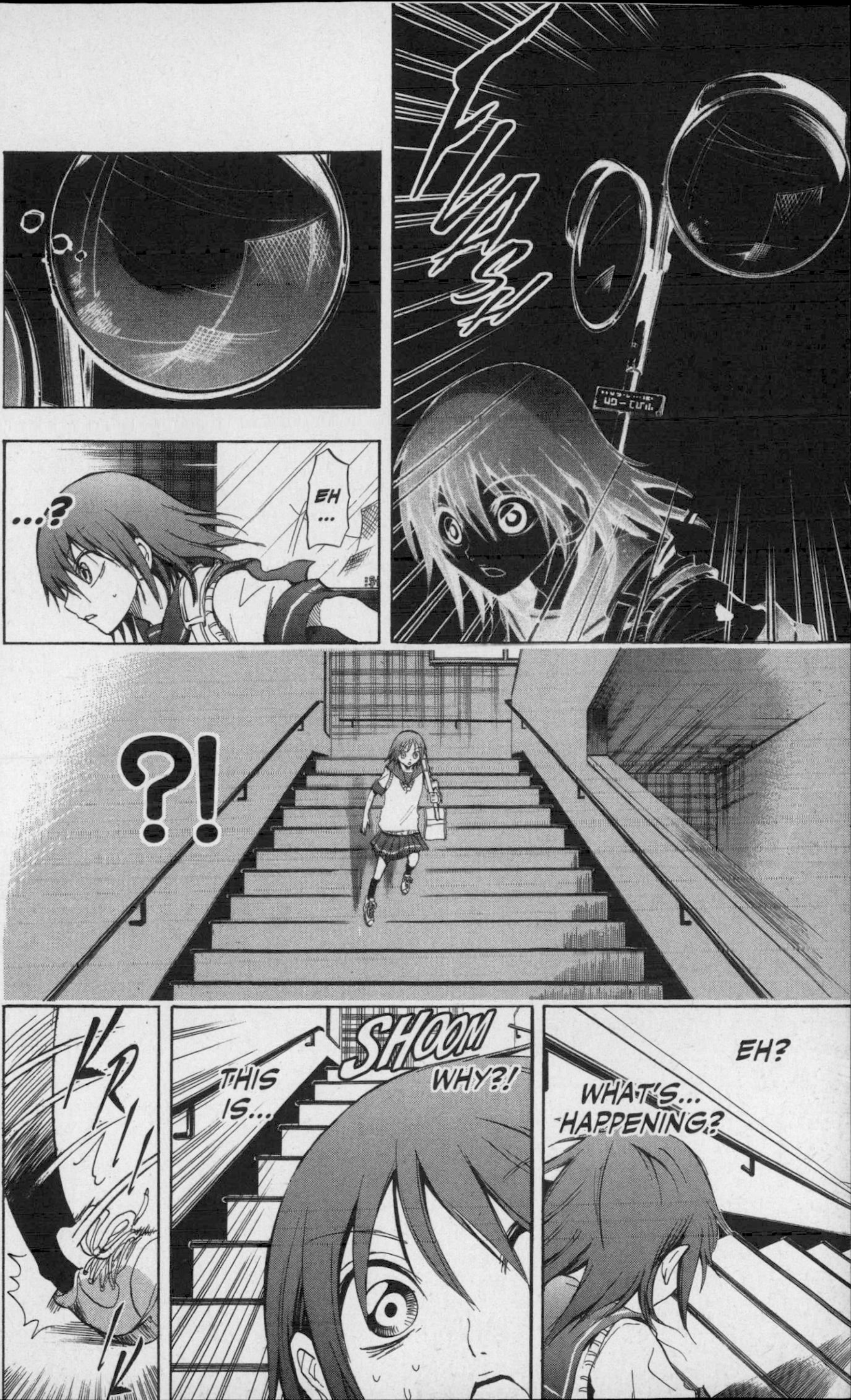
EH ...
...?
?!
EH?
WHAT'S... HAPPENING?
SHOOM
WHY?!
THIS IS...

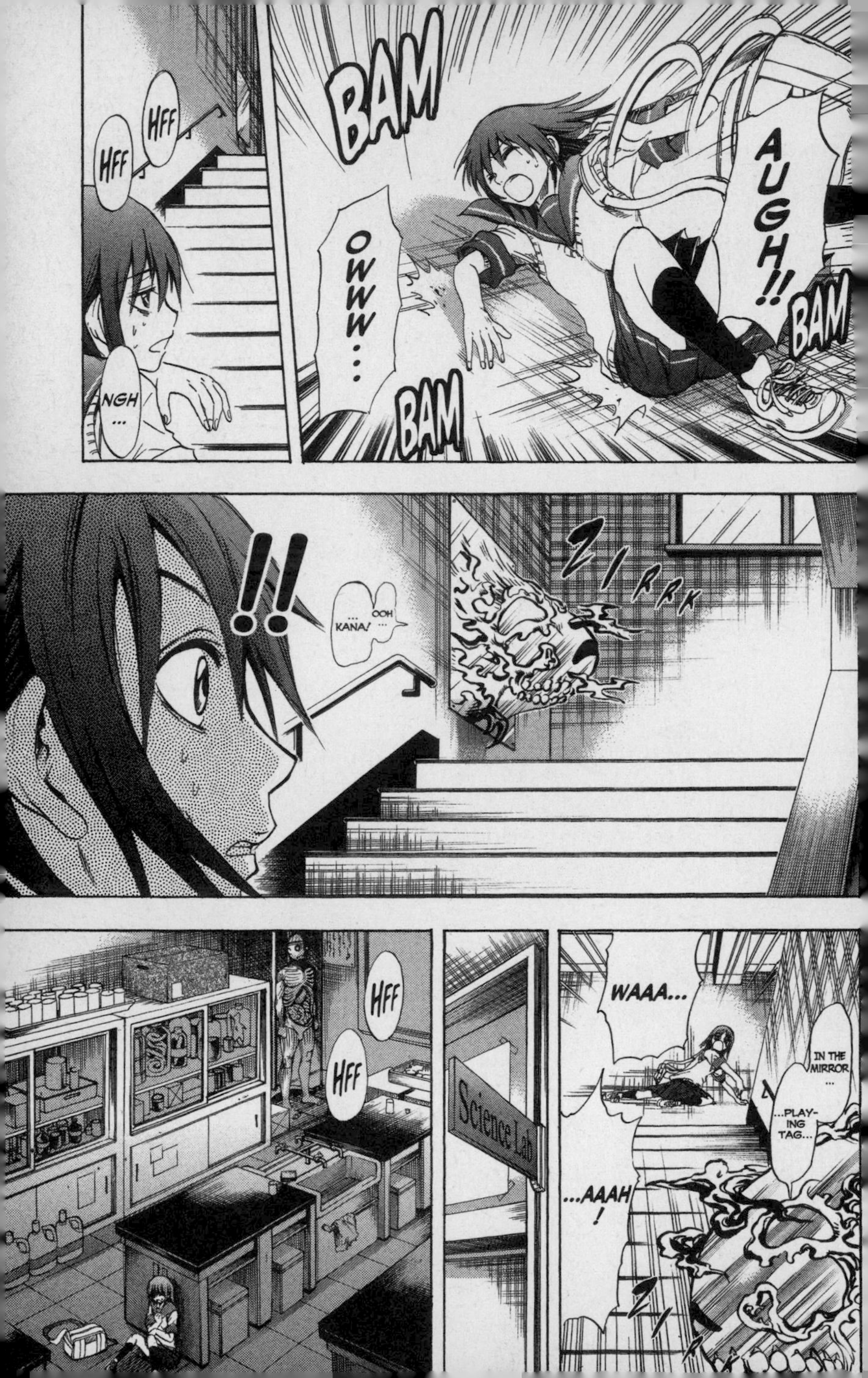
BAM
AUGH!!
BAM
OWWW...
BAM
HFF
HFF
NGH...
ZIRRK
OOH...
...KANA!
!!
IN THE MIRROR...
...PLAY-ING TAG...
WAAA...
...AAAH!
Science Lab
HFF
HFF

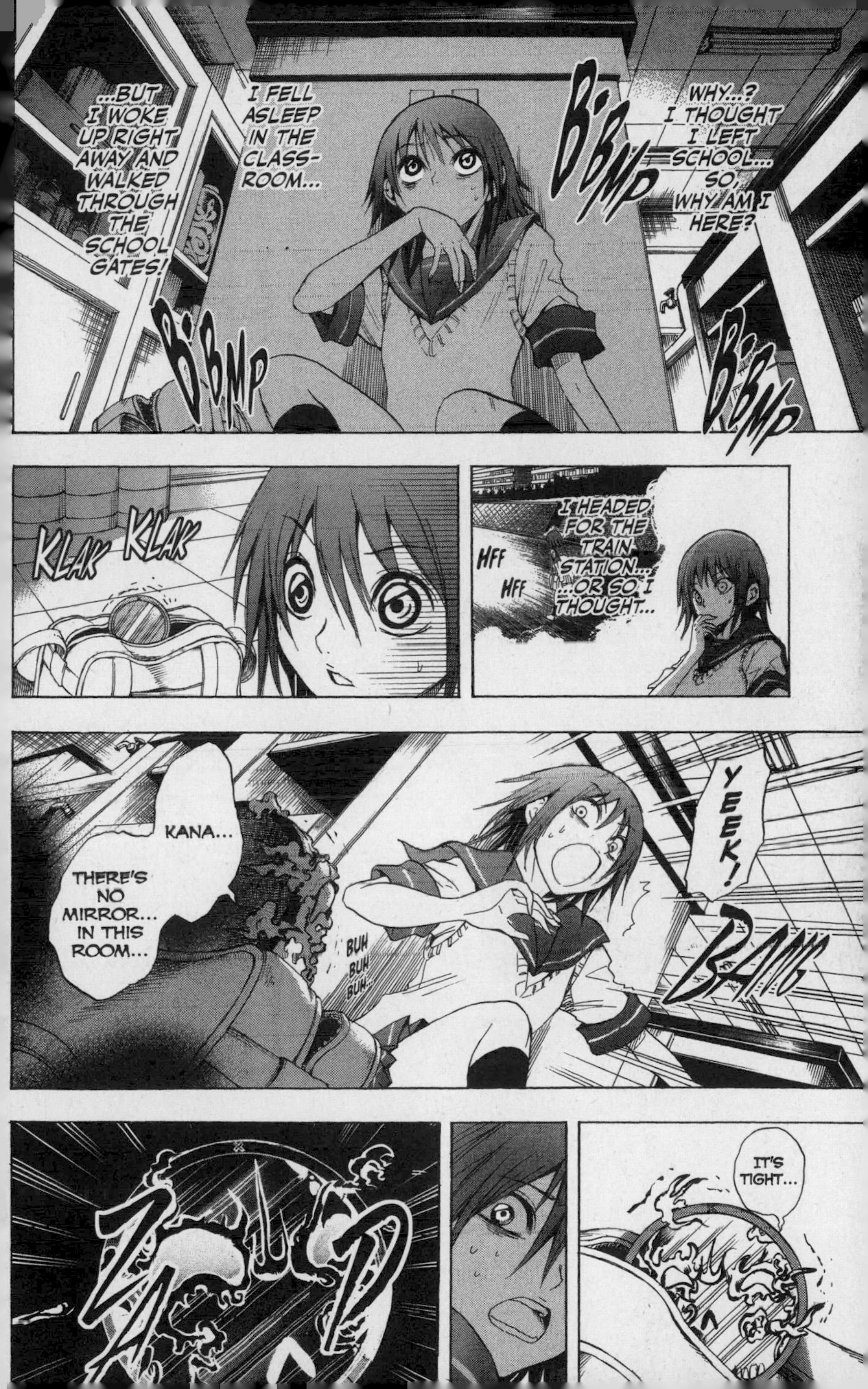
WHY...? I THOUGHT I LEFT SCHOOL... SO, WHY AM I HERE?
B-BMP
I FELL ASLEEP IN THE CLASS-ROOM...
...BUT I WOKE UP RIGHT AWAY AND WALKED THROUGH THE SCHOOL GATES!
B-BMP
B-BMP
I HEADED FOR THE TRAIN STATION... ...OR SO I THOUGHT...
HFF
HFF
KLAK KLAK
YEEK!
BANG
KANA...
THERE'S NO MIRROR... IN THIS ROOM...
BUH BUH BUH...
IT'S TIGHT...

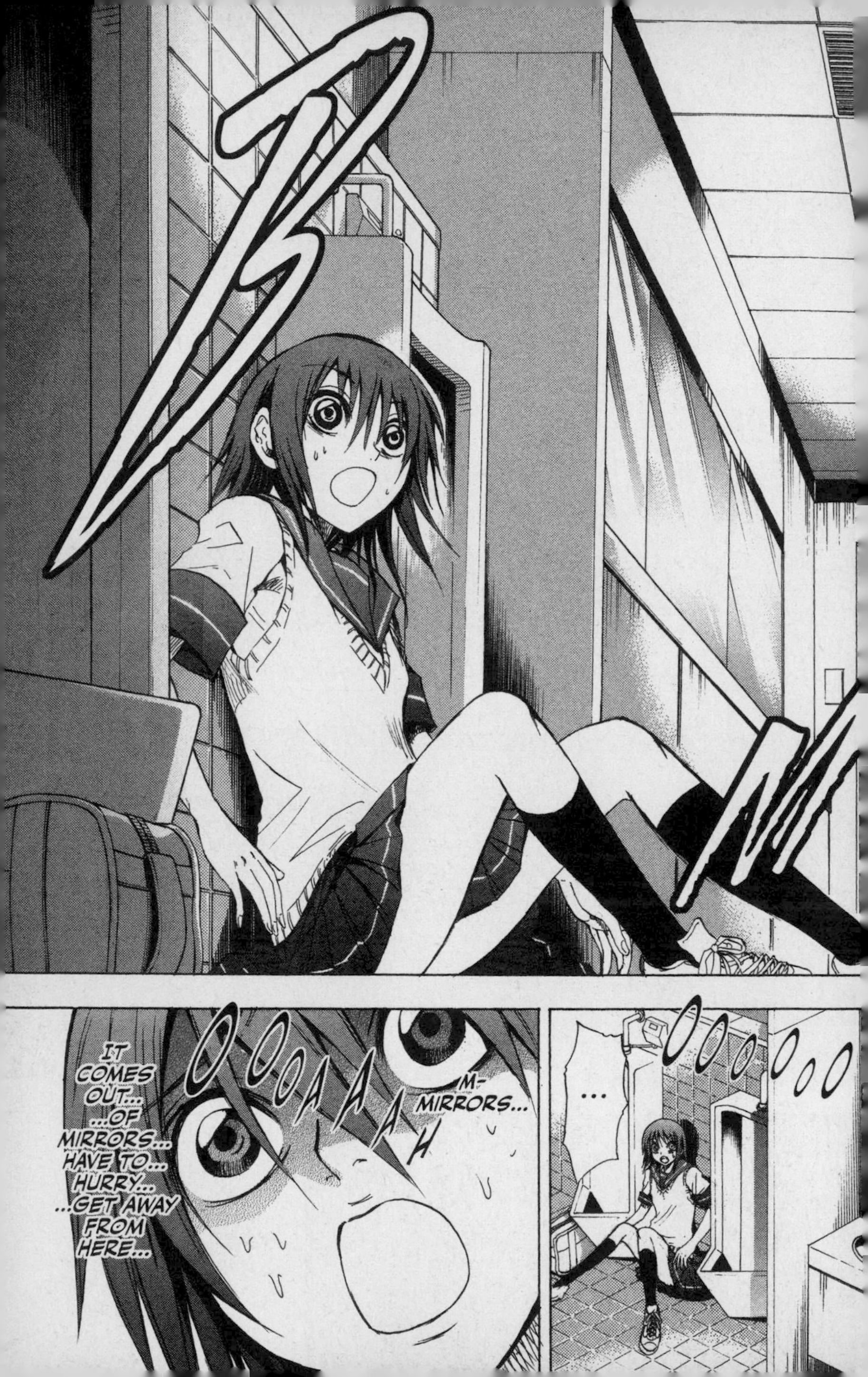
OOOOOOO
...
M-MIRRORS...
OOOAAAAAH
IT COMES OUT... ...OF MIRRORS... HAVE TO... HURRY... ...GET AWAY FROM HERE...

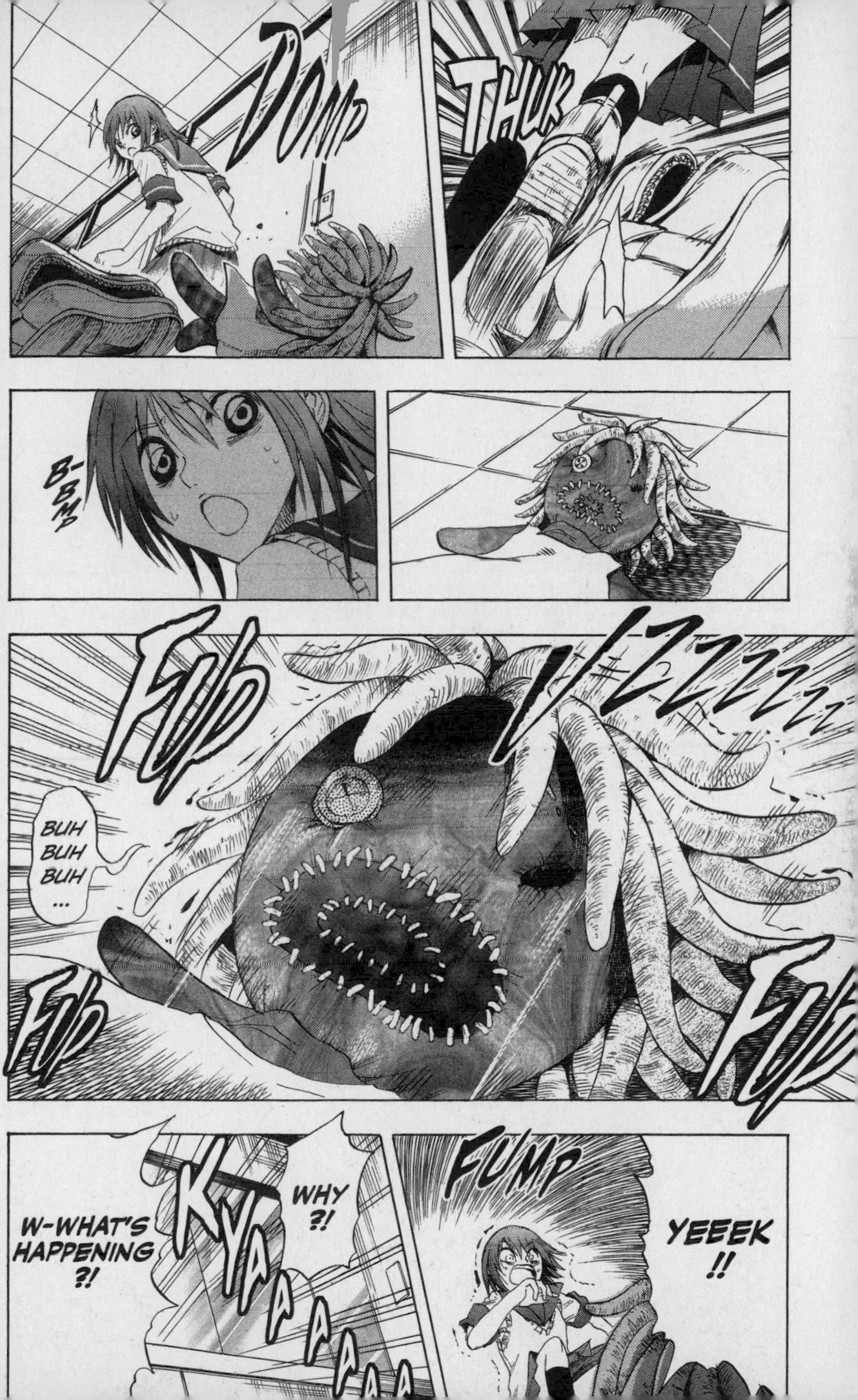
THUK
DOMP
B-BUMP
FLIP
BUH BUH BUH ...
FLIP
FLIP
FUMP
YEEEK !!
WHY ?!
KYAAAAAAA
W-WHAT'S HAPPENING ?!

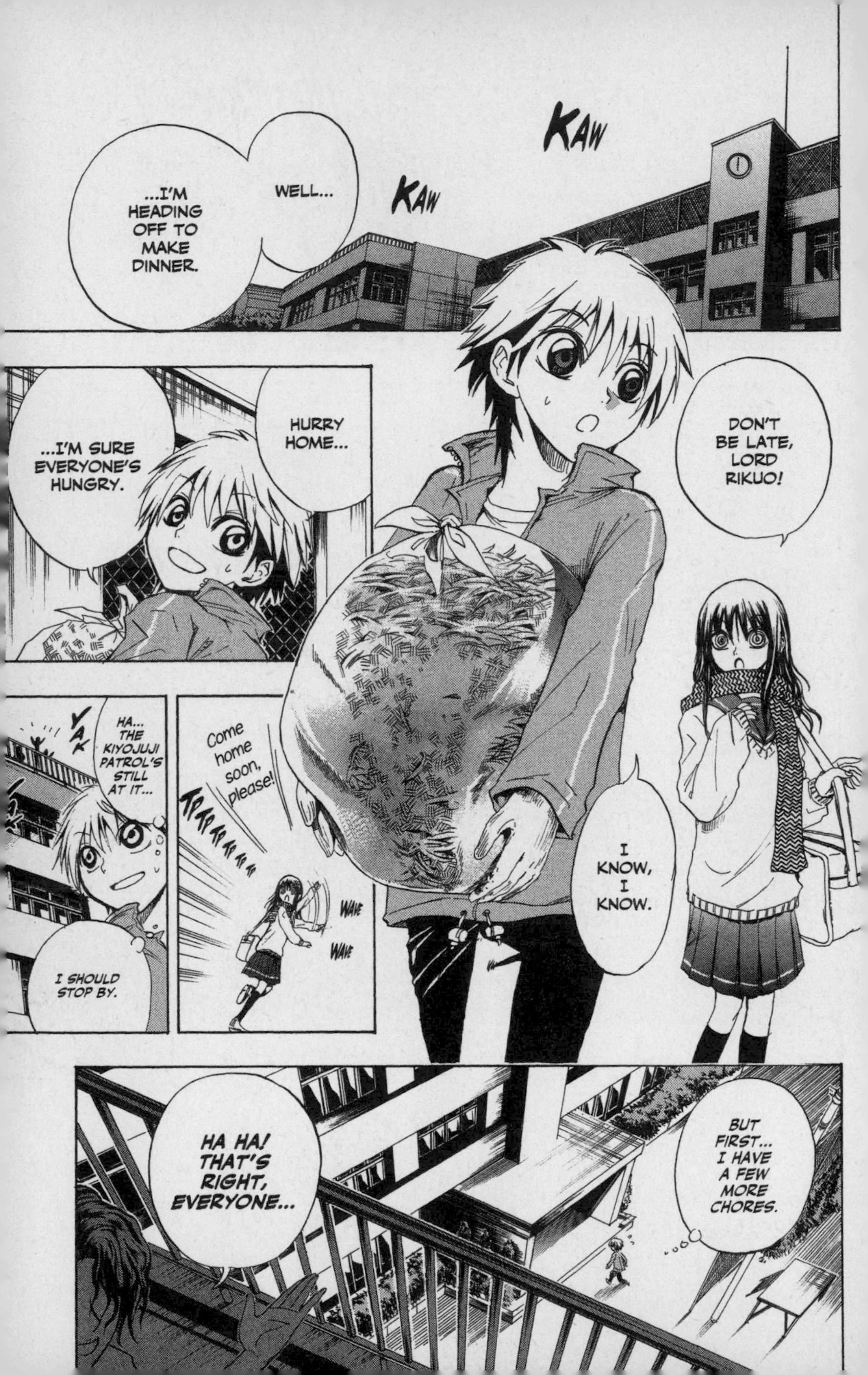
KAW
KAW
WELL...
...I'M HEADING OFF TO MAKE DINNER.
DON'T BE LATE, LORD RIKUO!
I KNOW, I KNOW.
HURRY HOME...
...I'M SURE EVERYONE'S HUNGRY.
Come home soon, please!
WAVE
WAVE
YAK
HA... THE KIYOJUJI PATROL'S STILL AT IT...
I SHOULD STOP BY.
BUT FIRST... I HAVE A FEW MORE CHORES.
HA HA! THAT'S RIGHT, EVERYONE...

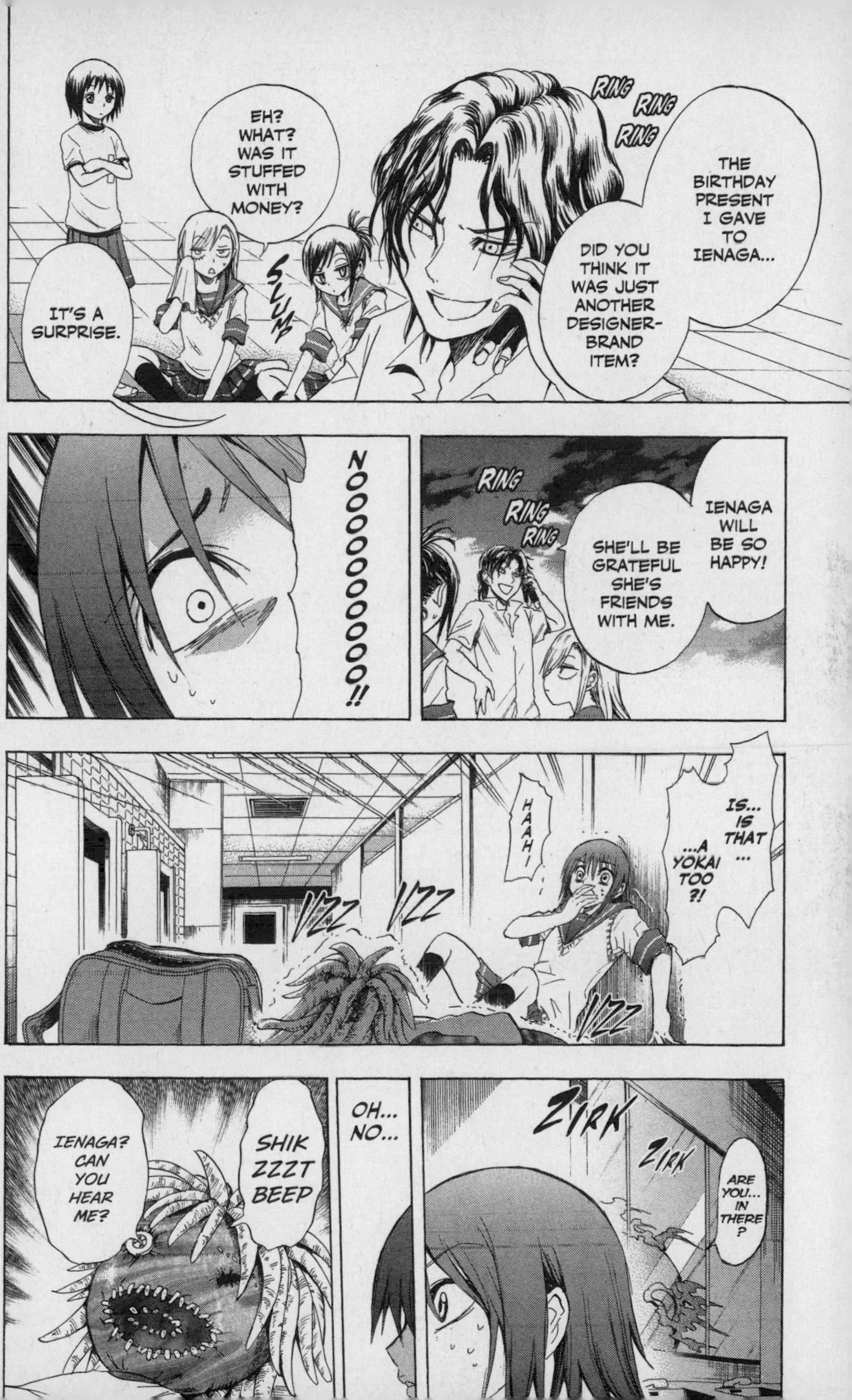
THE BIRTHDAY PRESENT I GAVE TO IENAGA...
RING RING RING
DID YOU THINK IT WAS JUST ANOTHER DESIGNER-BRAND ITEM?
SLUMP
EH? WHAT? WAS IT STUFFED WITH MONEY?
IT'S A SURPRISE.
IENAGA WILL BE SO HAPPY!
RING RING RING
SHE'LL BE GRATEFUL SHE'S FRIENDS WITH ME.
NOOOOOOOOOOOO!!
IS... IS THAT ...
...A YOKAI TOO?!
HAAH!
VZZ VZZ VZZ
ZIRK ZIRK
ARE YOU... IN THERE?
OH... NO...
SHIK ZZZT BEEP
IENAGA? CAN YOU HEAR ME?

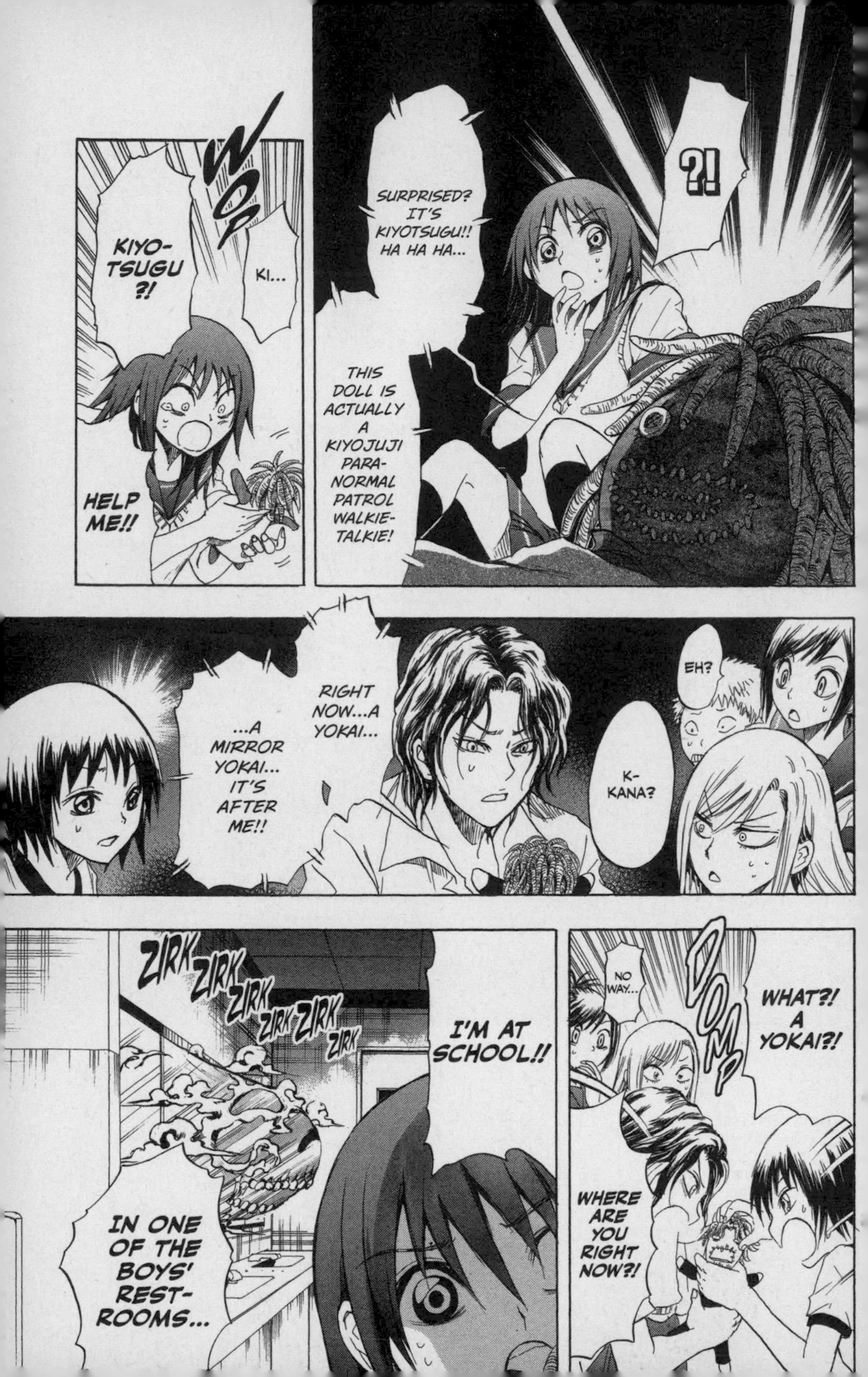
?!
SURPRISED? IT'S KIYOTSUGU!! HA HA HA...
THIS DOLL IS ACTUALLY A KIYOJUJI PARA-NORMAL PATROL WALKIE-TALKIE!
WOP
KI...
KIYO-TSUGU ?!
HELP ME!!
EH?
K-KANA?
RIGHT NOW...A YOKAI...
...A MIRROR YOKAI... IT'S AFTER ME!!
DOOM
WHAT?! A YOKAI?!
NO WAY...
WHERE ARE YOU RIGHT NOW?!
I'M AT SCHOOL!!
ZIRK ZIRK ZIRK ZIRK ZIRK ZIRK
IN ONE OF THE BOYS' REST-ROOMS...

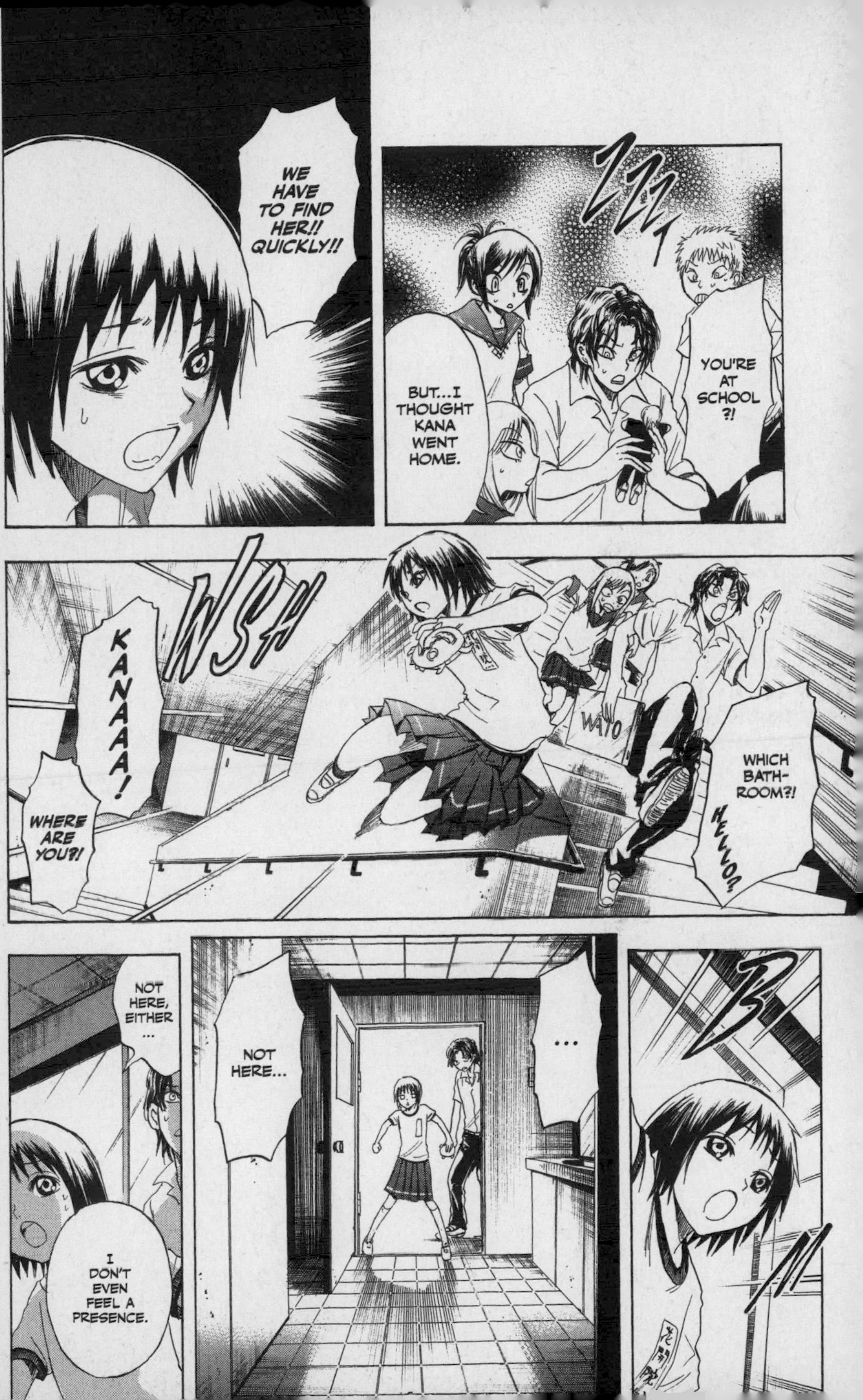
ZZZ
YOU'RE AT SCHOOL?!
BUT...I THOUGHT KANA WENT HOME.
WE HAVE TO FIND HER!! QUICKLY!!
WHICH BATHROOM?!
HELLO?
WSH
KANAAAA!
WHERE ARE YOU?!
B
...
NOT HERE...
NOT HERE, EITHER...
I DON'T EVEN FEEL A PRESENCE.

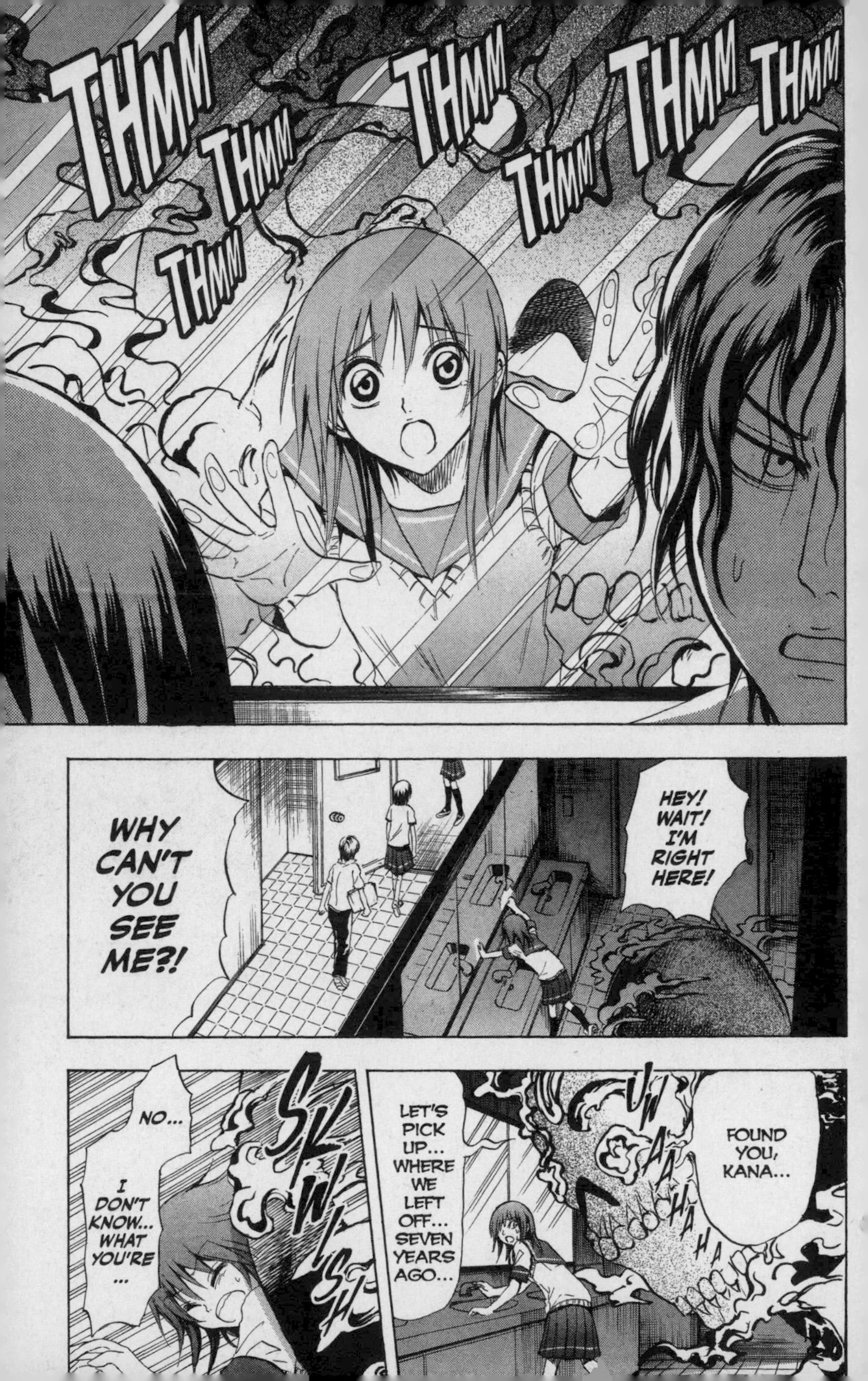
THMM
THMM
THMM
THMM
THMM
THMM
THMM
HEY! WAIT! I'M RIGHT HERE!
WHY CAN'T YOU SEE ME?!
FOUND YOU, KANA...
LET'S PICK UP... WHERE WE LEFT OFF... SEVEN YEARS AGO...
SKWISH
NO...
I DON'T KNOW... WHAT YOU'RE ...

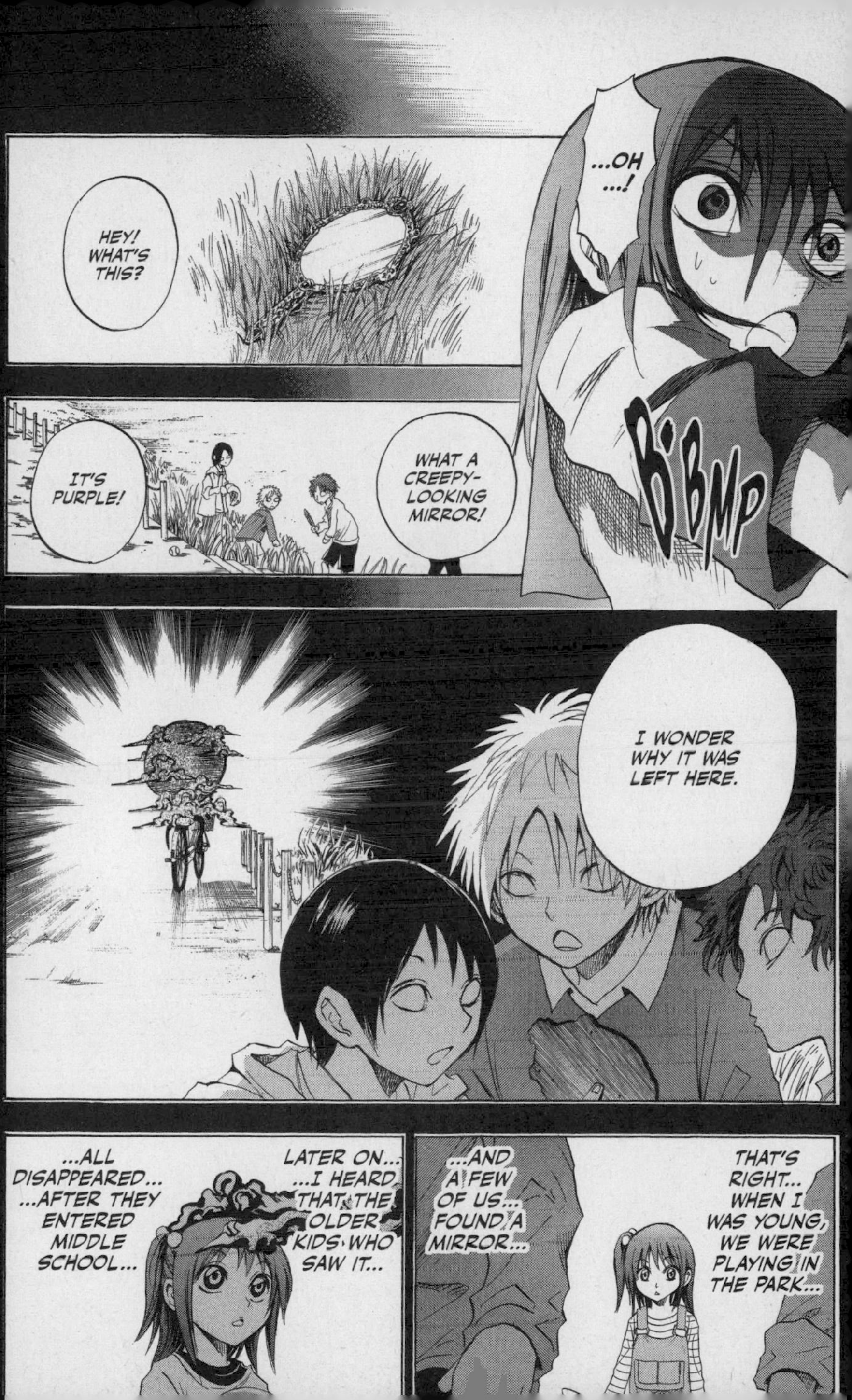
...OH ...!
BiBMP
HEY! WHAT'S THIS?
WHAT A CREEPY-LOOKING MIRROR!
IT'S PURPLE!
I WONDER WHY IT WAS LEFT HERE.
THAT'S RIGHT... WHEN I WAS YOUNG, WE WERE PLAYING IN THE PARK...
...AND A FEW OF US... FOUND A MIRROR...
LATER ON... ...I HEARD THAT THE OLDER KIDS WHO SAW IT...
...ALL DISAPPEARED... ...AFTER THEY ENTERED MIDDLE SCHOOL...

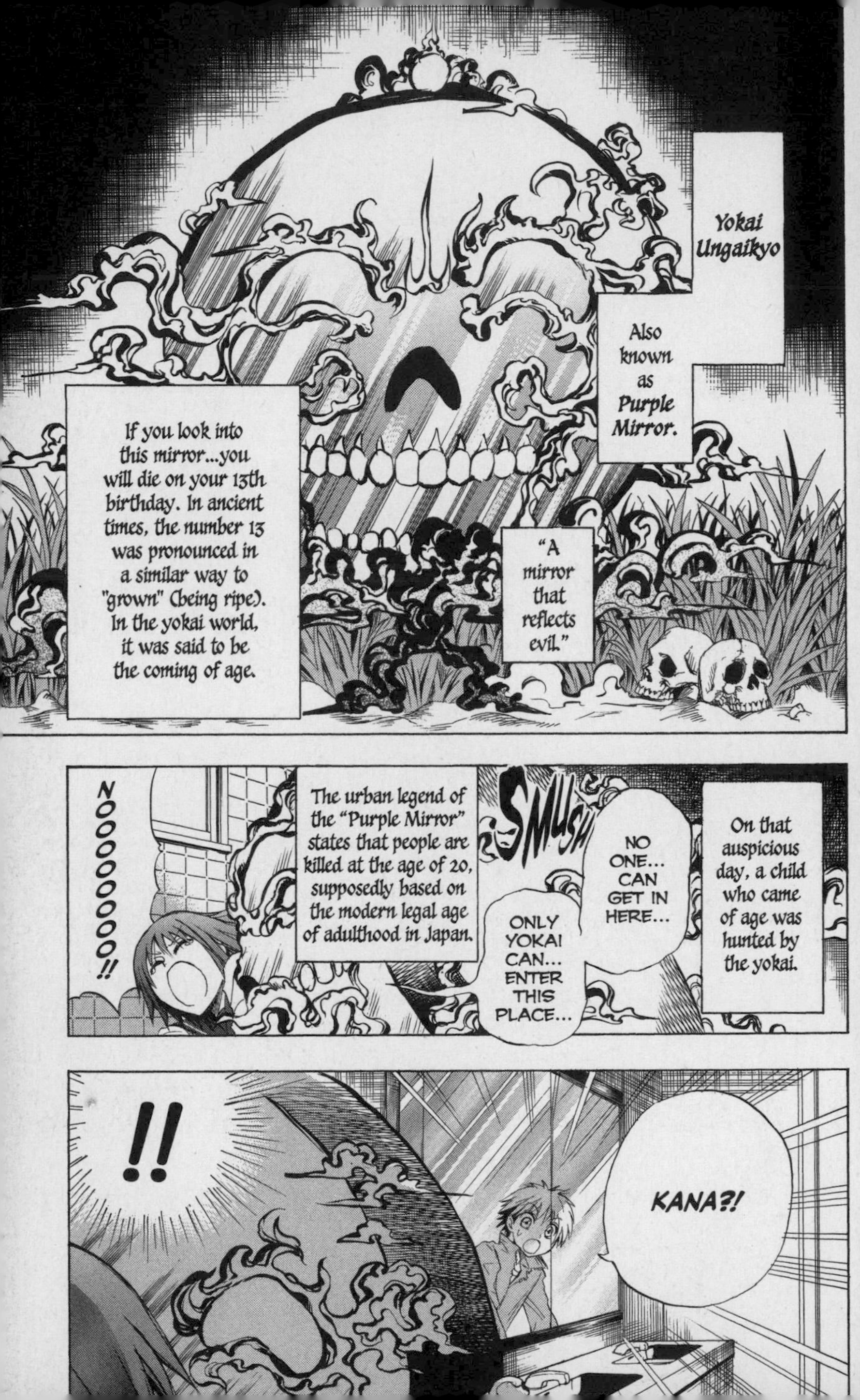
Yokai Ungaikyo
Also known as Purple Mirror.
"A mirror that reflects evil."
If you look into this mirror...you will die on your 13th birthday. In ancient times, the number 13 was pronounced in a similar way to "grown" (being ripe). In the yokai world, it was said to be the coming of age.
On that auspicious day, a child who came of age was hunted by the yokai.
NO ONE... CAN GET IN HERE...
ONLY YOKAI CAN... ENTER THIS PLACE...
SMUSH
The urban legend of the "Purple Mirror" states that people are killed at the age of 20, supposedly based on the modern legal age of adulthood in Japan.
NOOOOOOOOO!!
KANA?!
!!

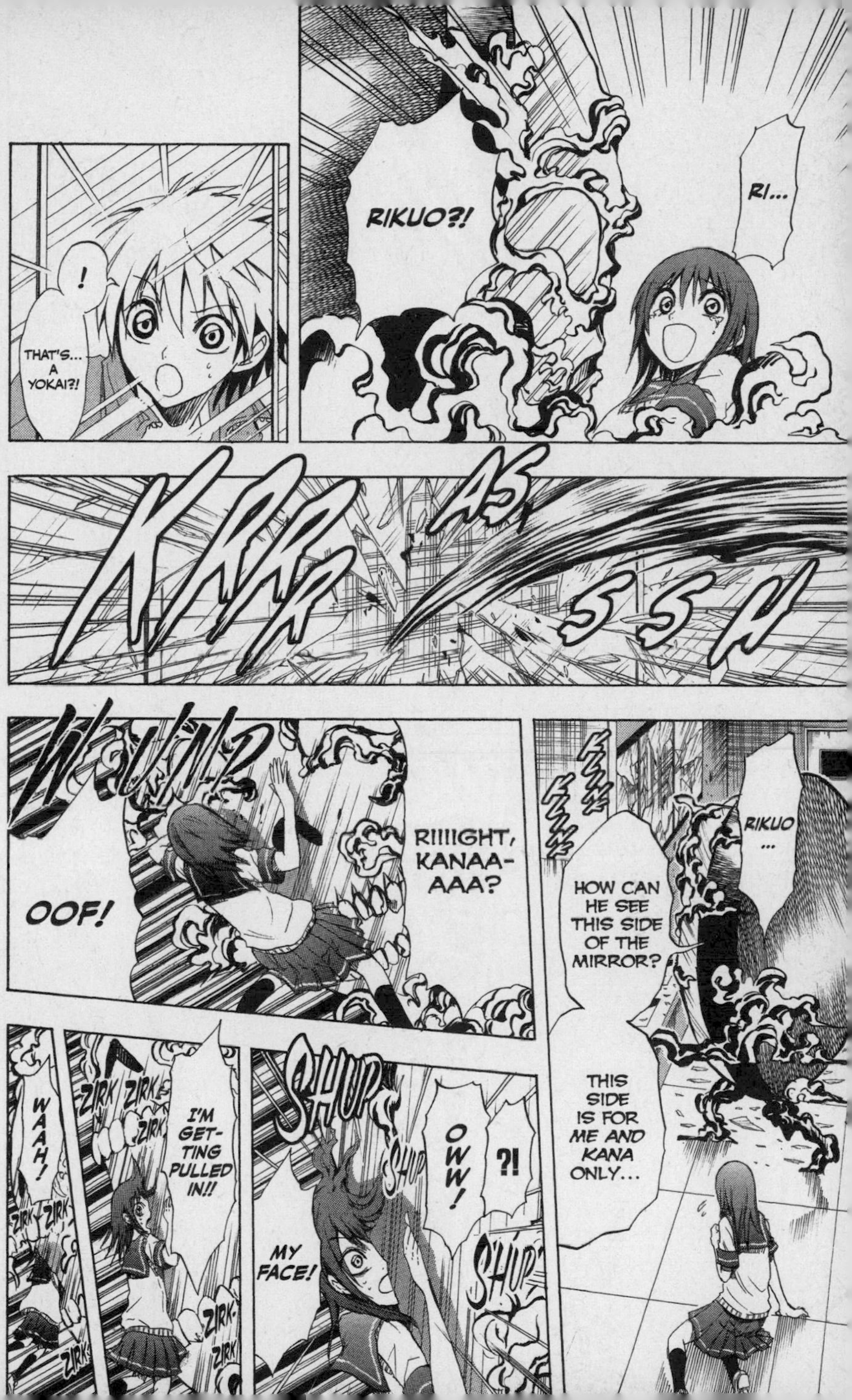
RI...
RIKUO?!
!
THAT'S... A YOKAI?!
RIKUO ...
HOW CAN HE SEE THIS SIDE OF THE MIRROR?
THIS SIDE IS FOR ME AND KANA ONLY...
RIIIIGHT, KANAA-AAA?
OOF!
SHUP
SHUP
?!
OWW!
SHUP
MY FACE!
ZIRK ZIRK ZIRK
I'M GET-TING PULLED IN!!
ZIRK-ZIRK
WAAAH!
ZIRK ZIRK
ZIRK

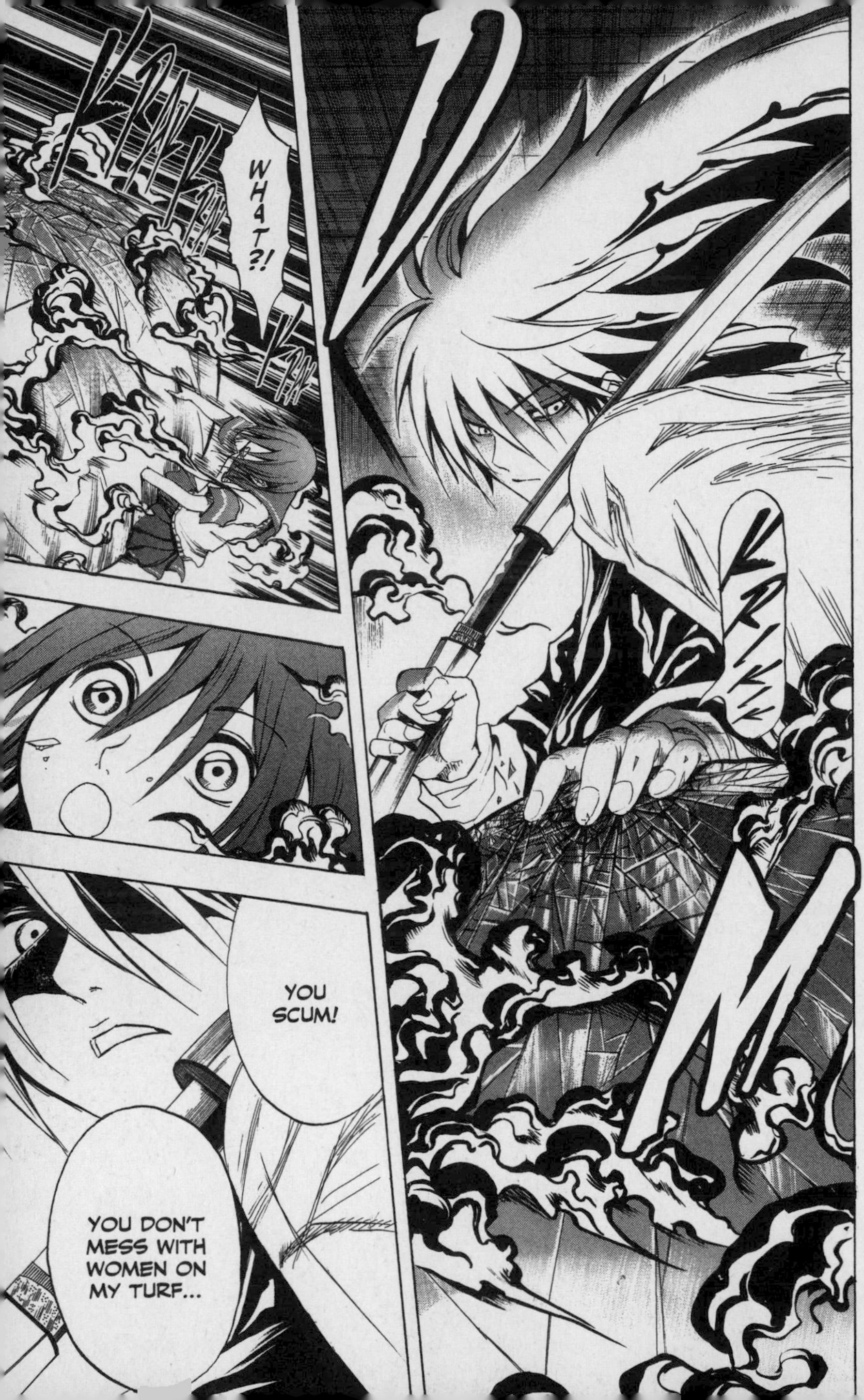
WHAT?!
YOU SCUM!
YOU DON'T MESS WITH WOMEN ON MY TURF...

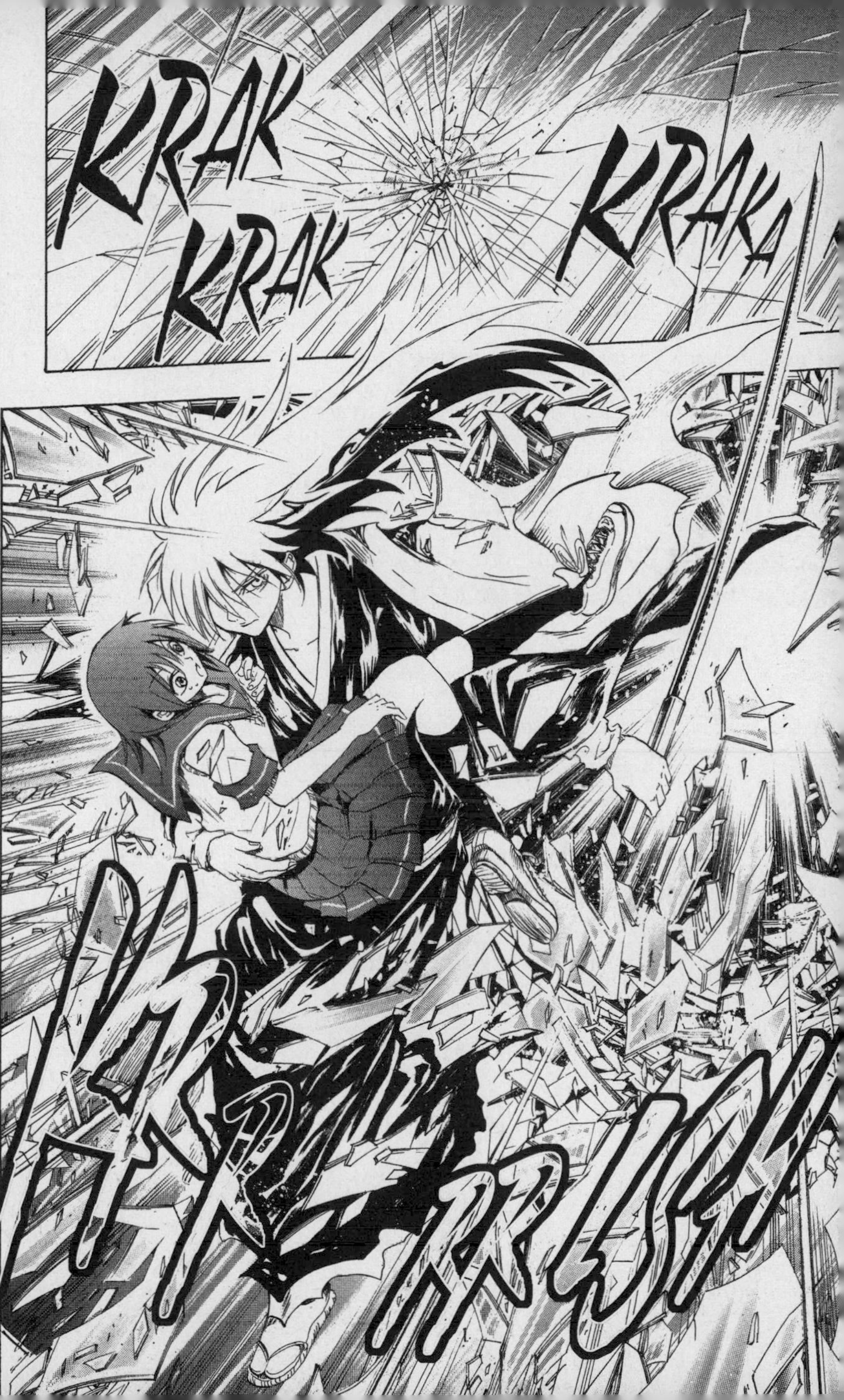
KRAKA
KRAK KRAK

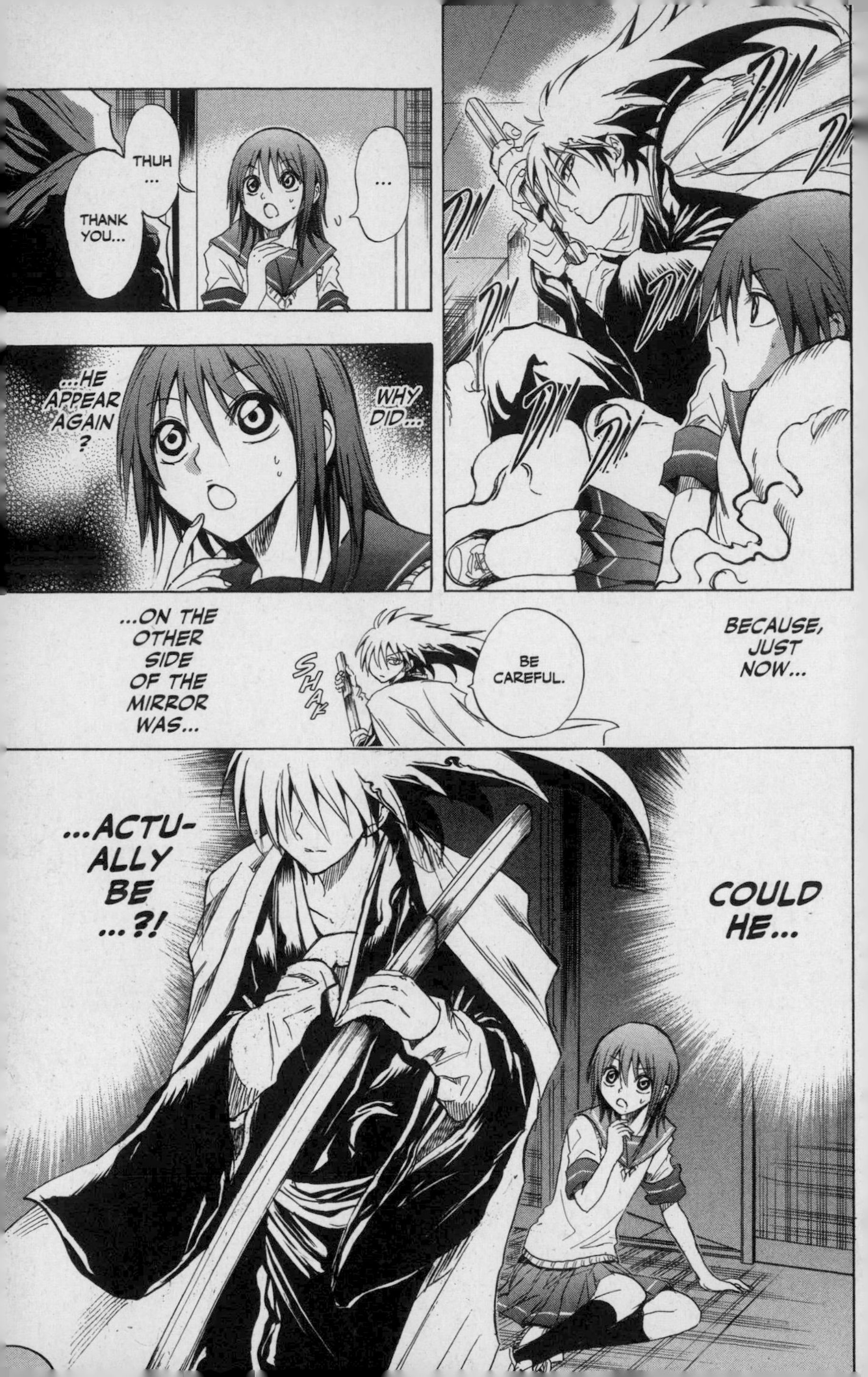
...
THUH... THANK YOU...
WHY DID...
...HE APPEAR AGAIN?
BECAUSE, JUST NOW...
BE CAREFUL.
SHAK
...ON THE OTHER SIDE OF THE MIRROR WAS...
COULD HE...
...ACTU-ALLY BE ...?!

Rikuo working hard as a human

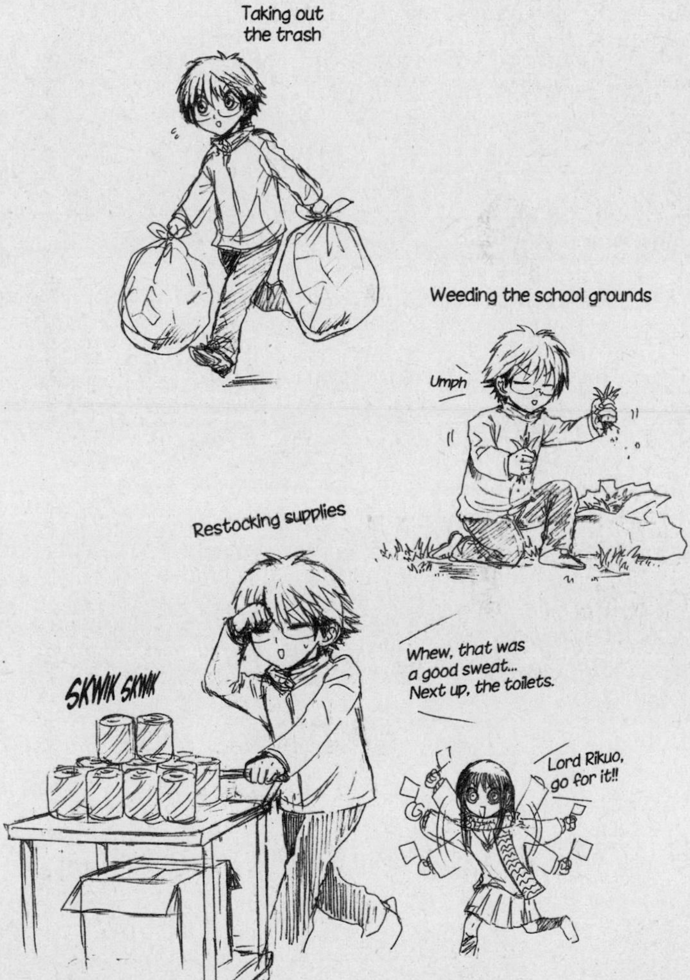
Taking out the trash
Weeding the school grounds
Umph
Restocking supplies
SKWIK SKWIK
Whew, that was a good sweat... Next up, the toilets.
Lord Rikuo, go for it!!

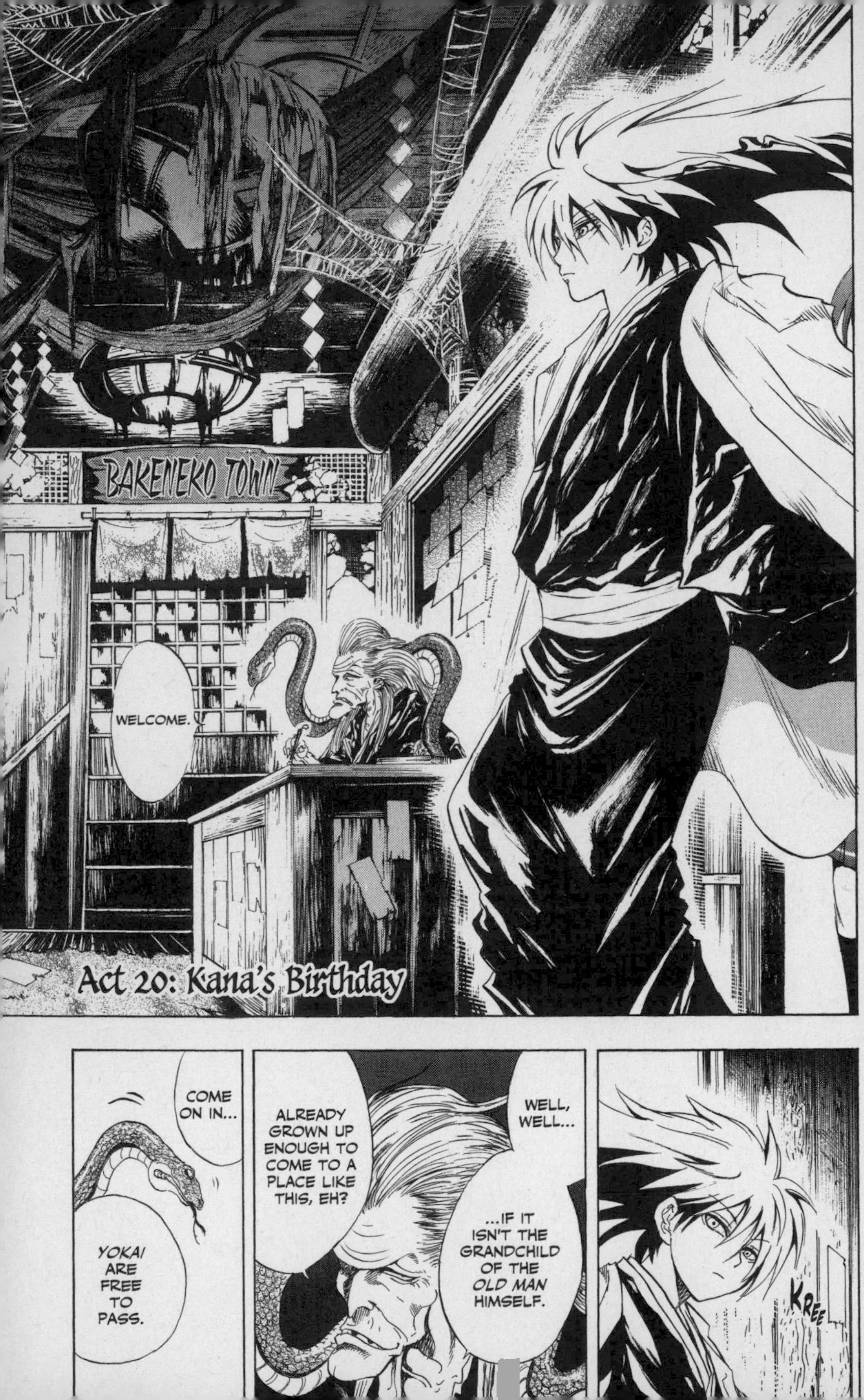
BAKENEKO TOWN
WELCOME.
Act 20: Kana's Birthday
KREE
WELL, WELL...
...IF IT ISN'T THE GRANDCHILD OF THE *OLD MAN* HIMSELF.
ALREADY GROWN UP ENOUGH TO COME TO A PLACE LIKE THIS, EH?
COME ON IN...
YOKAI ARE FREE TO PASS.

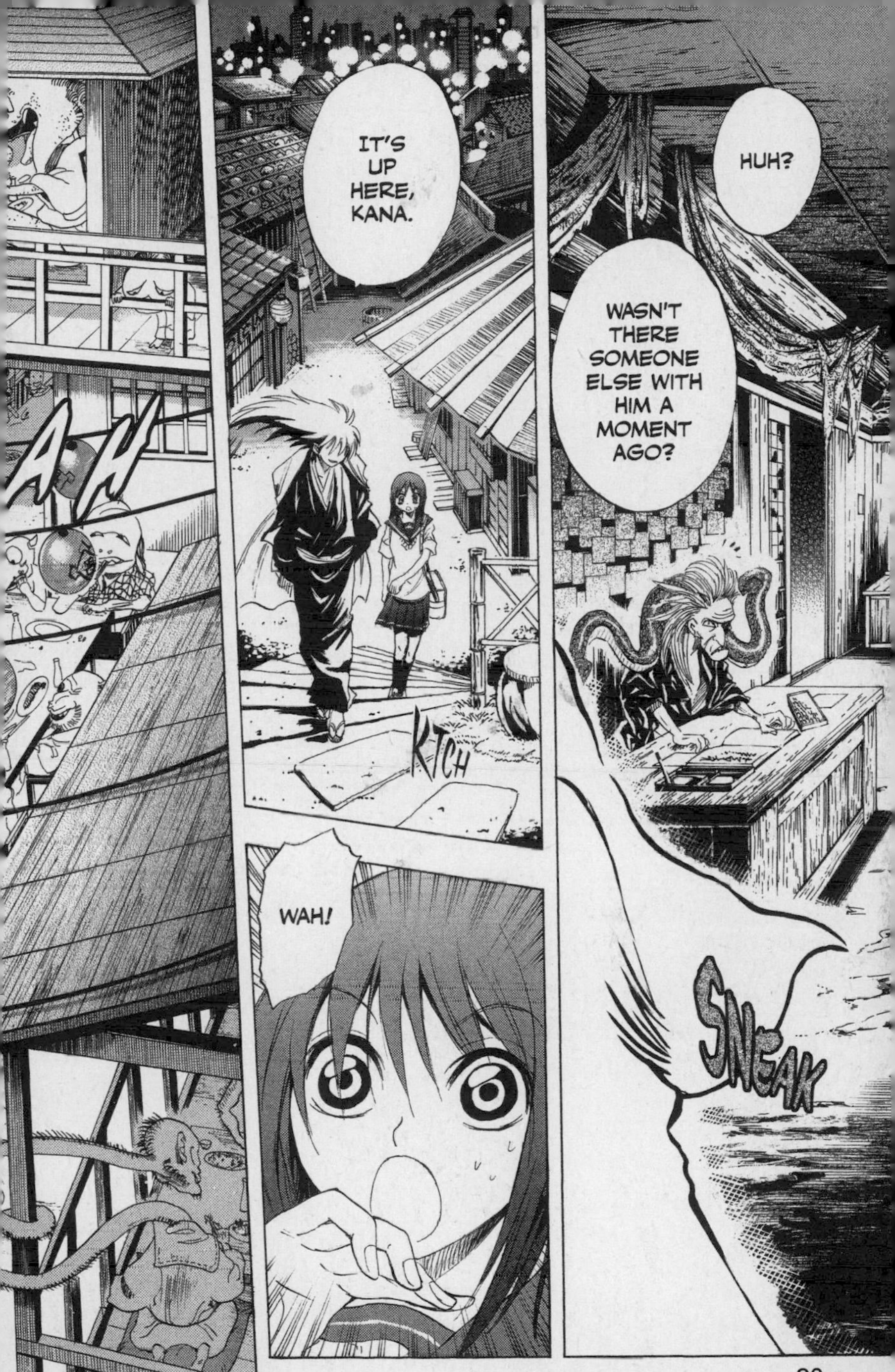
HUH?
WASN'T THERE SOMEONE ELSE WITH HIM A MOMENT AGO?
SNEAK
IT'S UP HERE, KANA.
KTCH
WAH!
AH

Act 20: Kana's Birthday

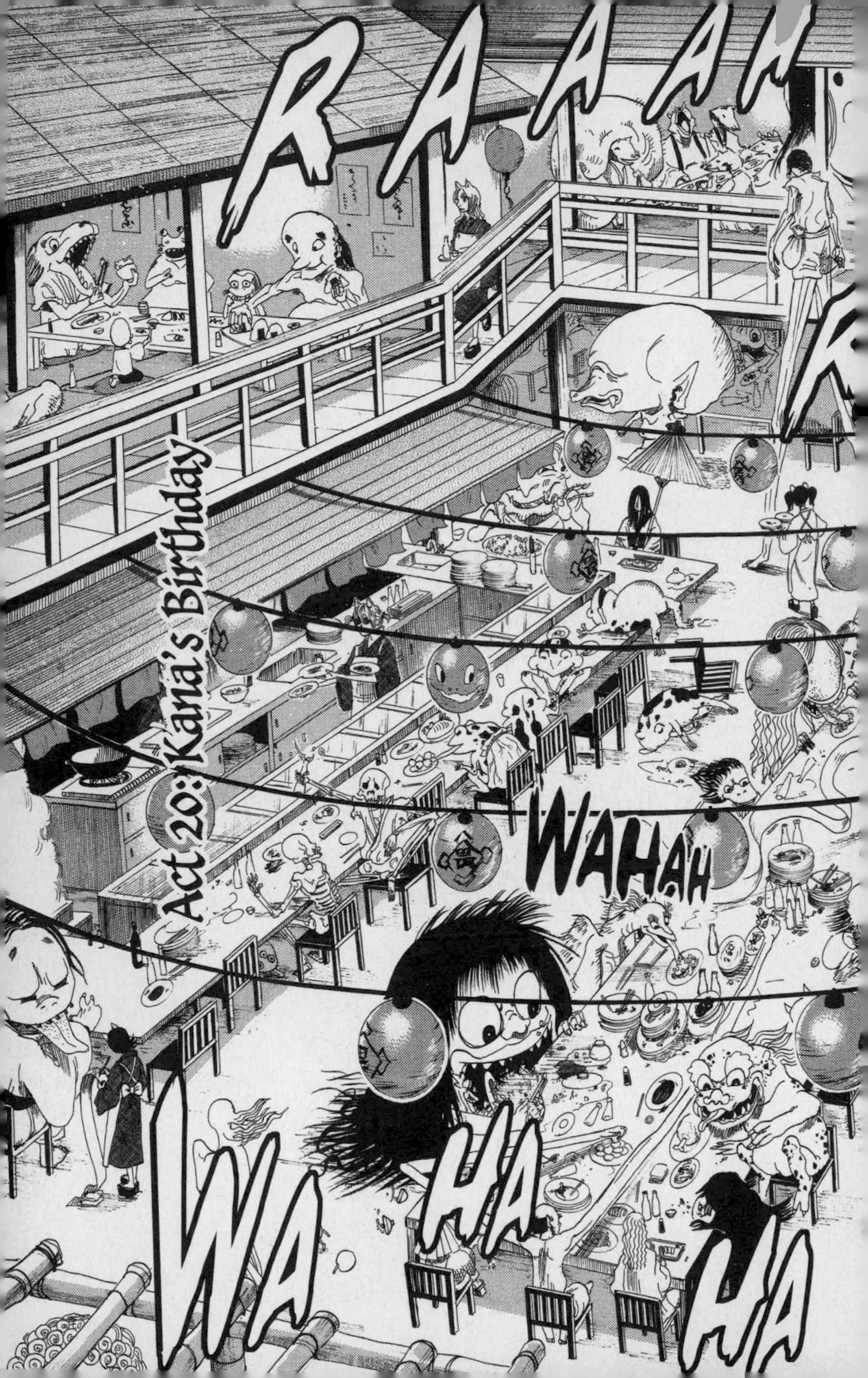
RAAAH
K
WAHAH
WA HA HA

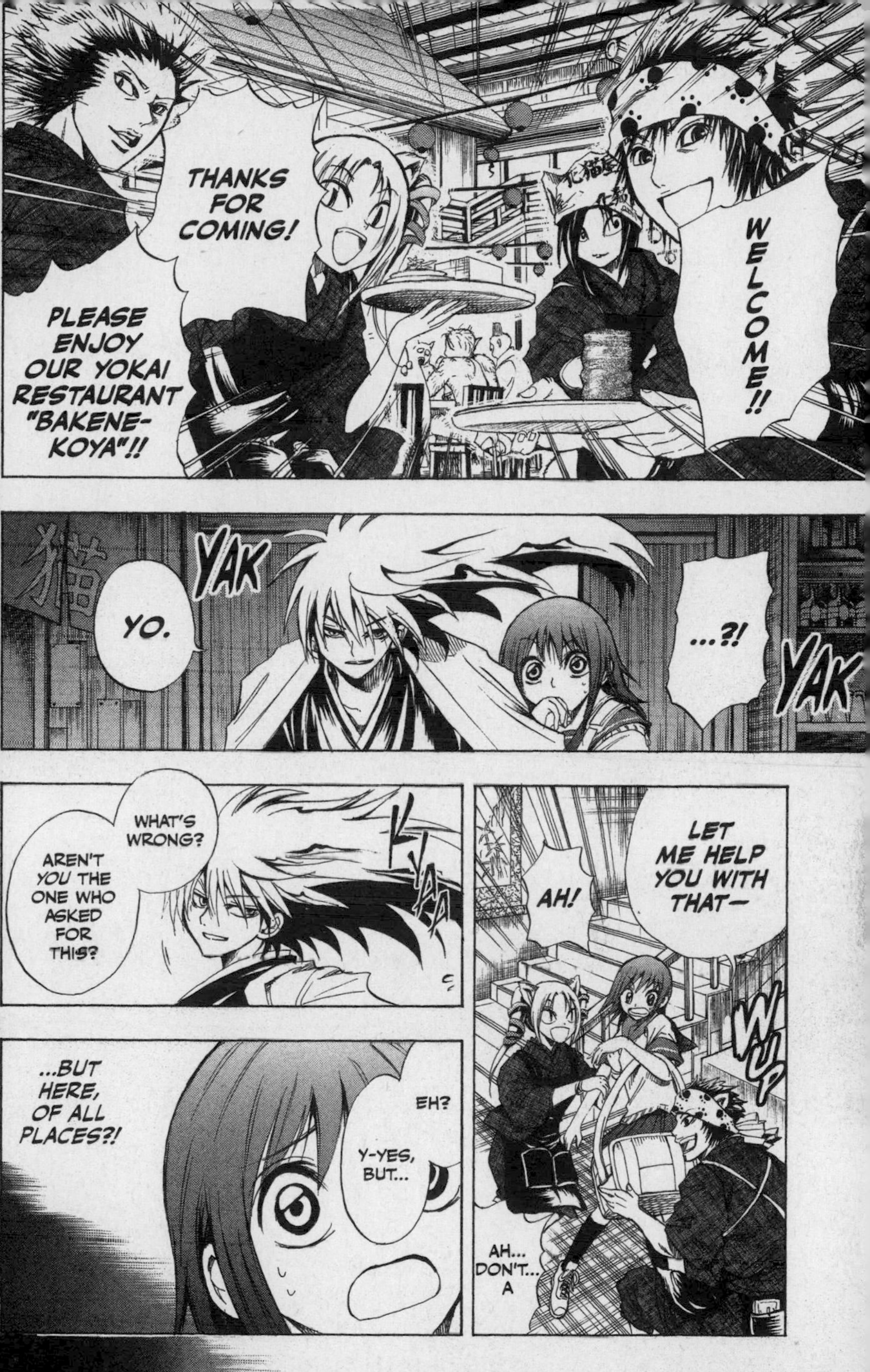
WELCOME!!
THANKS FOR COMING!
PLEASE ENJOY OUR YOKAI RESTAURANT "BAKENE-KOYA"!!
YAK
...?!
YO.
YAK
LET ME HELP YOU WITH THAT—
AH!
WUP
AH... DON'T... A
WHAT'S WRONG?
AREN'T YOU THE ONE WHO ASKED FOR THIS?
KYAA
EH?
Y-YES, BUT...
...BUT HERE, OF ALL PLACES?!

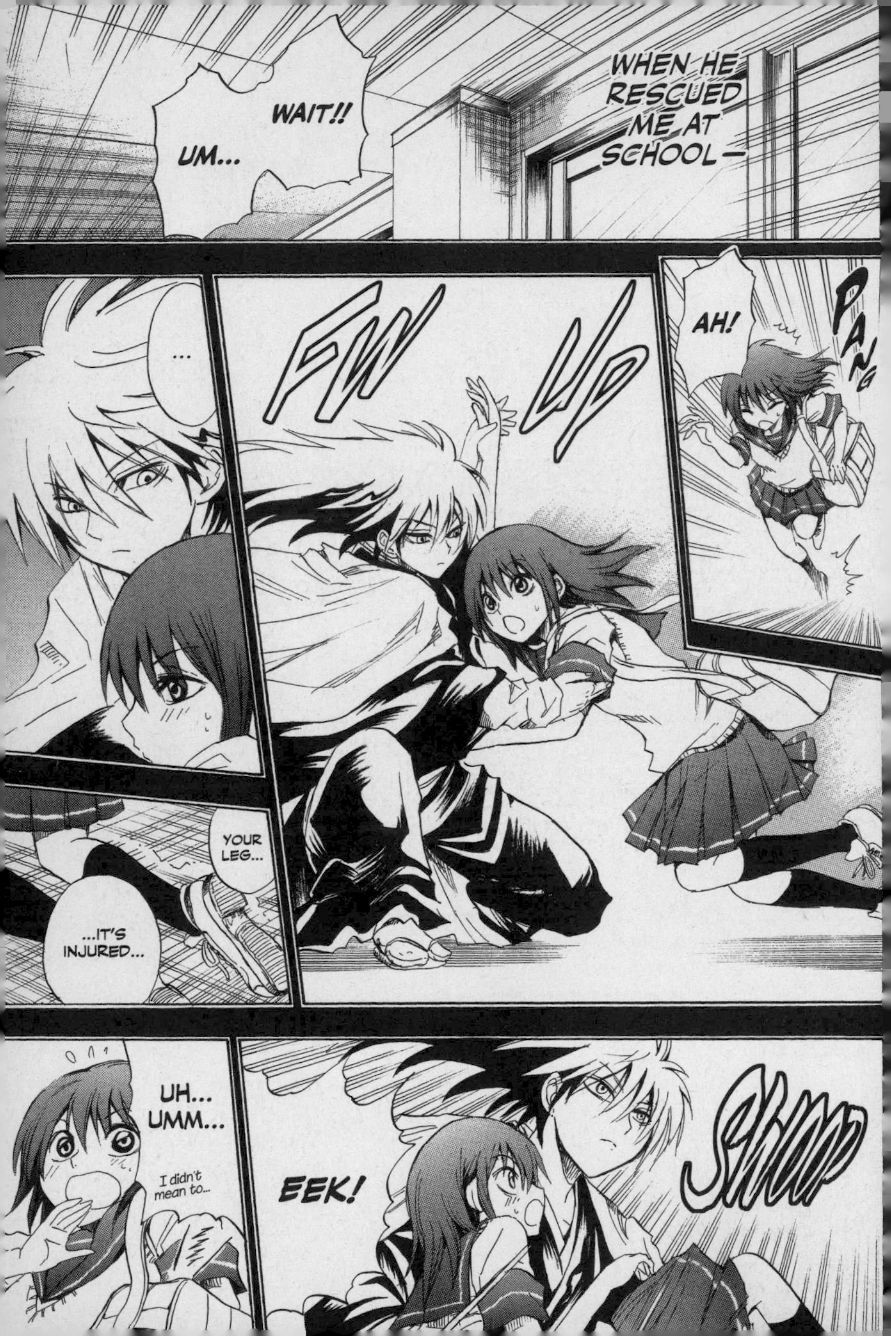
WHEN HE RESCUED ME AT SCHOOL—
WAIT!!
UM...
PANG
AH!
FWUP
...
YOUR LEG...
...IT'S INJURED...
EEK!
UH... UMM...
I didn't mean to...

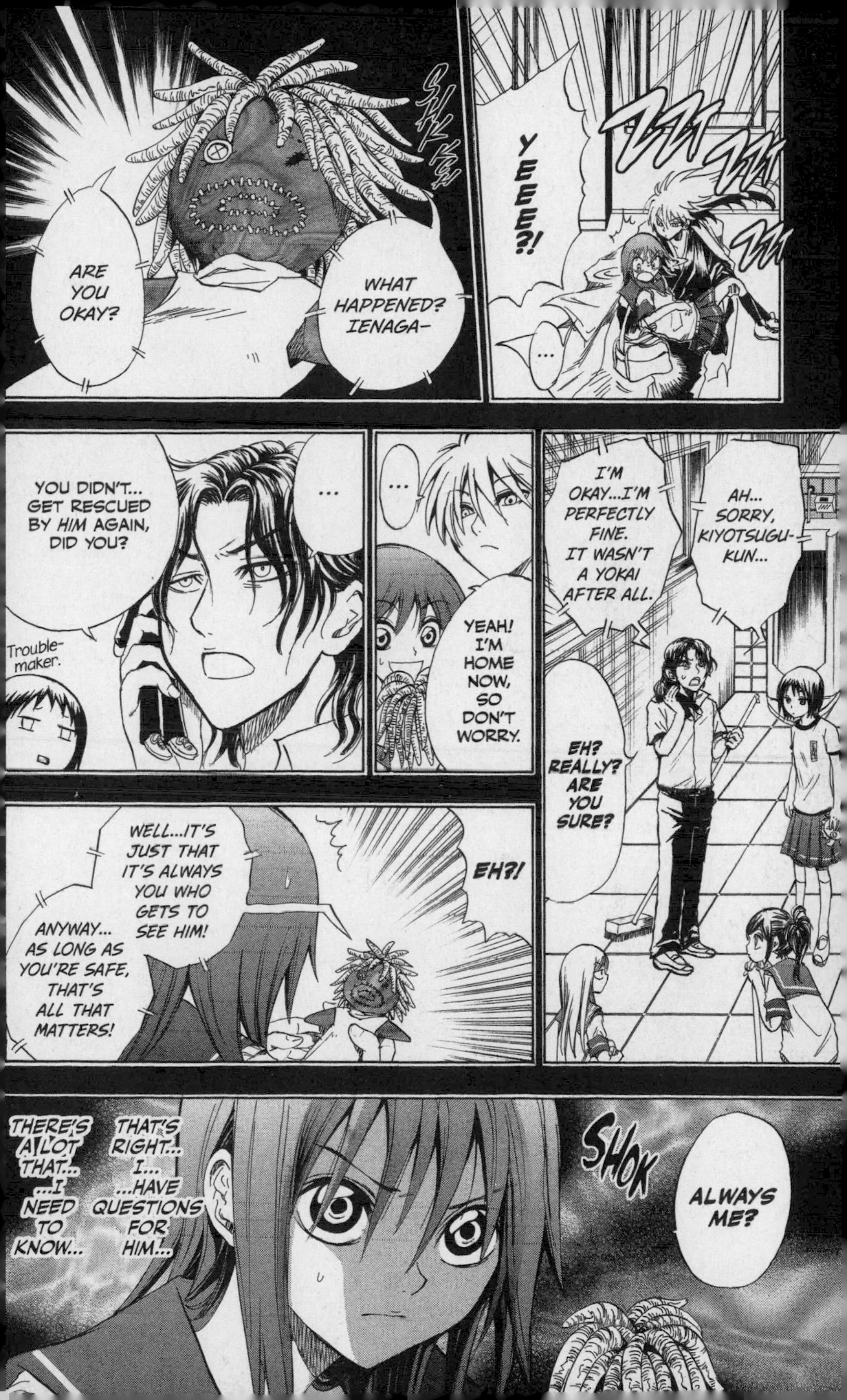
YEEEE?!
...
WHAT HAPPENED? IENAGA-
ARE YOU OKAY?
AH... SORRY, KIYOTSUGU-KUN...
I'M OKAY...I'M PERFECTLY FINE. IT WASN'T A YOKAI AFTER ALL.
EH? REALLY? ARE YOU SURE?
...
YEAH! I'M HOME NOW, SO DON'T WORRY.
...
YOU DIDN'T... GET RESCUED BY HIM AGAIN, DID YOU?
Trouble-maker.
EH?!
WELL...IT'S JUST THAT IT'S ALWAYS YOU WHO GETS TO SEE HIM!
ANYWAY... AS LONG AS YOU'RE SAFE, THAT'S ALL THAT MATTERS!
ALWAYS ME?
SHOK
THAT'S RIGHT... I... ...HAVE QUESTIONS FOR HIM...
THERE'S A LOT THAT... ...I NEED TO KNOW...

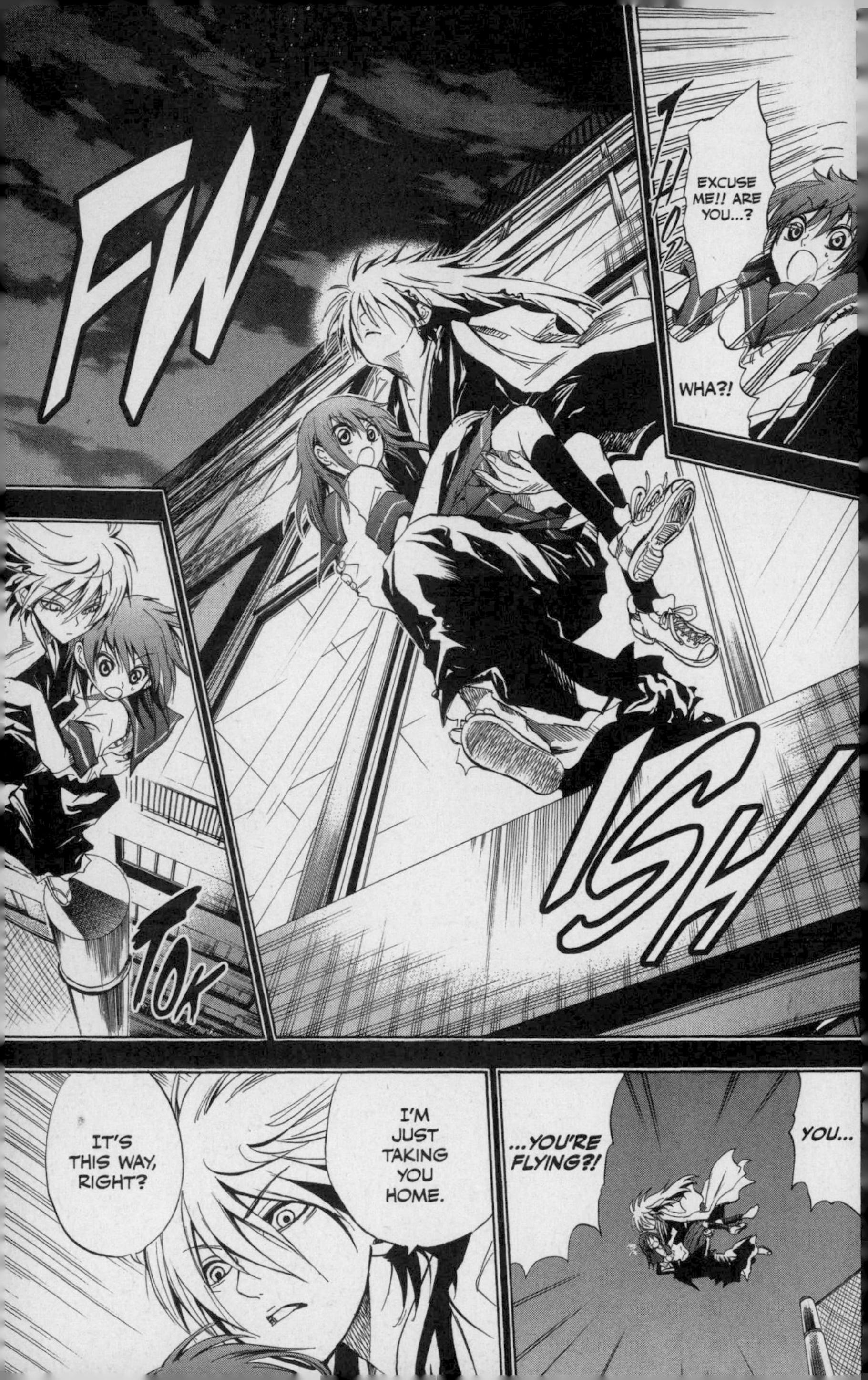
EXCUSE ME!! ARE YOU...?
WHA?!
FW
ISH
TOK
YOU...
...YOU'RE FLYING?!
I'M JUST TAKING YOU HOME.
IT'S THIS WAY, RIGHT?

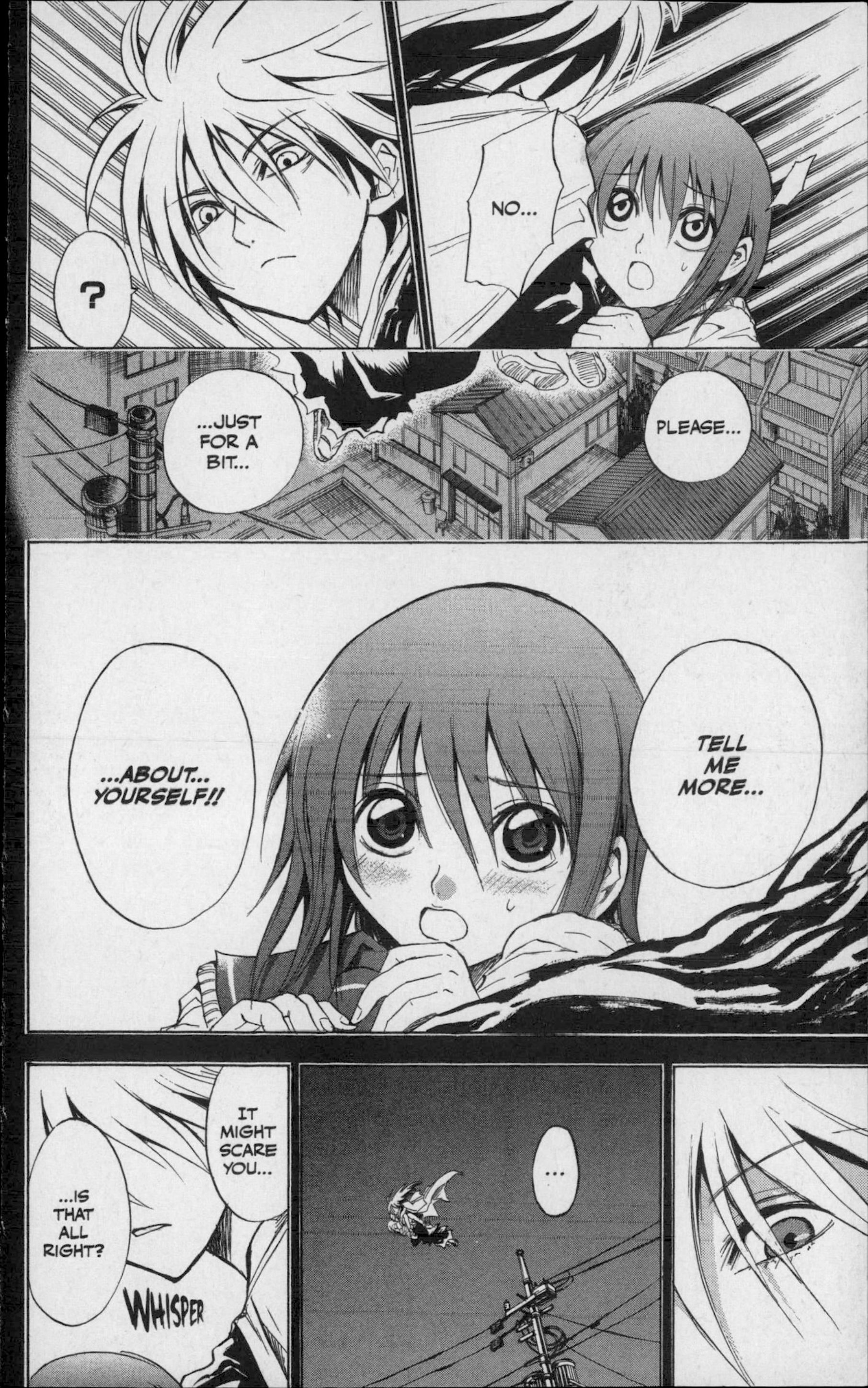
NO...
?
PLEASE...
...JUST FOR A BIT...
TELL ME MORE...
...ABOUT... YOURSELF!!
...
IT MIGHT SCARE YOU...
...IS THAT ALL RIGHT?
WHISPER

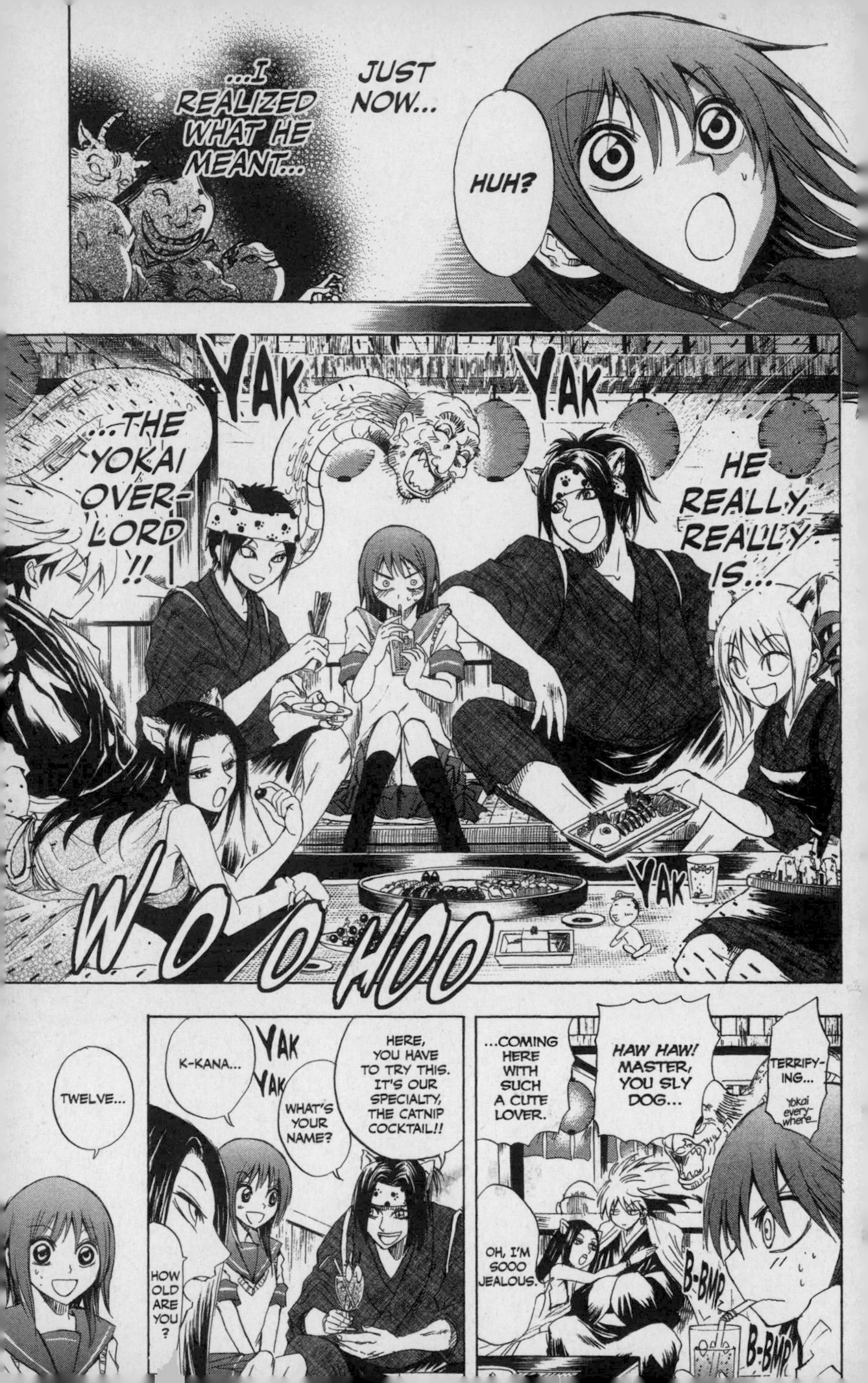
HUH?
JUST NOW...
...I REALIZED WHAT HE MEANT...
YAK
HE REALLY, REALLY IS...
YAK
...THE YOKAI OVER-LORD!!
YAK
WOO HOO
TERRIFY-ING...
Yokai every-where...
HAW HAW! MASTER, YOU SLY DOG...
...COMING HERE WITH SUCH A CUTE LOVER.
OH, I'M SOOO JEALOUS.
B-BMP
B-BMP
HERE, YOU HAVE TO TRY THIS. IT'S OUR SPECIALTY, THE CATNIP COCKTAIL!!
YAK
YAK
WHAT'S YOUR NAME?
K-KANA...
HOW OLD ARE YOU?
TWELVE...

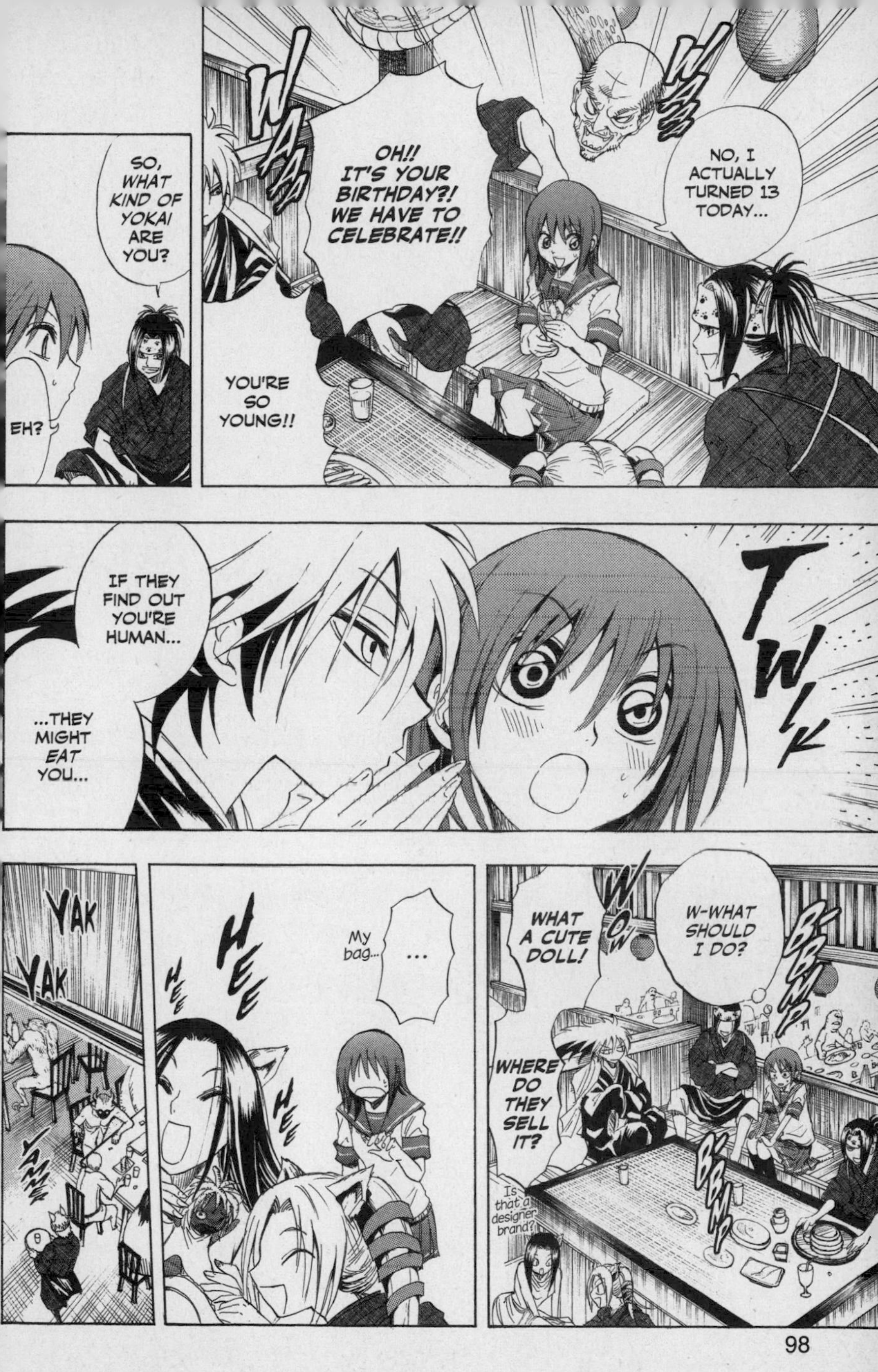
WAA
NO, I ACTUALLY TURNED 13 TODAY...
OH!! IT'S YOUR BIRTHDAY?! WE HAVE TO CELEBRATE!!
WAA
YOU'RE SO YOUNG!!
SO, WHAT KIND OF YOKAI ARE YOU?
EH?
TWIK
IF THEY FIND OUT YOU'RE HUMAN...
...THEY MIGHT EAT YOU...
W-WHAT SHOULD I DO?
WOW
WHAT A CUTE DOLL!
WHERE DO THEY SELL IT?
Is that a designer brand?
...
My bag...
HEE
HEE
HEE
HEE
YAK
YAK
YAMMER

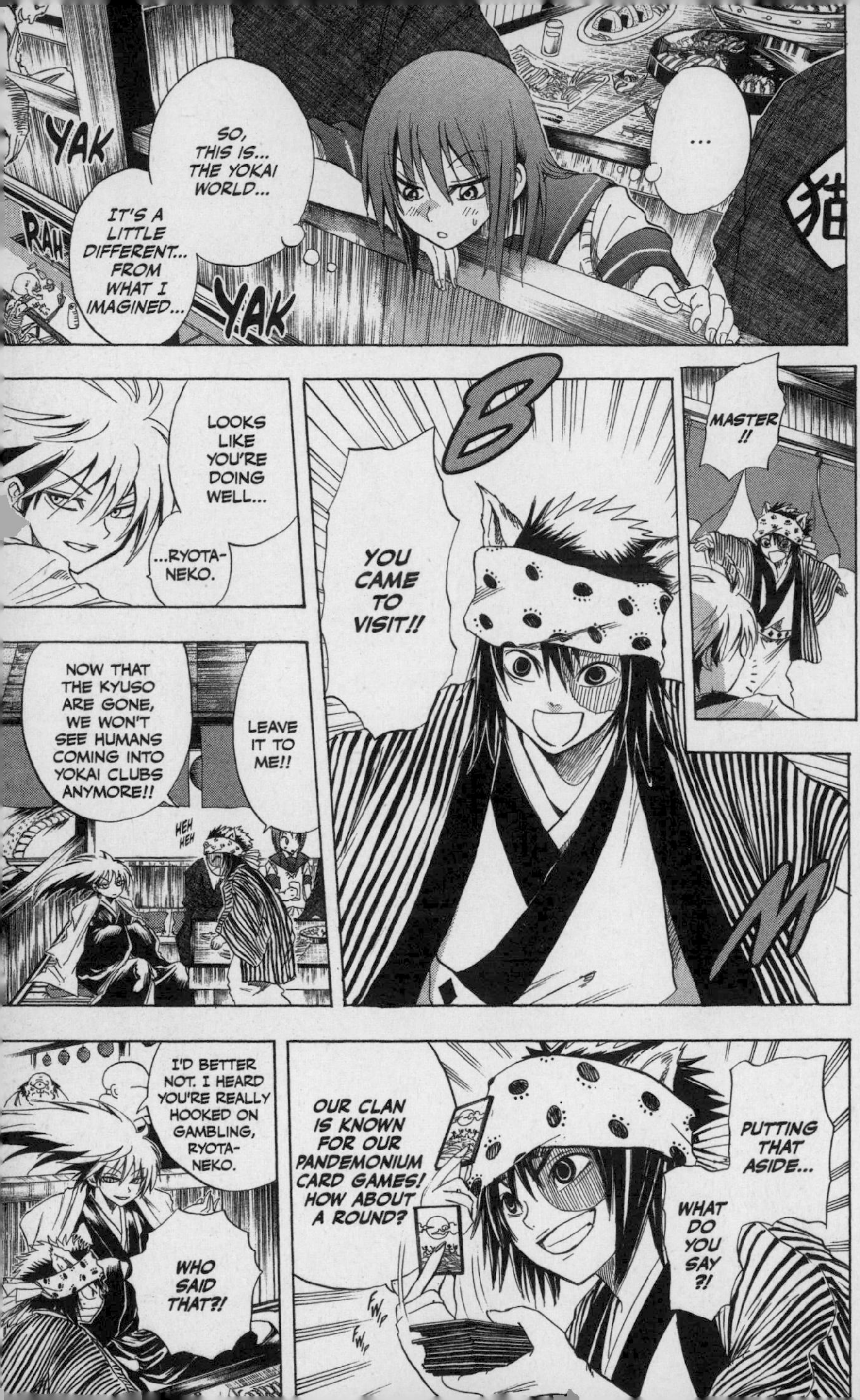
...
SO, THIS IS... THE YOKAI WORLD...
IT'S A LITTLE DIFFERENT... FROM WHAT I IMAGINED...
YAK
RAH
YAK
MASTER!!
B
YOU CAME TO VISIT!!
M
LOOKS LIKE YOU'RE DOING WELL...
...RYOTA-NEKO.
NOW THAT THE KYUSO ARE GONE, WE WON'T SEE HUMANS COMING INTO YOKAI CLUBS ANYMORE!!
LEAVE IT TO ME!!
HEH HEH
PUTTING THAT ASIDE...
WHAT DO YOU SAY?!
OUR CLAN IS KNOWN FOR OUR PANDEMONIUM CARD GAMES! HOW ABOUT A ROUND?
FWIP
FWIP
I'D BETTER NOT. I HEARD YOU'RE REALLY HOOKED ON GAMBLING, RYOTA-NEKO.
WHO SAID THAT?!

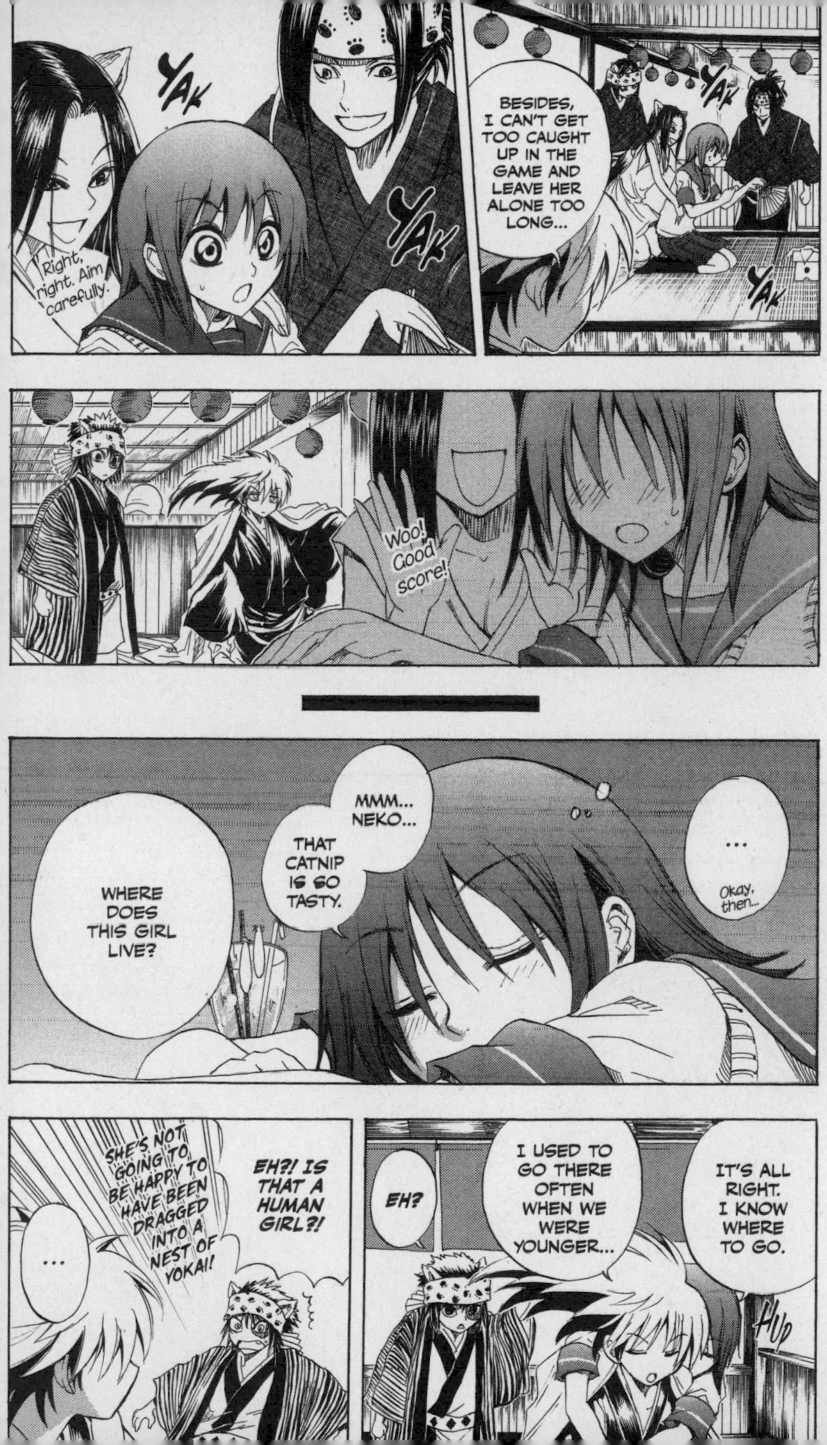

BESIDES, I CAN'T GET TOO CAUGHT UP IN THE GAME AND LEAVE HER ALONE TOO LONG...
YAK
YAK
YAK
YAK
Right, right. Aim carefully.
Woo! Good score!
...
Okay, then...
MMM... NEKO...
THAT CATNIP IS SO TASTY.
WHERE DOES THIS GIRL LIVE?
IT'S ALL RIGHT. I KNOW WHERE TO GO.
HUP
I USED TO GO THERE OFTEN WHEN WE WERE YOUNGER...
EH?
EH?! IS THAT A HUMAN GIRL?!
SHE'S NOT GOING TO BE HAPPY TO HAVE BEEN DRAGGED INTO A NEST OF YOKAI!
...

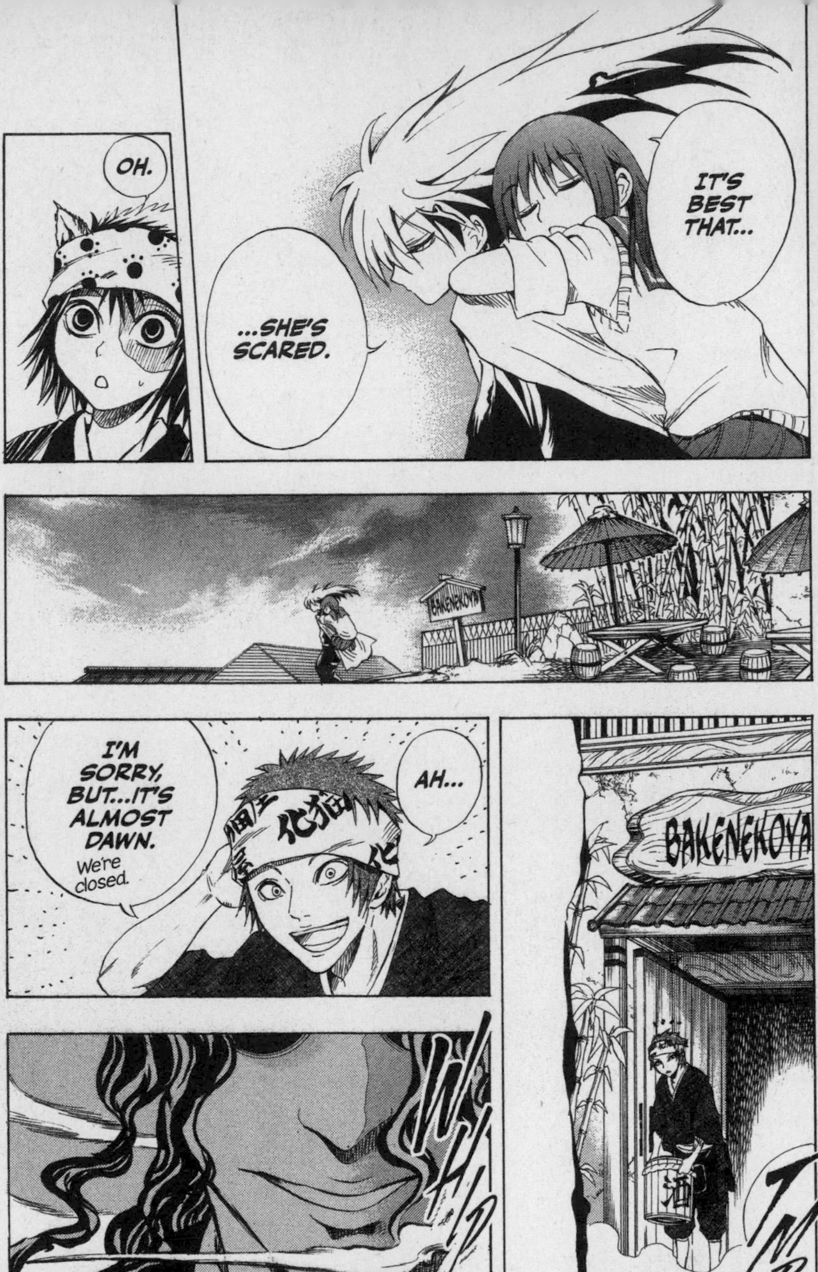
IT'S BEST THAT...
...SHE'S SCARED.
OH.
BAKENEKOYA
BAKENEKOYA
AH...
I'M SORRY, BUT...IT'S ALMOST DAWN.
We're closed.

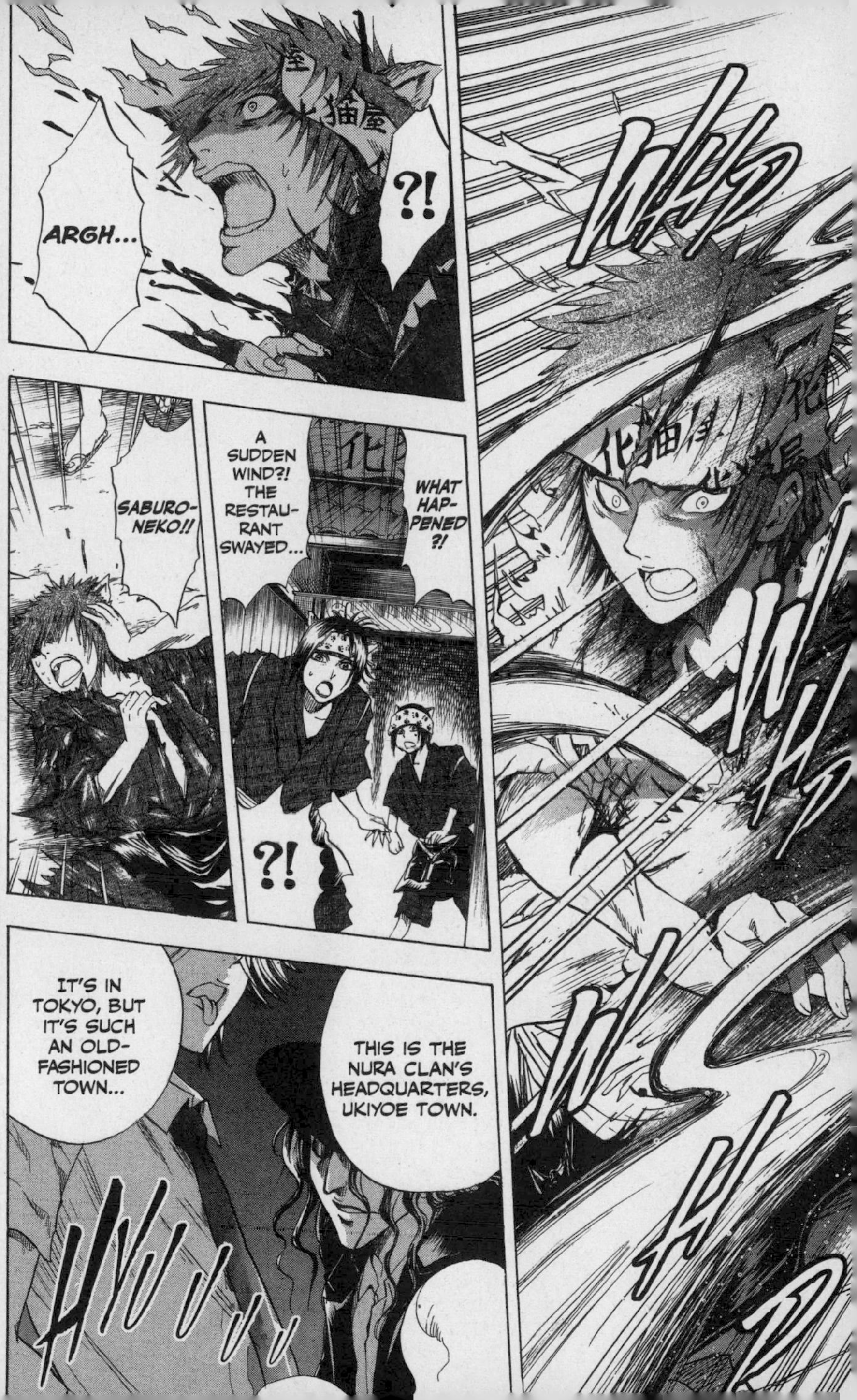
?!
ARGH...
WHAT HAPPENED?!
A SUDDEN WIND?! THE RESTAURANT SWAYED...
?!
SABURO-NEKO!!
THIS IS THE NURA CLAN'S HEADQUARTERS, UKIYOE TOWN.
IT'S IN TOKYO, BUT IT'S SUCH AN OLD-FASHIONED TOWN...

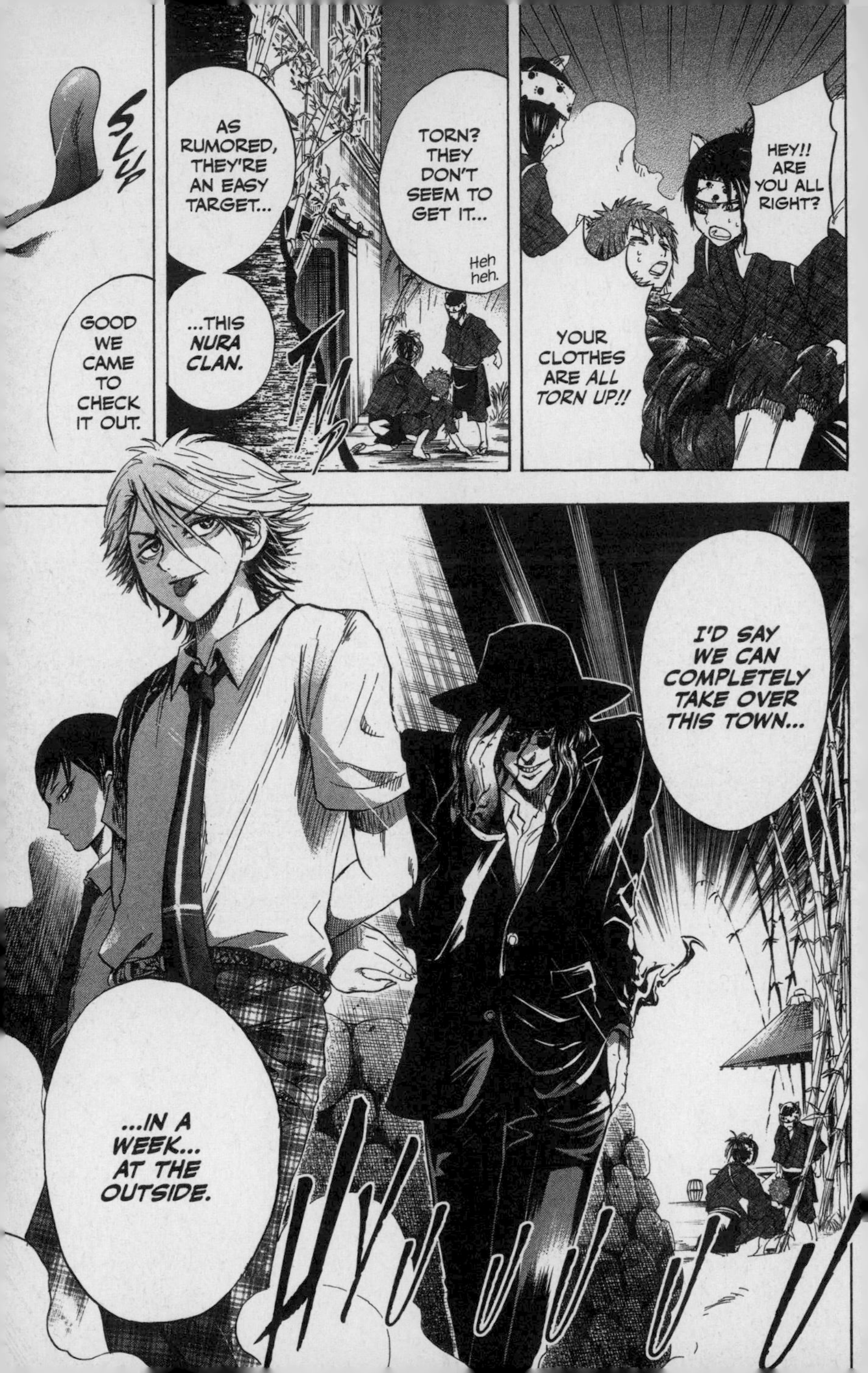
HEY!! ARE YOU ALL RIGHT?
YOUR CLOTHES ARE ALL TORN UP!!
TORN? THEY DON'T SEEM TO GET IT...
Heh heh.
AS RUMORED, THEY'RE AN EASY TARGET...
...THIS NURA CLAN.
SLUP
GOOD WE CAME TO CHECK IT OUT.
I'D SAY WE CAN COMPLETELY TAKE OVER THIS TOWN...
...IN A WEEK... AT THE OUTSIDE.

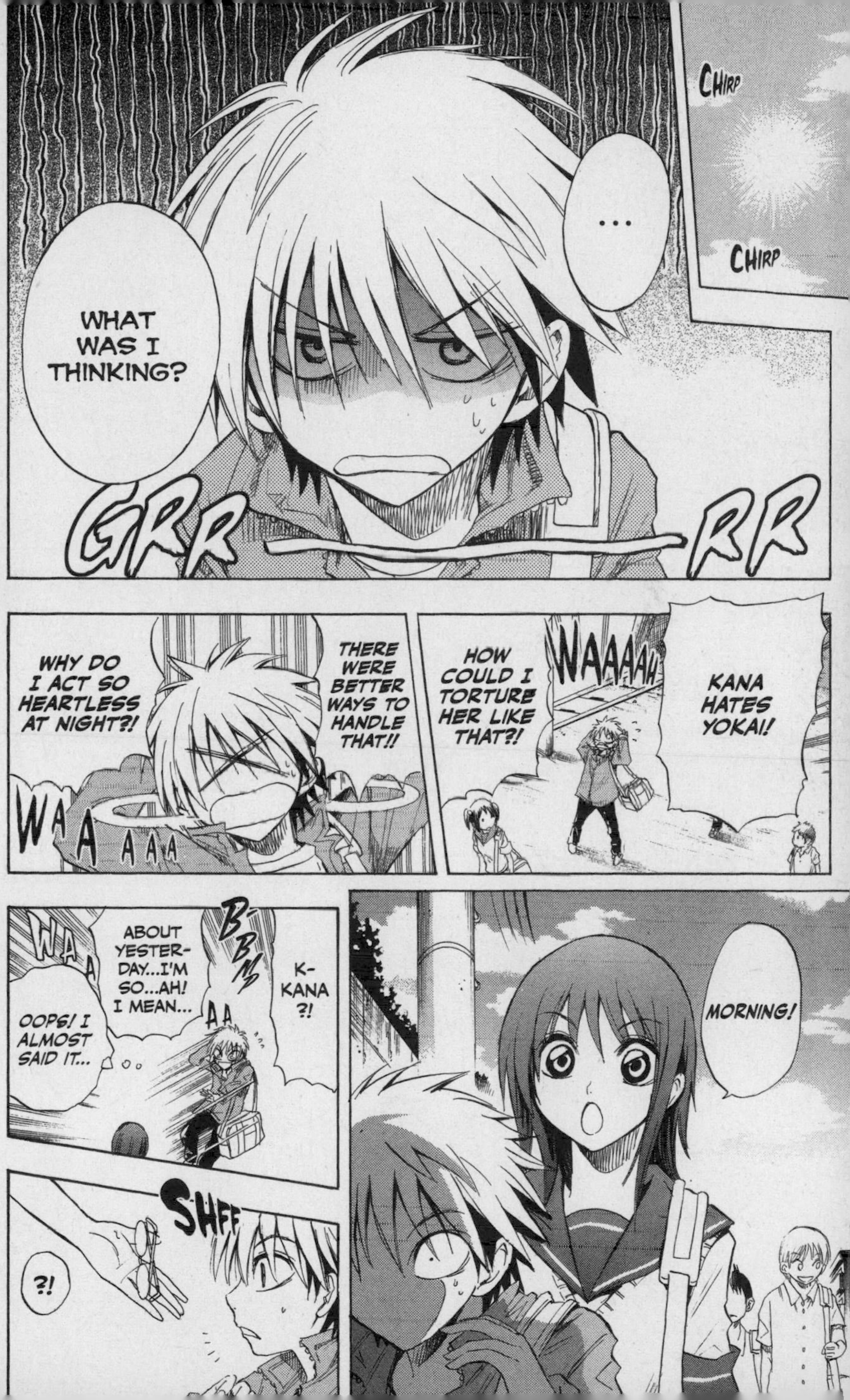

CHIRP
CHIRP
...
WHAT WAS I THINKING?
GRR—RR
KANA HATES YOKAI!
WAAAAH
HOW COULD I TORTURE HER LIKE THAT?!
THERE WERE BETTER WAYS TO HANDLE THAT!!
WHY DO I ACT SO HEARTLESS AT NIGHT?!
WA A A A A
MORNING!
K-KANA?!
B-BM
ABOUT YESTER-DAY...I'M SO...AH! I MEAN...
AA
WA A A
OOPS! I ALMOST SAID IT...
SHFF
?!

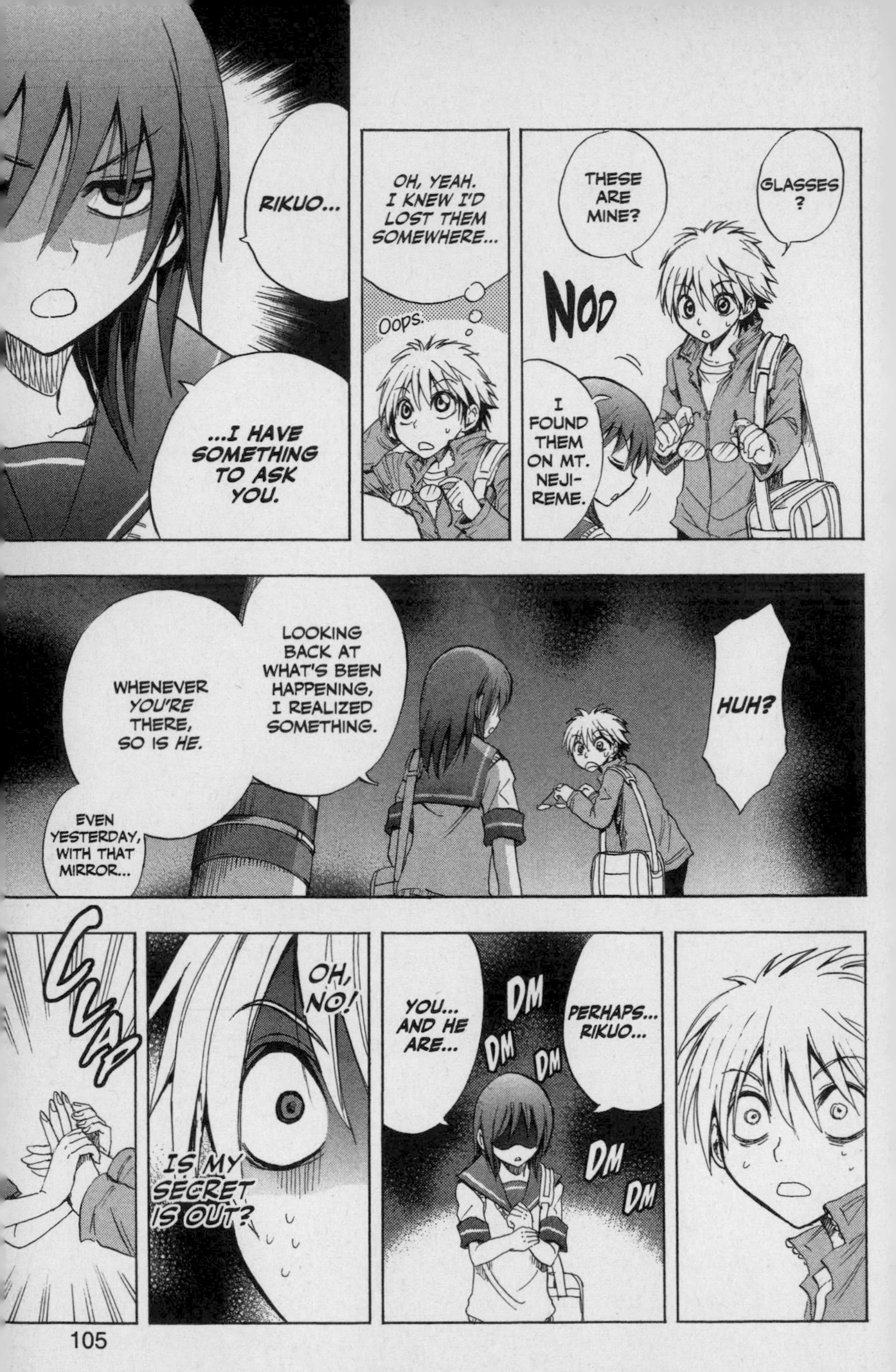

GLASSES?
THESE ARE MINE?
NOD
I FOUND THEM ON MT. NEJI-REME.
OH, YEAH. I KNEW I'D LOST THEM SOMEWHERE...
Oops.
RIKUO...
...I HAVE SOMETHING TO ASK YOU.
HUH?
LOOKING BACK AT WHAT'S BEEN HAPPENING, I REALIZED SOMETHING.
WHENEVER YOU'RE THERE, SO IS HE.
EVEN YESTERDAY, WITH THAT MIRROR...
PERHAPS... RIKUO...
DM
DM
DM
DM
DM
DM
YOU... AND HE ARE...
OH, NO!
IS MY SECRET IS OUT?

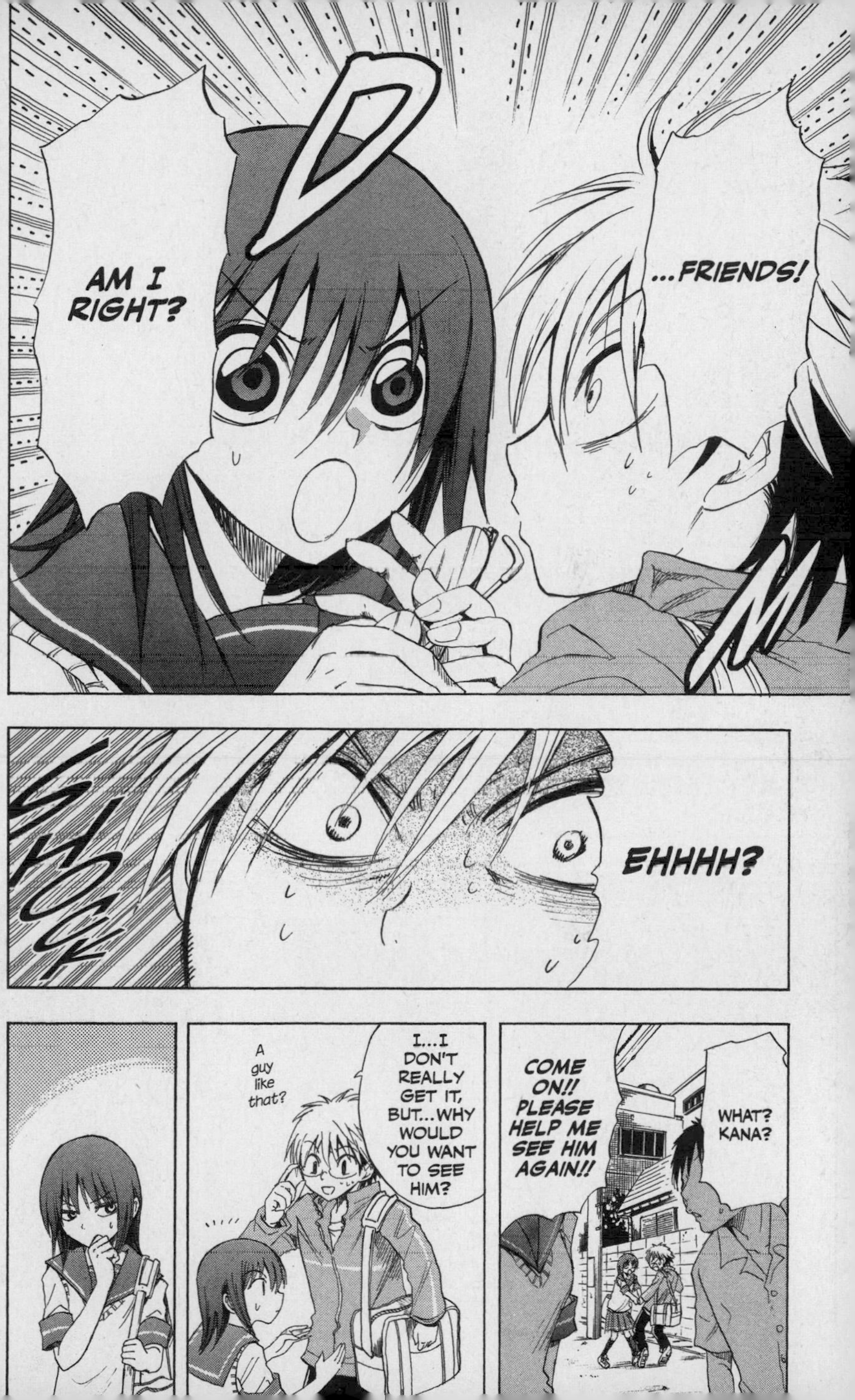
...FRIENDS!
AM I RIGHT?
EHHHH?
SHOCK
WHAT? KANA?
COME ON!! PLEASE HELP ME SEE HIM AGAIN!!
I...I DON'T REALLY GET IT, BUT...WHY WOULD YOU WANT TO SEE HIM?
A guy like that?

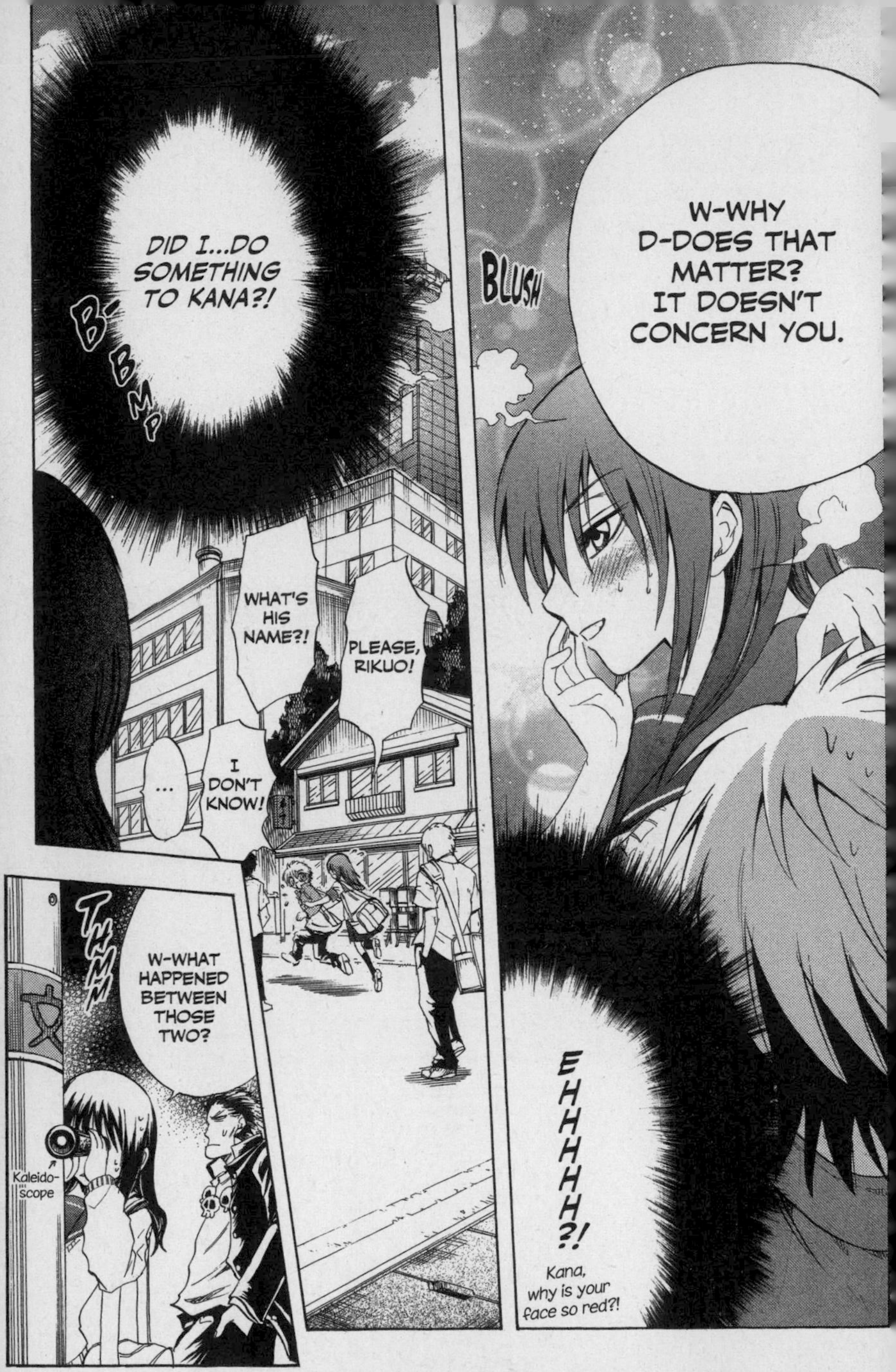
W-WHY D-DOES THAT MATTER? IT DOESN'T CONCERN YOU.
BLUSH
EHHHHHH?!
Kana, why is your face so red?!
DID I...DO SOMETHING TO KANA?!
B-BMP
PLEASE, RIKUO!
WHAT'S HIS NAME?!
I DON'T KNOW!
...
THMM
W-WHAT HAPPENED BETWEEN THOSE TWO?
Kaleido-scope

Kana Ienaga

Birthday: June 23
(Blood Type: A, Sign: Cancer)
Height: 4'11"
Weight: 86 lbs.
Items Carried: Handheld Mirror,
Binoculars, Doll

[Kyotsugu's Kana Analysis]
She doesn't know
anything about yokai!!
But she seems to run
into yokai quite often.
I really envy her for
that. In that sense,
she's our team's ace!

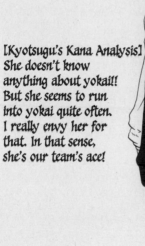
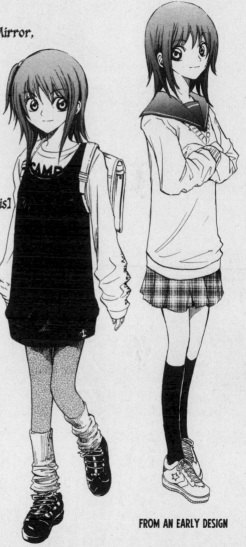

FROM AN EARLY DESIGN

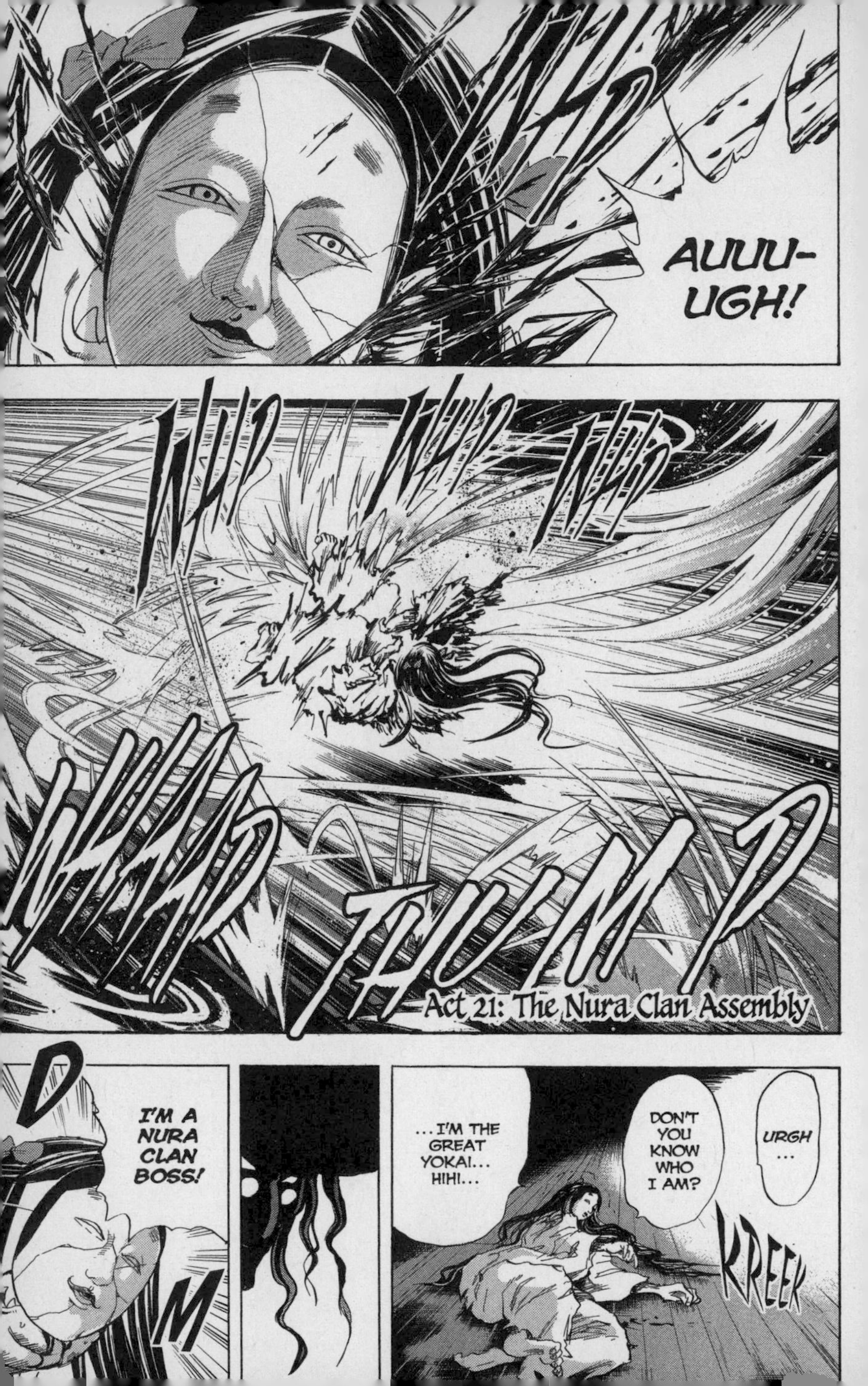
AUUU-UGH!
WHIP
WHIP
WHIP
WHAM
THUMP
Act 21: The Nura Clan Assembly
URGH ...
DON'T YOU KNOW WHO I AM?
...I'M THE GREAT YOKAI... HIHI...
KREEK
I'M A NURA CLAN BOSS!

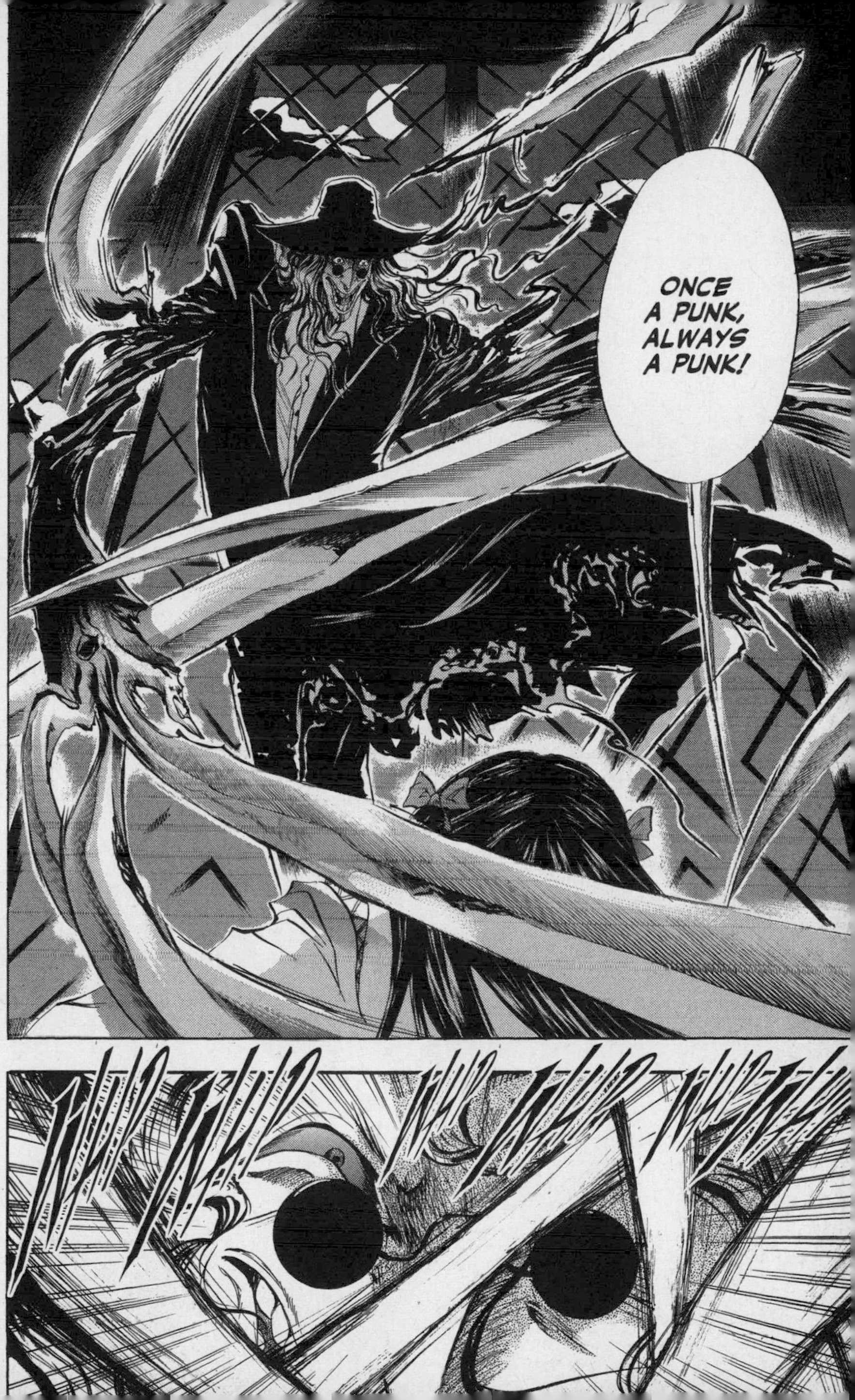
ONCE A PUNK, ALWAYS A PUNK!

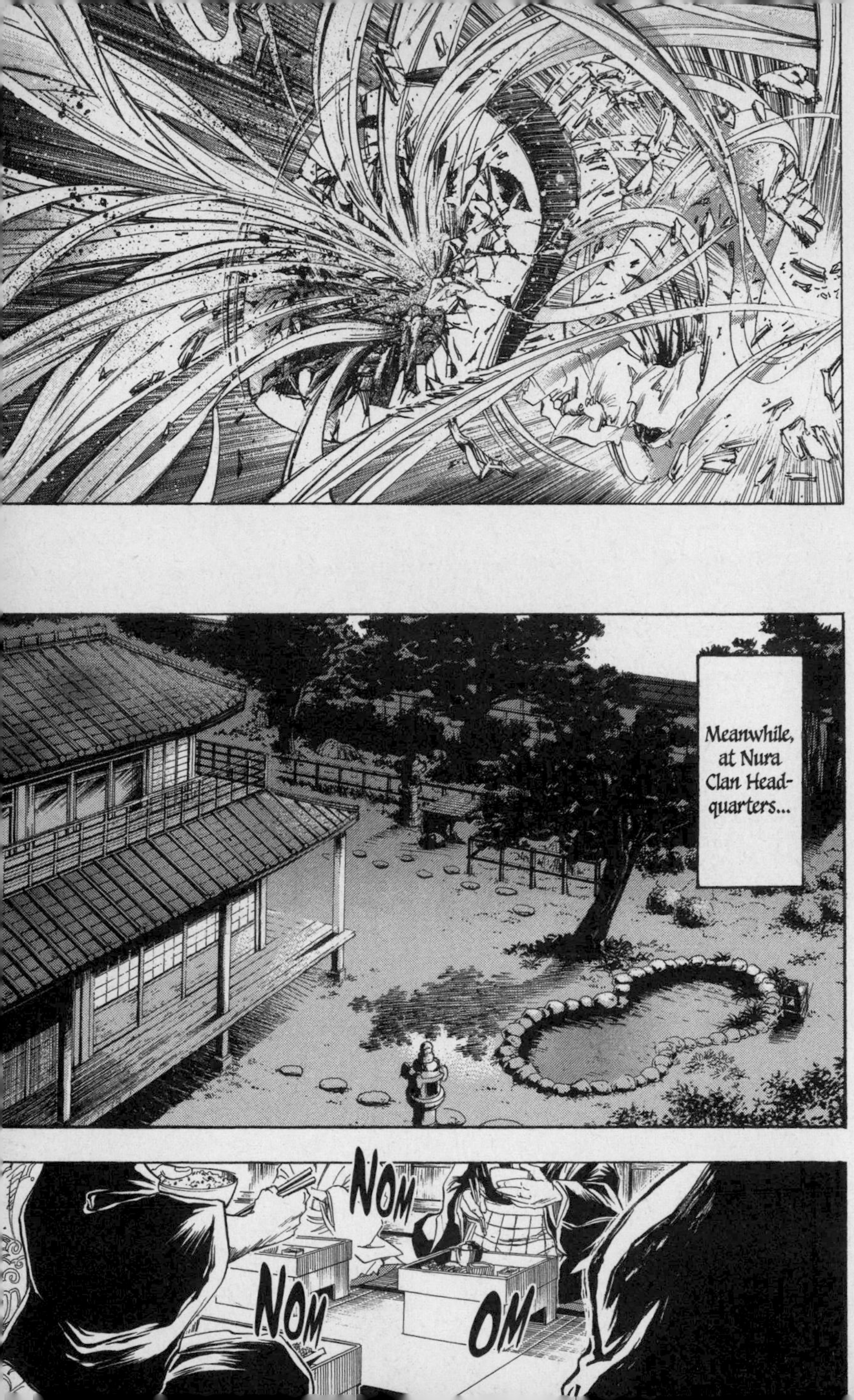
Meanwhile, at Nura Clan Head-quarters...
NOM
OM
NOM

Act 21: The Nura Clan Assembly

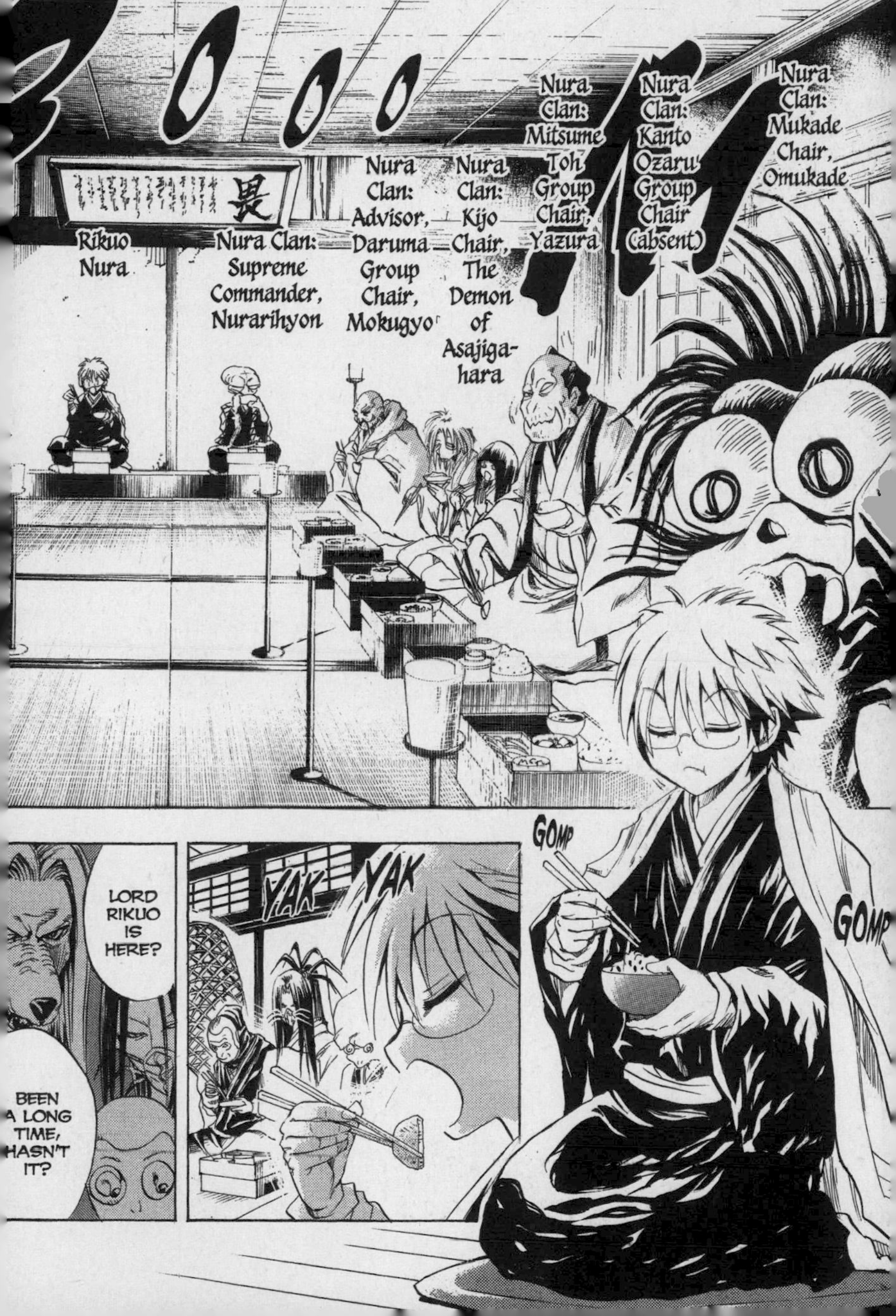
Nura Clan: Mukade Chair, Omukade
Nura Clan: Kanto Ozaru Group Chair (absent)
Nura Clan: Mitsume Toh Group Chair, Yazura
Nura Clan: Kijo Chair, The Demon of Asajiga-hara
Nura Clan: Advisor, Daruma Group Chair, Mokugyo
Nura Clan: Supreme Commander, Nurarihyon
Rikuo Nura
GOMP
GOMP
YAK
YAK
LORD RIKUO IS HERE?
BEEN A LONG TIME, HASN'T IT?

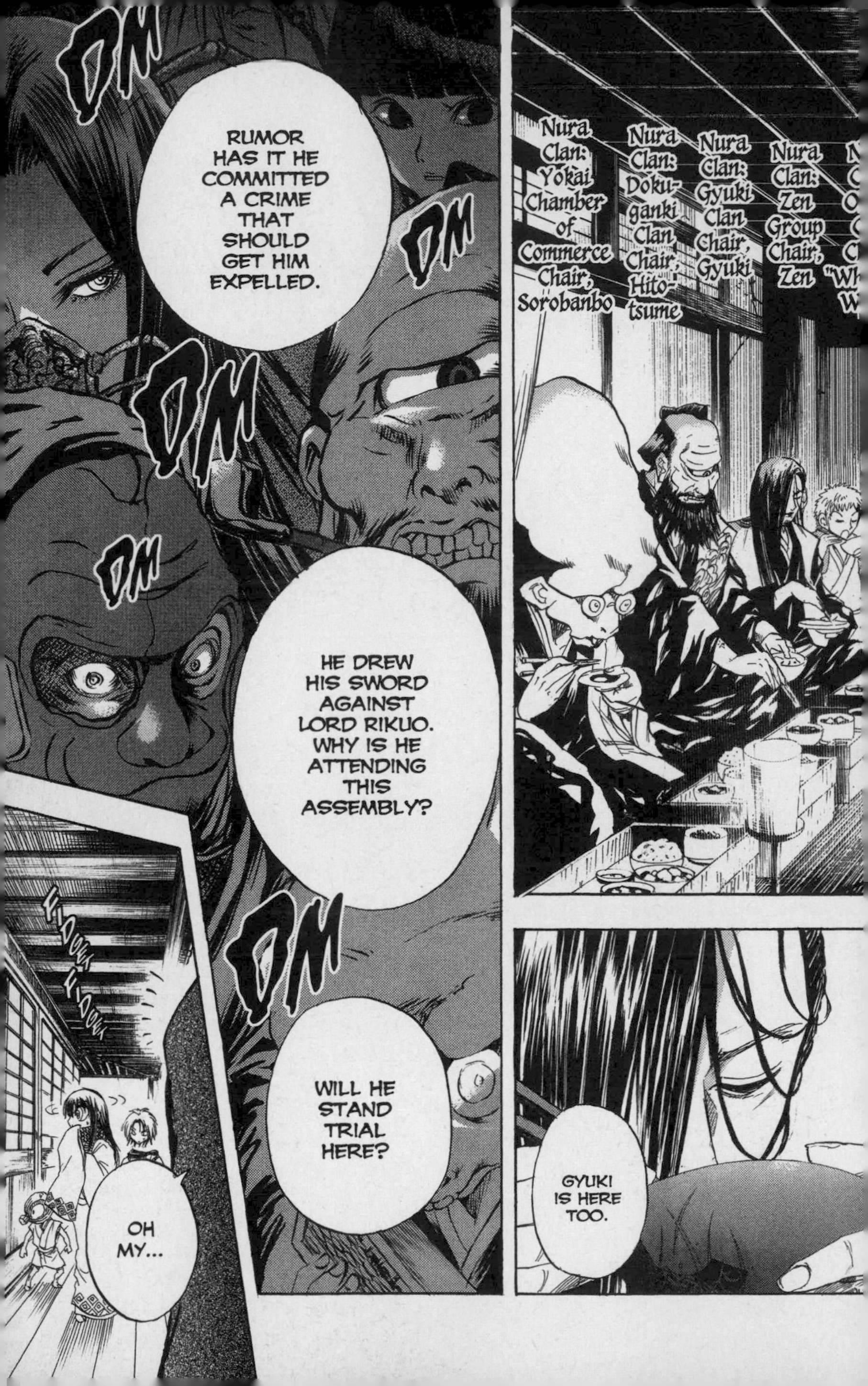

Nura Clan: Yokai Chamber of Commerce Chair, Sorobanbo
Nura Clan: Doku-ganki Clan Chair, Hito-tsume
Nura Clan: Gyuki Clan Chair, Gyuki
Nura Clan: Zen Group Chair, Zen
DM
RUMOR HAS IT HE COMMITTED A CRIME THAT SHOULD GET HIM EXPELLED.
DM
DM
DM
HE DREW HIS SWORD AGAINST LORD RIKUO. WHY IS HE ATTENDING THIS ASSEMBLY?
DM
WILL HE STAND TRIAL HERE?
GYUKI IS HERE TOO.
OH MY...

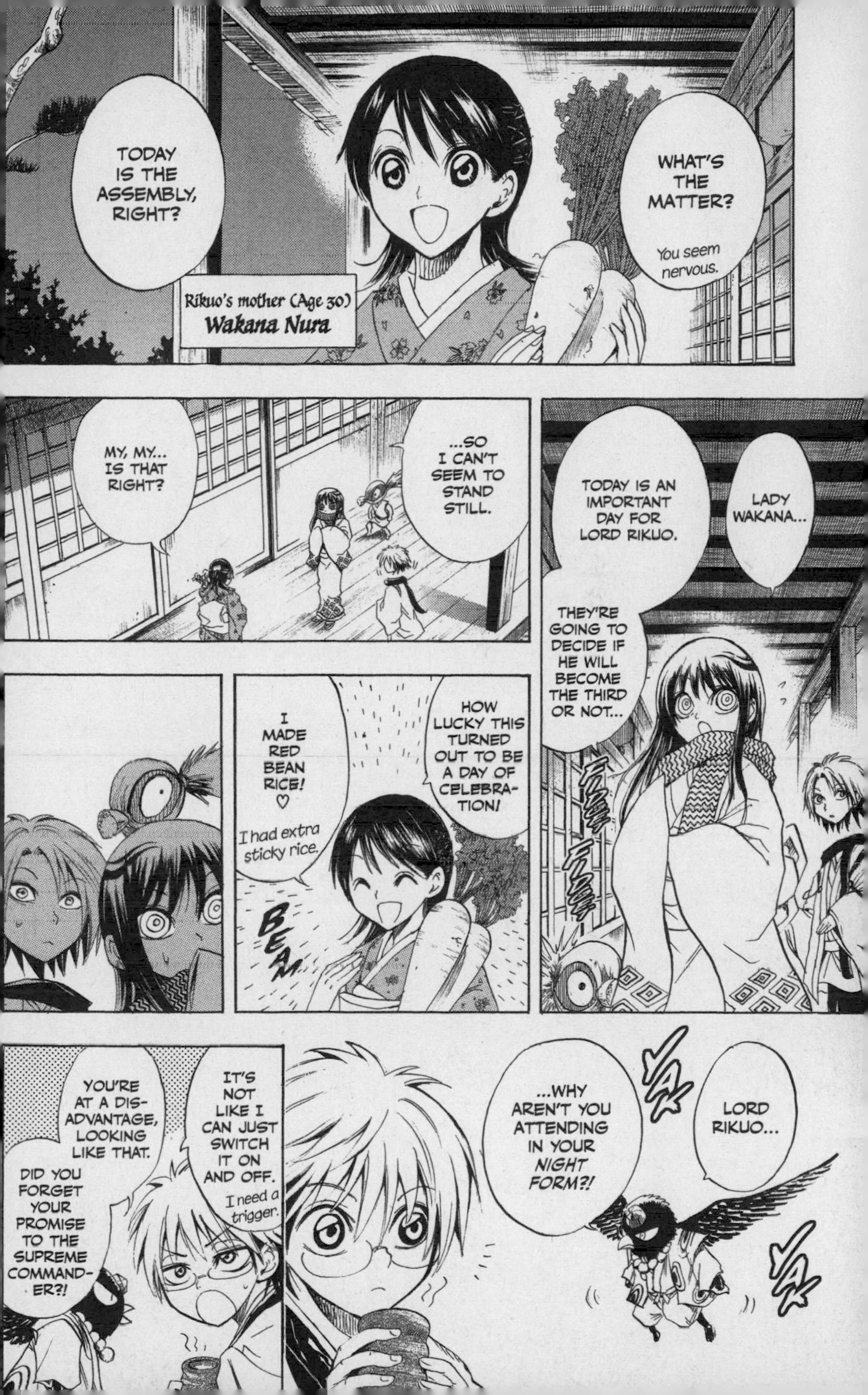
WHAT'S THE MATTER?
You seem nervous.
TODAY IS THE ASSEMBLY, RIGHT?
Rikuo's mother (Age 30) Wakana Nura
LADY WAKANA...
TODAY IS AN IMPORTANT DAY FOR LORD RIKUO.
THEY'RE GOING TO DECIDE IF HE WILL BECOME THE THIRD OR NOT...
...SO I CAN'T SEEM TO STAND STILL.
MY, MY... IS THAT RIGHT?
HOW LUCKY THIS TURNED OUT TO BE A DAY OF CELEBRA-TION!
I MADE RED BEAN RICE! ♡
I had extra sticky rice.
BEAM
YAK
LORD RIKUO...
...WHY AREN'T YOU ATTENDING IN YOUR NIGHT FORM?!
YAK
IT'S NOT LIKE I CAN JUST SWITCH IT ON AND OFF.
I need a trigger.
YOU'RE AT A DIS-ADVANTAGE, LOOKING LIKE THAT.
DID YOU FORGET YOUR PROMISE TO THE SUPREME COMMAND-ER?!

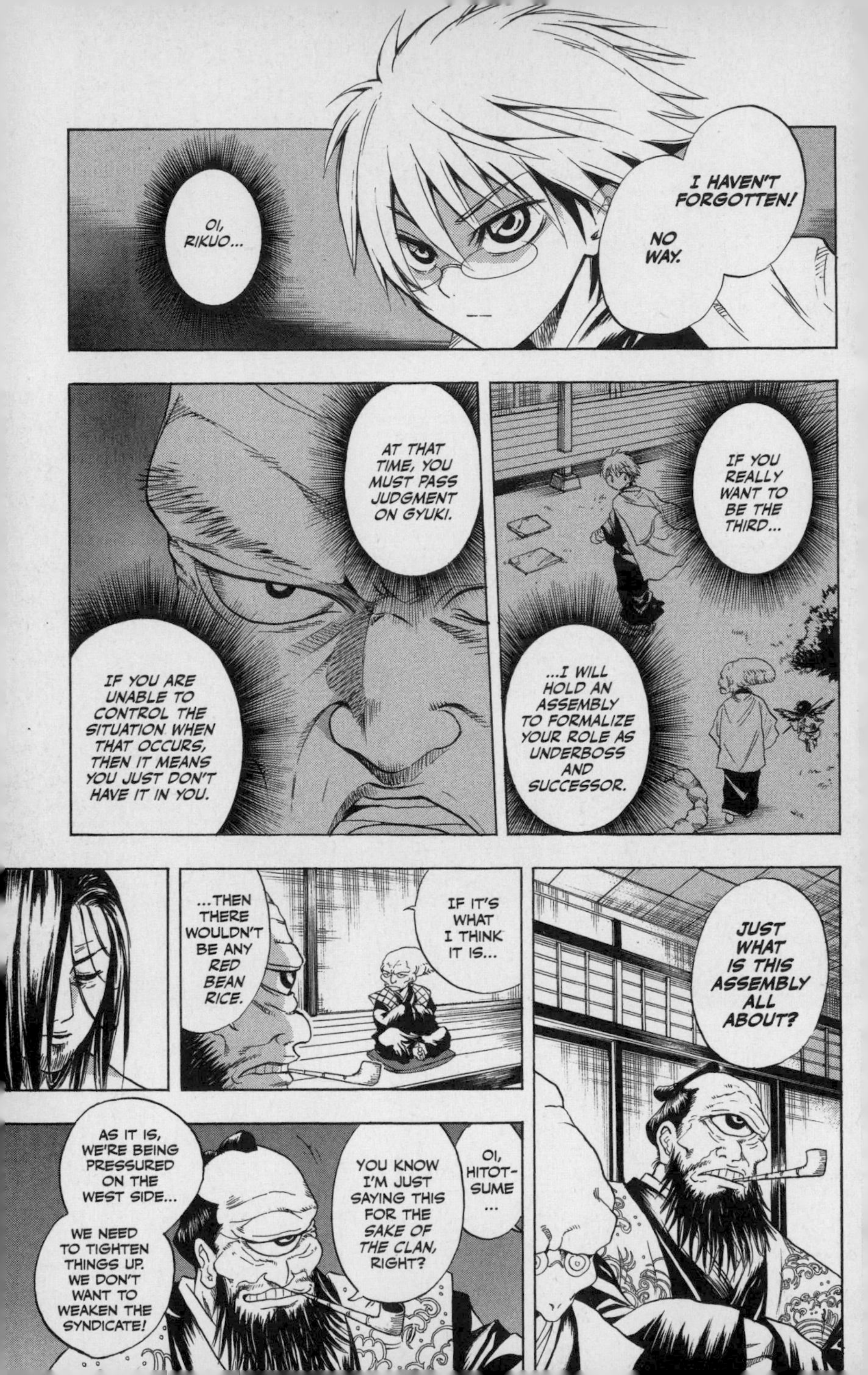
I HAVEN'T FORGOTTEN!
NO WAY.
OI, RIKUO...
IF YOU REALLY WANT TO BE THE THIRD...
...I WILL HOLD AN ASSEMBLY TO FORMALIZE YOUR ROLE AS UNDERBOSS AND SUCCESSOR.
AT THAT TIME, YOU MUST PASS JUDGMENT ON GYUKI.
IF YOU ARE UNABLE TO CONTROL THE SITUATION WHEN THAT OCCURS, THEN IT MEANS YOU JUST DON'T HAVE IT IN YOU.
JUST WHAT IS THIS ASSEMBLY ALL ABOUT?
IF IT'S WHAT I THINK IT IS...
...THEN THERE WOULDN'T BE ANY RED BEAN RICE.
OI, HITOT-SUME ...
YOU KNOW I'M JUST SAYING THIS FOR THE SAKE OF THE CLAN, RIGHT?
AS IT IS, WE'RE BEING PRESSURED ON THE WEST SIDE...
WE NEED TO TIGHTEN THINGS UP. WE DON'T WANT TO WEAKEN THE SYNDICATE!

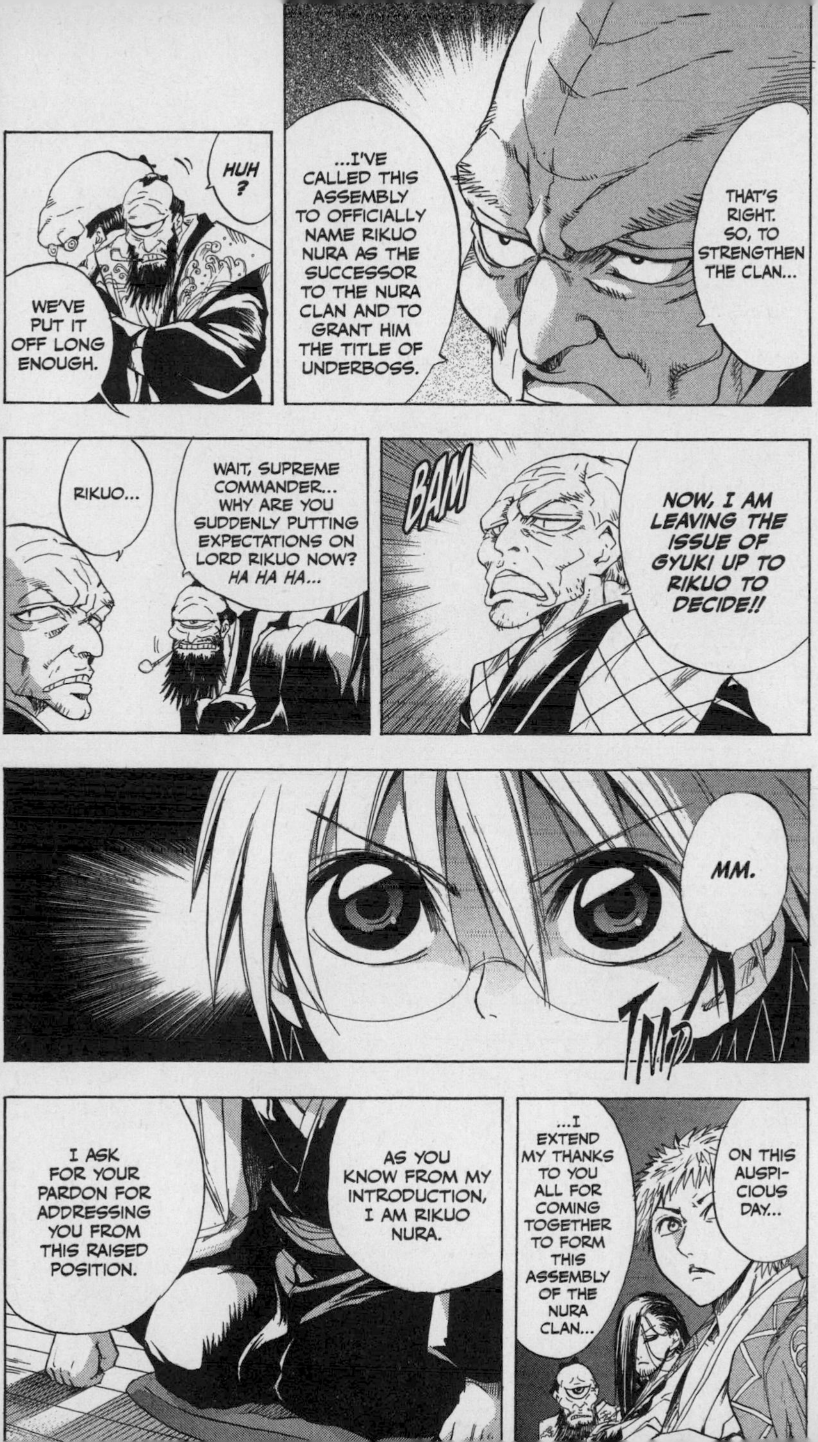
THAT'S RIGHT. SO, TO STRENGTHEN THE CLAN...
...I'VE CALLED THIS ASSEMBLY TO OFFICIALLY NAME RIKUO NURA AS THE SUCCESSOR TO THE NURA CLAN AND TO GRANT HIM THE TITLE OF UNDERBOSS.
HUH?
WE'VE PUT IT OFF LONG ENOUGH.
NOW, I AM LEAVING THE ISSUE OF GYUKI UP TO RIKUO TO DECIDE!!
BAM
WAIT, SUPREME COMMANDER... WHY ARE YOU SUDDENLY PUTTING EXPECTATIONS ON LORD RIKUO NOW? HA HA HA...
RIKUO...
MM.
TMP
ON THIS AUSPICIOUS DAY...
...I EXTEND MY THANKS TO YOU ALL FOR COMING TOGETHER TO FORM THIS ASSEMBLY OF THE NURA CLAN...
AS YOU KNOW FROM MY INTRODUCTION, I AM RIKUO NURA.
I ASK FOR YOUR PARDON FOR ADDRESSING YOU FROM THIS RAISED POSITION.

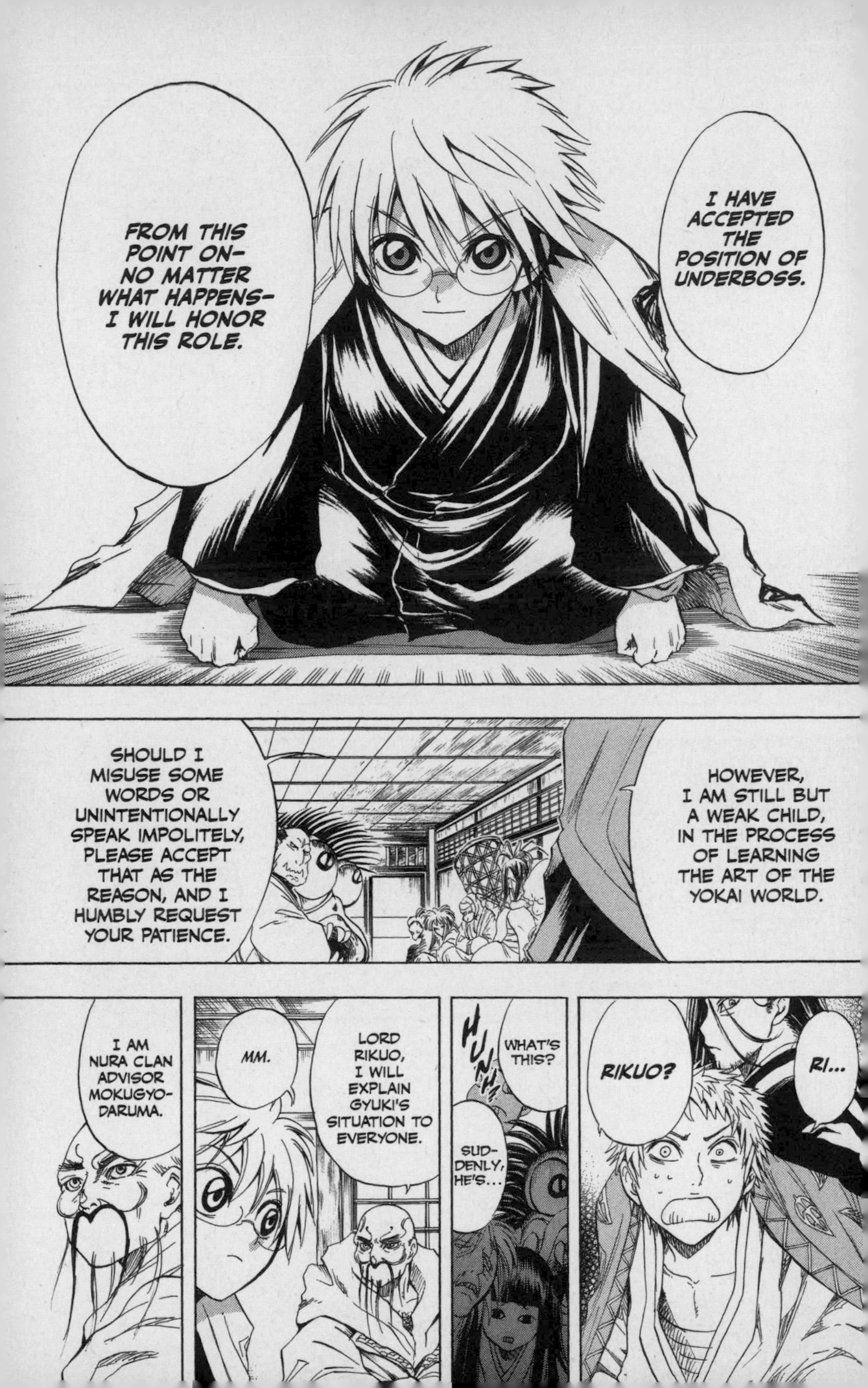

I HAVE ACCEPTED THE POSITION OF UNDERBOSS.
FROM THIS POINT ON— NO MATTER WHAT HAPPENS— I WILL HONOR THIS ROLE.
HOWEVER, I AM STILL BUT A WEAK CHILD, IN THE PROCESS OF LEARNING THE ART OF THE YOKAI WORLD.
SHOULD I MISUSE SOME WORDS OR UNINTENTIONALLY SPEAK IMPOLITELY, PLEASE ACCEPT THAT AS THE REASON, AND I HUMBLY REQUEST YOUR PATIENCE.
RI...
RIKUO?
HUNH!
WHAT'S THIS?
SUD-DENLY, HE'S...
LORD RIKUO, I WILL EXPLAIN GYUKI'S SITUATION TO EVERYONE.
MM.
I AM NURA CLAN ADVISOR MOKUGYO-DARUMA.

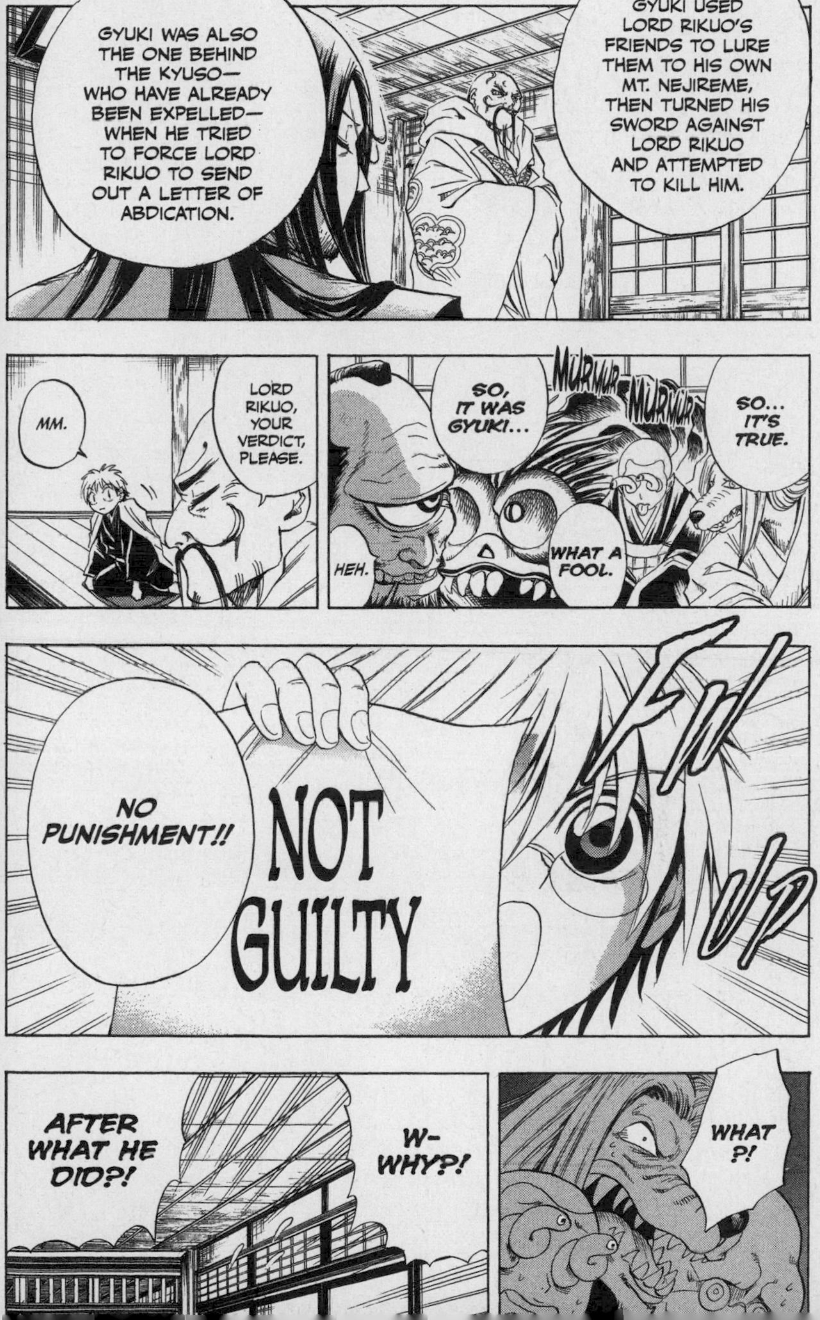
THE OTHER DAY, GYUKI USED LORD RIKUO'S FRIENDS TO LURE THEM TO HIS OWN MT. NEJIREME, THEN TURNED HIS SWORD AGAINST LORD RIKUO AND ATTEMPTED TO KILL HIM.
GYUKI WAS ALSO THE ONE BEHIND THE KYUSO—WHO HAVE ALREADY BEEN EXPELLED—WHEN HE TRIED TO FORCE LORD RIKUO TO SEND OUT A LETTER OF ABDICATION.
SO... IT'S TRUE.
MURMUR MURMUR
SO, IT WAS GYUKI...
WHAT A FOOL.
HEH.
LORD RIKUO, YOUR VERDICT, PLEASE.
MM.
NOT GUILTY
NO PUNISHMENT!!
WHAT ?!
W- WHY?!
AFTER WHAT HE DID?!

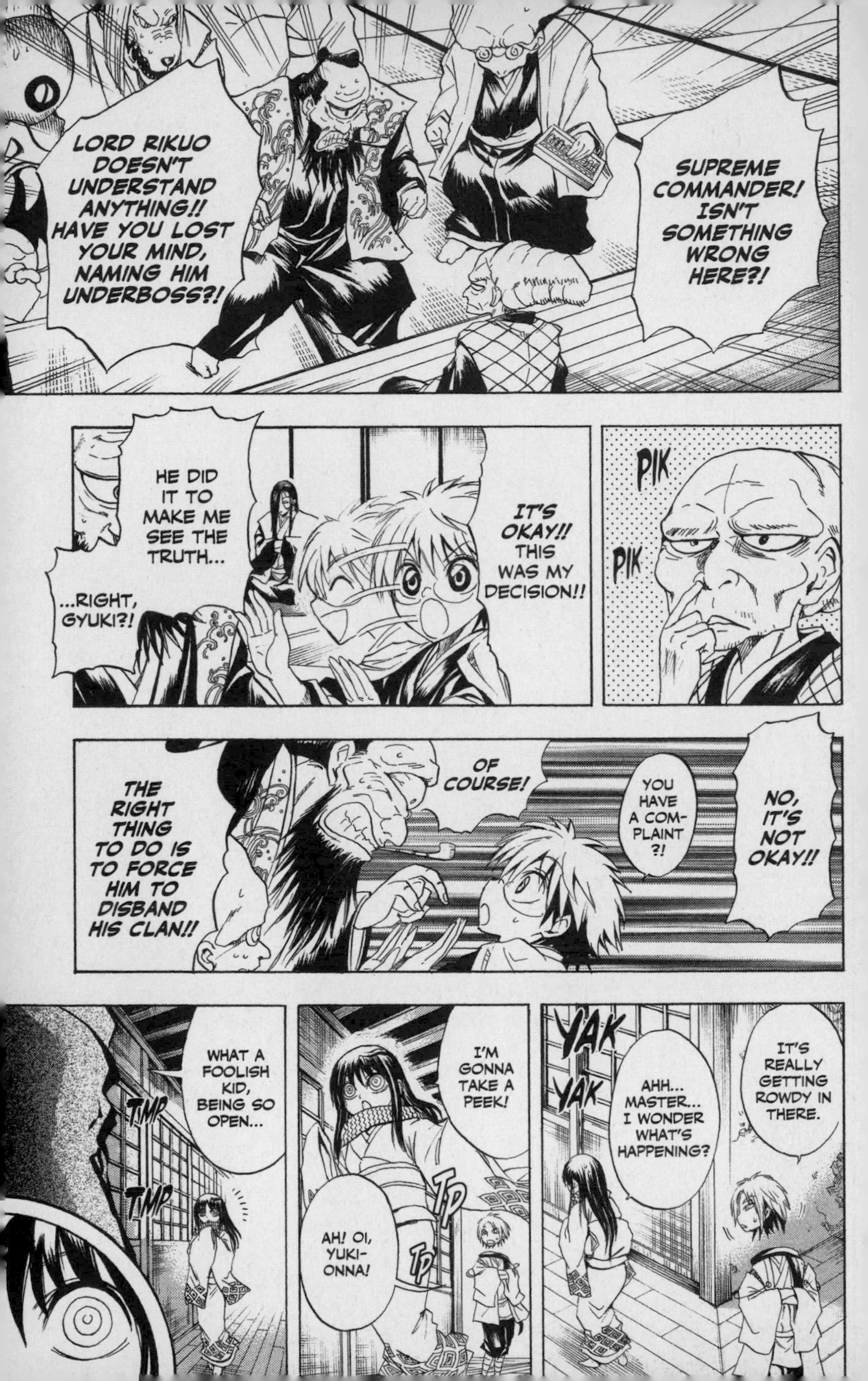
SUPREME COMMANDER! ISN'T SOMETHING WRONG HERE?!
LORD RIKUO DOESN'T UNDERSTAND ANYTHING!! HAVE YOU LOST YOUR MIND, NAMING HIM UNDERBOSS?!
PIK
PIK
IT'S OKAY!! THIS WAS MY DECISION!!
HE DID IT TO MAKE ME SEE THE TRUTH...
...RIGHT, GYUKI?!
NO, IT'S NOT OKAY!!
YOU HAVE A COM-PLAINT?!
OF COURSE!
THE RIGHT THING TO DO IS TO FORCE HIM TO DISBAND HIS CLAN!!
YAK
YAK
IT'S REALLY GETTING ROWDY IN THERE.
AHH... MASTER... I WONDER WHAT'S HAPPENING?
I'M GONNA TAKE A PEEK!
TP
TP
AH! OI, YUKI-ONNA!
WHAT A FOOLISH KID, BEING SO OPEN...
TMP
TMP

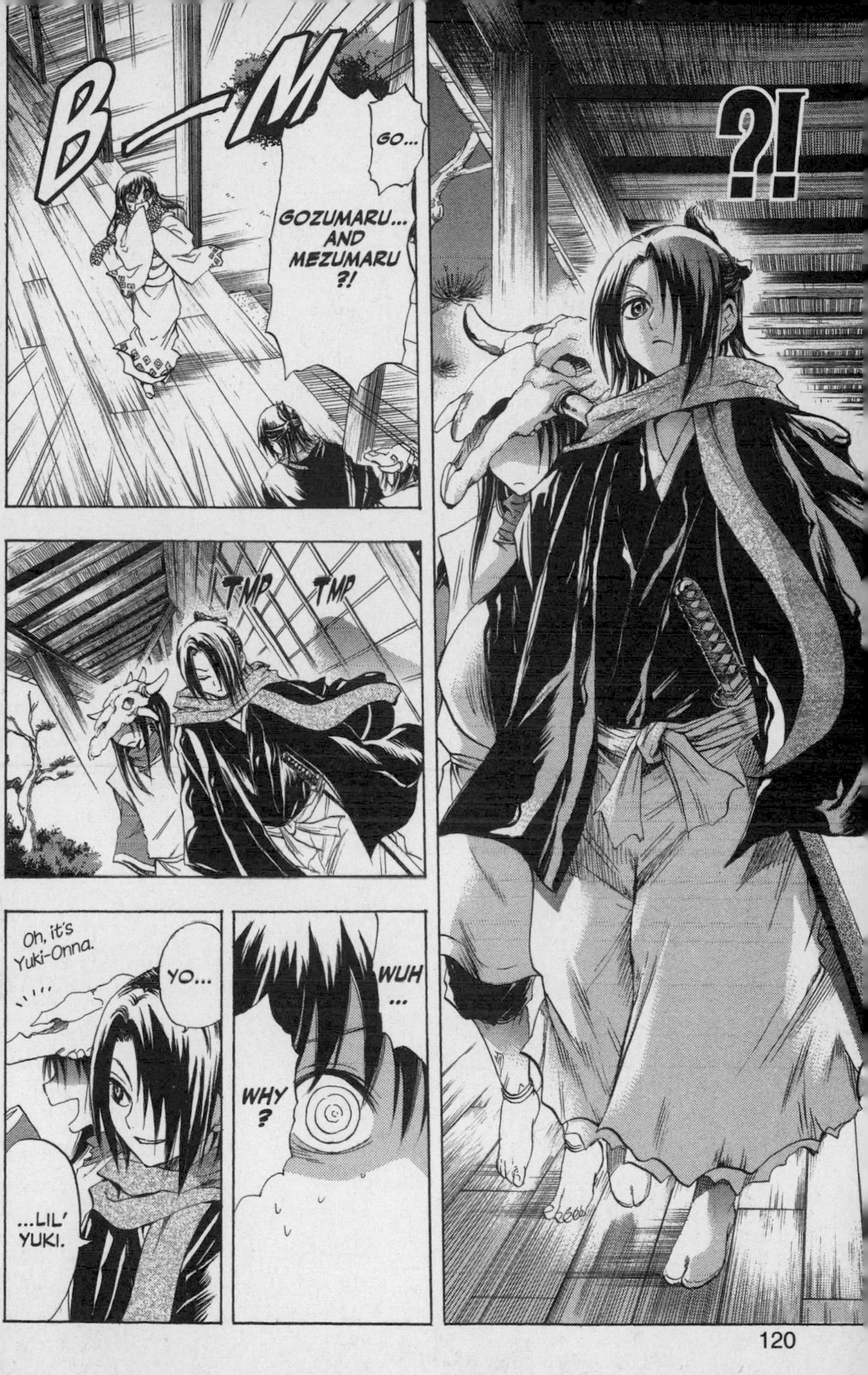
?!
B—M
GO...
GOZUMARU... AND MEZUMARU ?!
TMP TMP
WUH ...
WHY ?
Oh, it's Yuki-Onna.
YO...
...LIL' YUKI.

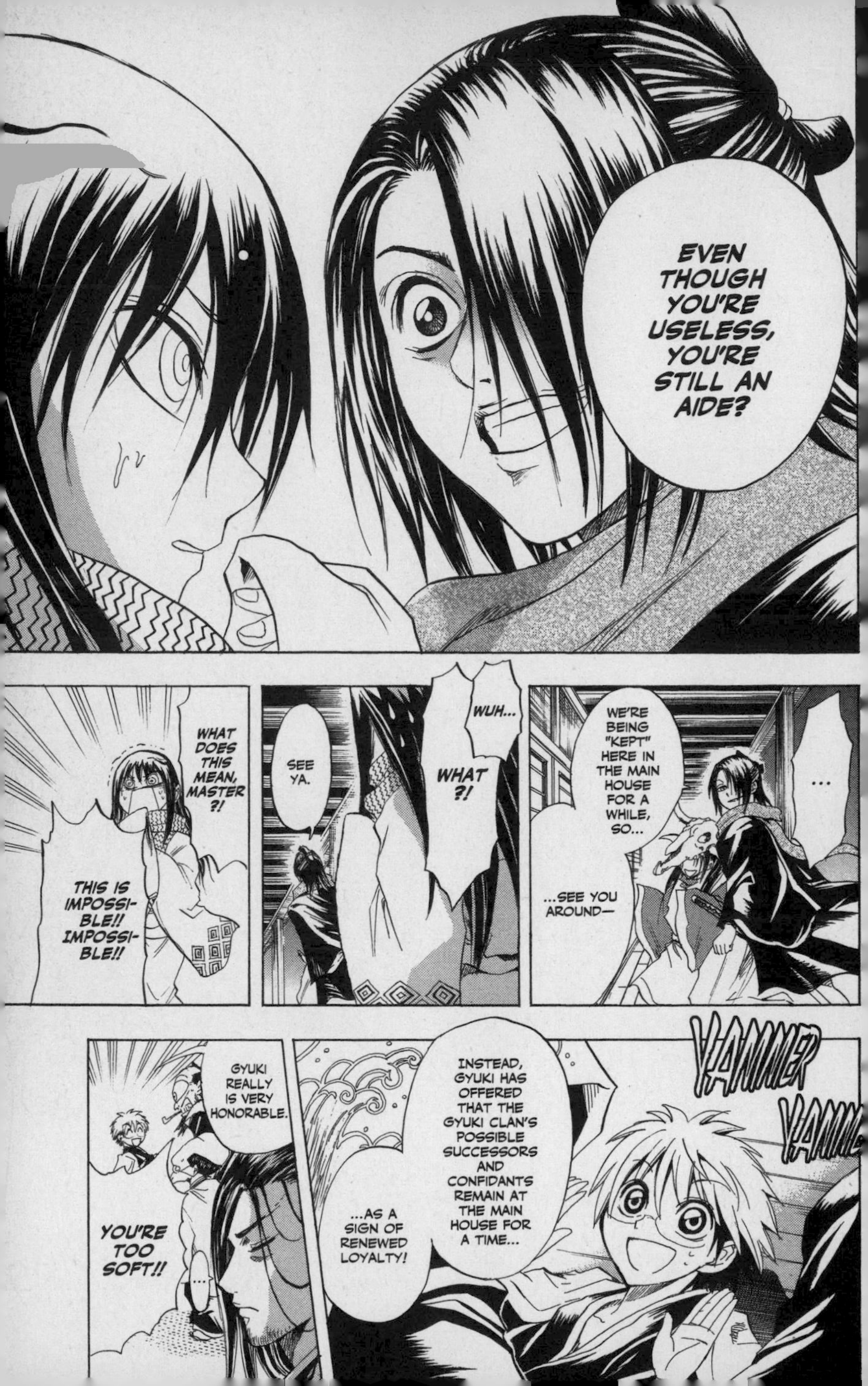
EVEN THOUGH YOU'RE USELESS, YOU'RE STILL AN AIDE?
...
WE'RE BEING "KEPT" HERE IN THE MAIN HOUSE FOR A WHILE, SO...
...SEE YOU AROUND—
WUH...
WHAT?!
SEE YA.
WHAT DOES THIS MEAN, MASTER?!
THIS IS IMPOSSIBLE!! IMPOSSIBLE!!
YAMMER
INSTEAD, GYUKI HAS OFFERED THAT THE GYUKI CLAN'S POSSIBLE SUCCESSORS AND CONFIDANTS REMAIN AT THE MAIN HOUSE FOR A TIME...
...AS A SIGN OF RENEWED LOYALTY!
GYUKI REALLY IS VERY HONORABLE.
YOU'RE TOO SOFT!!
...

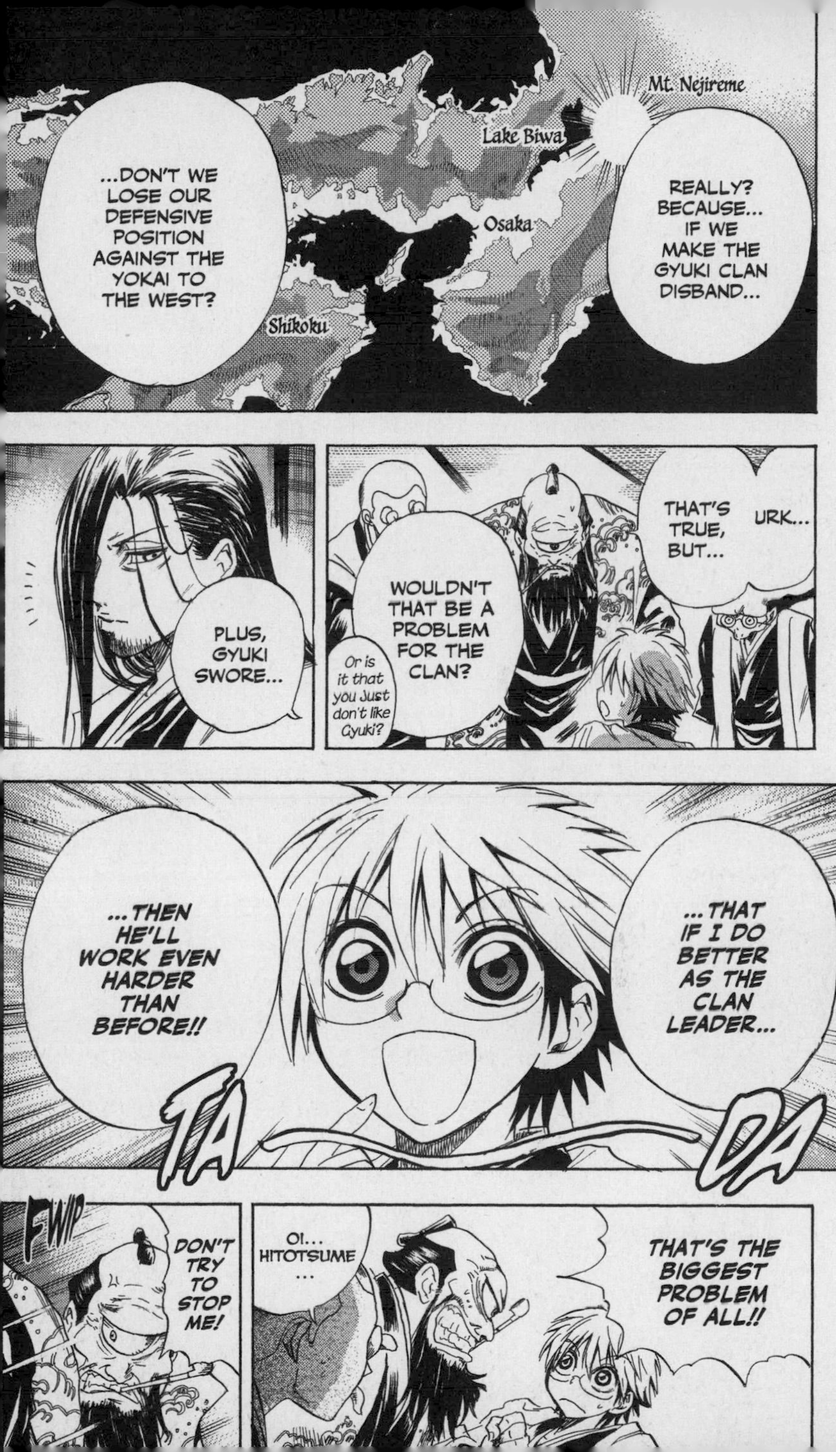
Mt. Nejireme
Lake Biwa
Osaka
Shikoku
REALLY? BECAUSE... IF WE MAKE THE GYUKI CLAN DISBAND...
...DON'T WE LOSE OUR DEFENSIVE POSITION AGAINST THE YOKAI TO THE WEST?
URK...
THAT'S TRUE, BUT...
WOULDN'T THAT BE A PROBLEM FOR THE CLAN?
Or is it that you just don't like Gyuki?
PLUS, GYUKI SWORE...
...THAT IF I DO BETTER AS THE CLAN LEADER...
...THEN HE'LL WORK EVEN HARDER THAN BEFORE!!
TA DA
THAT'S THE BIGGEST PROBLEM OF ALL!!
OI... HITOTSUME ...
FWIP
DON'T TRY TO STOP ME!

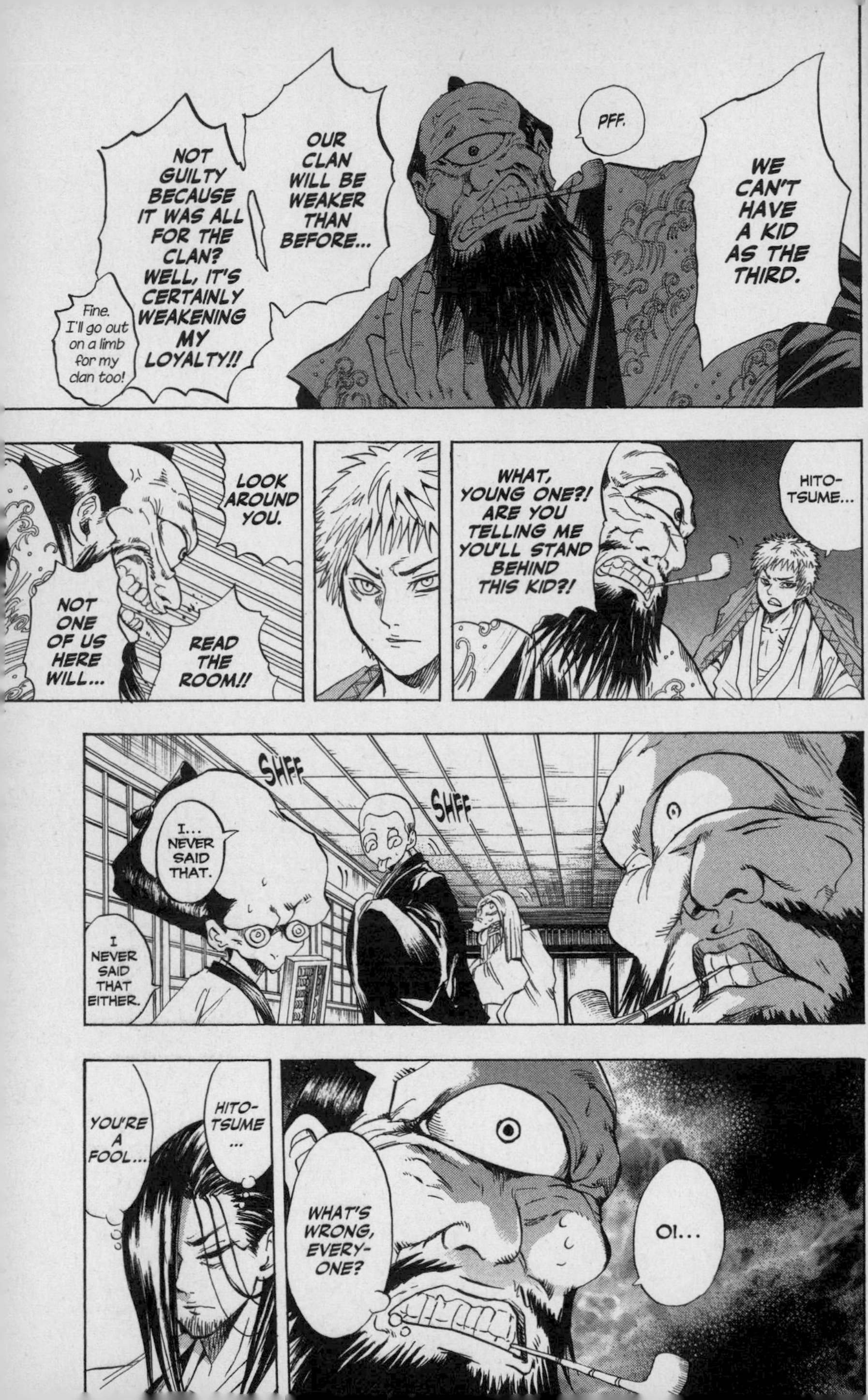
WE CAN'T HAVE A KID AS THE THIRD.
PFF.
OUR CLAN WILL BE WEAKER THAN BEFORE...
NOT GUILTY BECAUSE IT WAS ALL FOR THE CLAN? WELL, IT'S CERTAINLY WEAKENING MY LOYALTY!!
Fine. I'll go out on a limb for my clan too!
HITO-TSUME...
WHAT, YOUNG ONE?! ARE YOU TELLING ME YOU'LL STAND BEHIND THIS KID?!
LOOK AROUND YOU.
READ THE ROOM!!
NOT ONE OF US HERE WILL...
SHFF
SHFF
I... NEVER SAID THAT.
I NEVER SAID THAT EITHER.
OI...
WHAT'S WRONG, EVERY-ONE?
HITO-TSUME ...
YOU'RE A FOOL...

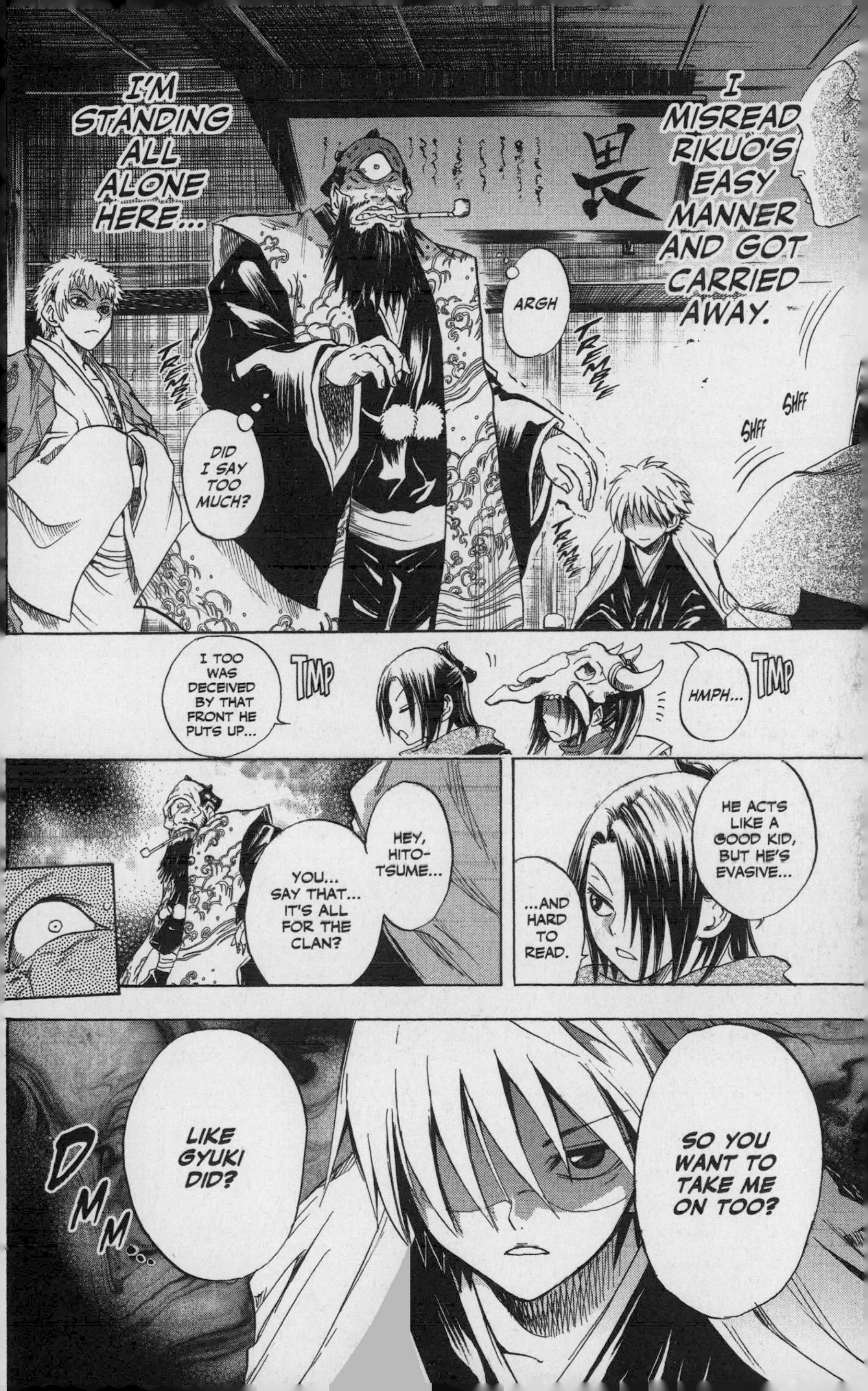
I MISREAD RIKUO'S EASY MANNER AND GOT CARRIED AWAY.
SHFF
SHFF
ARGH
I'M STANDING ALL ALONE HERE...
DID I SAY TOO MUCH?
TMP
HMPH...
I TOO WAS DECEIVED BY THAT FRONT HE PUTS UP...
TMP
HE ACTS LIKE A GOOD KID, BUT HE'S EVASIVE...
...AND HARD TO READ.
HEY, HITO-TSUME...
YOU... SAY THAT... IT'S ALL FOR THE CLAN?
SO YOU WANT TO TAKE ME ON TOO?
LIKE GYUKI DID?
DMM...

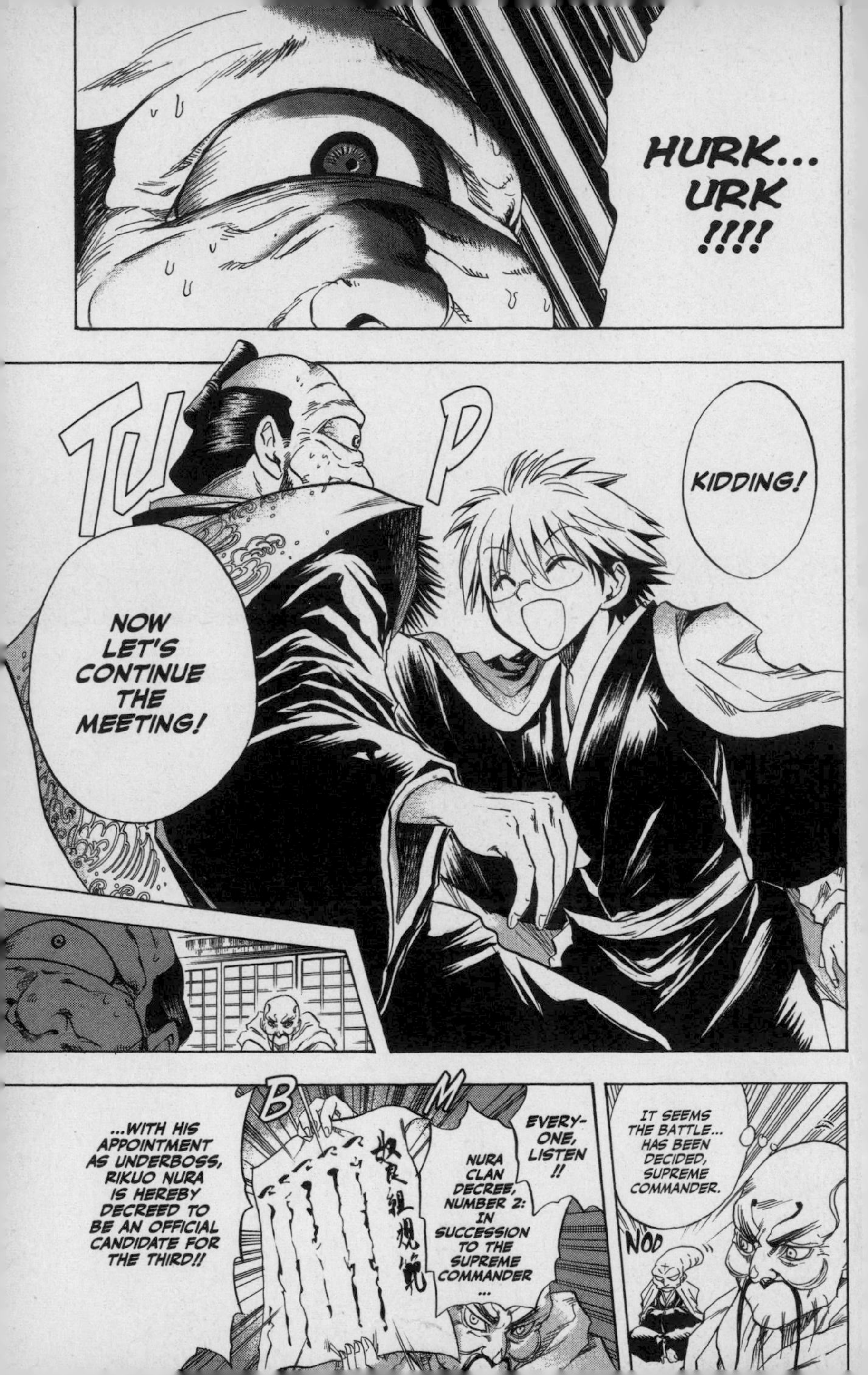
HURK... URK !!!!
KIDDING!
TUP
NOW LET'S CONTINUE THE MEETING!
IT SEEMS THE BATTLE... HAS BEEN DECIDED, SUPREME COMMANDER.
NOD
BM
EVERY-ONE, LISTEN !!
奴良組規範
NURA CLAN DECREE, NUMBER 2: IN SUCCESSION TO THE SUPREME COMMANDER ...
...WITH HIS APPOINTMENT AS UNDERBOSS, RIKUO NURA IS HEREBY DECREED TO BE AN OFFICIAL CANDIDATE FOR THE THIRD!!

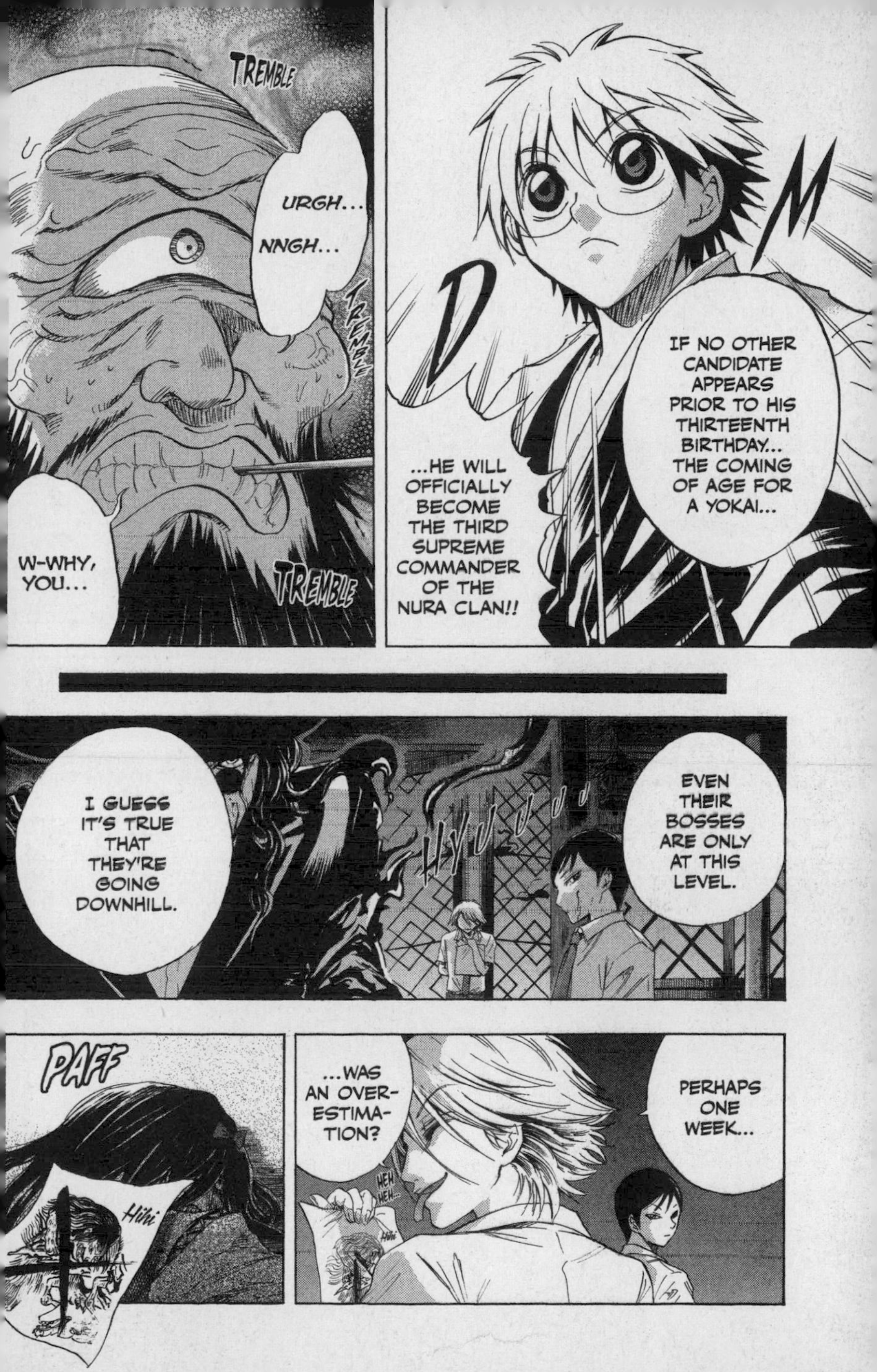
IF NO OTHER CANDIDATE APPEARS PRIOR TO HIS THIRTEENTH BIRTHDAY... THE COMING OF AGE FOR A YOKAI...
...HE WILL OFFICIALLY BECOME THE THIRD SUPREME COMMANDER OF THE NURA CLAN!!
TREMBLE
URGH... NNGH...
TREMBLE
W-WHY, YOU...
TREMBLE
EVEN THEIR BOSSES ARE ONLY AT THIS LEVEL.
HYUUUU
I GUESS IT'S TRUE THAT THEY'RE GOING DOWNHILL.
PERHAPS ONE WEEK...
...WAS AN OVER-ESTIMATION?
HEH HEH...
Hihi
PAFF
Hihi

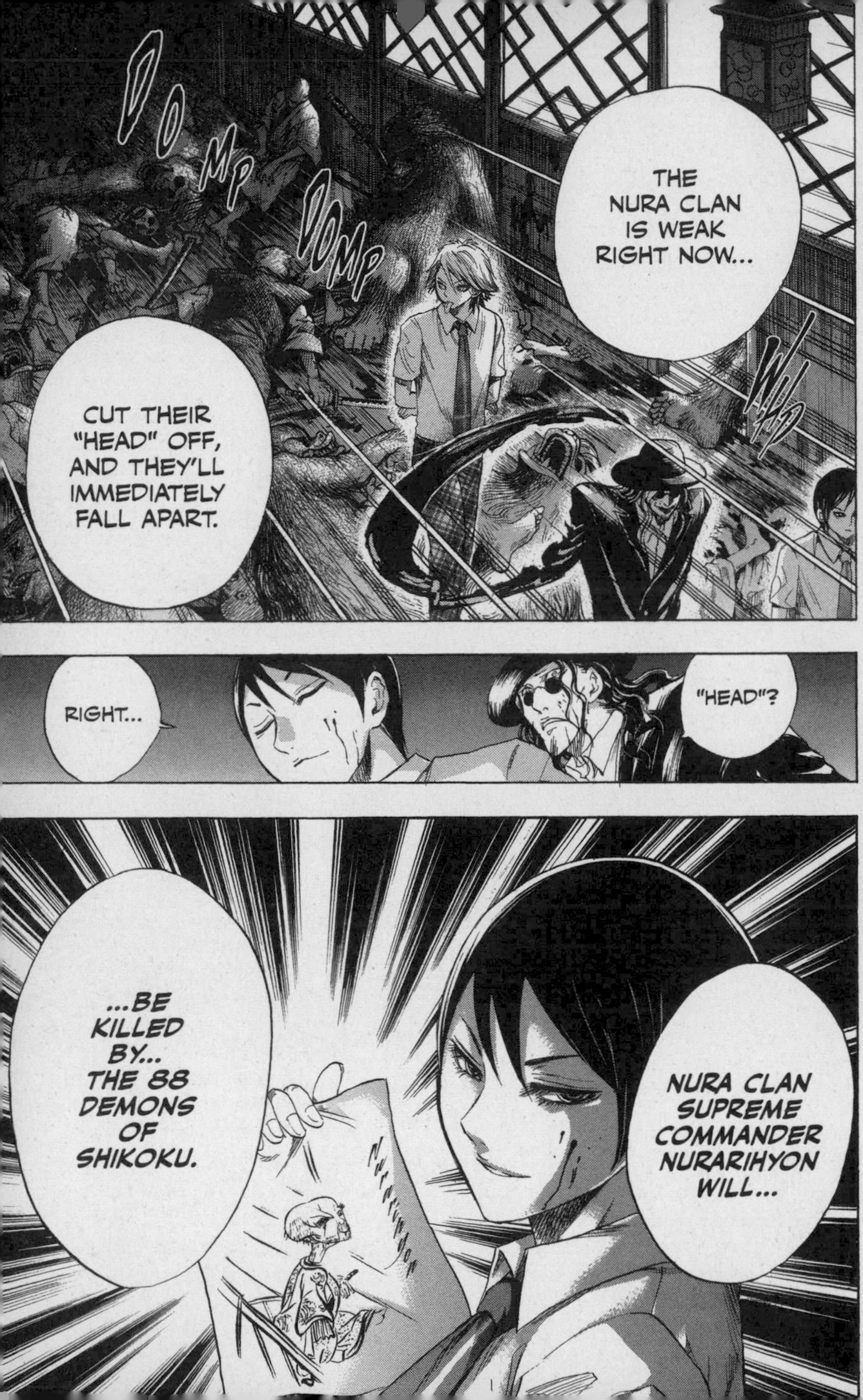
DOMP
DOMP
THE NURA CLAN IS WEAK RIGHT NOW...
CUT THEIR "HEAD" OFF, AND THEY'LL IMMEDIATELY FALL APART.
"HEAD"?
RIGHT...
NURA CLAN SUPREME COMMANDER NURARIHYON WILL...
...BE KILLED BY... THE 88 DEMONS OF SHIKOKU.

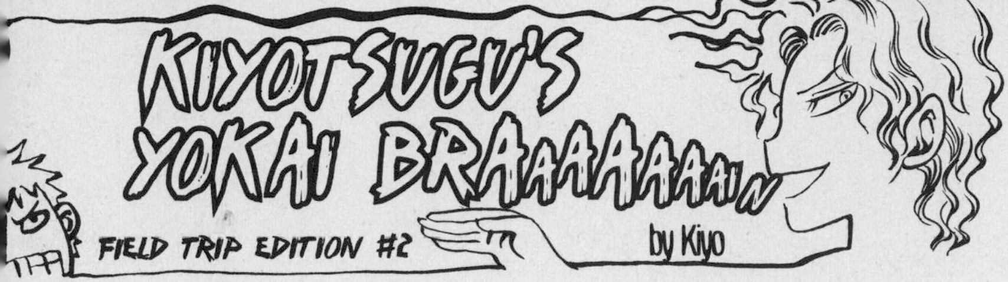
KIYOTSUGU'S YOKAI BRAAAAAAAIN
FIELD TRIP EDITION #2
by Kiyo

Kiyo: Hmm? What's this question about? I don't quite understand it. Oh, there's another user comment...

RE: The young masters like to climb trees too, at night. —*Karasu-Tengu, Tokyo*

Kiyo: It's that person again!! What's going on here?

Question 6: What kind of yokai are Kubinashi and Ryota-Neko? —*Yokai Kamaitachi, Ibaragi Prefecture.*

Kiyo: Kubinashi? I've never heard of such a yokai...

RE: Kubinashi is a member of the "Nukekubi" family of yokai. Nukekubi are also known as "Rokurokubi." Ryota-Neko is a Nekomata. There are many cat yokai, so I guess you would need to be specific... —*Karasu-Tengu, Tokyo.*

Kiyo: What's with this guy?! He lives on my site!! Oh, Nura—!! Look at this!! Who do you think this is? This Karasu-Tengu!?

Rikuo: Ah... *Karasu-Tengu must be surfing the net with his recently acquired cell phone skills...*

S-some maniac?

Kiyo: Hmm. Seems that there is more to the yokai world that I am not aware of. All right, I will continue my research until the next volume!! Keep those questions coming!!
Deep!! Very Deep!!

Kiyo: Hey!! How did you like the profile of Ienaga on page 108? We'll do other members next time around!! I wonder where they all went, anyway? Okay, let's continue!!

Question 4: Why is it that only Yura's uniform has a ribbon on it? —*Red Butterfly, Iwate Prefecture.*

Kiyo: Hmm?! That has nothing to do with yokai! I can't answer this question without Keikain, but let's think about it from the other side. Why don't the other girls wear ribbons too? Ienaga, please tell us!!

Kana: Eh? Because...it's a bother?

Kiyo: Which means, the uniform actually does come with a ribbon?

Kana: Yeah.

Kiyo: You know what you all are? You're *lazy.* Look at Nura...he wears his jersey underneath his uniform. A disturbance of a uniform is a disturbance of the heart!! Remember!! I make sure even my collar is properly buttoned!! A person who's really serious about yokai is also serious about their uniform... But, of course, it's almost time for summer uniforms, so it won't really matter. For some reason, Keikain wears her P.E. outfit *all the time* lately.

Question 5: Do Gozumaru and Mezumaru like to be up in trees? —*Chachamaru, Shizuoka Prefecture*

Act 22: Yokai of the Wind

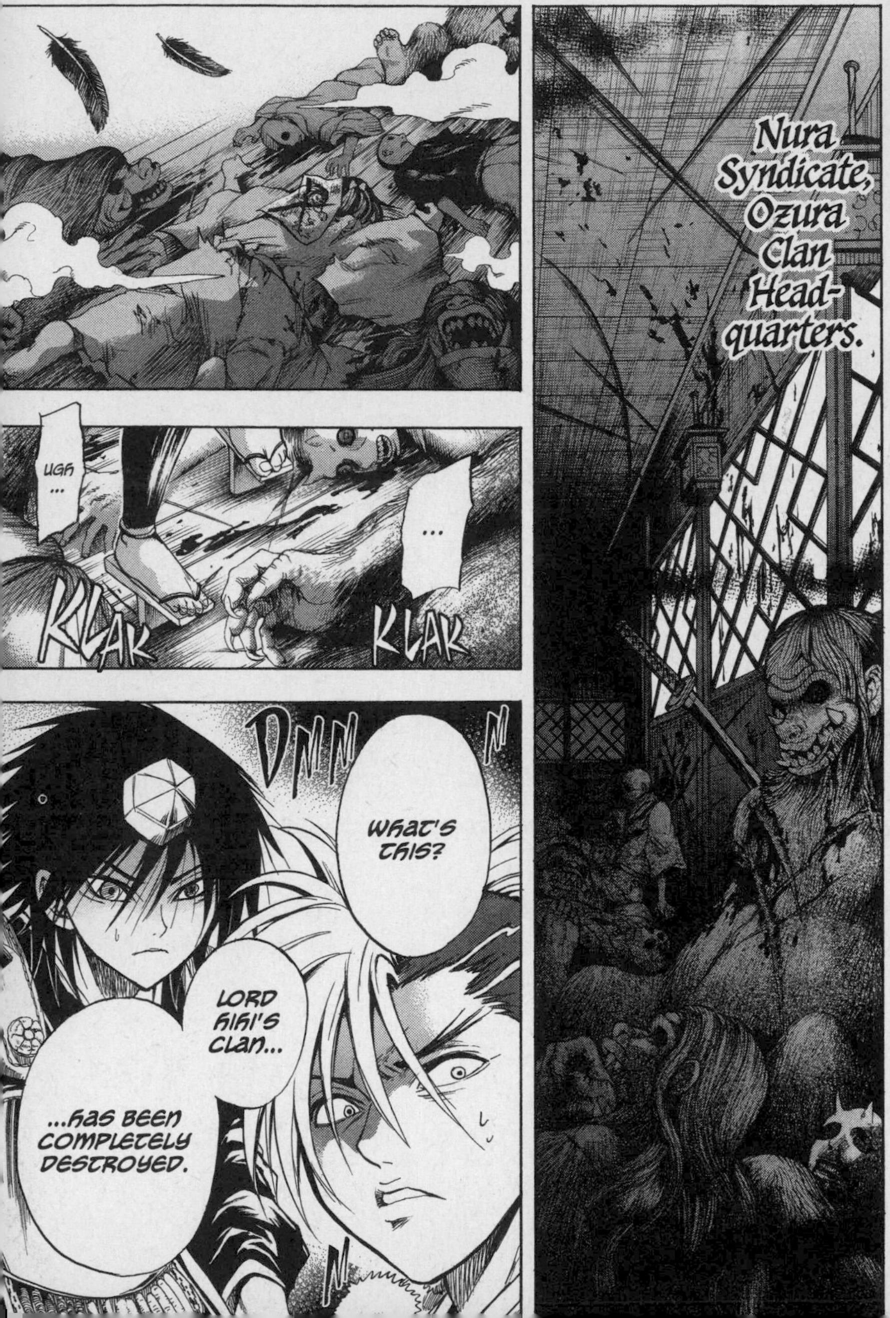
Nura Syndicate, Ozura Clan Head-quarters.
...
UGH ...
KLAK
KLAK
DNNN
WHAT'S THIS?
LORD HIHI'S CLAN...
...HAS BEEN COMPLETELY DESTROYED.

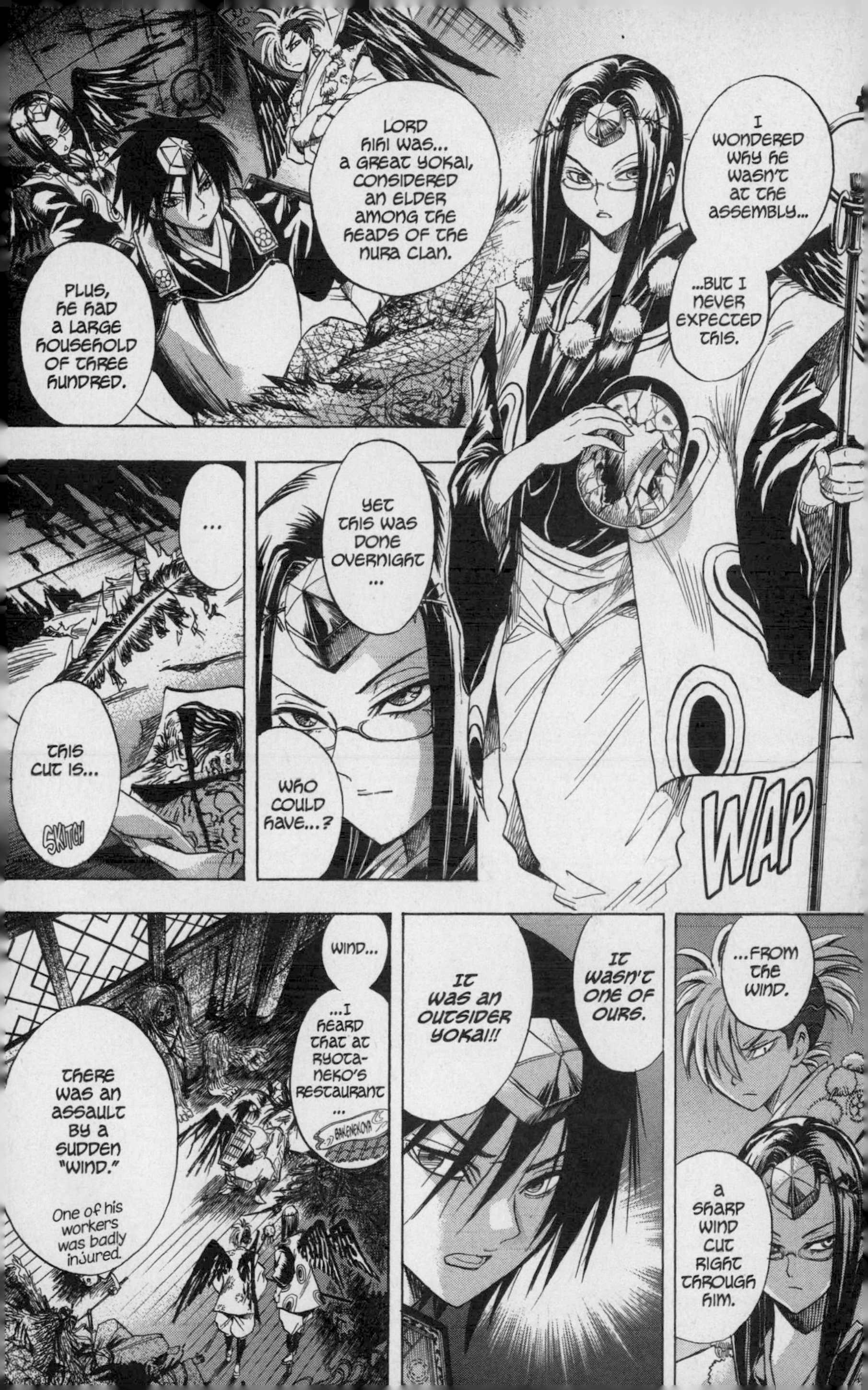
I WONDERED WHY HE WASN'T AT THE ASSEMBLY...
...BUT I NEVER EXPECTED THIS.
WAP
LORD HIHI WAS... A GREAT YOKAI, CONSIDERED AN ELDER AMONG THE HEADS OF THE NURA CLAN.
PLUS, HE HAD A LARGE HOUSEHOLD OF THREE HUNDRED.
YET THIS WAS DONE OVERNIGHT...
WHO COULD HAVE...?
...
THIS CUT IS...
SKITCH
...FROM THE WIND.
A SHARP WIND CUT RIGHT THROUGH HIM.
IT WASN'T ONE OF OURS.
IT WAS AN OUTSIDER YOKAI!!
WIND...
...I HEARD THAT AT RYOTA-NEKO'S RESTAURANT...
BAKENEKOYA
THERE WAS AN ASSAULT BY A SUDDEN "WIND."
One of his workers was badly injured.

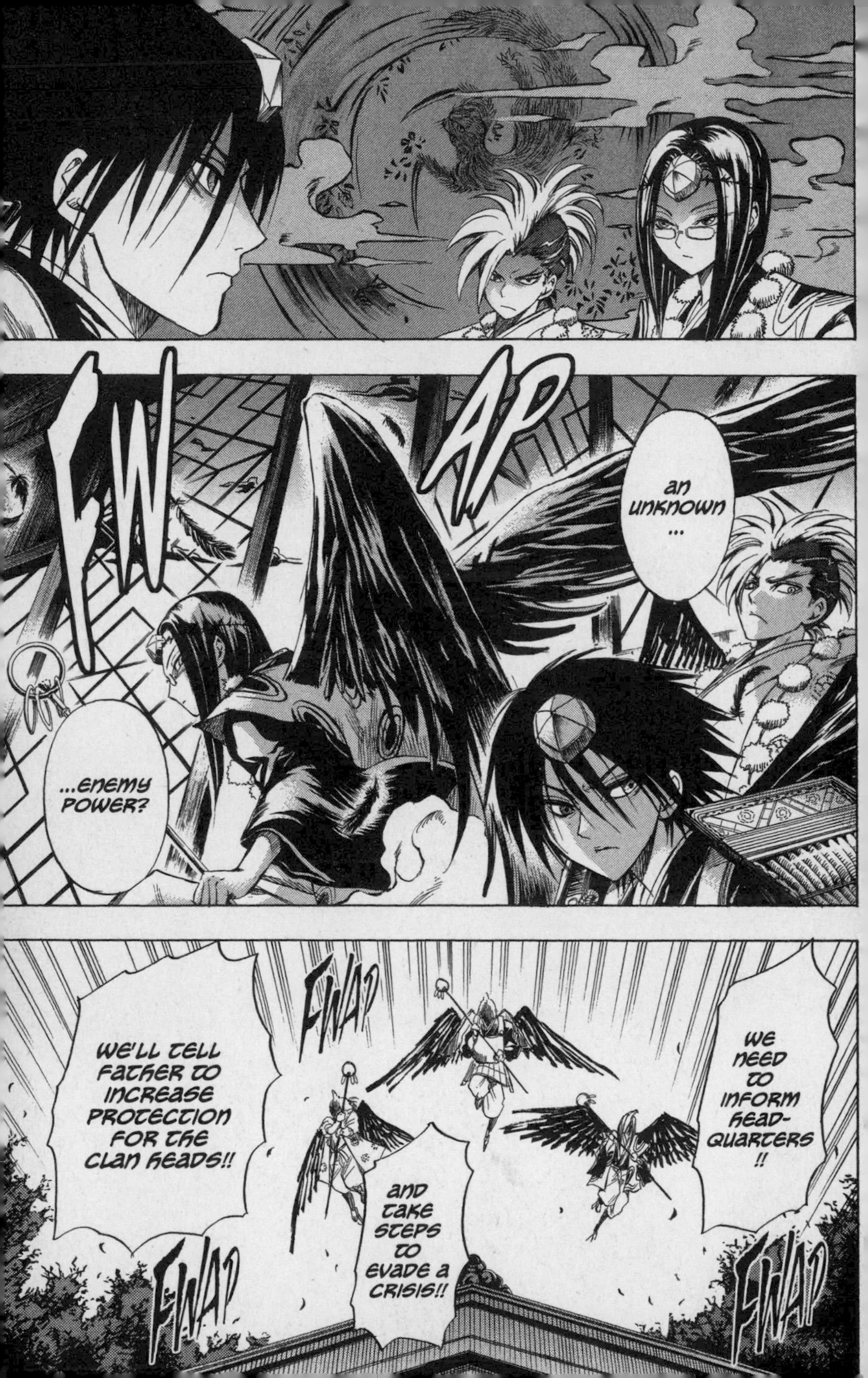
FW
AP
an unknown...
...enemy power?
FWAP
We need to inform head-quarters!!
We'll tell father to increase protection for the clan heads!!
and take steps to evade a crisis!!
FWAP
FWAP

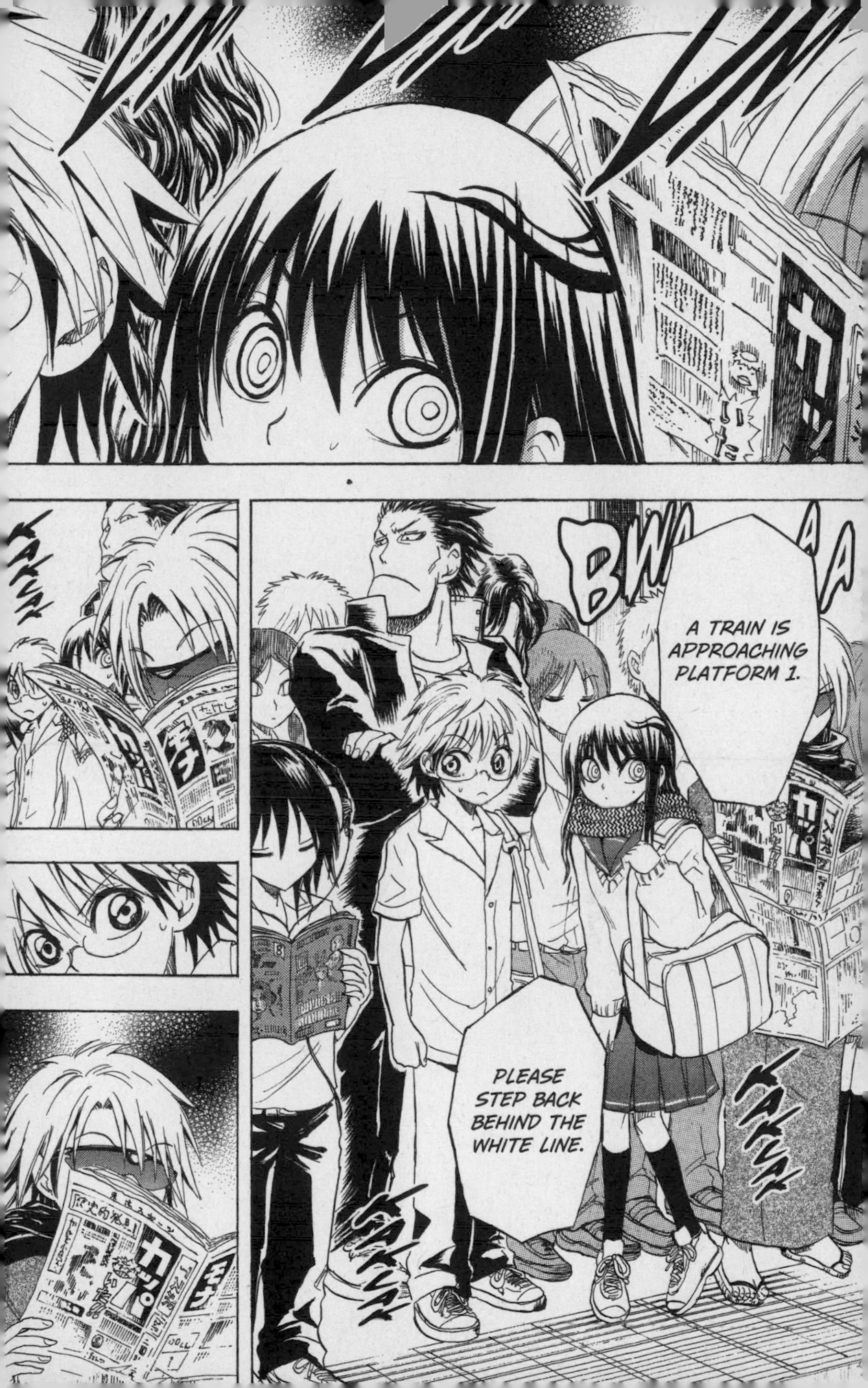
A TRAIN IS APPROACHING PLATFORM 1.
PLEASE STEP BACK BEHIND THE WHITE LINE.

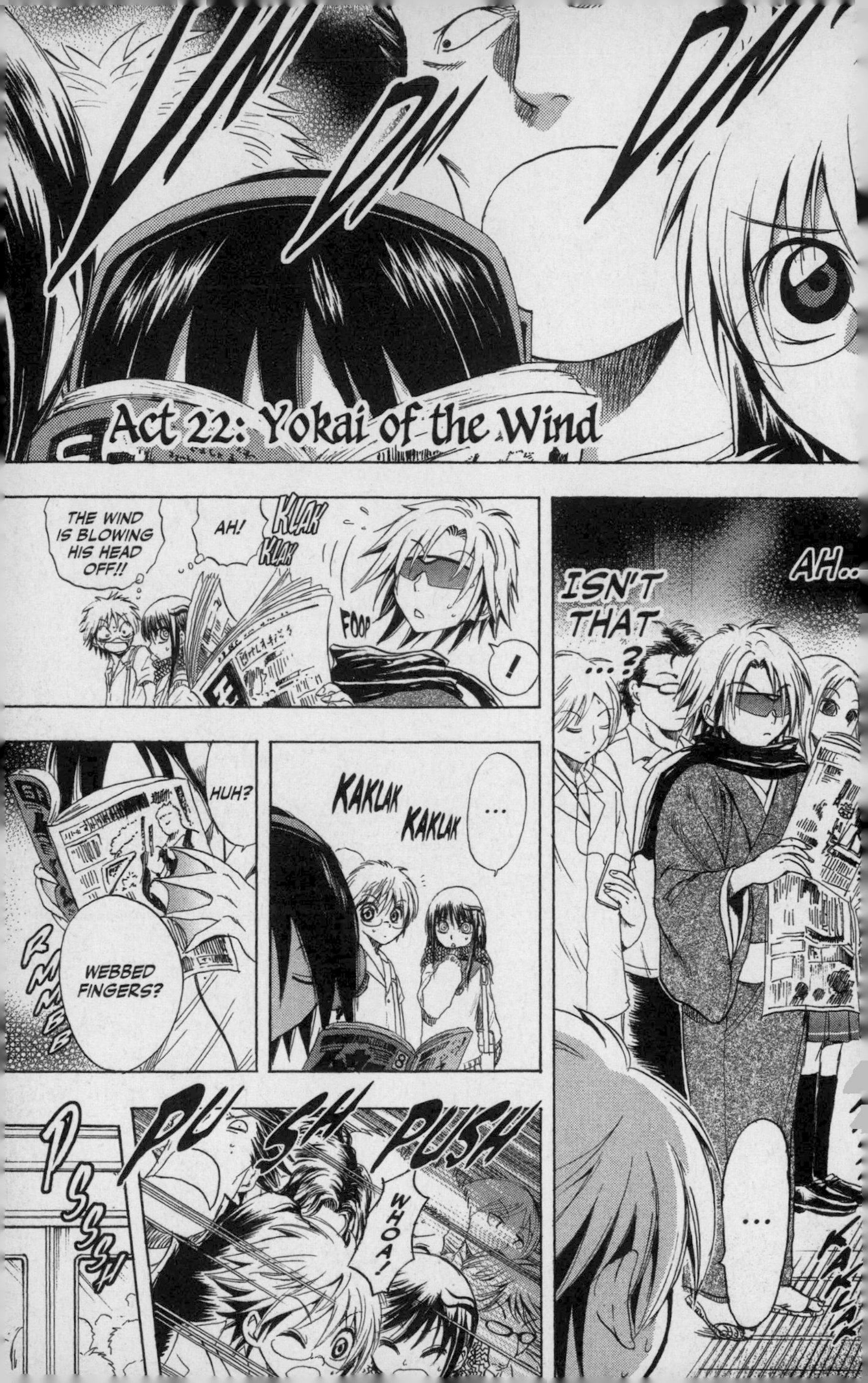
Act 22: Yokai of the Wind
AH...
ISN'T THAT ...?
...
KAKLAK
!
FOOP
KLAK
KLAK
AH!
THE WIND IS BLOWING HIS HEAD OFF!!
...
KAKLAK
KAKLAK
HUH?
WEBBED FINGERS?
PUSH
PUSH
WHOA!
PSSSH

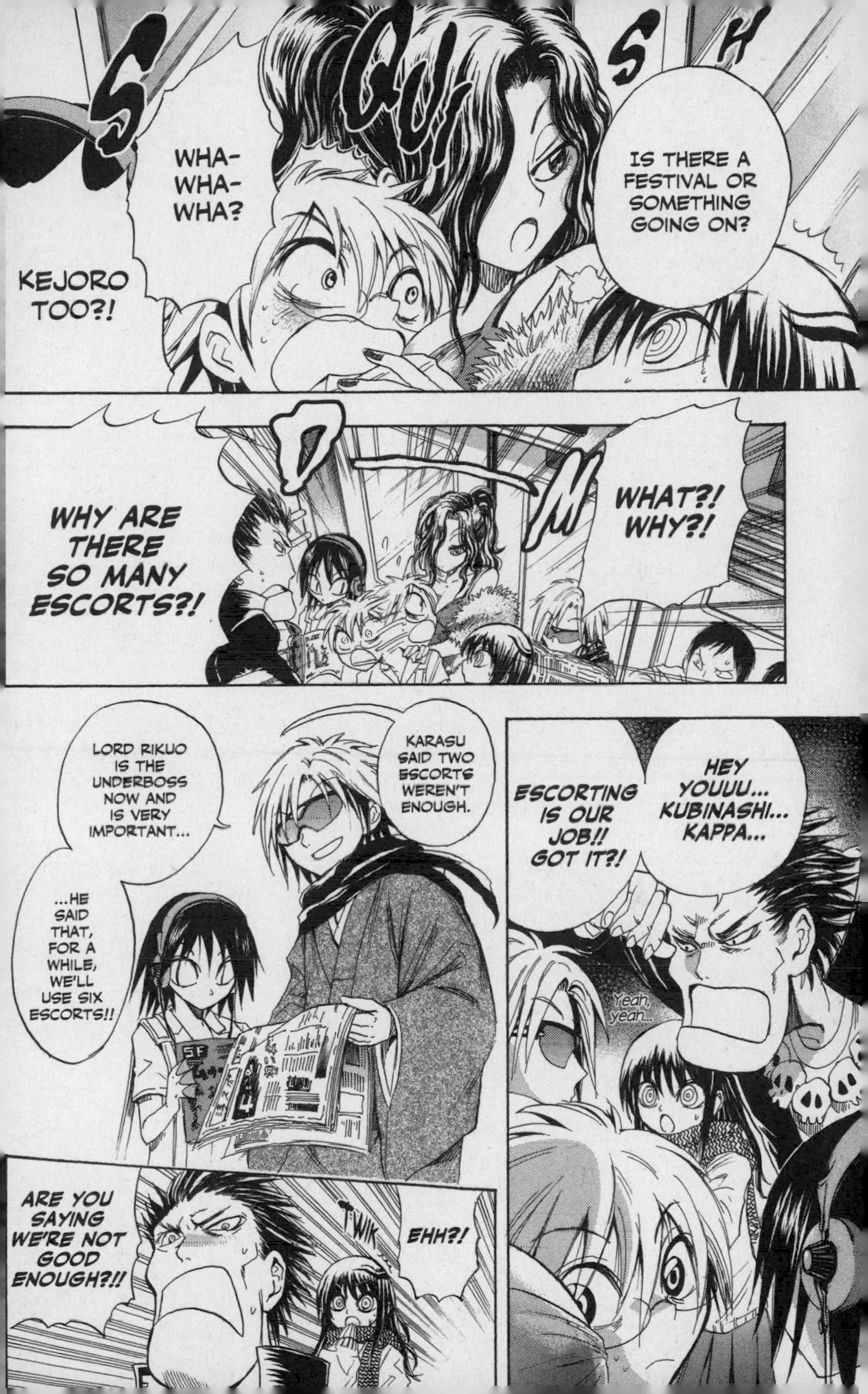
SGUSH
IS THERE A FESTIVAL OR SOMETHING GOING ON?
WHA-WHA-WHA?
KEJORO TOO?!
DM
WHAT?! WHY?!
WHY ARE THERE SO MANY ESCORTS?!
HEY YOUUU... KUBINASHI... KAPPA...
ESCORTING IS OUR JOB!! GOT IT?!
Yeah, yeah...
KARASU SAID TWO ESCORTS WEREN'T ENOUGH.
LORD RIKUO IS THE UNDERBOSS NOW AND IS VERY IMPORTANT...
...HE SAID THAT, FOR A WHILE, WE'LL USE SIX ESCORTS!!
EHH?!
TWIK
ARE YOU SAYING WE'RE NOT GOOD ENOUGH?!!

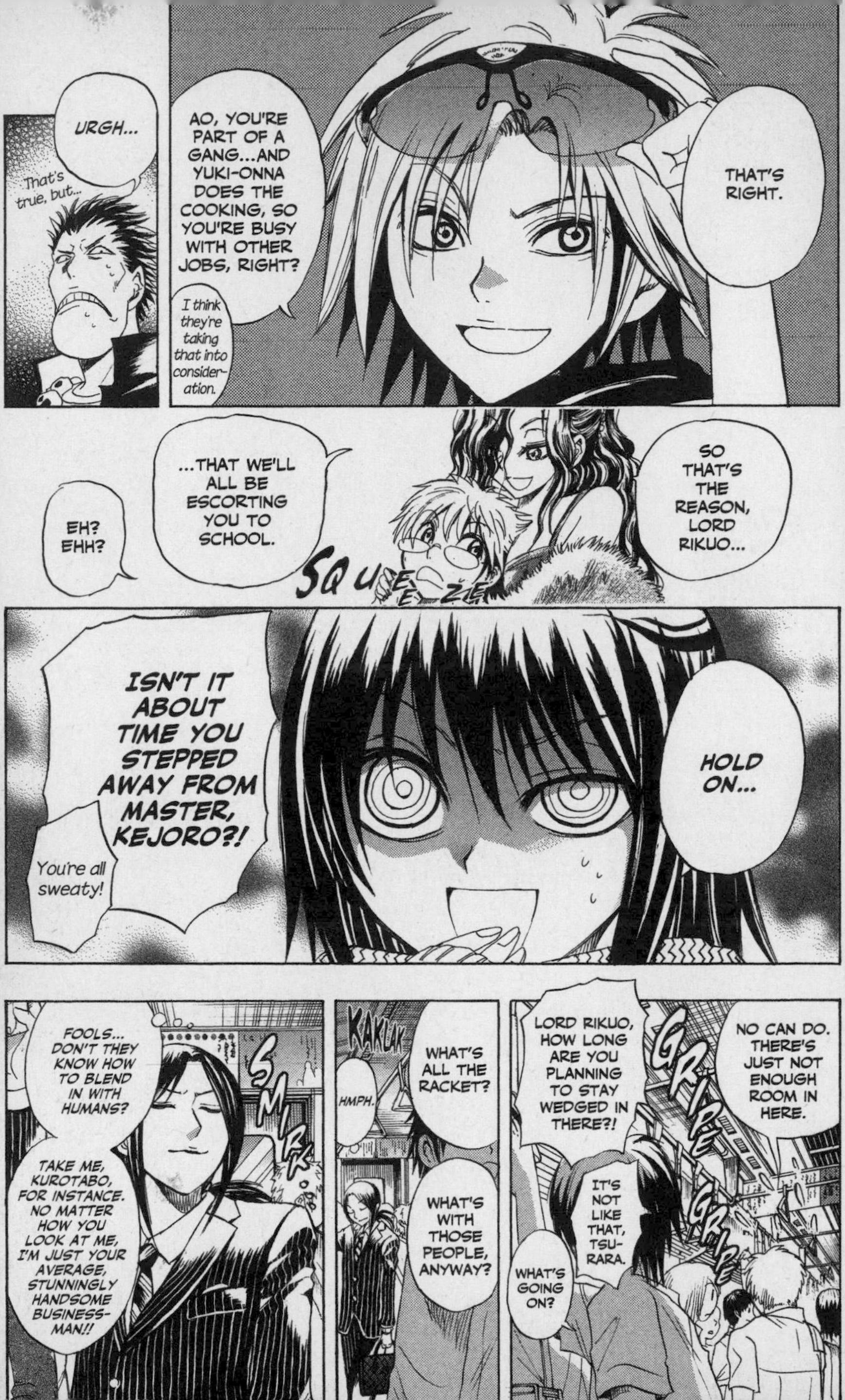
THAT'S RIGHT.
AO, YOU'RE PART OF A GANG...AND YUKI-ONNA DOES THE COOKING, SO YOU'RE BUSY WITH OTHER JOBS, RIGHT?
I think they're taking that into consider-ation.
URGH...
That's true, but...
SO THAT'S THE REASON, LORD RIKUO...
...THAT WE'LL ALL BE ESCORTING YOU TO SCHOOL.
SQUEEZE
EH? EHH?
HOLD ON...
ISN'T IT ABOUT TIME YOU STEPPED AWAY FROM MASTER, KEJORO?!
You're all sweaty!
NO CAN DO. THERE'S JUST NOT ENOUGH ROOM IN HERE.
GRIPE GRIPE
LORD RIKUO, HOW LONG ARE YOU PLANNING TO STAY WEDGED IN THERE?!
IT'S NOT LIKE THAT, TSURARA.
WHAT'S GOING ON?
KAKLAK
WHAT'S ALL THE RACKET?
HMPH.
WHAT'S WITH THOSE PEOPLE, ANYWAY?
FOOLS... DON'T THEY KNOW HOW TO BLEND IN WITH HUMANS?
SMIRK
TAKE ME, KUROTABO, FOR INSTANCE. NO MATTER HOW YOU LOOK AT ME, I'M JUST YOUR AVERAGE, STUNNINGLY HANDSOME BUSINESS-MAN!!

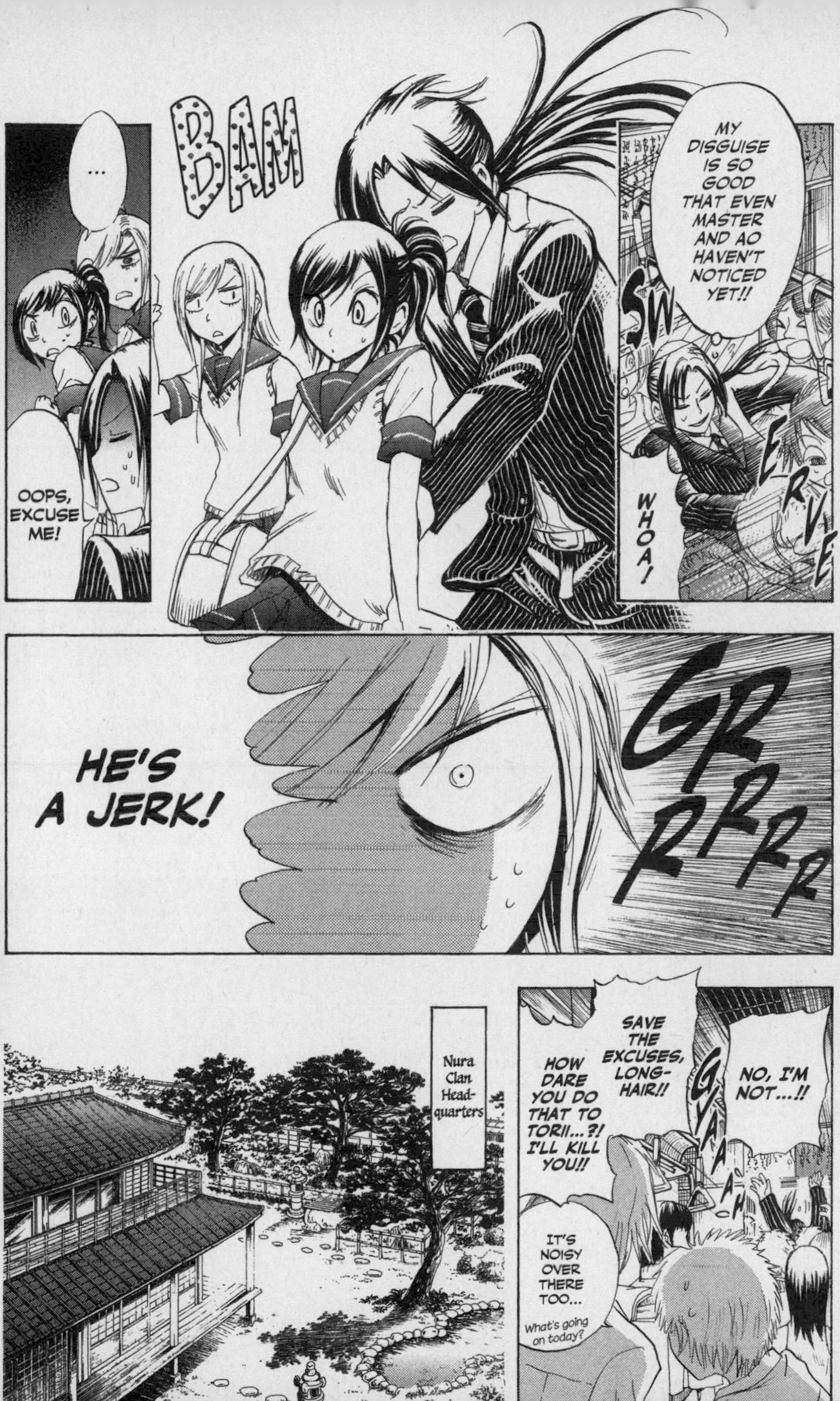
MY DISGUISE IS SO GOOD THAT EVEN MASTER AND AO HAVEN'T NOTICED YET!!
SWERVE
WHOA!
BAM
...
OOPS, EXCUSE ME!
GRRRRRR
HE'S A JERK!
NO, I'M NOT...!!
GYAAAH
SAVE THE EXCUSES, LONG-HAIR!!
HOW DARE YOU DO THAT TO TORII...?! I'LL KILL YOU!!
IT'S NOISY OVER THERE TOO...
What's going on today?
Nura Clan Head-quarters

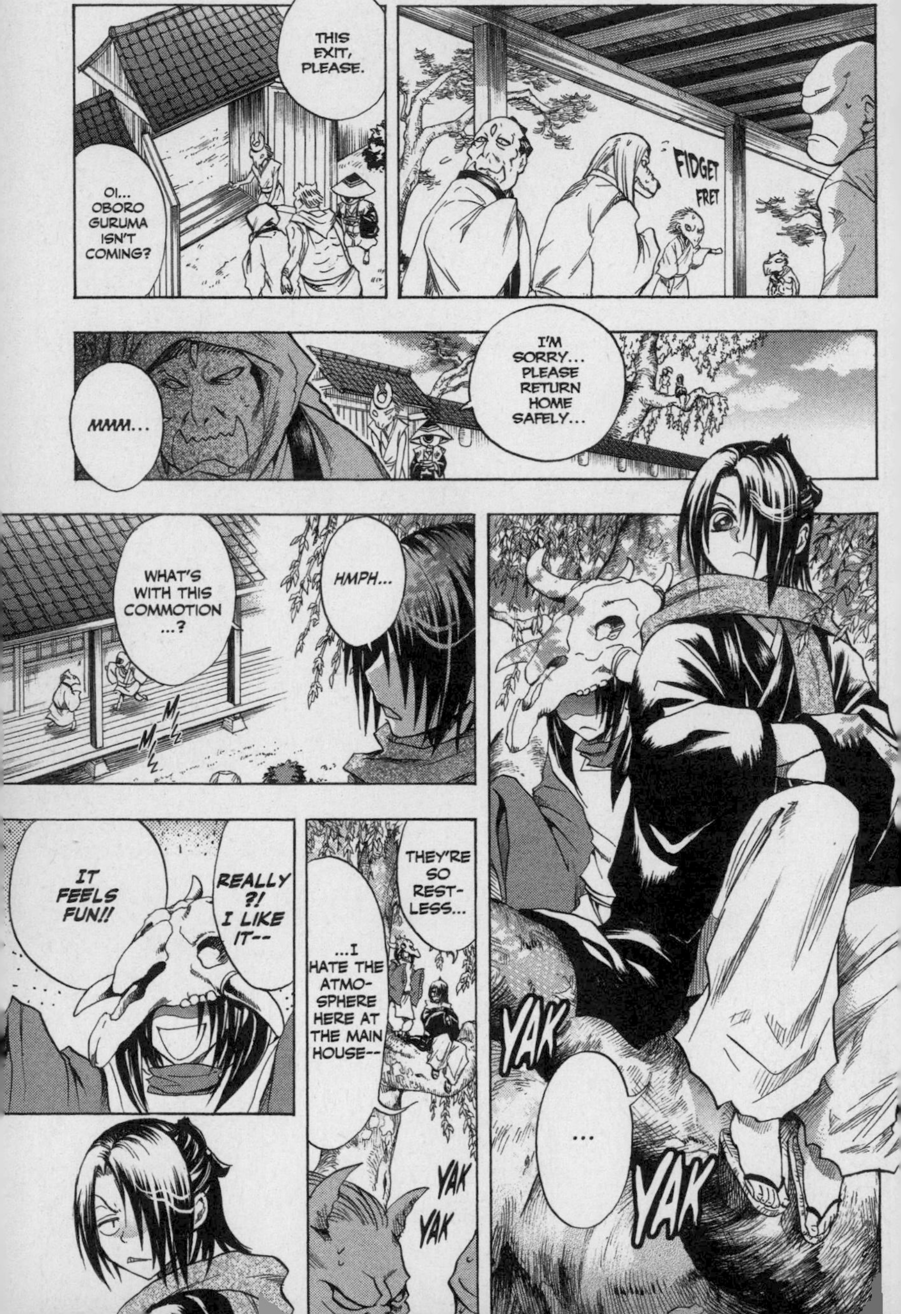
FIDGET
FRET
THIS EXIT, PLEASE.
OI... OBORO GURUMA ISN'T COMING?
I'M SORRY... PLEASE RETURN HOME SAFELY...
MMM...
YAK
...
YAK
HMPH...
WHAT'S WITH THIS COMMOTION ...?
M M M
THEY'RE SO REST-LESS...
...I HATE THE ATMOSPHERE HERE AT THE MAIN HOUSE--
YAK
YAK
REALLY ?! I LIKE IT--
IT FEELS FUN!!

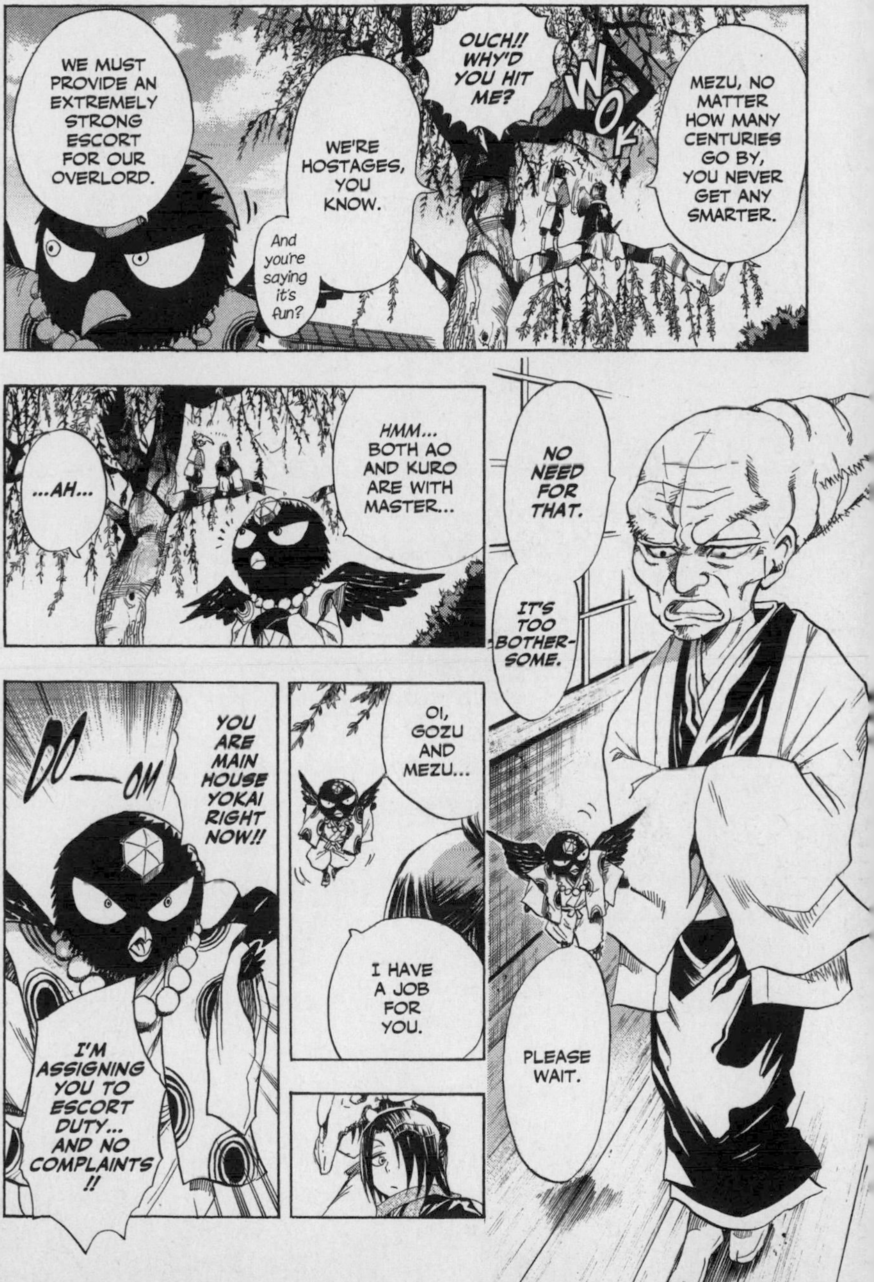
MEZU, NO MATTER HOW MANY CENTURIES GO BY, YOU NEVER GET ANY SMARTER.
WOK
OUCH!! WHY'D YOU HIT ME?
WE'RE HOSTAGES, YOU KNOW.
And you're saying it's fun?
WE MUST PROVIDE AN EXTREMELY STRONG ESCORT FOR OUR OVERLORD.
NO NEED FOR THAT.
IT'S TOO BOTHER-SOME.
PLEASE WAIT.
HMM... BOTH AO AND KURO ARE WITH MASTER...
...AH...
OI, GOZU AND MEZU...
I HAVE A JOB FOR YOU.
DO—OM
YOU ARE MAIN HOUSE YOKAI RIGHT NOW!!
I'M ASSIGNING YOU TO ESCORT DUTY... AND NO COMPLAINTS!!

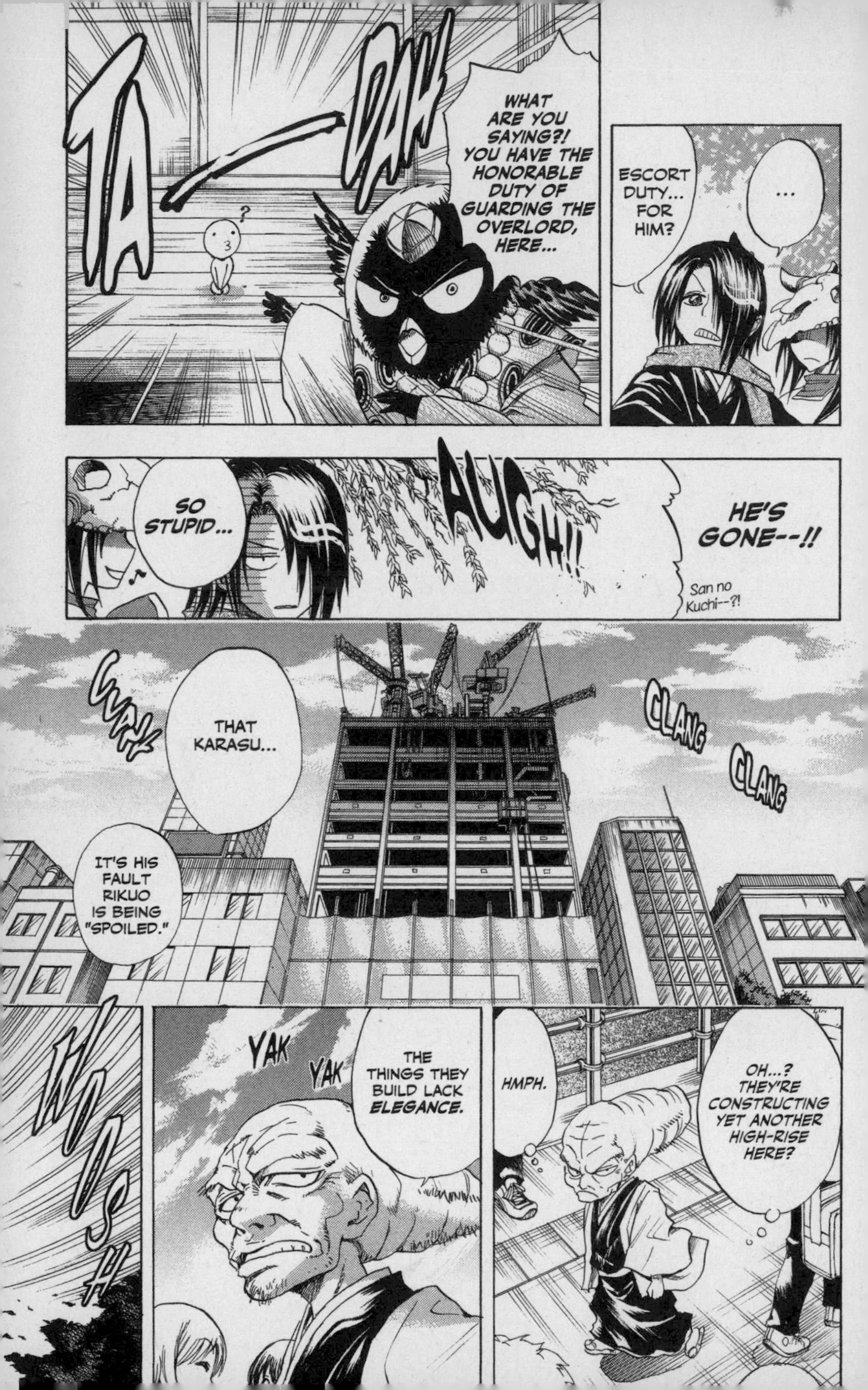
...
ESCORT DUTY... FOR HIM?
WHAT ARE YOU SAYING?! YOU HAVE THE HONORABLE DUTY OF GUARDING THE OVERLORD, HERE...
TA—DAH
?
HE'S GONE--!!
San no Kuchi--?!
AUGH!!
SO STUPID...
CLANG
CLANG
THAT KARASU...
IT'S HIS FAULT RIKUO IS BEING "SPOILED."
OH...? THEY'RE CONSTRUCTING YET ANOTHER HIGH-RISE HERE?
HMPH.
THE THINGS THEY BUILD LACK ELEGANCE.
YAK
YAK
WHOOSH

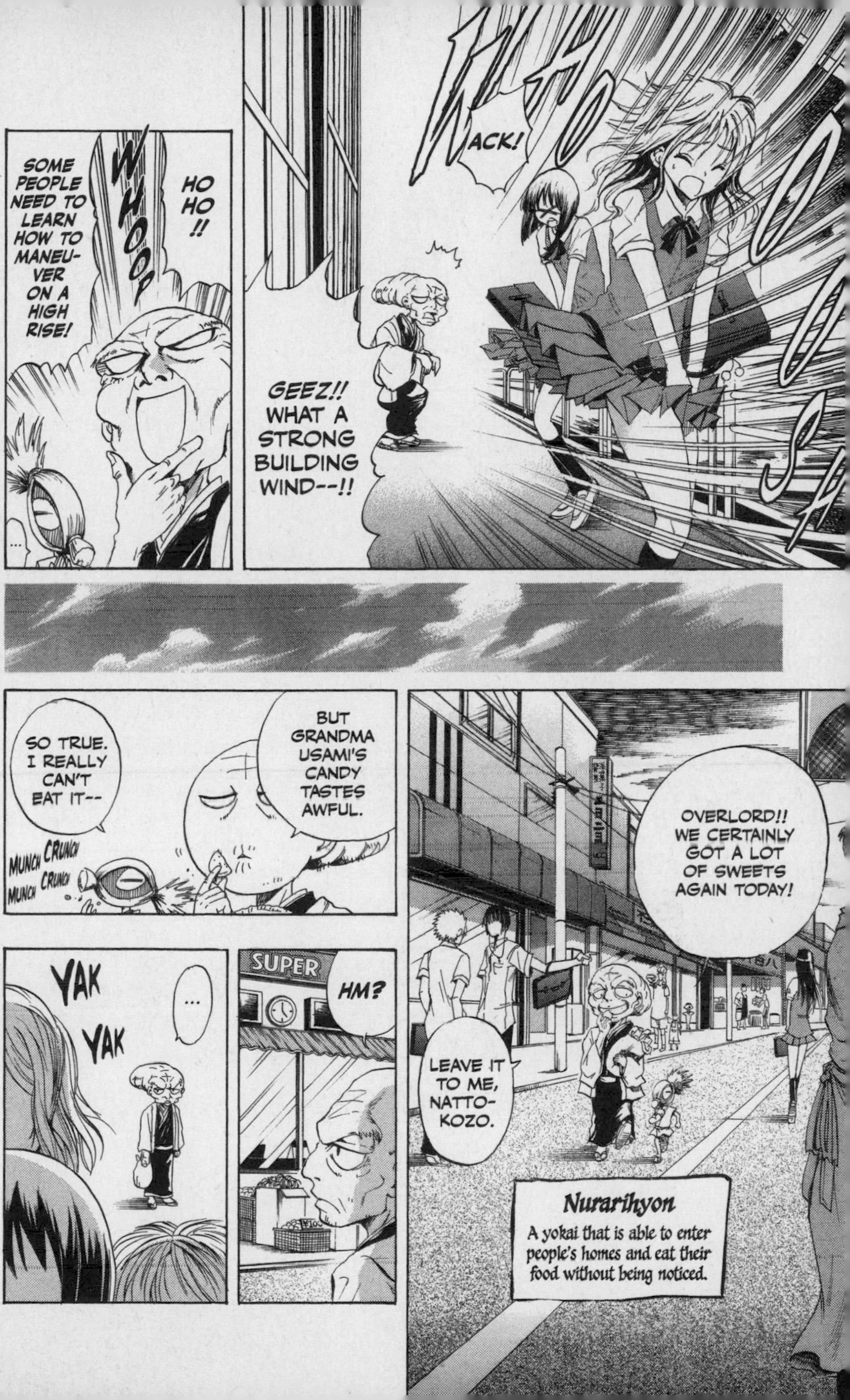
ACK!
GEEZ!! WHAT A STRONG BUILDING WIND--!!
HO HO !!
WHOOP
SOME PEOPLE NEED TO LEARN HOW TO MANEU-VER ON A HIGH RISE!
...
OVERLORD!! WE CERTAINLY GOT A LOT OF SWEETS AGAIN TODAY!
LEAVE IT TO ME, NATTO-KOZO.
Nurarihyon
A yokai that is able to enter people's homes and eat their food without being noticed.
BUT GRANDMA USAMI'S CANDY TASTES AWFUL.
SO TRUE. I REALLY CAN'T EAT IT--
MUNCH CRUNCH MUNCH CRUNCH
SUPER
HM?
...
YAK YAK

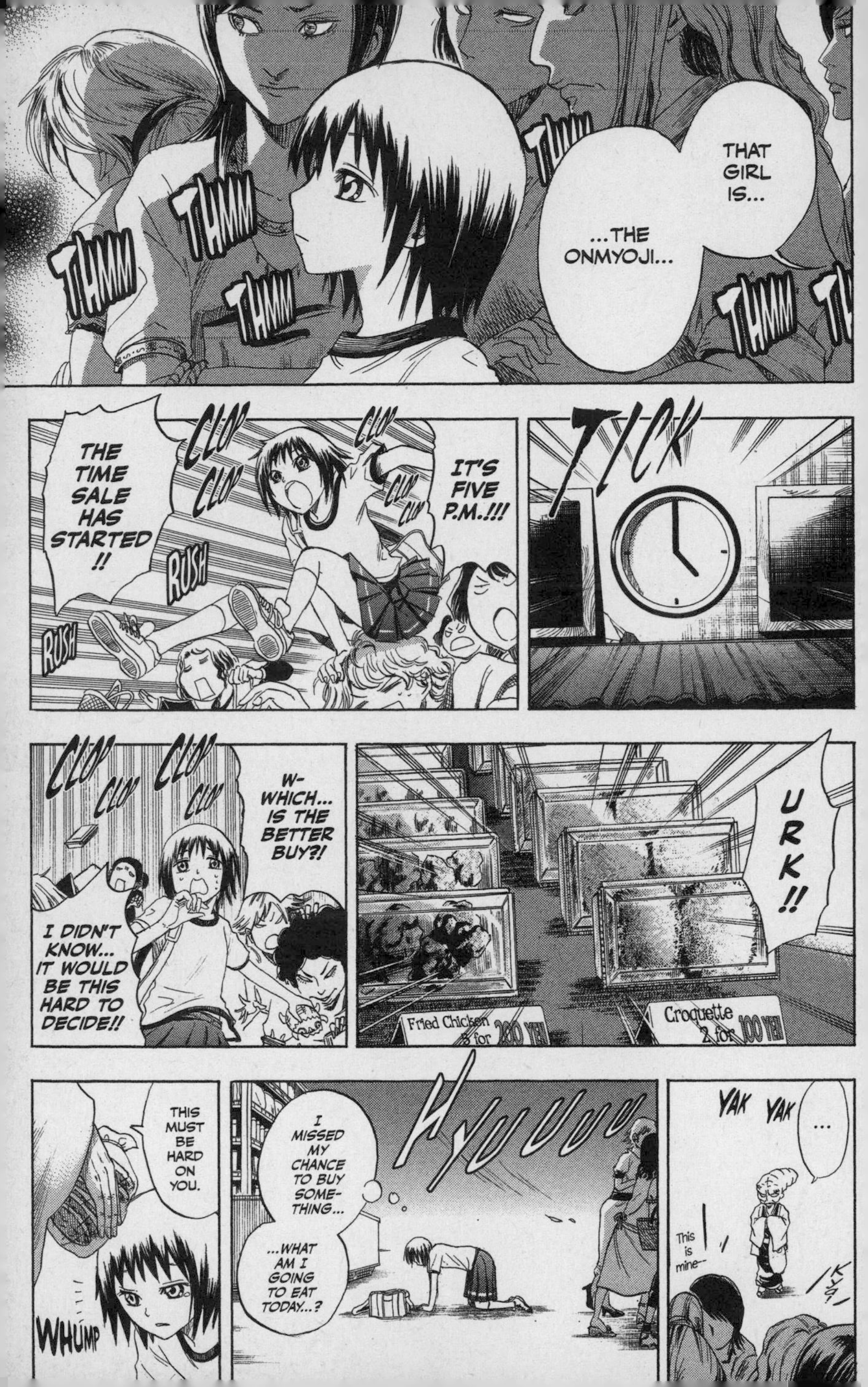
THMM
THAT GIRL IS...
...THE ONMYOJI...
THMM
THMM
THMM
THMM
TICK
IT'S FIVE P.M.!!!
CLOP CLOP CLOP CLOP
THE TIME SALE HAS STARTED!!
RUSH
RUSH
URK!!
Croquette 2 for 100 YEN
Fried Chicken 3 for 200 YEN
W-WHICH... IS THE BETTER BUY?!
CLOP CLOP CLOP CLOP
I DIDN'T KNOW... IT WOULD BE THIS HARD TO DECIDE!!
YAK YAK
...
This is mine—
HYUUUUU
I MISSED MY CHANCE TO BUY SOMETHING...
...WHAT AM I GOING TO EAT TODAY...?
THIS MUST BE HARD ON YOU.
WHUMP

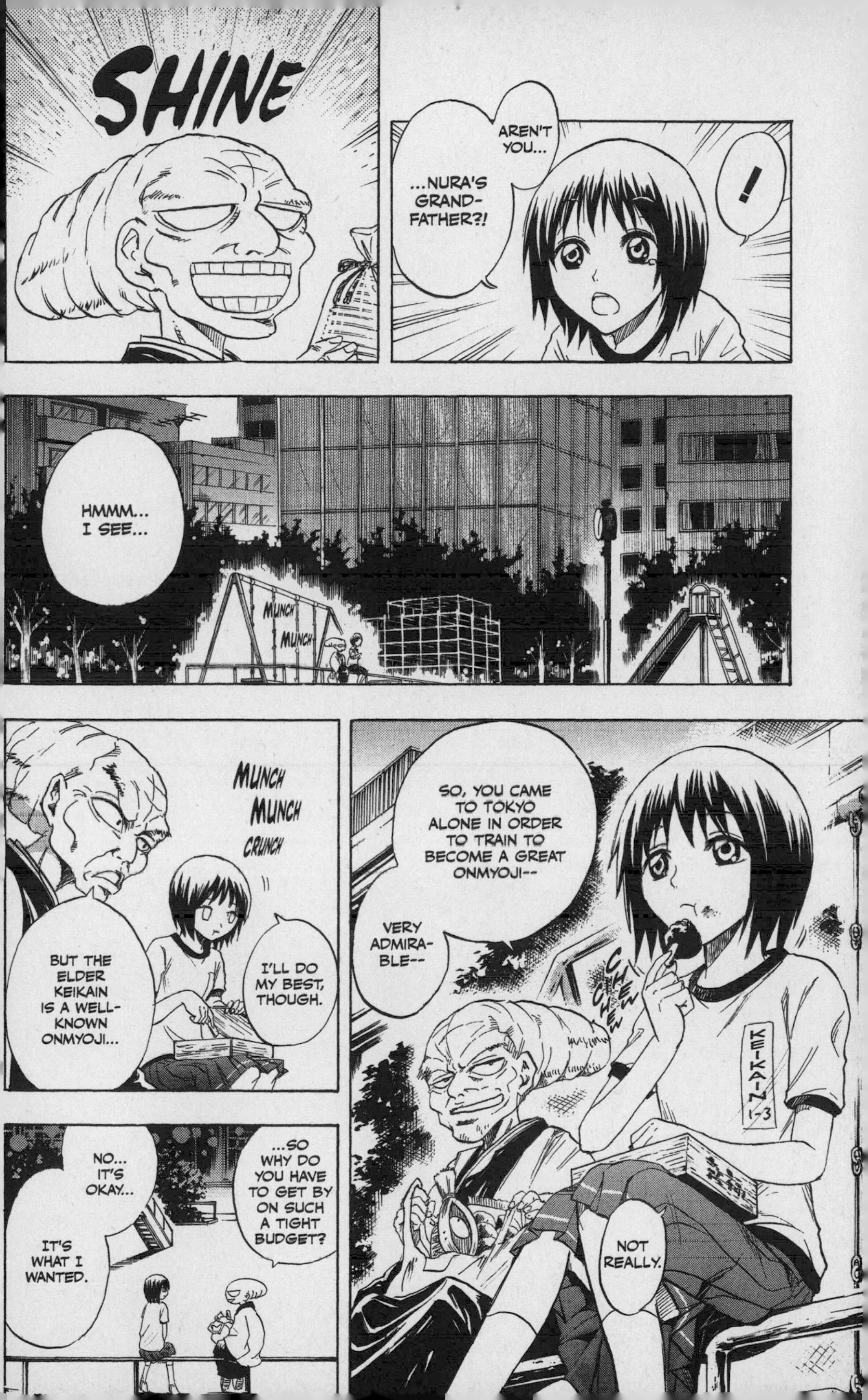
!
AREN'T YOU...
...NURA'S GRAND-FATHER?!
SHINE
HMMM... I SEE...
MUNCH
MUNCH
SO, YOU CAME TO TOKYO ALONE IN ORDER TO TRAIN TO BECOME A GREAT ONMYOJI--
VERY ADMIRA-BLE--
CHEW CHEW
KEIKAIN 1-3
NOT REALLY.
MUNCH MUNCH
CRUNCH
I'LL DO MY BEST, THOUGH.
BUT THE ELDER KEIKAIN IS A WELL-KNOWN ONMYOJI...
...SO WHY DO YOU HAVE TO GET BY ON SUCH A TIGHT BUDGET?
NO... IT'S OKAY...
IT'S WHAT I WANTED.

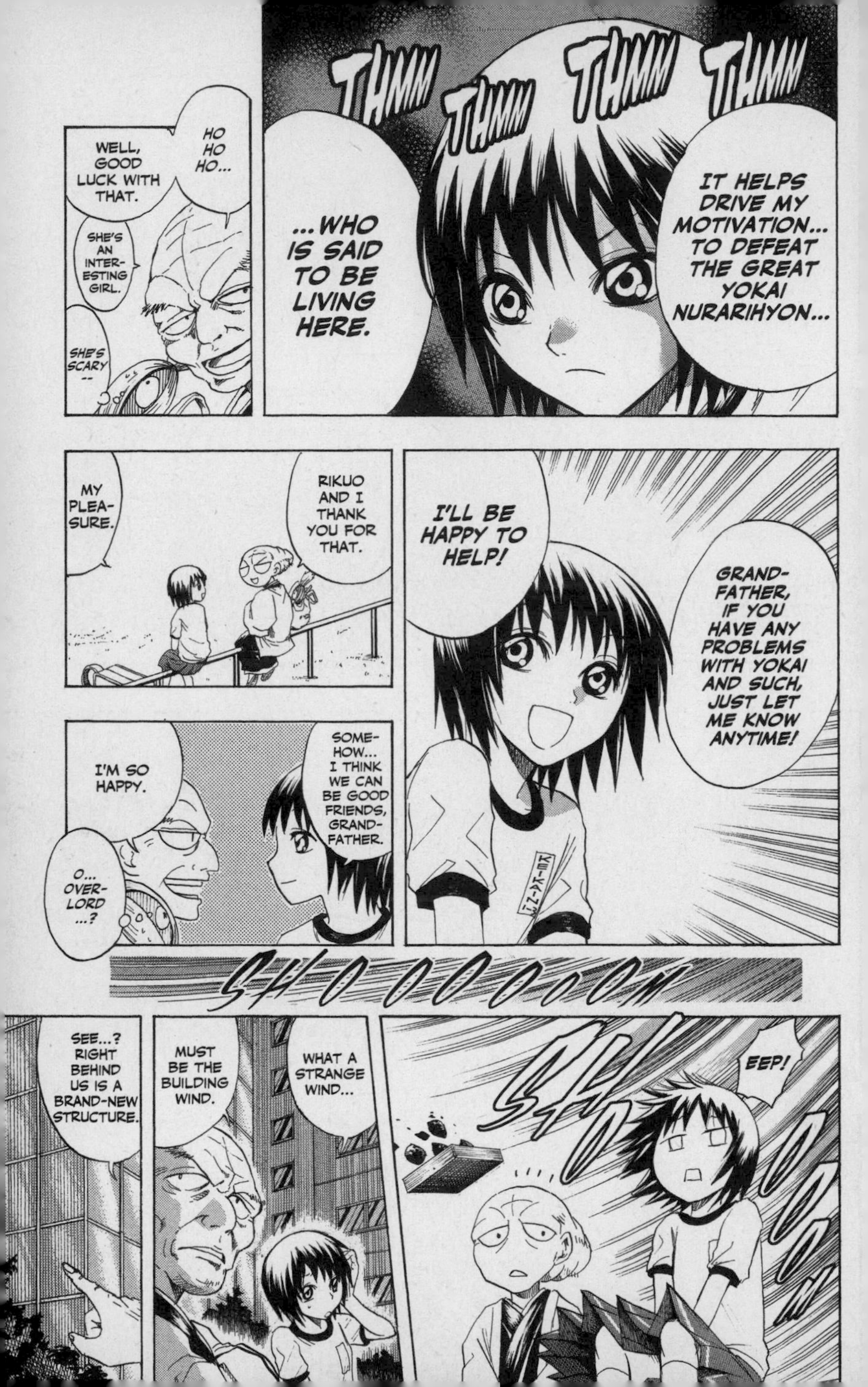
THMM THMM THMM THMM
IT HELPS DRIVE MY MOTIVATION... TO DEFEAT THE GREAT YOKAI NURARIHYON...
...WHO IS SAID TO BE LIVING HERE.
HO HO HO...
WELL, GOOD LUCK WITH THAT.
SHE'S AN INTER-ESTING GIRL.
SHE'S SCARY --
GRAND-FATHER, IF YOU HAVE ANY PROBLEMS WITH YOKAI AND SUCH, JUST LET ME KNOW ANYTIME!
I'LL BE HAPPY TO HELP!
KEIKAIN
RIKUO AND I THANK YOU FOR THAT.
MY PLEA-SURE.
SOME-HOW... I THINK WE CAN BE GOOD FRIENDS, GRAND-FATHER.
I'M SO HAPPY.
O... OVER-LORD ...?
SHOOOOOOOM
SHHOOOOOOM
EEP!
WHAT A STRANGE WIND...
MUST BE THE BUILDING WIND.
SEE...? RIGHT BEHIND US IS A BRAND-NEW STRUCTURE.

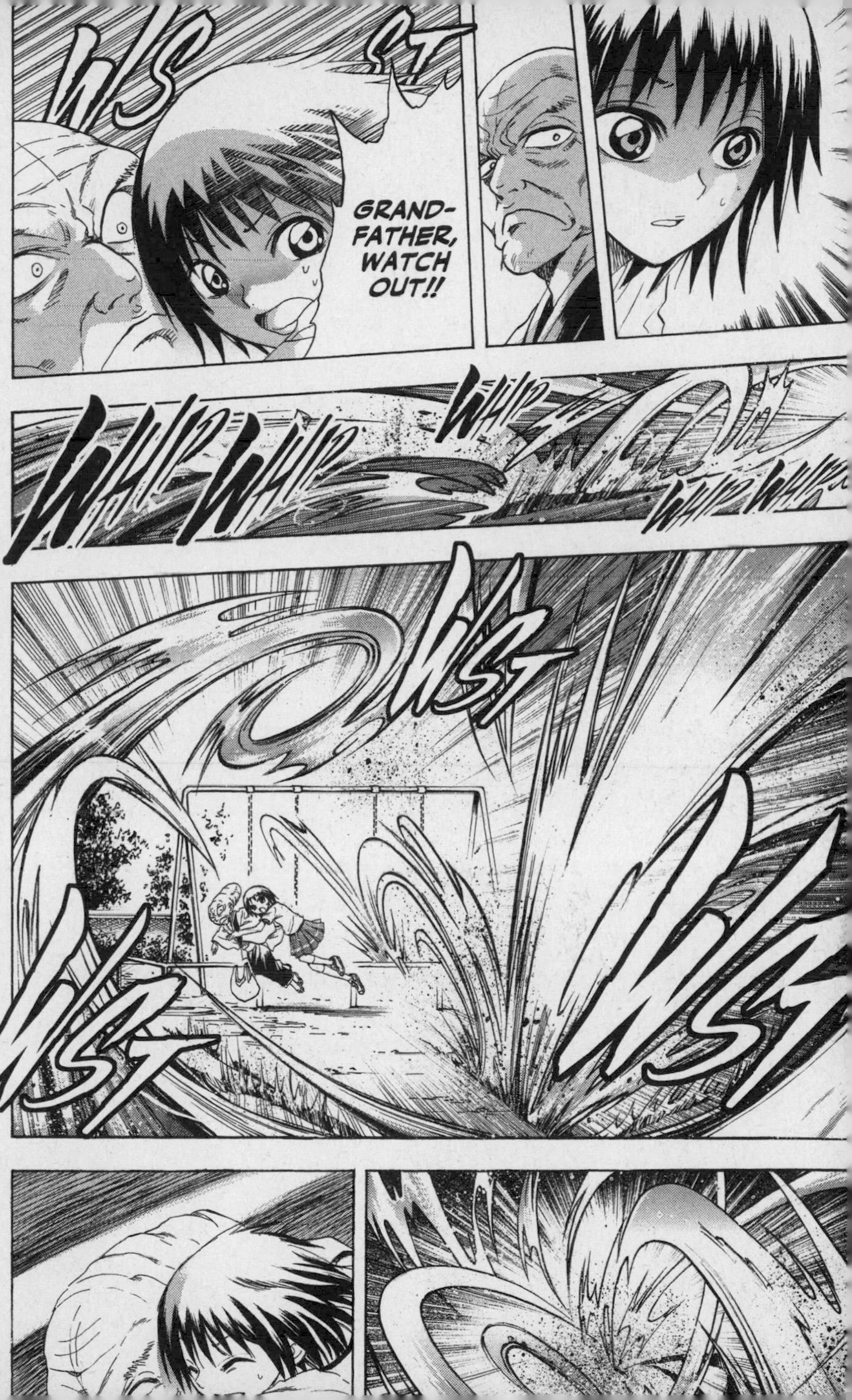
GRAND-FATHER, WATCH OUT!!

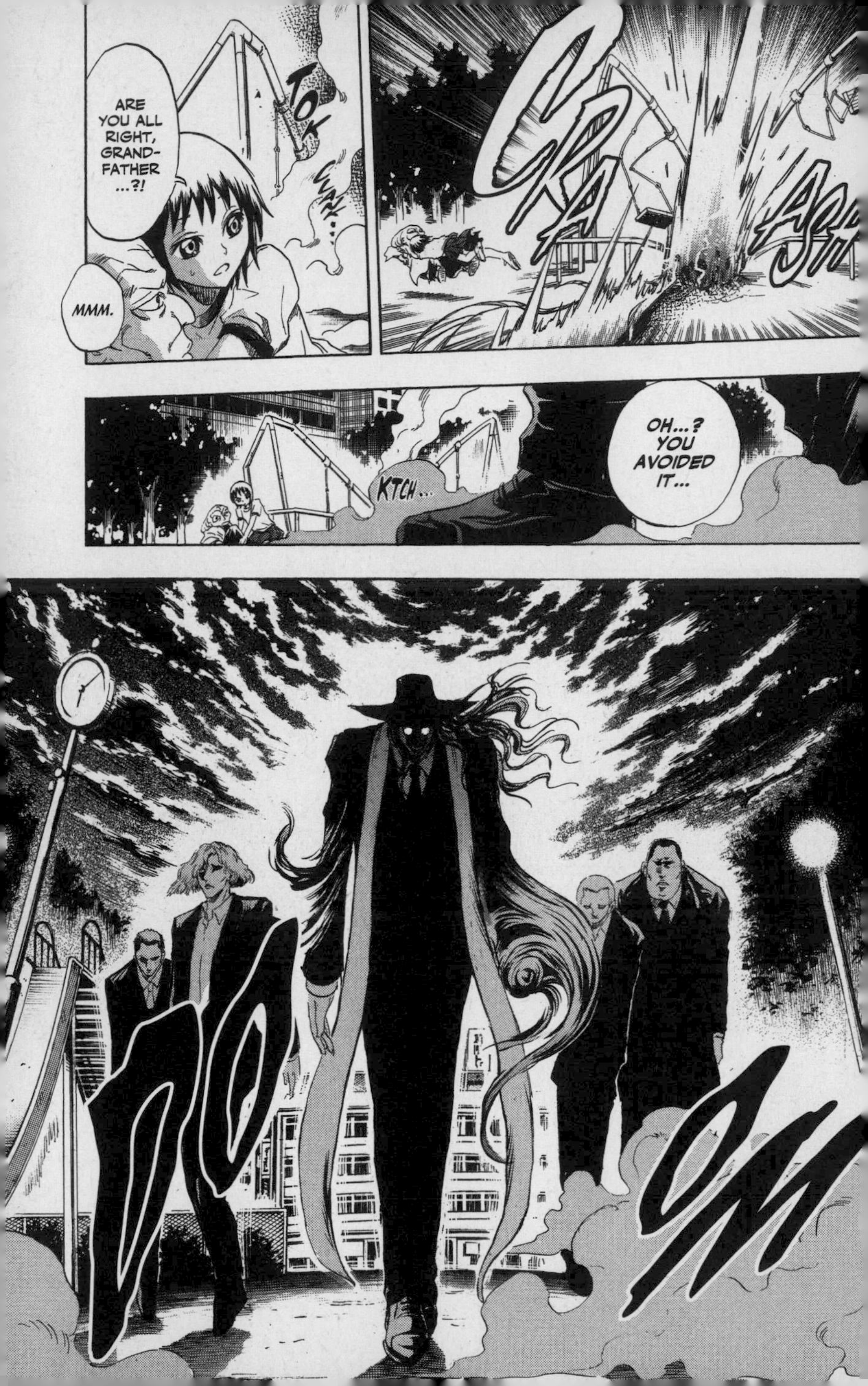
CRASH
TOK
CLANK...
ARE YOU ALL RIGHT, GRAND-FATHER ...?!
MMM.
OH...? YOU AVOIDED IT...
KTCH...

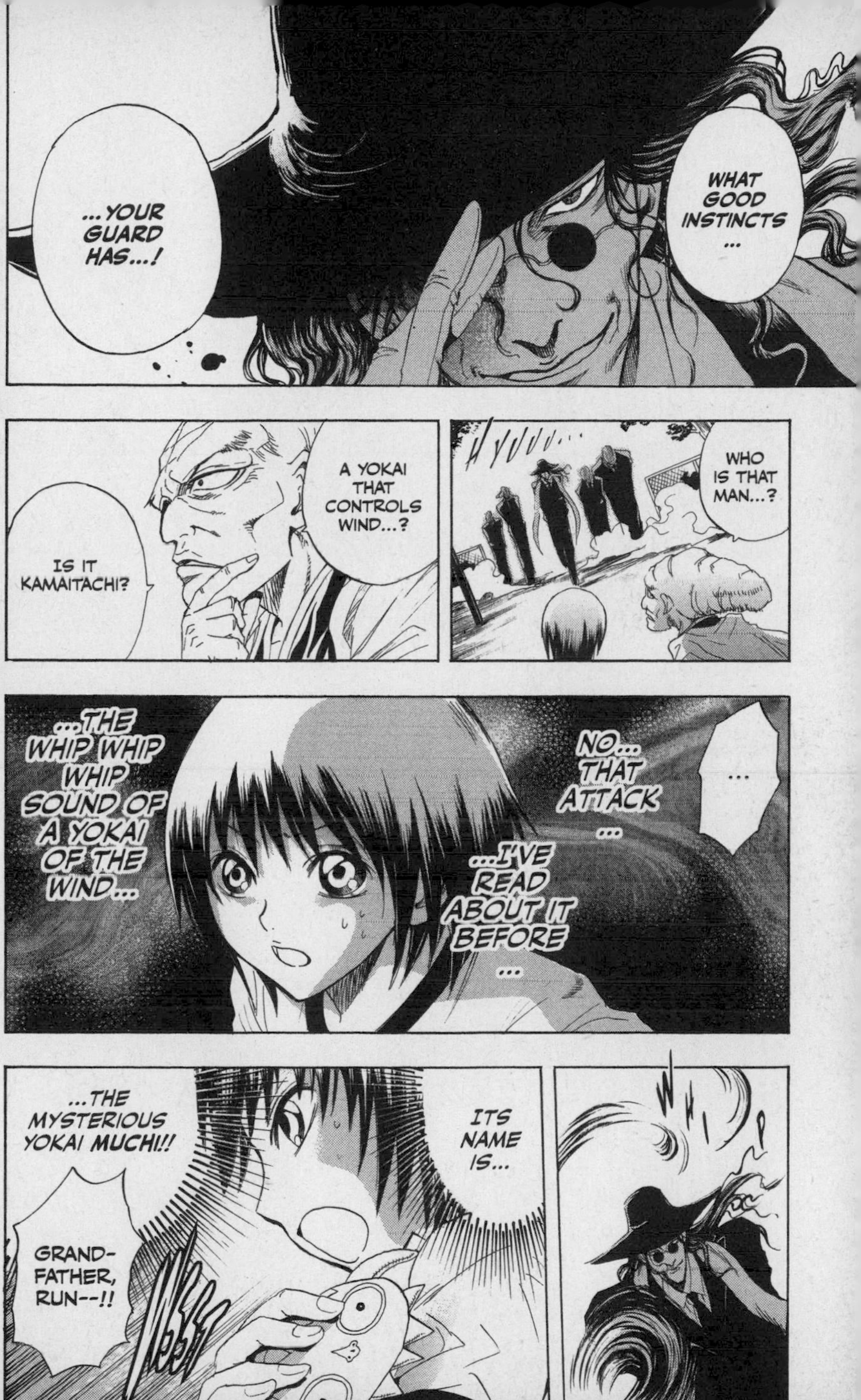
WHAT GOOD INSTINCTS ...
...YOUR GUARD HAS...!
WHO IS THAT MAN...?
A YOKAI THAT CONTROLS WIND...?
IS IT KAMAITACHI?
...
NO... THAT ATTACK ...
...I'VE READ ABOUT IT BEFORE ...
...THE WHIP WHIP WHIP SOUND OF A YOKAI OF THE WIND...
WHIP
ITS NAME IS...
...THE MYSTERIOUS YOKAI MUCHI!!
GRAND-FATHER, RUN--!!

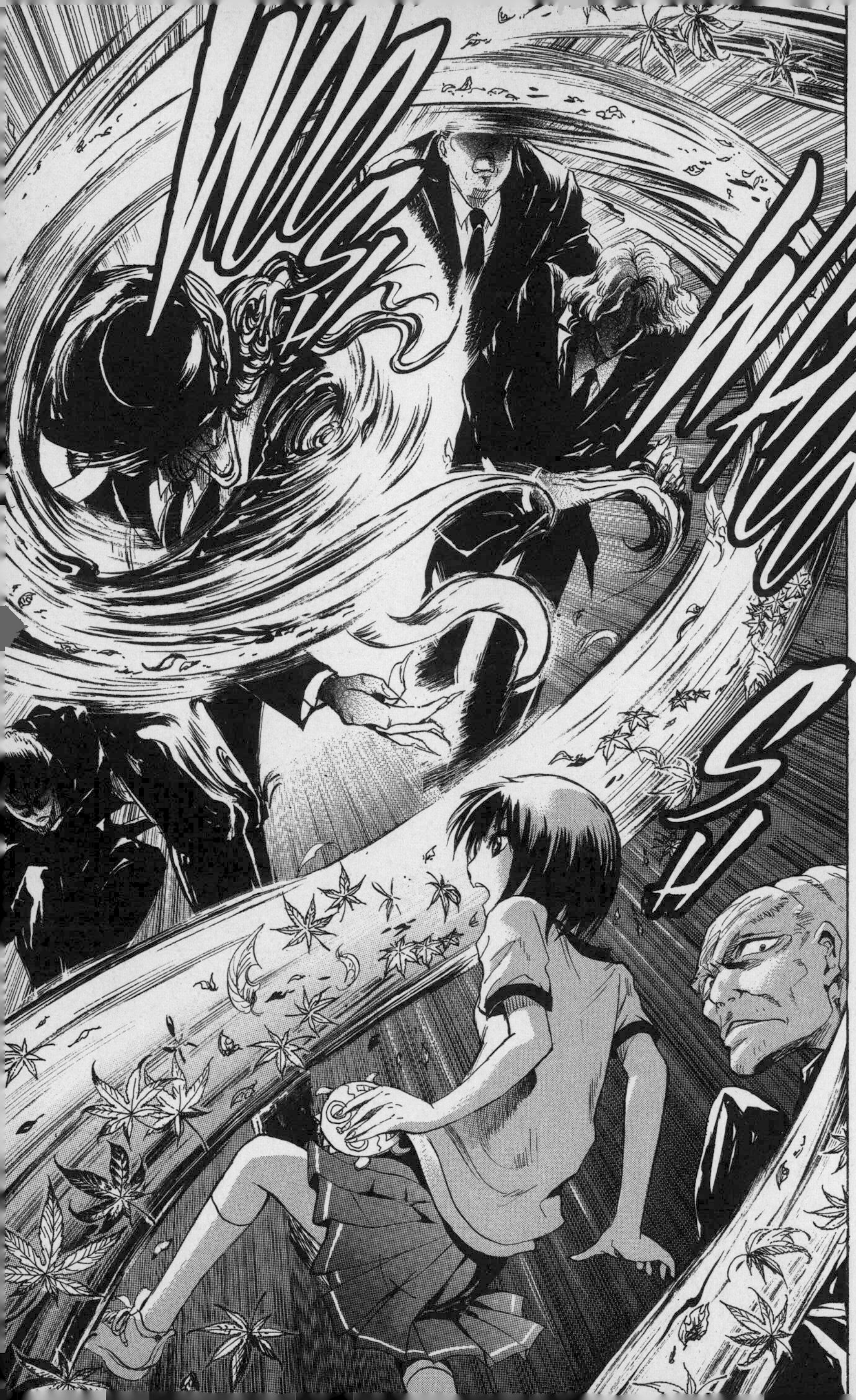
WHOOSH
WOOSH

Waaaah! It's benifuku *droooool*. They say it's really delicious. My granddad used to receive them often and always said they were famous, but this is the first time I'll get to eat one... Really? Can I really have one, Grandfather Nura? Really? Thank you. What? All of it? I feel bad, but maybe just two or three. Oooh, I'm so tired after training everyone, and this sweet taste really hits the spot. Maybe two or three more...no, wait...I don't want to eat them all now. You're giving them to me, right? Then I'm taking these home as a replacement for the croquette. Hey, what's that wind?

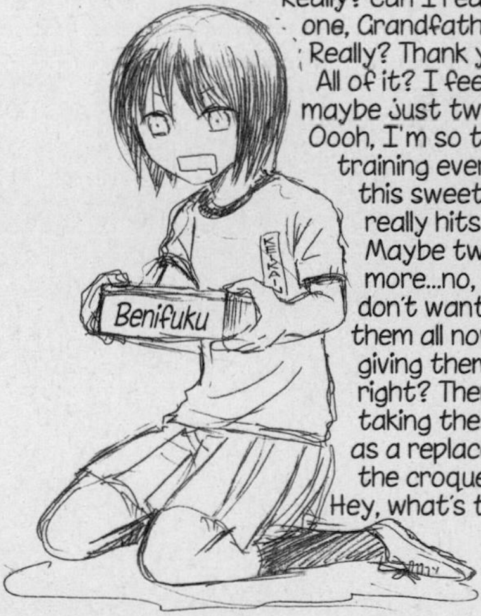
Benifuku

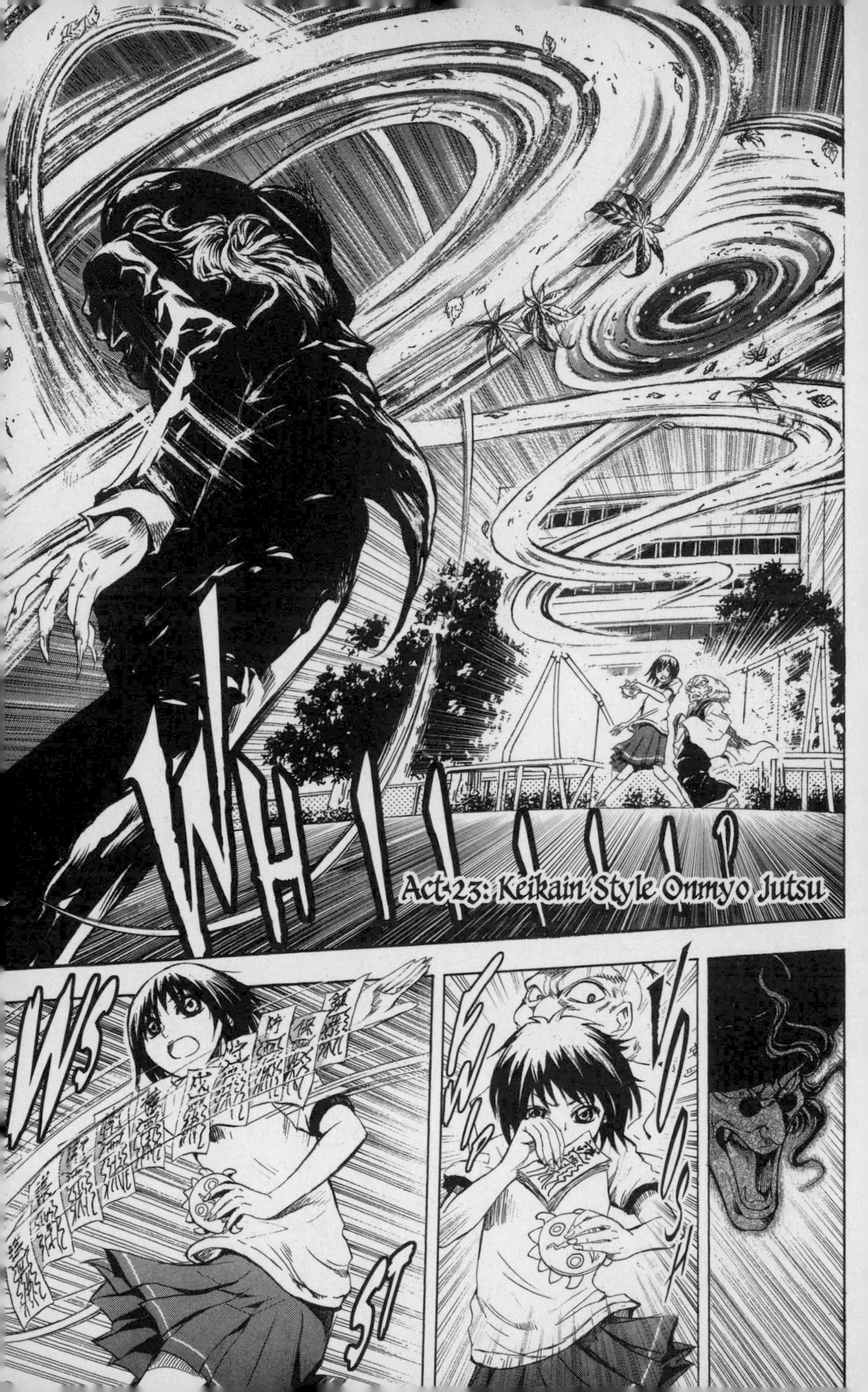
Act 23: Keikain Style Onmyo Jutsu

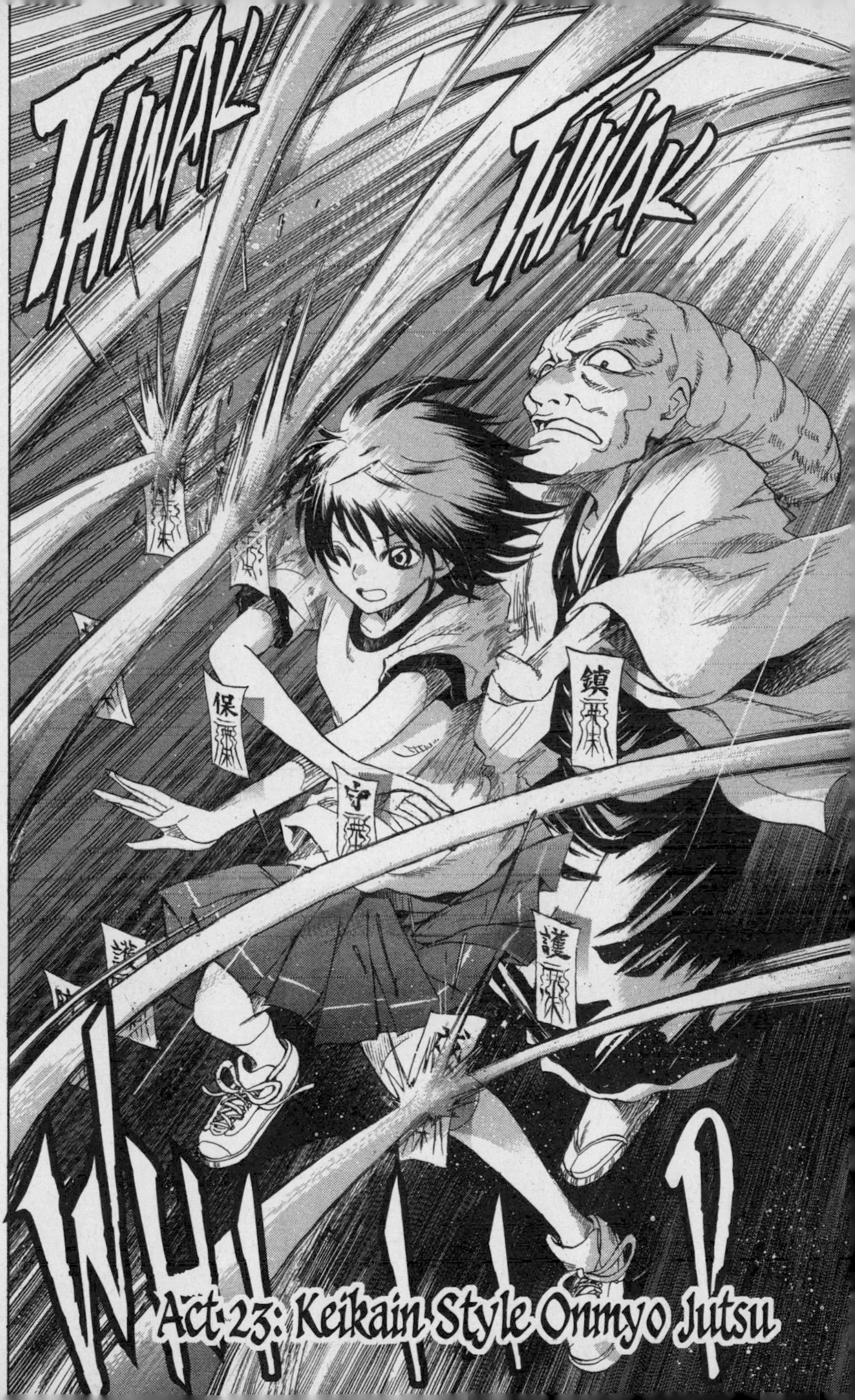
THWAK
THWAK
THWAK!

Act 23: Keikain Style Onmyo Jutsu

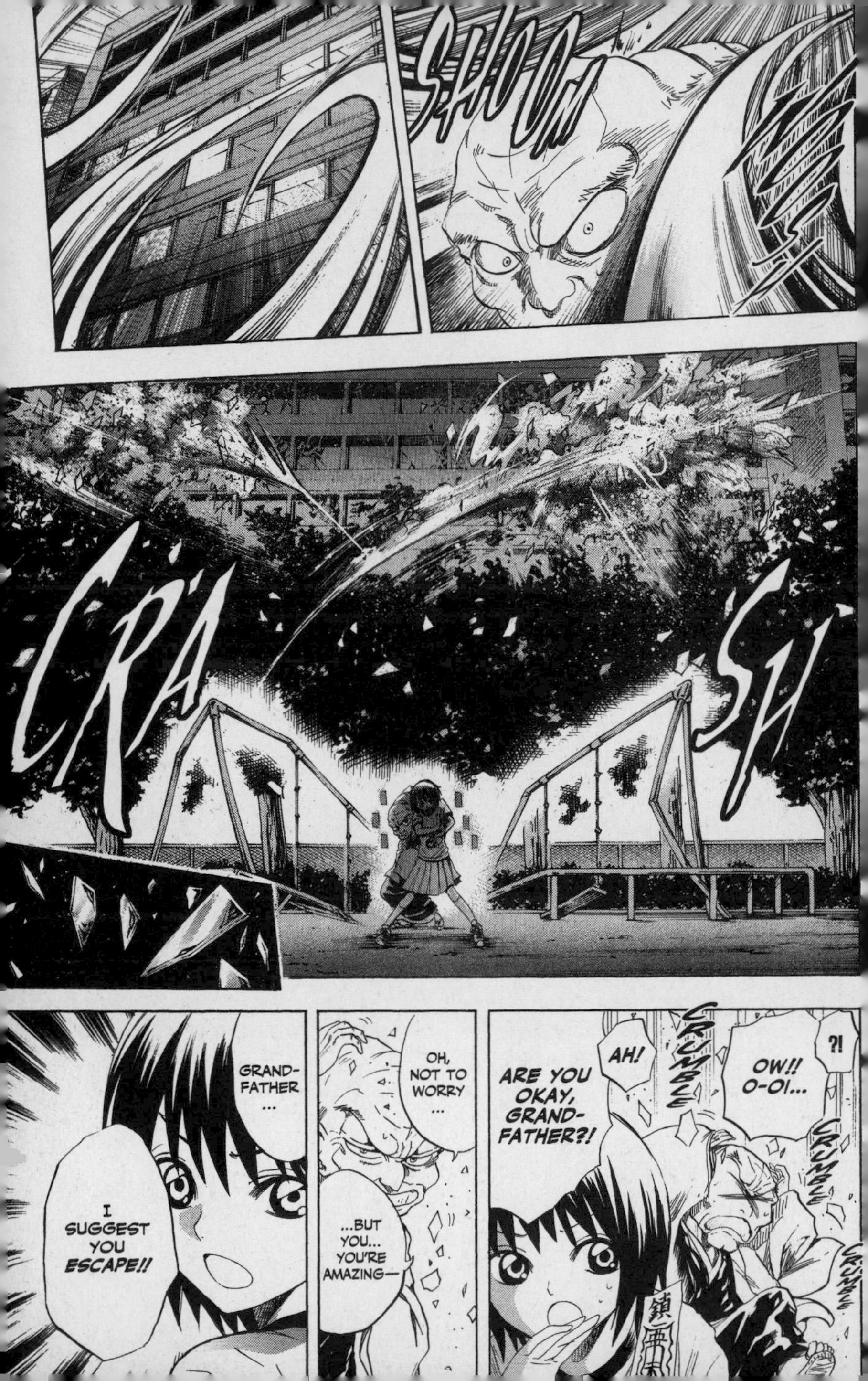
CRA
SH
?!
OW!! O-OI...
CRUMBLE
AH!
ARE YOU OKAY, GRANDFATHER?!
CRUMBLE
CRUMBLE
OH, NOT TO WORRY...
...BUT YOU... YOU'RE AMAZING—
GRANDFATHER...
I SUGGEST YOU *ESCAPE!!*

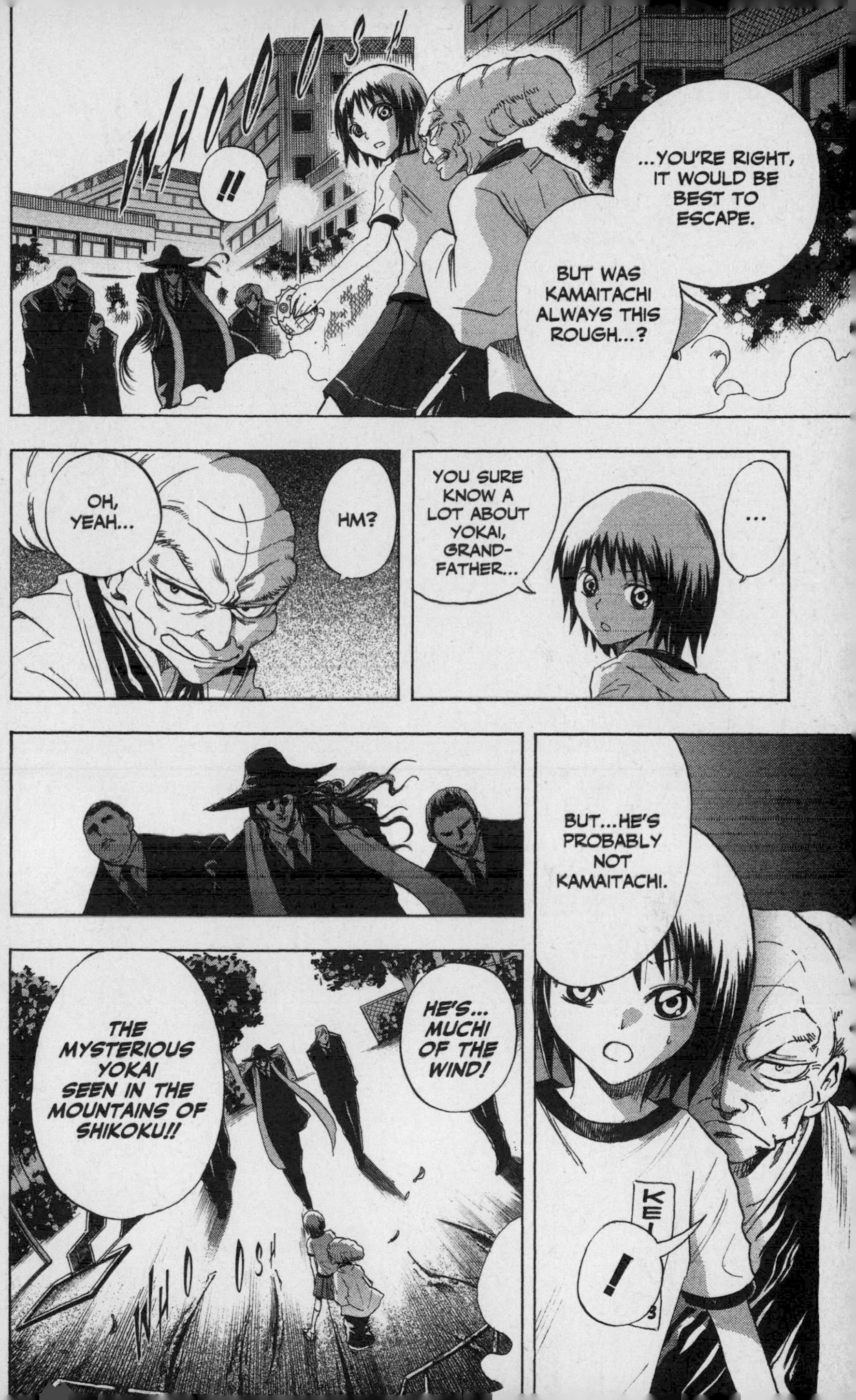
...YOU'RE RIGHT, IT WOULD BE BEST TO ESCAPE.
BUT WAS KAMAITACHI ALWAYS THIS ROUGH...?
!!
WHOOOSH
...
YOU SURE KNOW A LOT ABOUT YOKAI, GRANDFATHER...
HM?
OH, YEAH...
BUT...HE'S PROBABLY NOT KAMAITACHI.
!
HE'S... MUCHI OF THE WIND!
THE MYSTERIOUS YOKAI SEEN IN THE MOUNTAINS OF SHIKOKU!!
WHOOSH

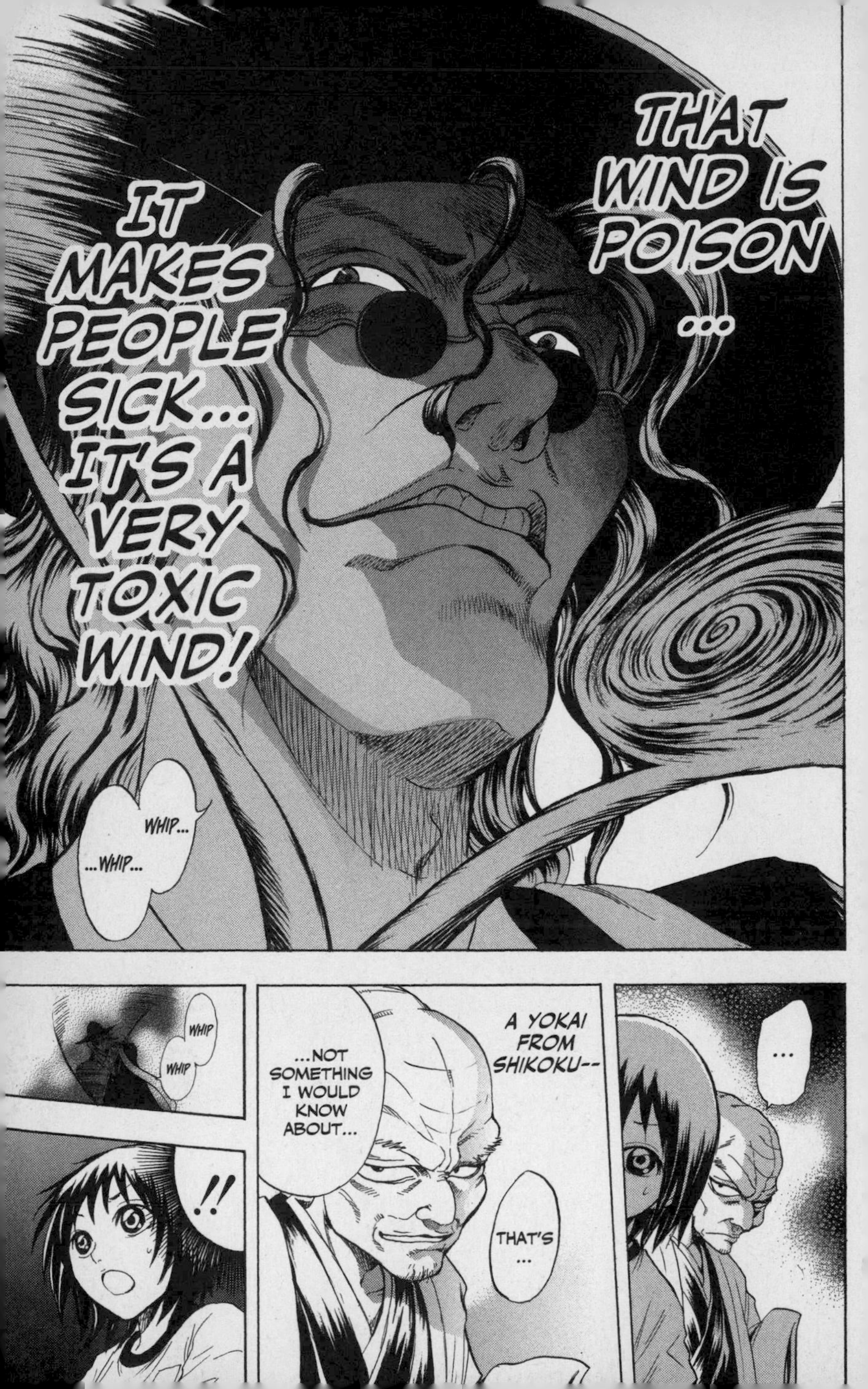
THAT WIND IS POISON...
IT MAKES PEOPLE SICK... IT'S A VERY TOXIC WIND!
WHIP... ...WHIP...
...
A YOKAI FROM SHIKOKU--
...NOT SOMETHING I WOULD KNOW ABOUT...
THAT'S ...
WHIP WHIP
!!

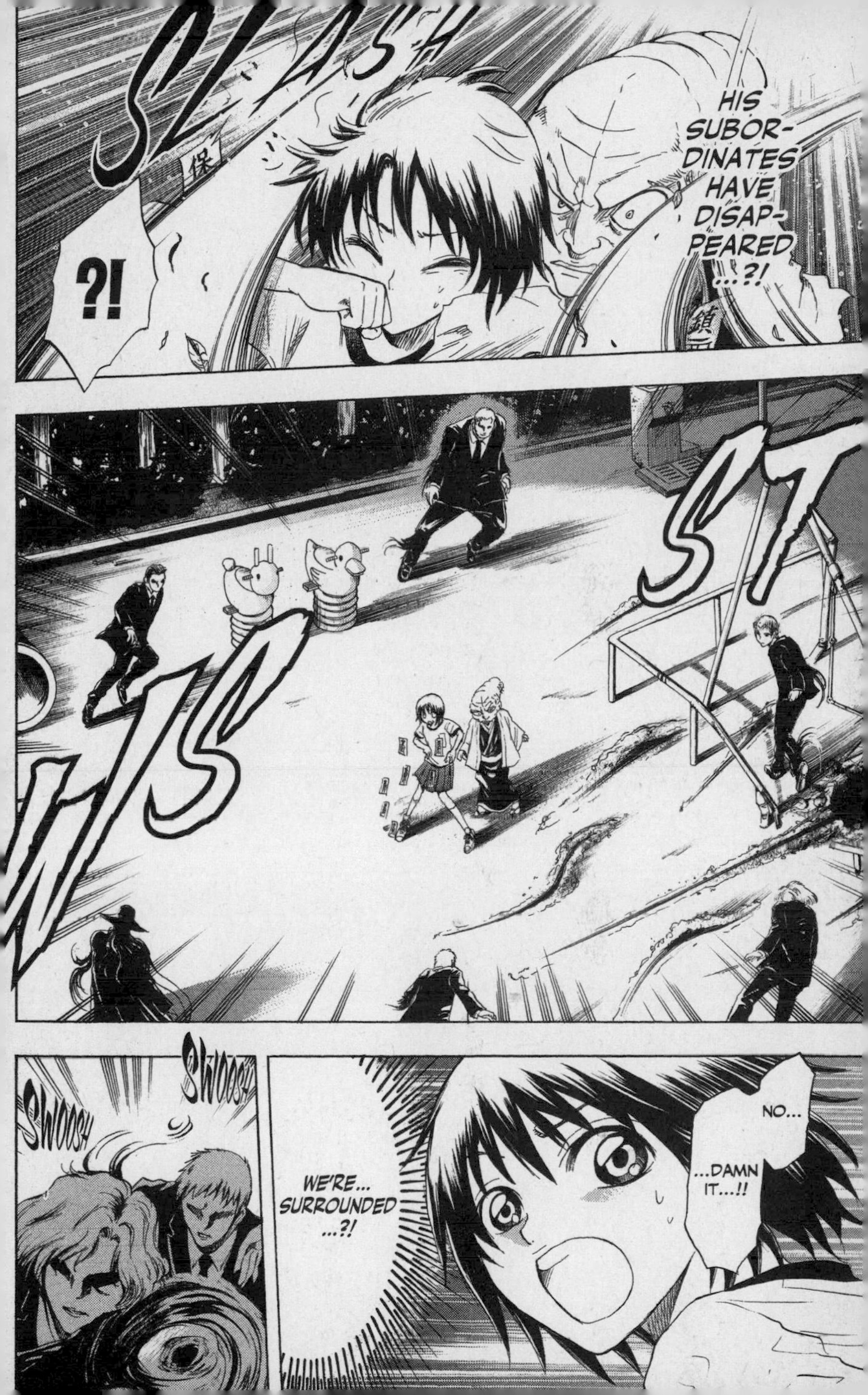
HIS SUBOR-DINATES HAVE DISAP-PEARED ...?!
SLASH
?!
NO...
...DAMN IT...!!
WE'RE... SURROUNDED ...?!
SWOOSH
SWOOSH

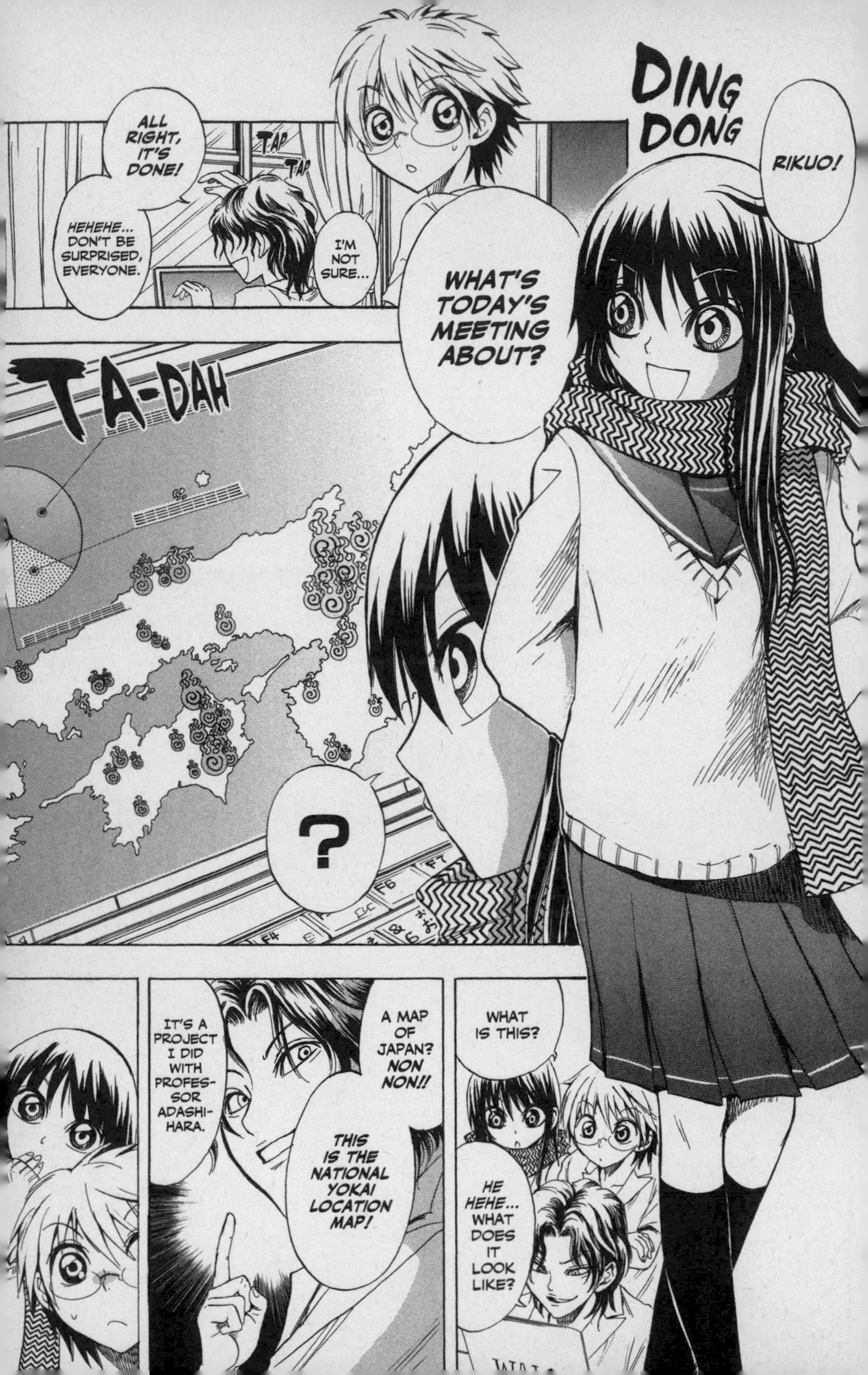
DING DONG
RIKUO!
WHAT'S TODAY'S MEETING ABOUT?
TAP
TAP
I'M NOT SURE...
ALL RIGHT, IT'S DONE!
HEHEHE... DON'T BE SURPRISED, EVERYONE.
TA-DAH
?
WHAT IS THIS?
HE HEHE... WHAT DOES IT LOOK LIKE?
A MAP OF JAPAN? NON NON!!
IT'S A PROJECT I DID WITH PROFES-SOR ADASHI-HARA.
THIS IS THE NATIONAL YOKAI LOCATION MAP!

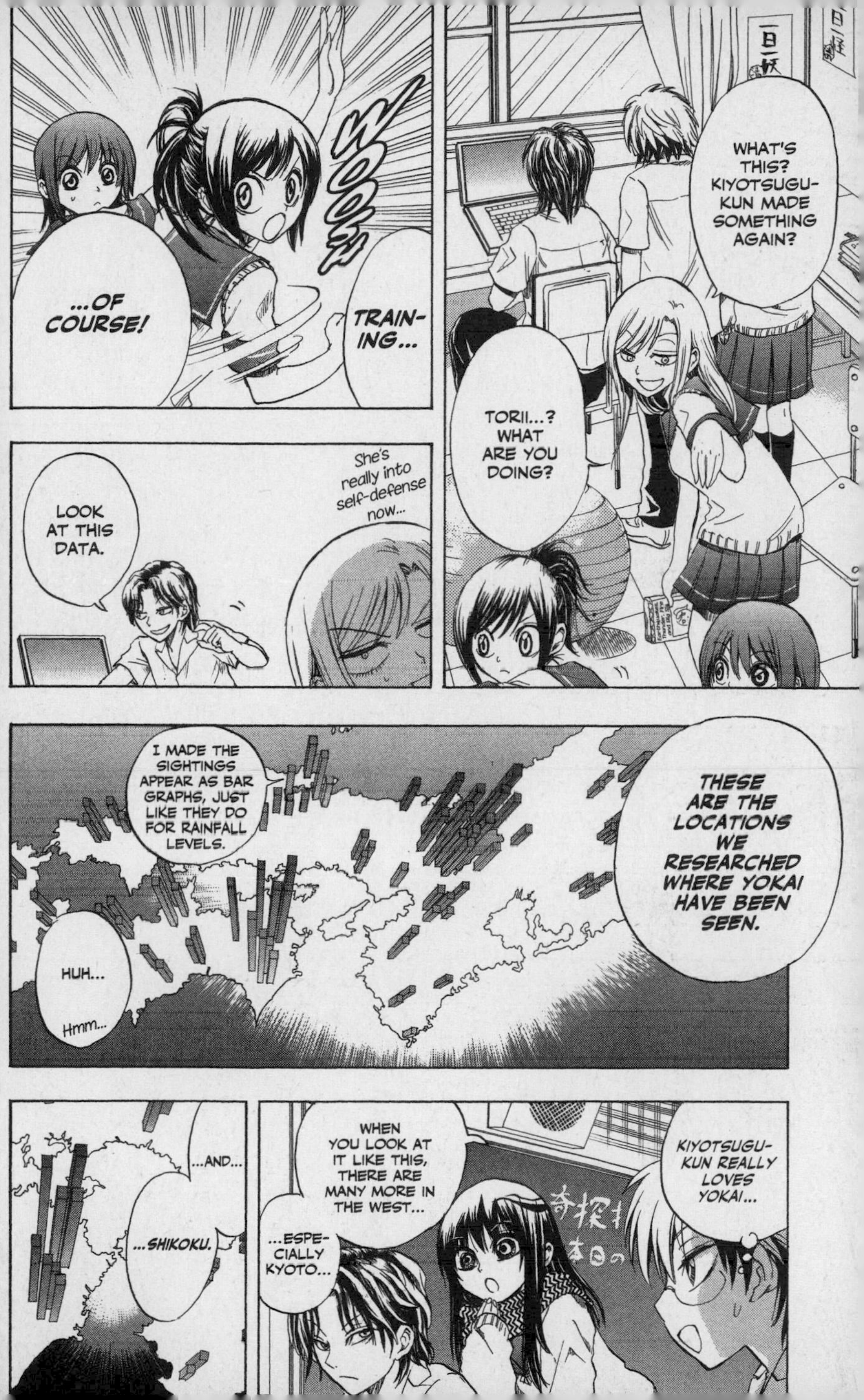
WHAT'S THIS? KIYOTSUGU-KUN MADE SOMETHING AGAIN?
TORII...? WHAT ARE YOU DOING?
TRAINING...
...OF COURSE!
She's really into self-defense now...
LOOK AT THIS DATA.
THESE ARE THE LOCATIONS WE RESEARCHED WHERE YOKAI HAVE BEEN SEEN.
I MADE THE SIGHTINGS APPEAR AS BAR GRAPHS, JUST LIKE THEY DO FOR RAINFALL LEVELS.
HUH...
Hmm...
KIYOTSUGU-KUN REALLY LOVES YOKAI...
WHEN YOU LOOK AT IT LIKE THIS, THERE ARE MANY MORE IN THE WEST...
...ESPECIALLY KYOTO...
...AND...
...SHIKOKU.

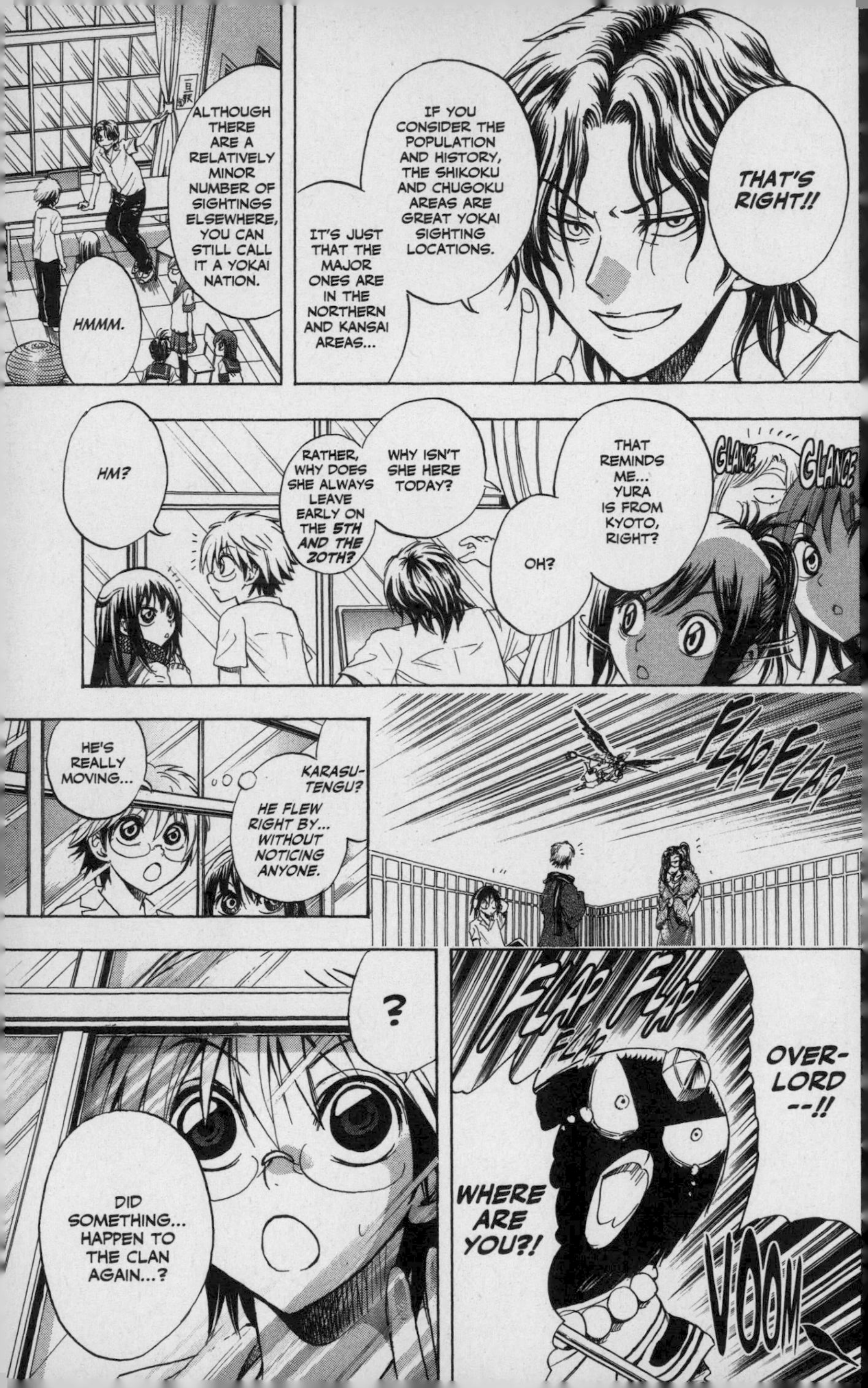
THAT'S RIGHT!!
IF YOU CONSIDER THE POPULATION AND HISTORY, THE SHIKOKU AND CHUGOKU AREAS ARE GREAT YOKAI SIGHTING LOCATIONS.
IT'S JUST THAT THE MAJOR ONES ARE IN THE NORTHERN AND KANSAI AREAS...
ALTHOUGH THERE ARE A RELATIVELY MINOR NUMBER OF SIGHTINGS ELSEWHERE, YOU CAN STILL CALL IT A YOKAI NATION.
HMMM.
GLANCE
GLANCE
THAT REMINDS ME... YURA IS FROM KYOTO, RIGHT?
OH?
WHY ISN'T SHE HERE TODAY?
RATHER, WHY DOES SHE ALWAYS LEAVE EARLY ON THE 5TH AND THE 20TH?
HM?
FLAP FLAP
KARASU-TENGU? HE FLEW RIGHT BY... WITHOUT NOTICING ANYONE.
HE'S REALLY MOVING...
FLAP FLAP
FLAP
OVER-LORD--!!
WHERE ARE YOU?!
VOOM
?
DID SOMETHING... HAPPEN TO THE CLAN AGAIN...?

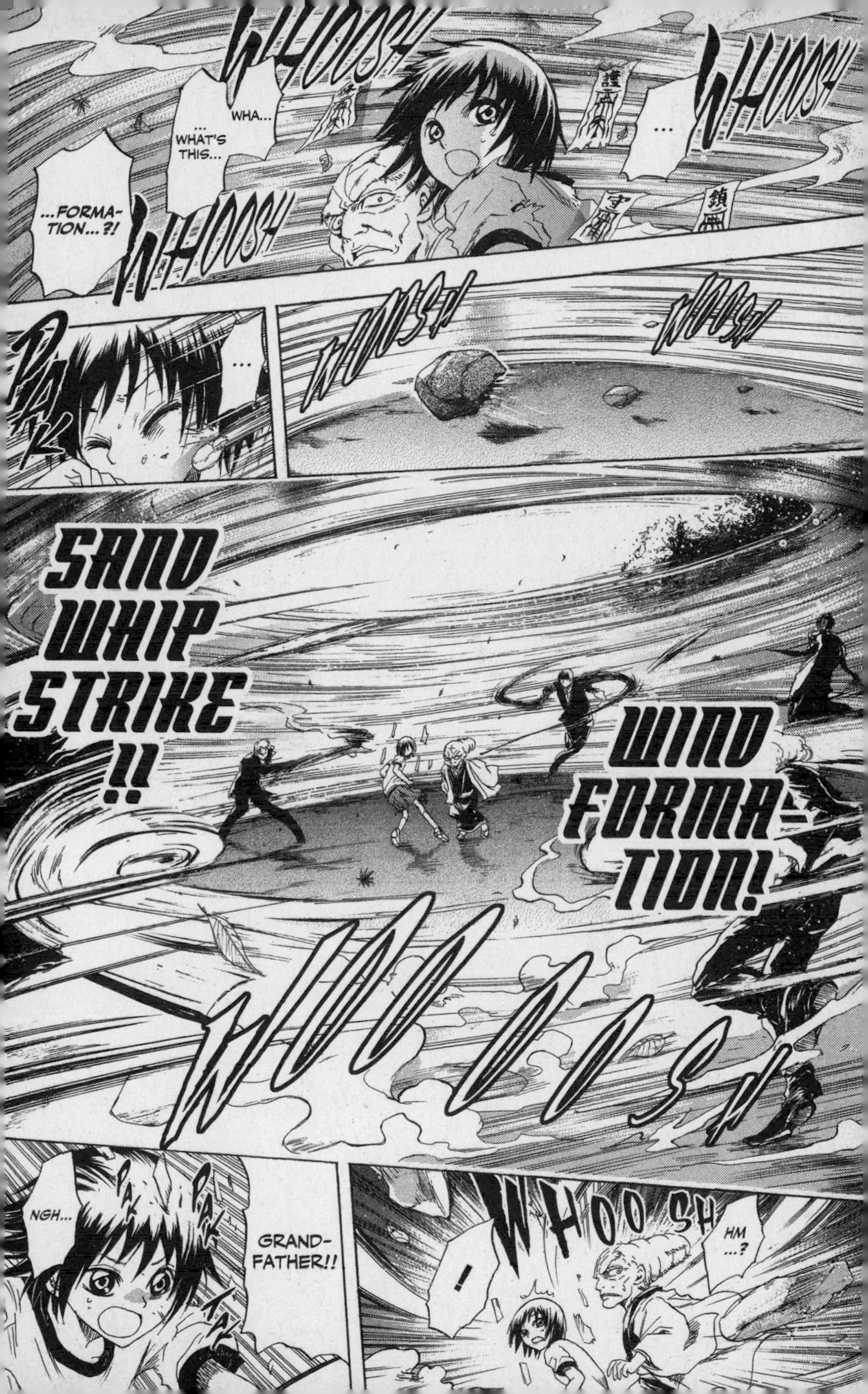
WHOOSH
...
WHOOSH
WHA...
... WHAT'S THIS...
...FORMA-TION...?!
WHOOSH
WHOOSH
WHOOSH
...
PAK
WIND FORMA-TION!
SAND WHIP STRIKE !!
WHOOOOSH
WHOOSH
HM ...?
!
GRAND-FATHER!!
PAK
PAK
NGH...

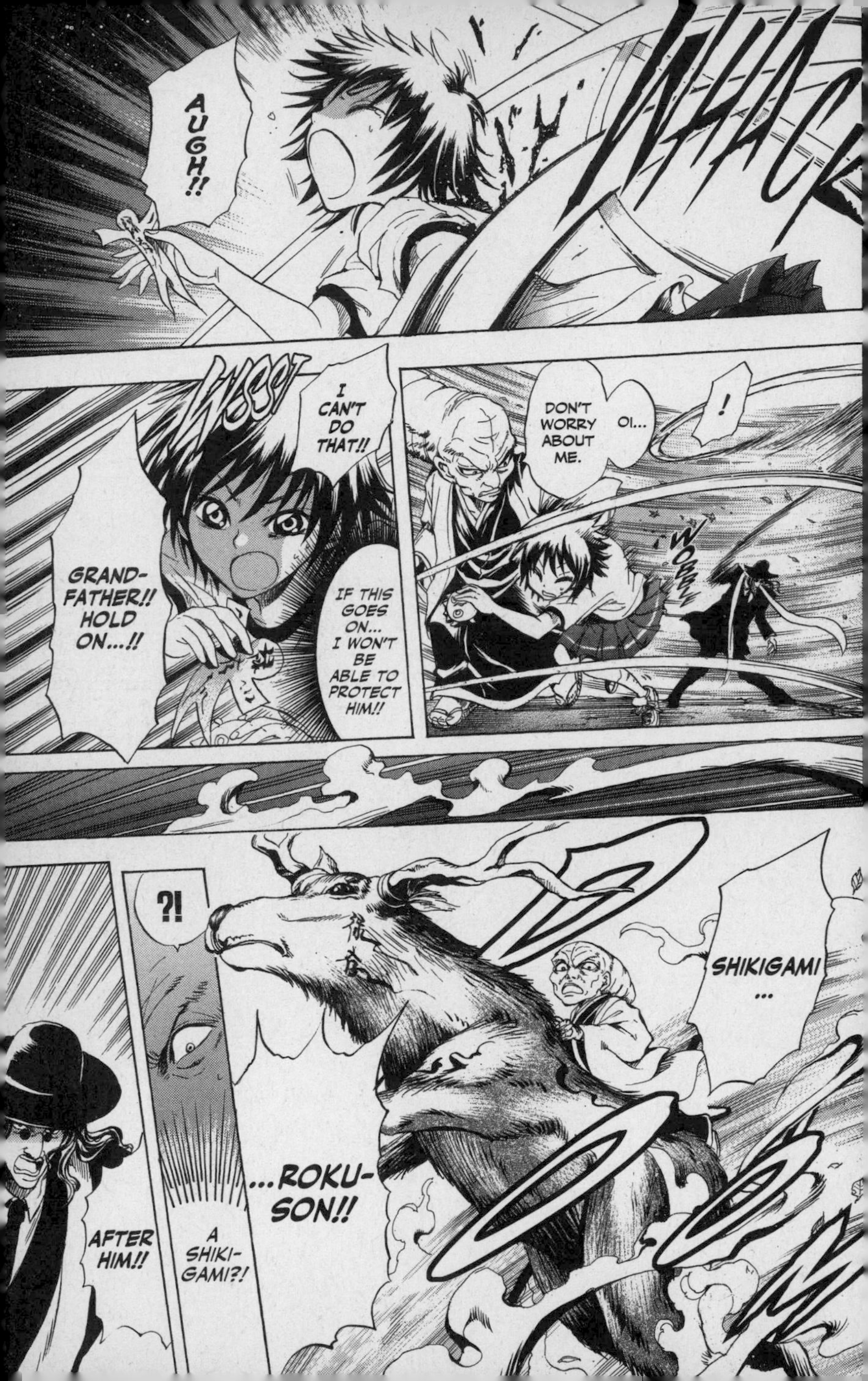
WHACK
AUGH!!
!
OI...
DON'T WORRY ABOUT ME.
I CAN'T DO THAT!!
IF THIS GOES ON... I WON'T BE ABLE TO PROTECT HIM!!
GRAND-FATHER!! HOLD ON...!!
SHIKIGAMI ...
...ROKU-SON!!
?!
A SHIKI-GAMI?!
AFTER HIM!!

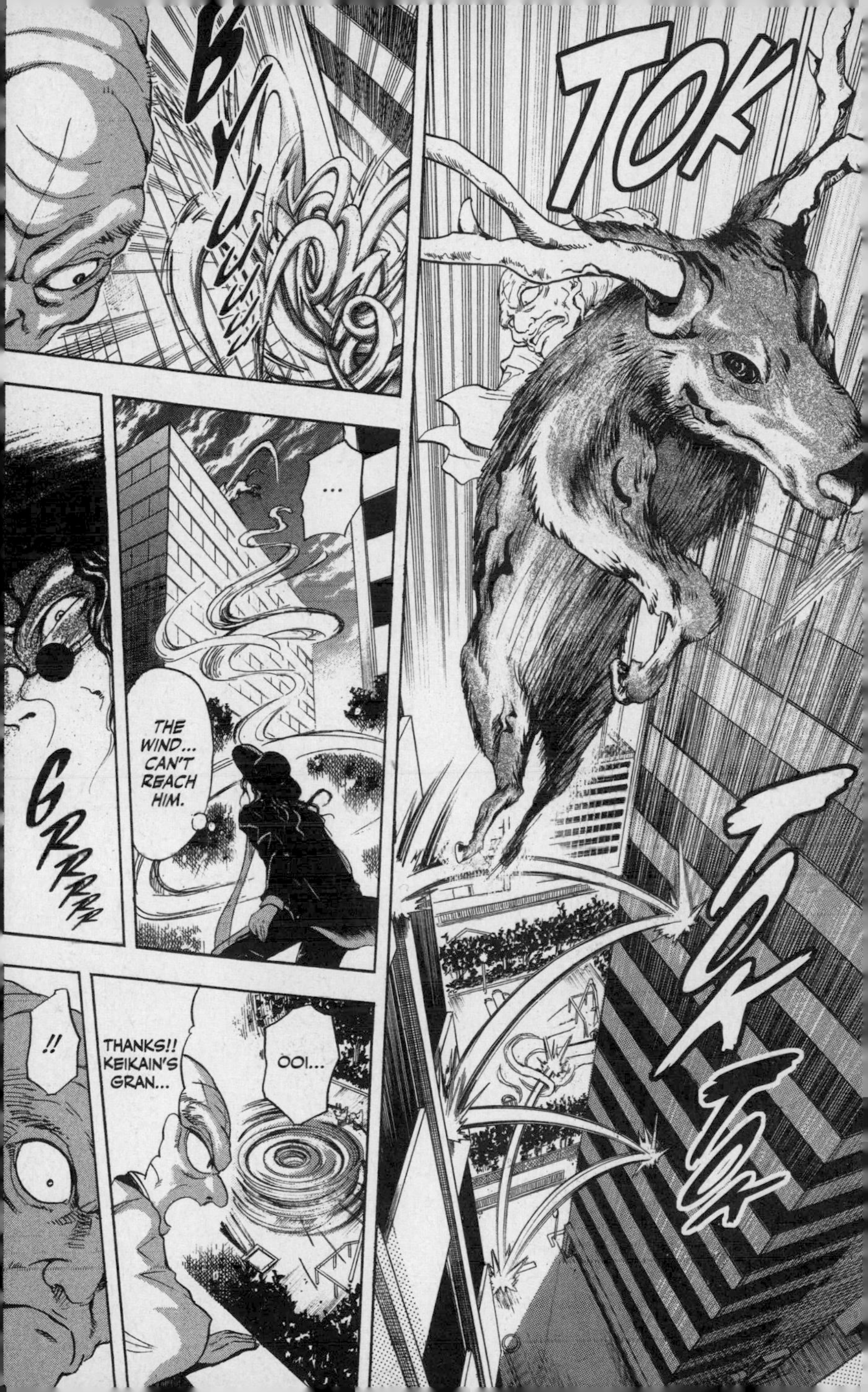
TOK
TOK TOK
...
THE WIND... CAN'T REACH HIM.
GRRRR
OOI...
THANKS!! KEIKAIN'S GRAN...
!!

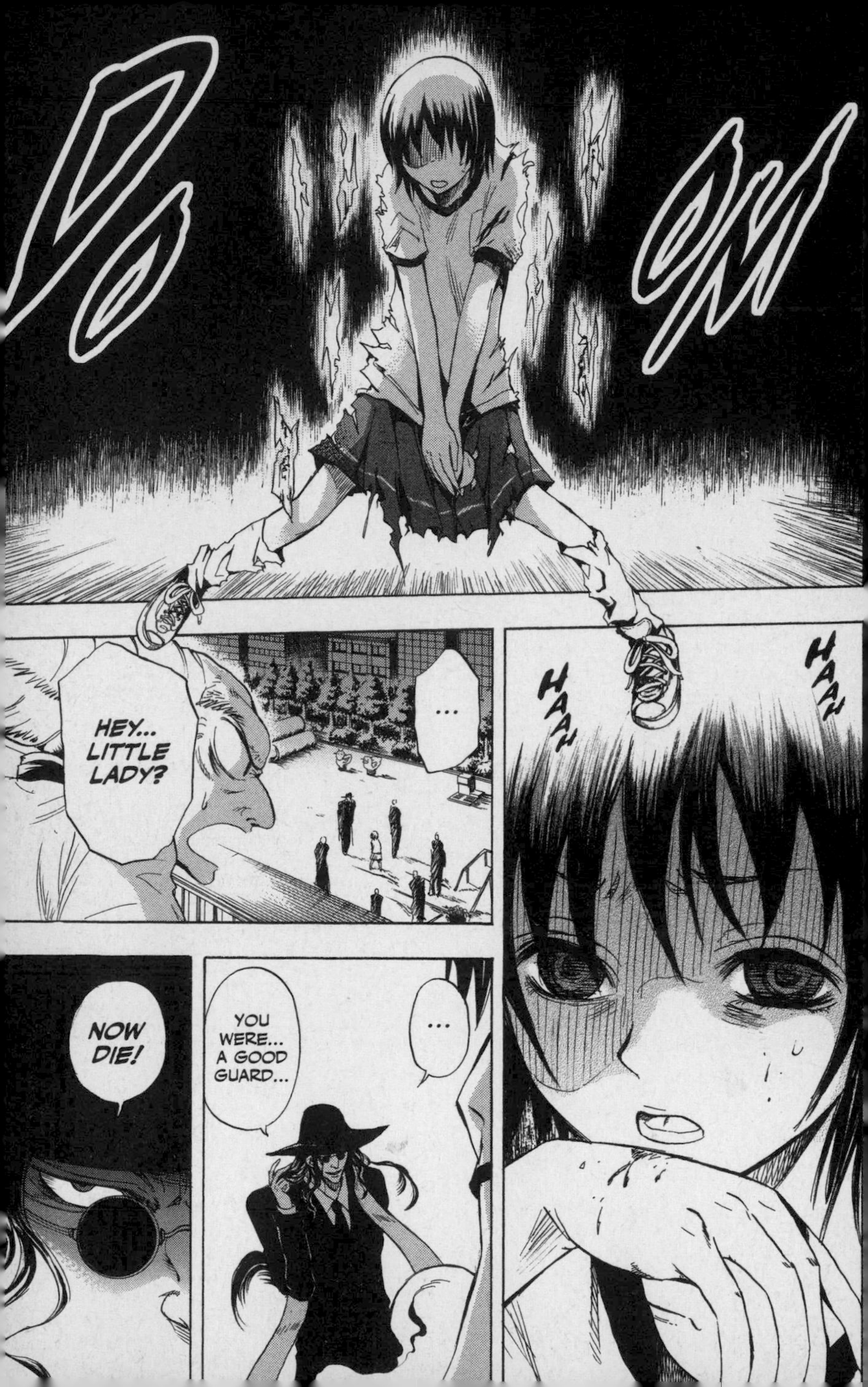
DOOM
HAAH
HAAH
...
HEY... LITTLE LADY?
...
YOU WERE... A GOOD GUARD...
NOW DIE!

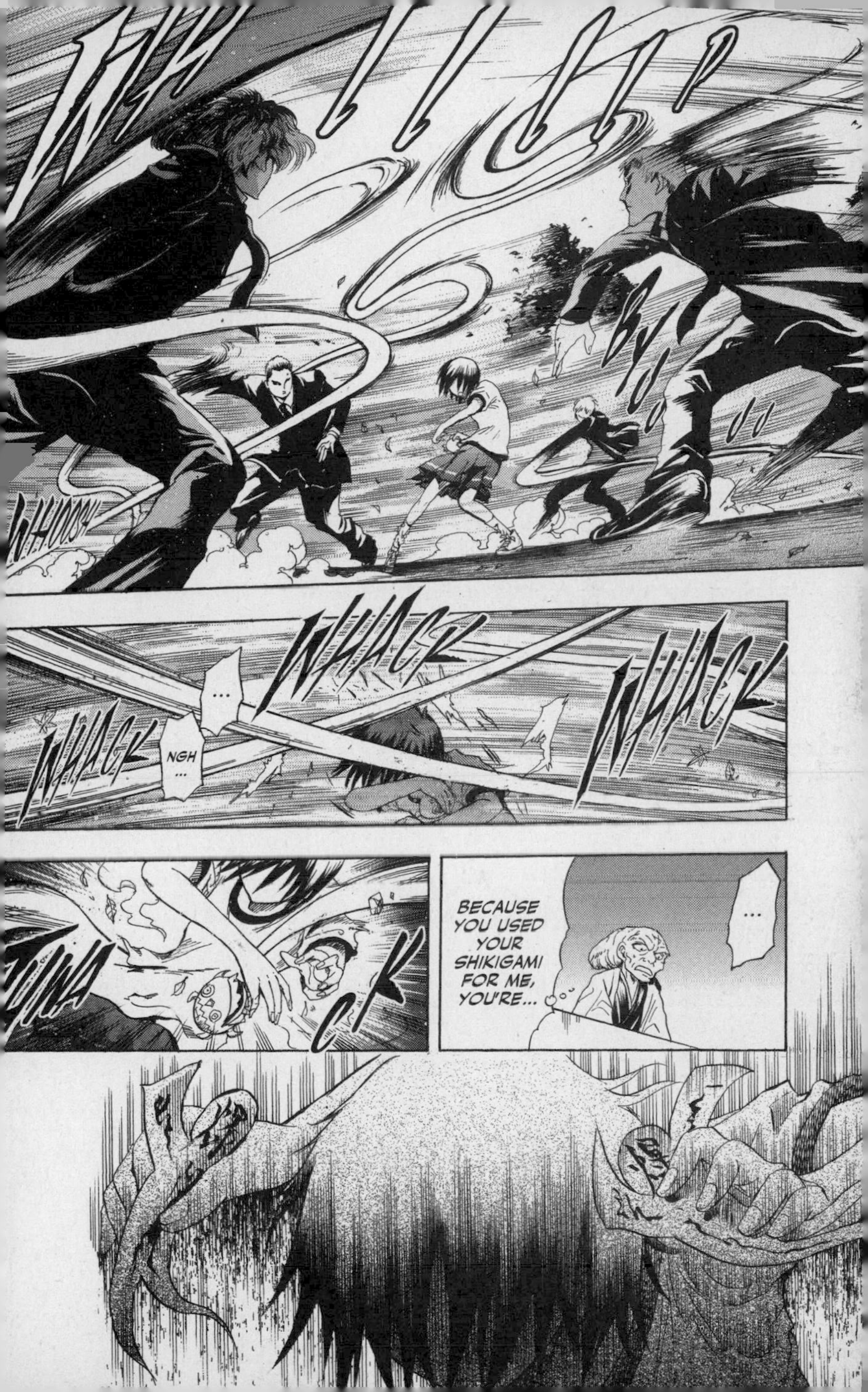
WHOOSH
WHACK
WHACK
...
NGH ...
WHACK
...
BECAUSE YOU USED YOUR SHIKIGAMI FOR ME, YOU'RE...

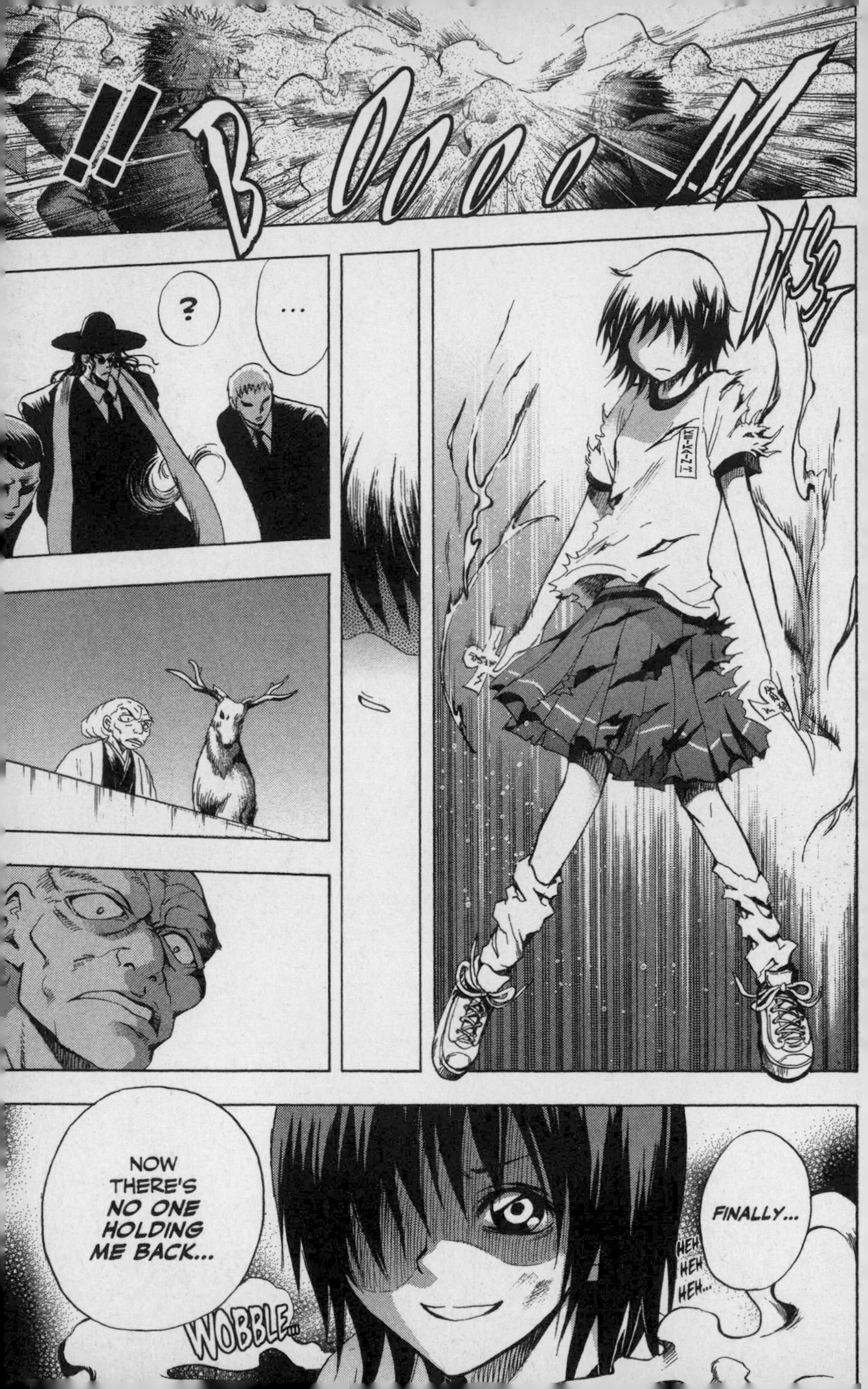
BOOOOM!!
...
?
FINALLY...
HEH HEH HEH...
NOW THERE'S NO ONE HOLDING ME BACK...
WOBBLE...

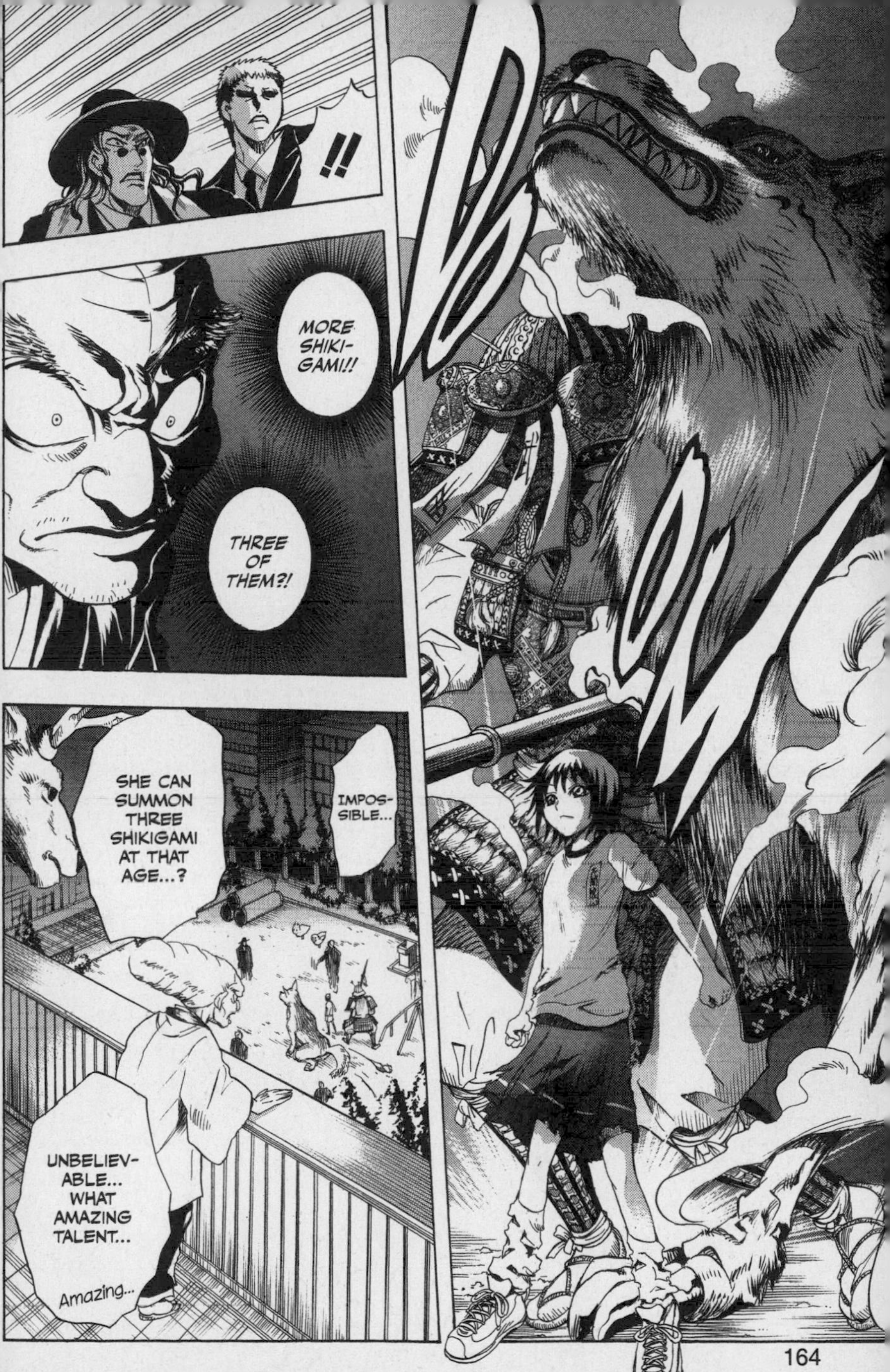
!!
MORE SHIKI-GAMI!!
THREE OF THEM?!
IMPOS-SIBLE...
SHE CAN SUMMON THREE SHIKIGAMI AT THAT AGE...?
UNBELIEV-ABLE... WHAT AMAZING TALENT...
Amazing...

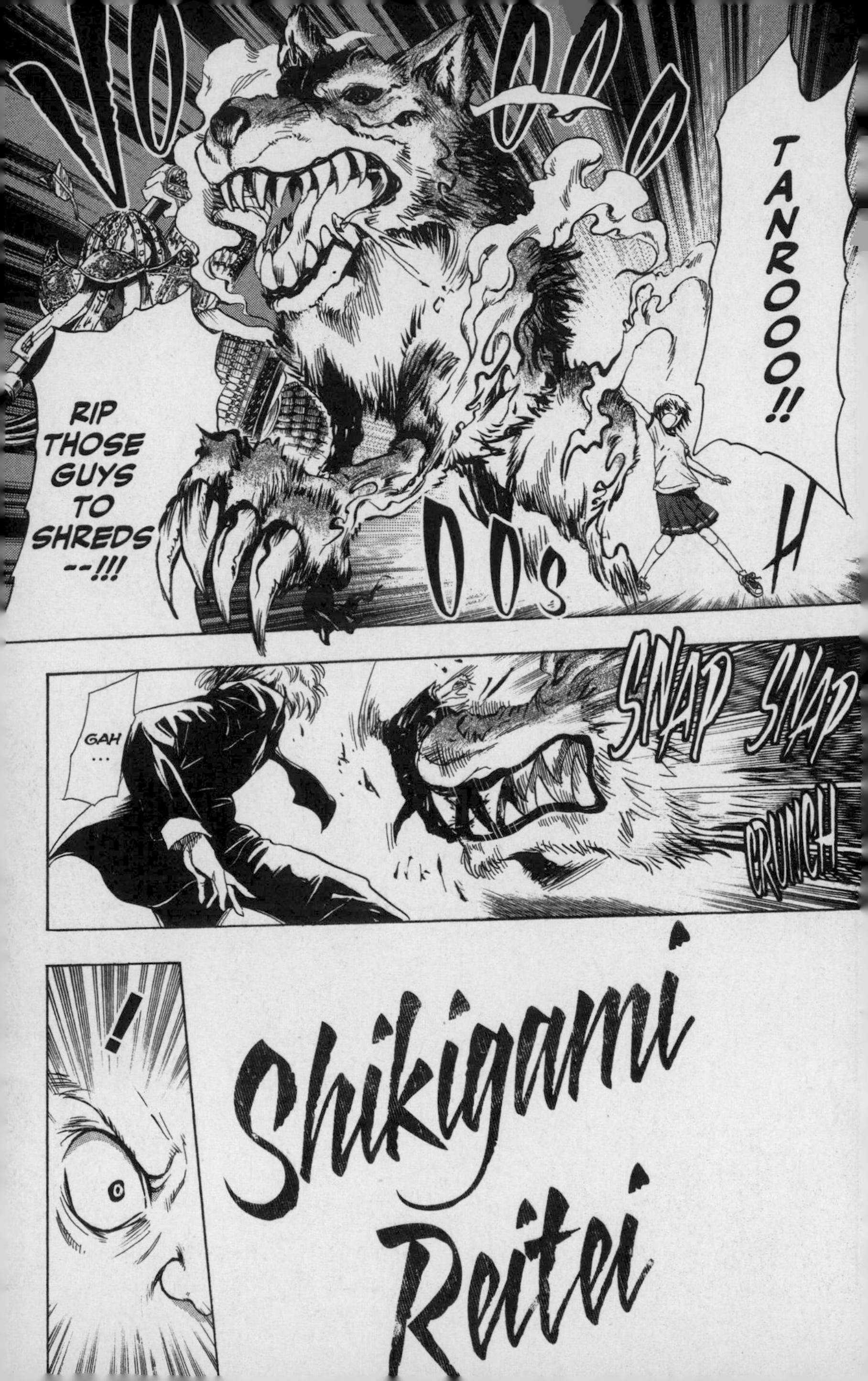
TANROOOO!!
VOOOOOOOOOSH
RIP THOSE GUYS TO SHREDS--!!!
SNAP SNAP
CRUNCH
GAH ...
Shikigami Reitei
!

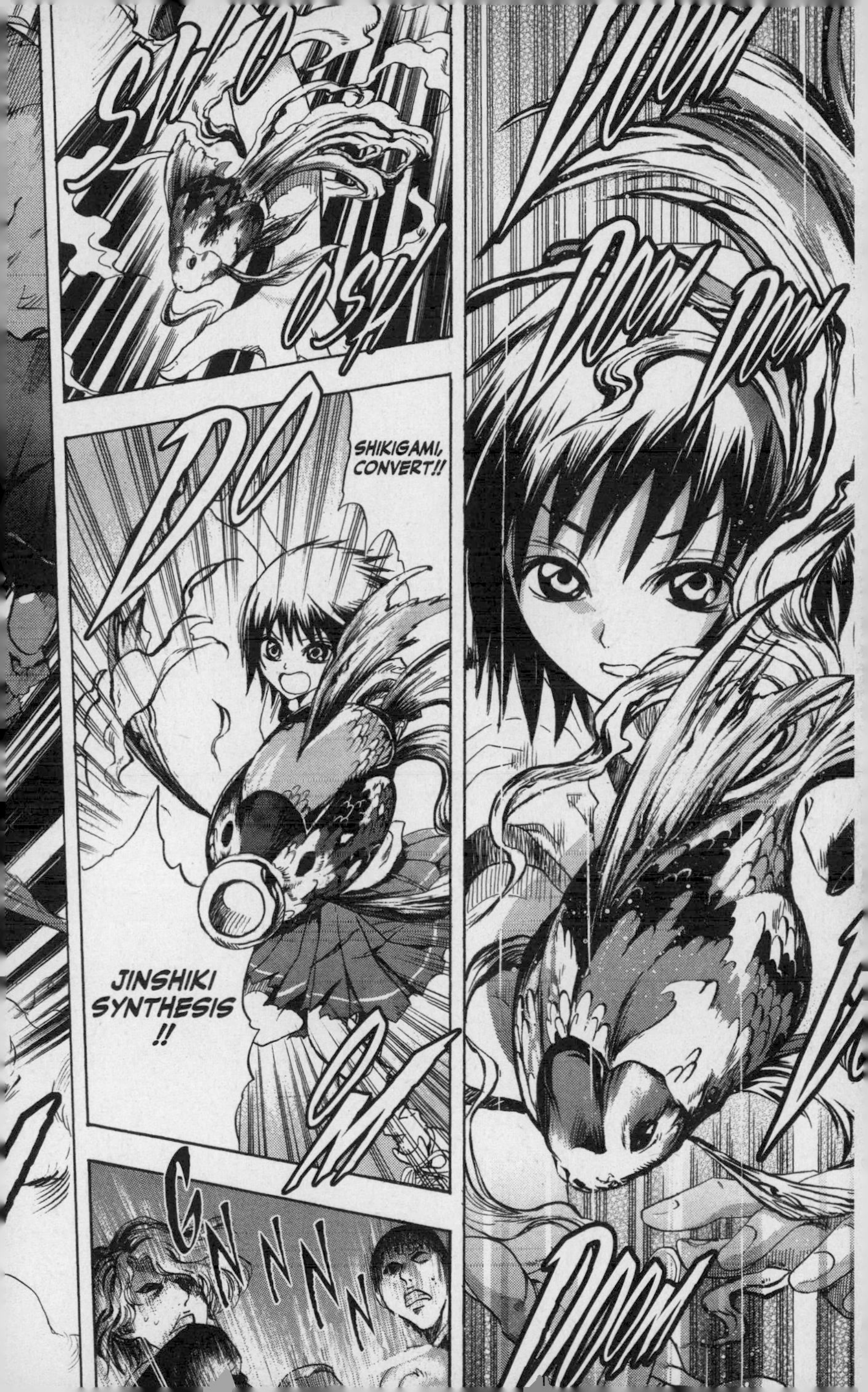
SHIKIGAMI, CONVERT!!
JINSHIKI SYNTHESIS !!

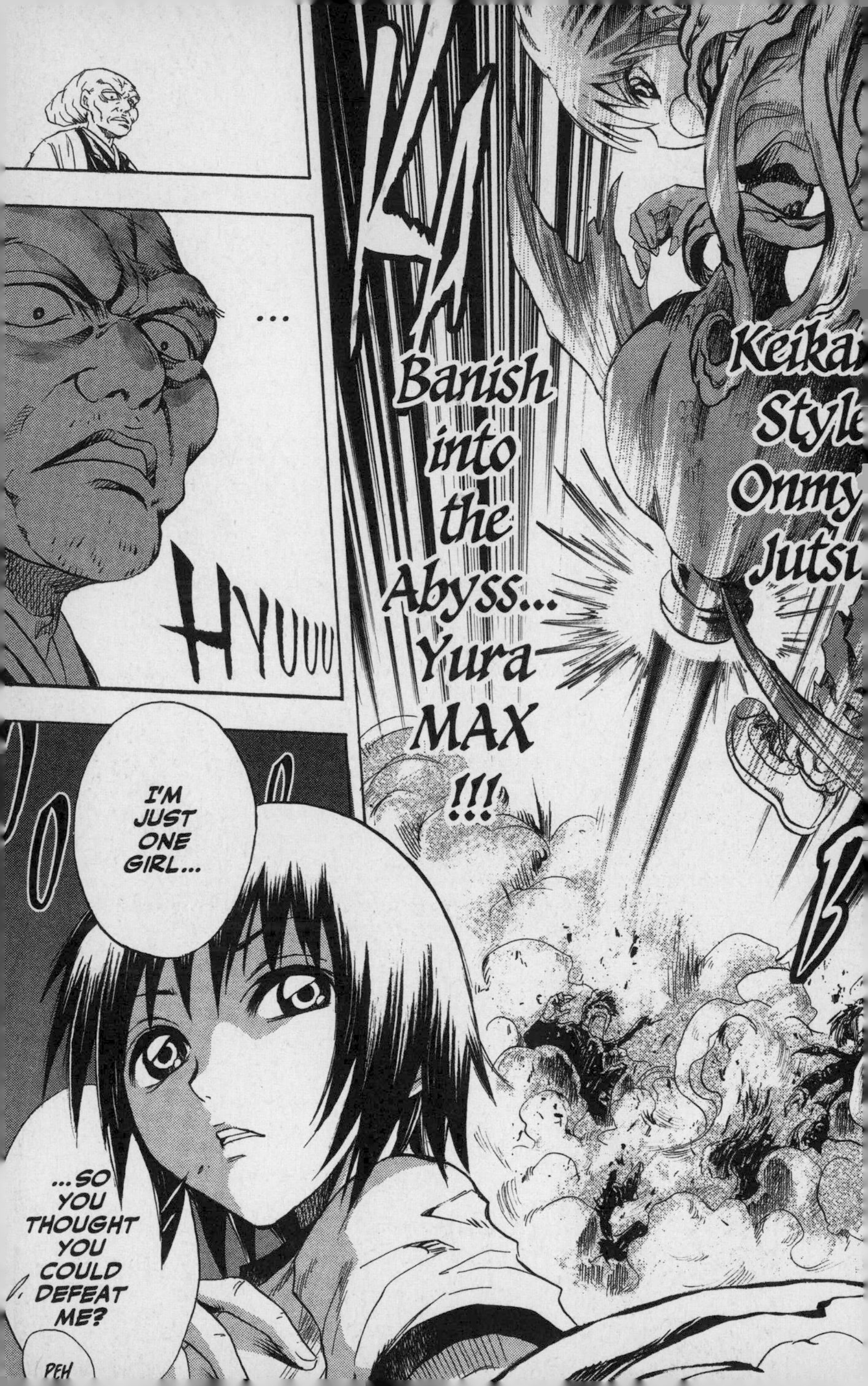

Keika Style Onmy Jutsu
Banish into the Abyss... Yura MAX!!!
...
HYUUU
I'M JUST ONE GIRL...
...SO YOU THOUGHT YOU COULD DEFEAT ME?
PEH

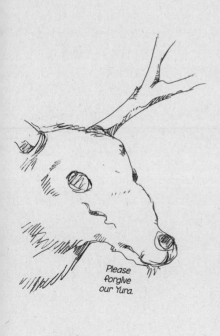

Please
forgive
our Yura.

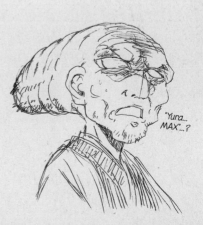

"Yura...
MAX"...?

Act 24: Nurarihyon's Power

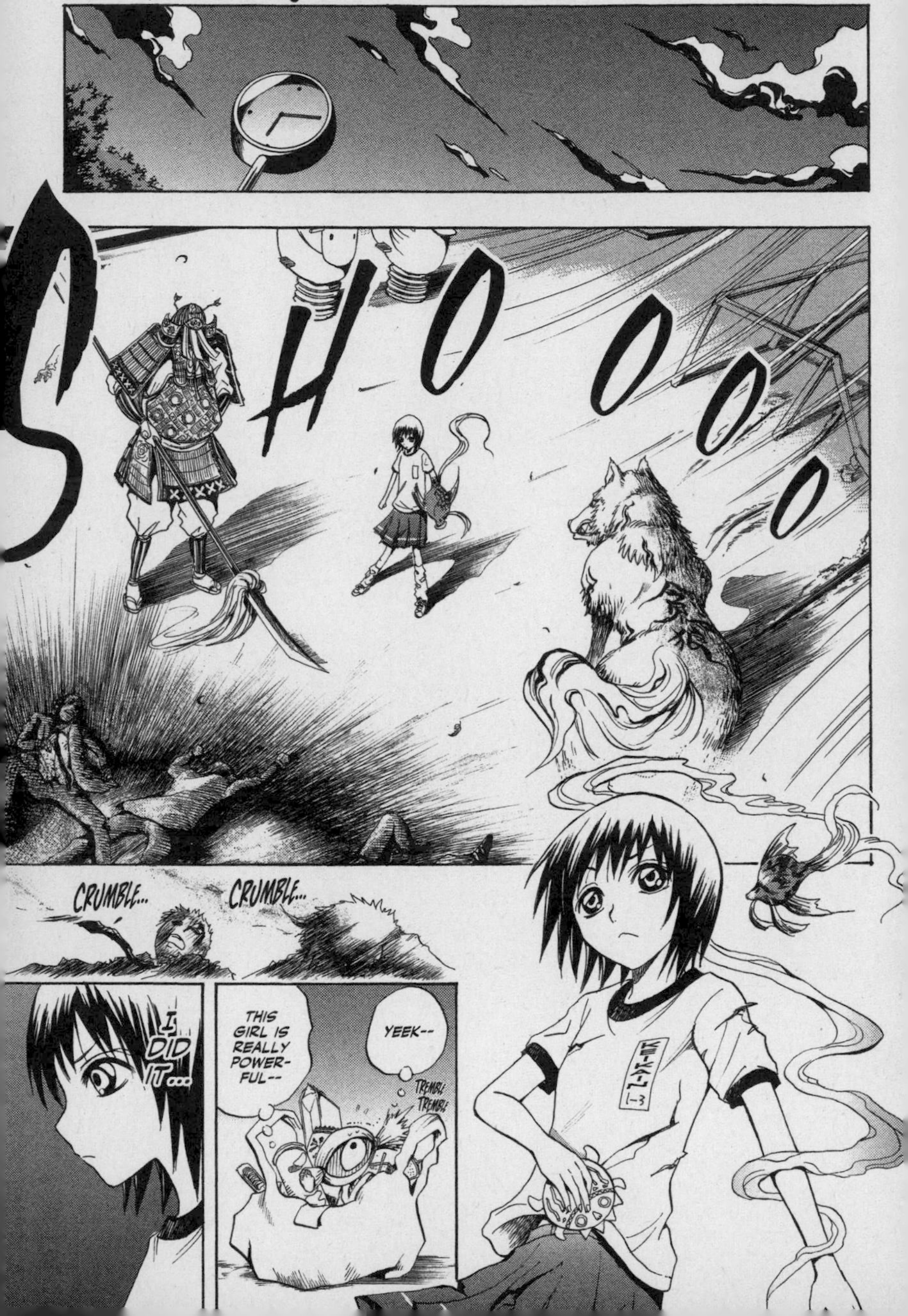
SHOOOOO
CRUMBLE... CRUMBLE...
YEEK--
THIS GIRL IS REALLY POWER-FUL--
TREMBLE TREMBLE
I DID IT...

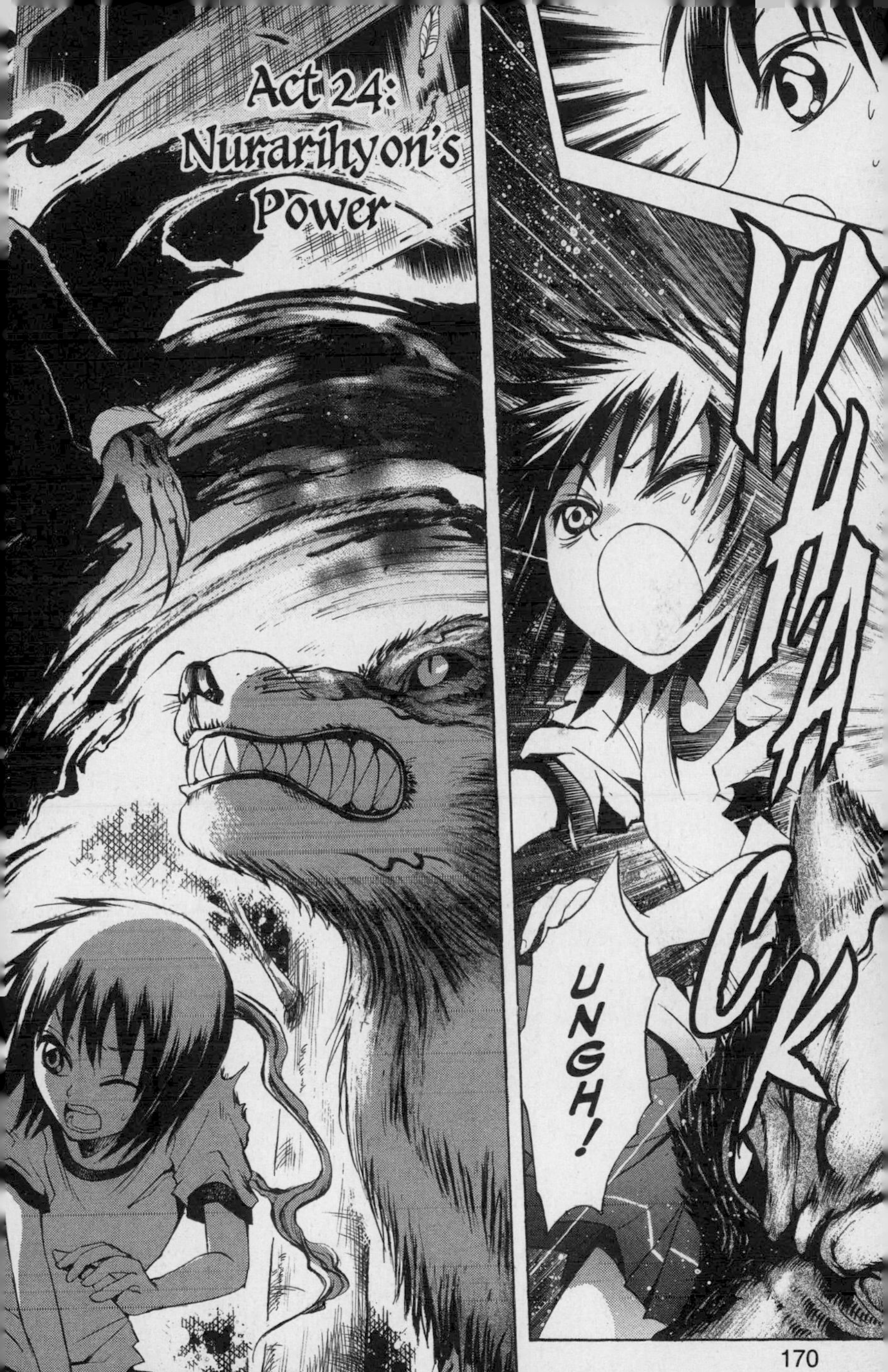
WHACK
UNGH!
Act 24: Nurarihyon's Power

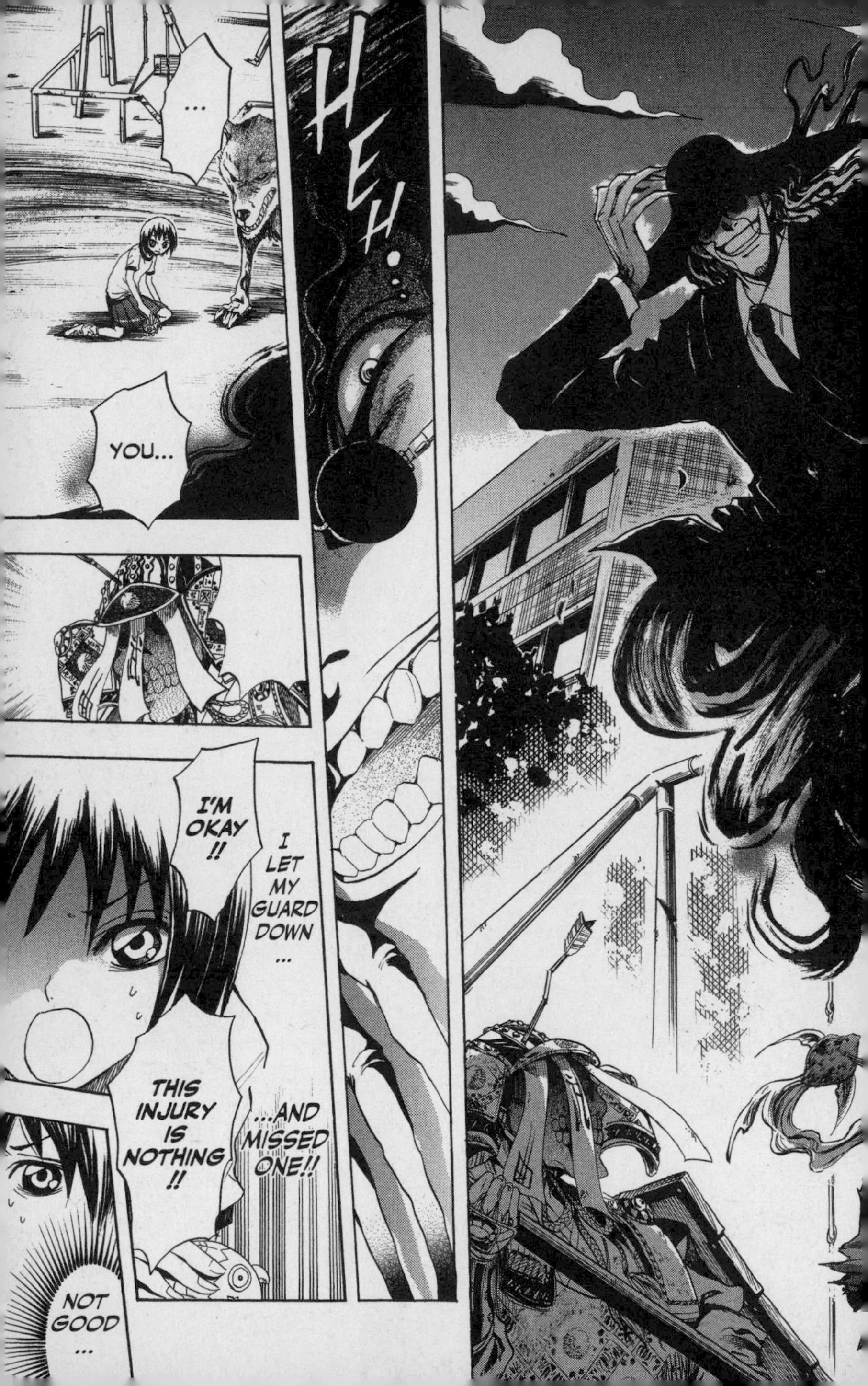
HEH
...
YOU...
I LET MY GUARD DOWN...
...AND MISSED ONE!!
I'M OKAY!!
THIS INJURY IS NOTHING!!
NOT GOOD...

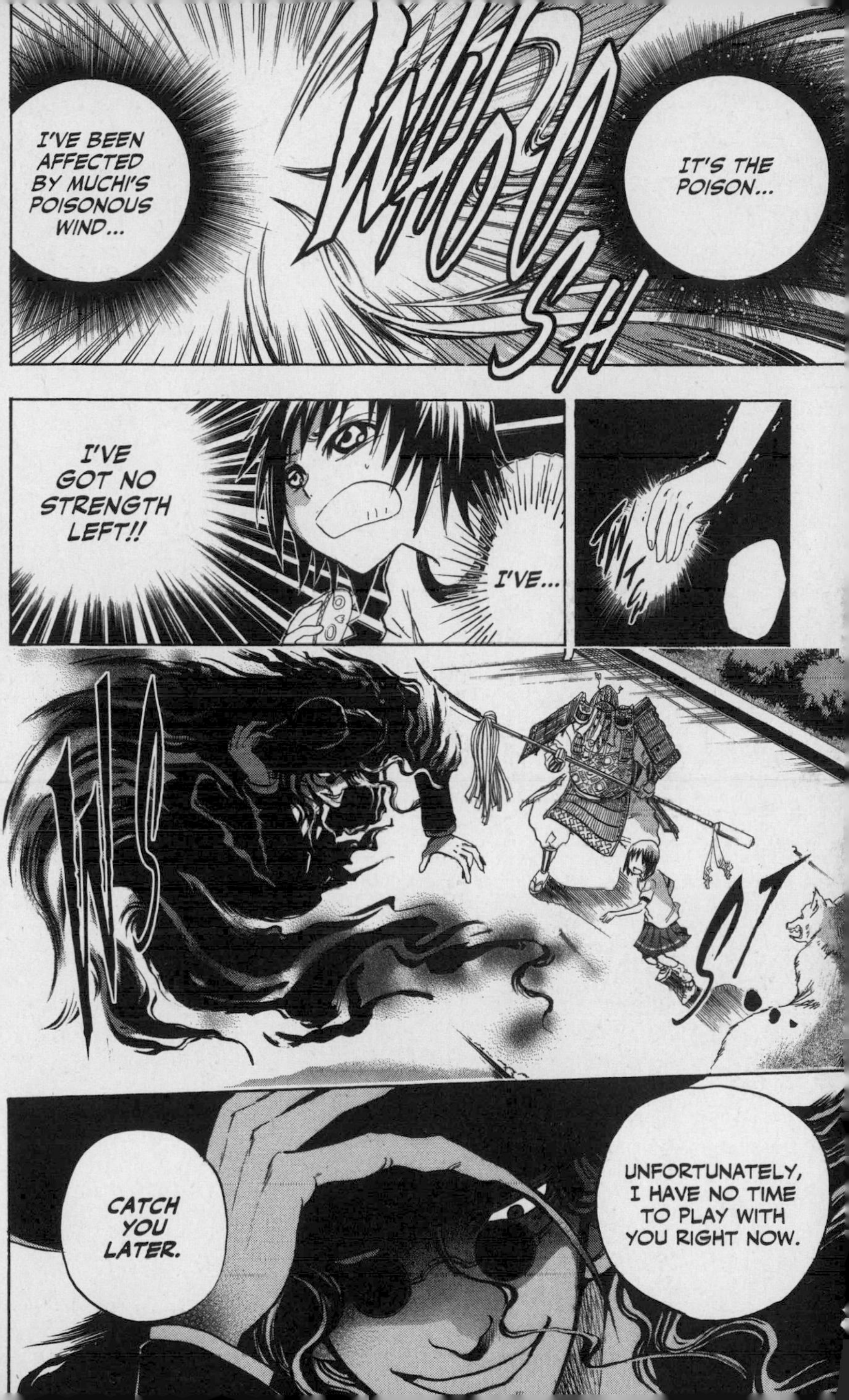
IT'S THE POISON...
WHOOSH
I'VE BEEN AFFECTED BY MUCHI'S POISONOUS WIND...
I'VE...
I'VE GOT NO STRENGTH LEFT!!
UNFORTUNATELY, I HAVE NO TIME TO PLAY WITH YOU RIGHT NOW.
CATCH YOU LATER.

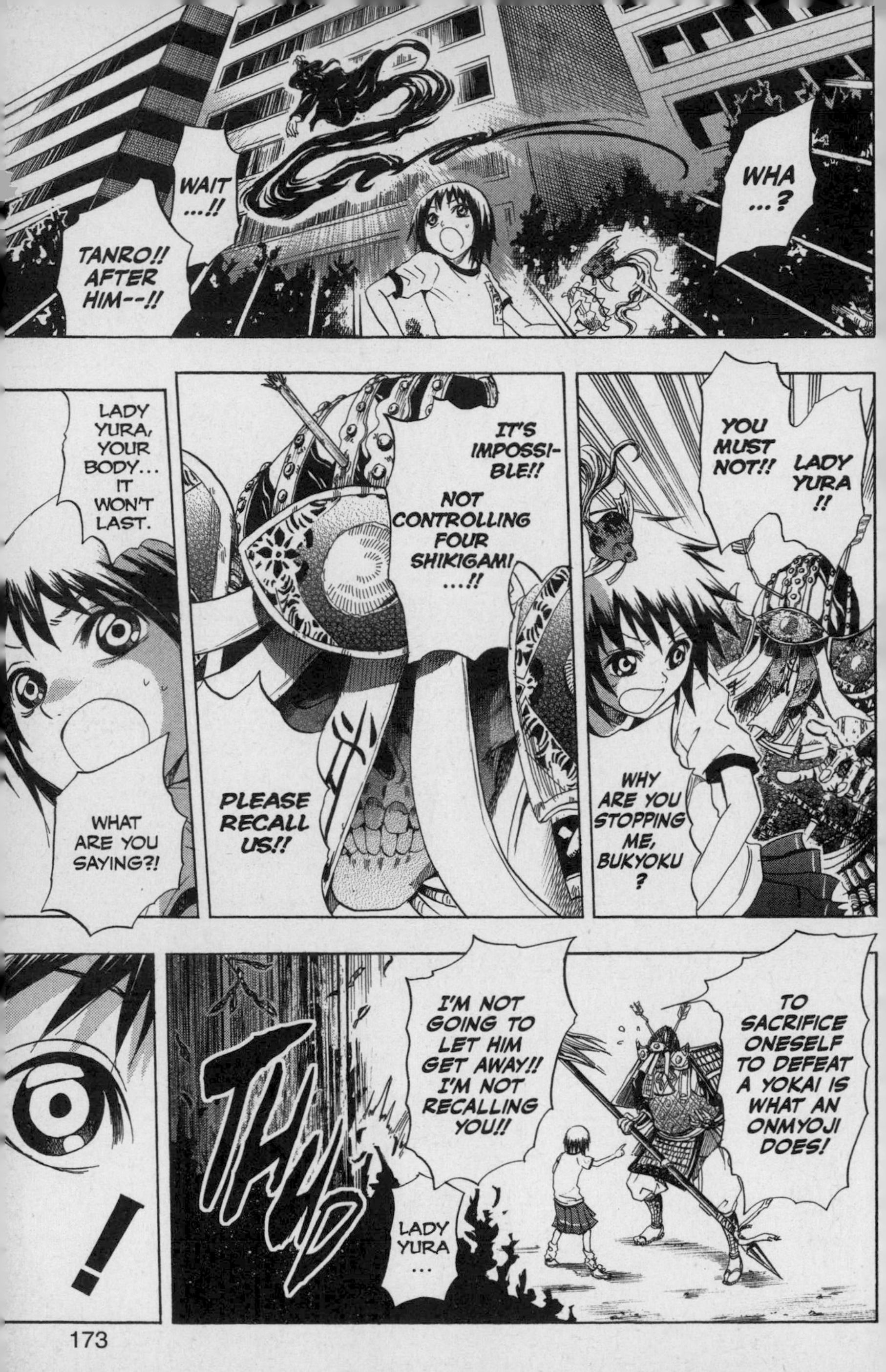
WHA ...?
WAIT ...!!
TANRO!! AFTER HIM--!!
LADY YURA!!
YOU MUST NOT!!
WHY ARE YOU STOPPING ME, BUKYOKU?
IT'S IMPOSSI-BLE!!
NOT CONTROLLING FOUR SHIKIGAMI ...!!
PLEASE RECALL US!!
LADY YURA, YOUR BODY... IT WON'T LAST.
WHAT ARE YOU SAYING?!
TO SACRIFICE ONESELF TO DEFEAT A YOKAI IS WHAT AN ONMYOJI DOES!
I'M NOT GOING TO LET HIM GET AWAY!! I'M NOT RECALLING YOU!!
LADY YURA ...
THUD
!

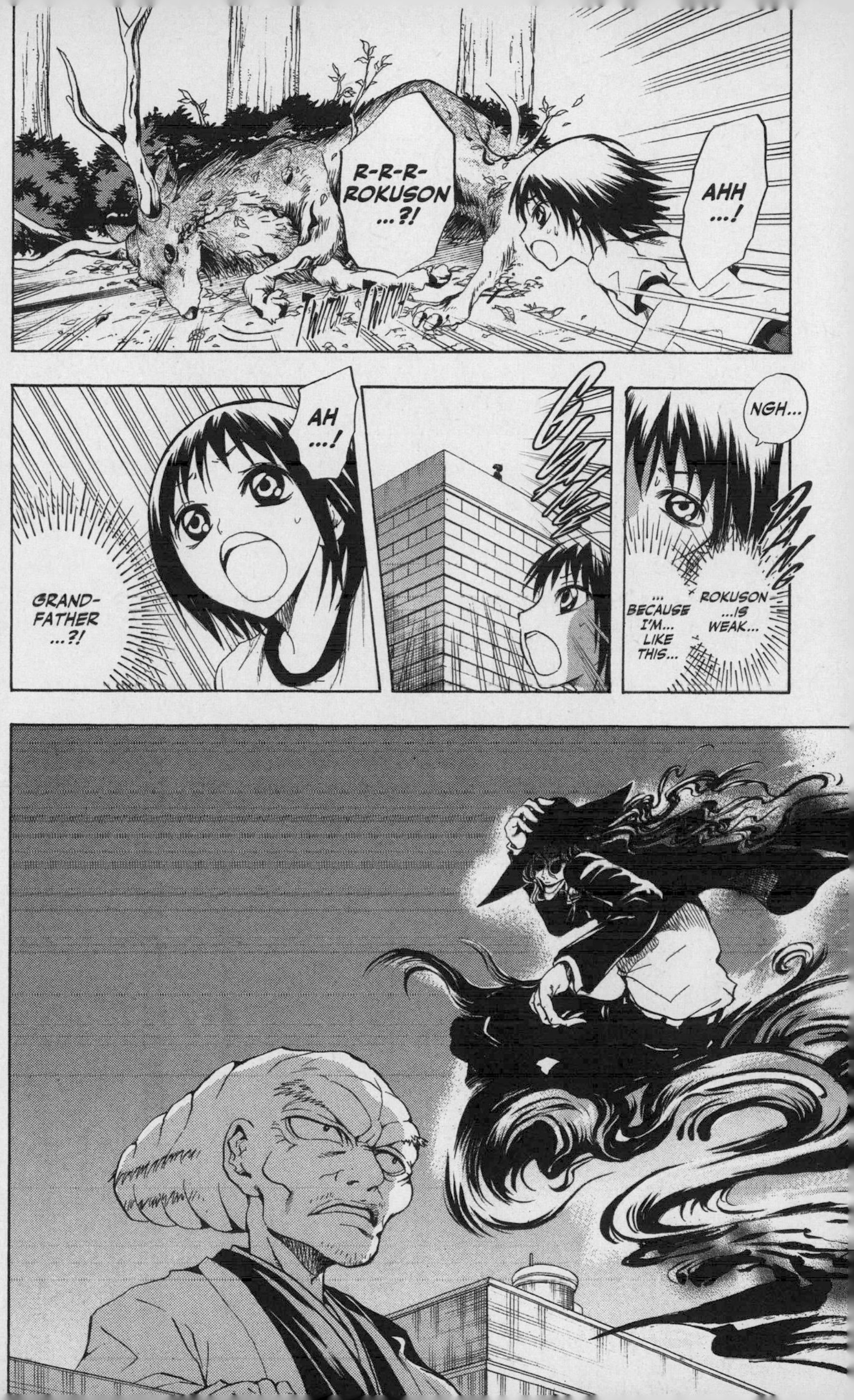
AHH ...!
R-R-R-ROKUSON ...?!
TWITCH TWITCH
NGH...
ROKUSON ...IS WEAK...
... BECAUSE I'M... LIKE THIS...
AH ...!
GRAND-FATHER ...?!

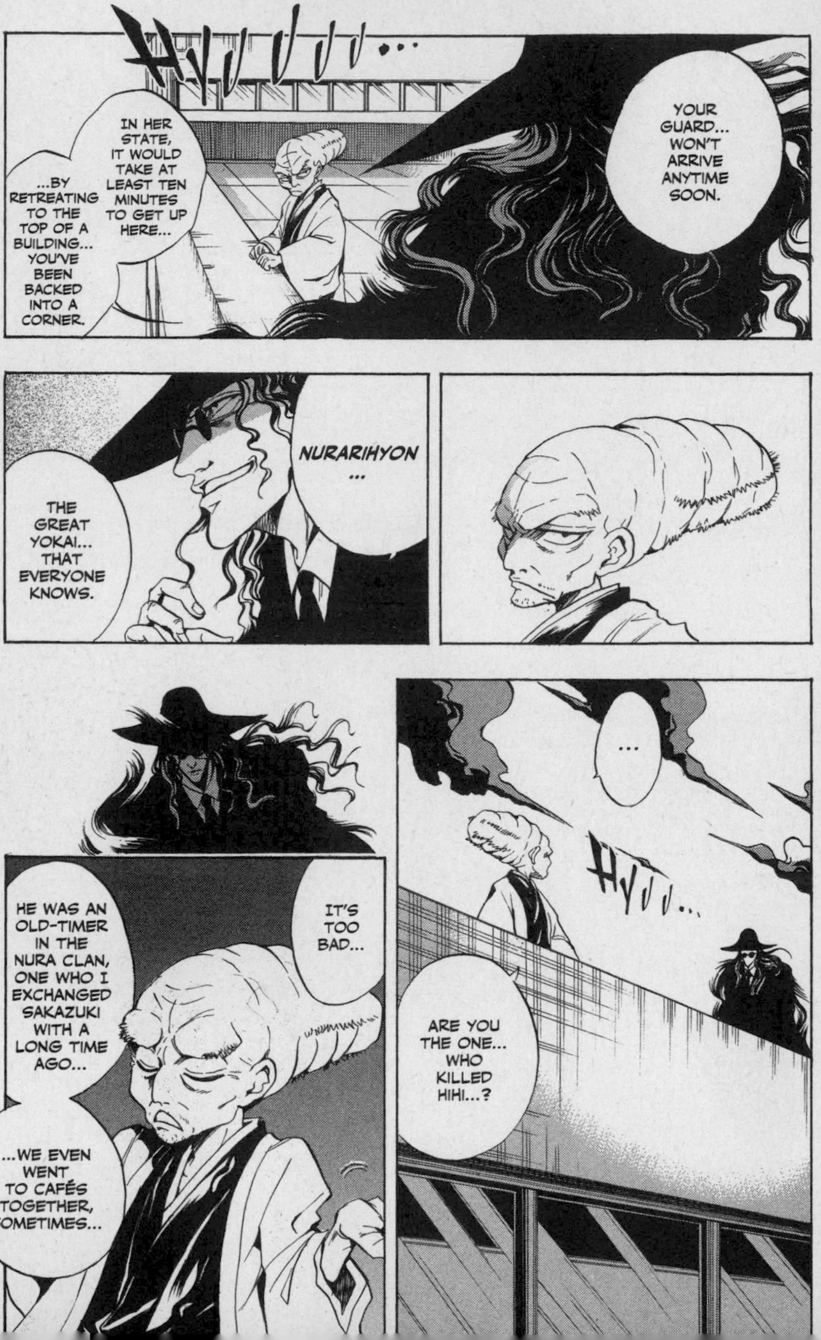
HYUUUUU...
YOUR GUARD... WON'T ARRIVE ANYTIME SOON.
IN HER STATE, IT WOULD TAKE AT LEAST TEN MINUTES TO GET UP HERE...
...BY RETREATING TO THE TOP OF A BUILDING... YOU'VE BEEN BACKED INTO A CORNER.
NURARIHYON...
THE GREAT YOKAI... THAT EVERYONE KNOWS.
...
HYUU...
ARE YOU THE ONE... WHO KILLED HIHI...?
IT'S TOO BAD...
HE WAS AN OLD-TIMER IN THE NURA CLAN, ONE WHO I EXCHANGED SAKAZUKI WITH A LONG TIME AGO...
...WE EVEN WENT TO CAFÉS TOGETHER, SOMETIMES...

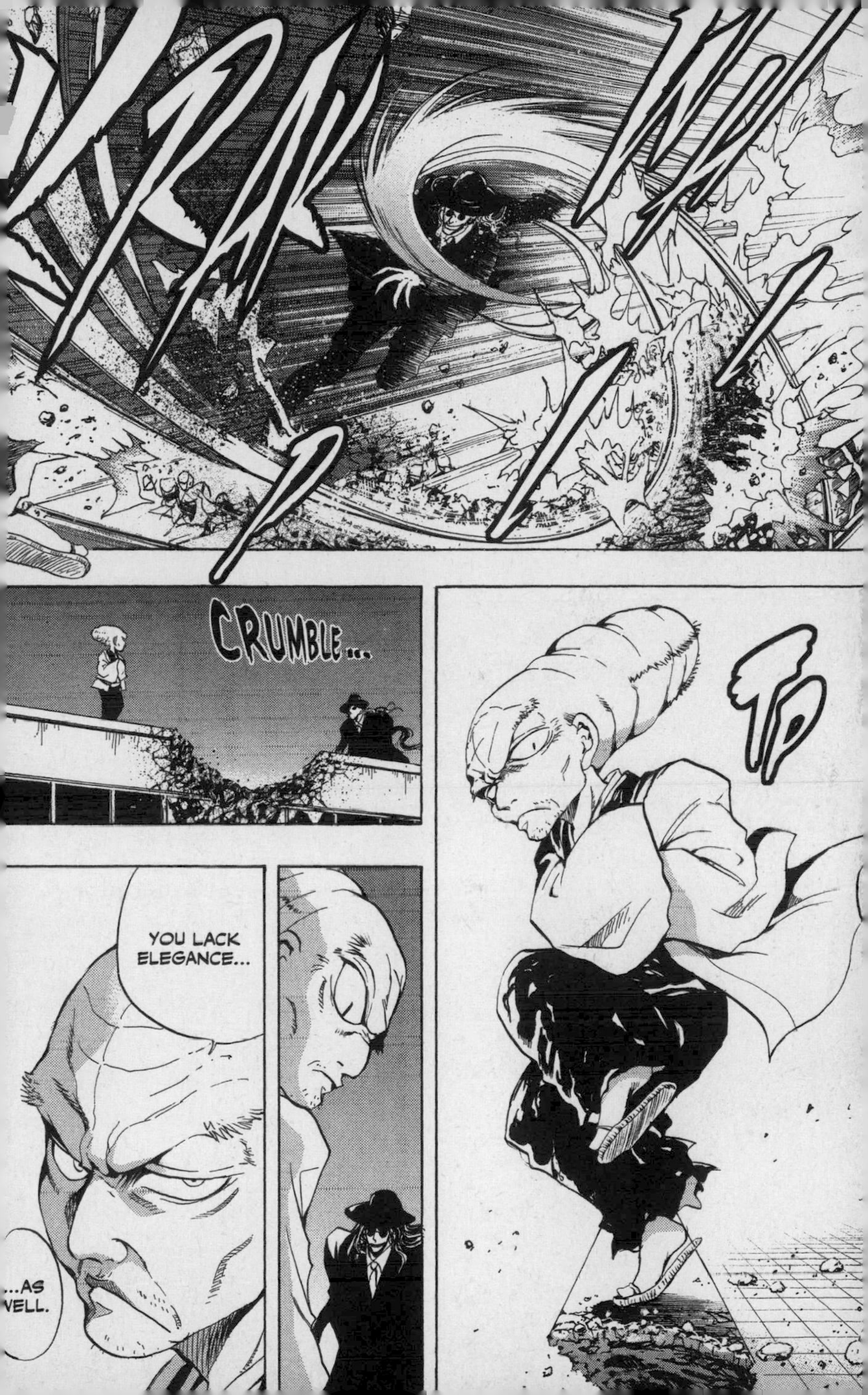
CRUMBLE...
YOU LACK ELEGANCE...
...AS WELL.

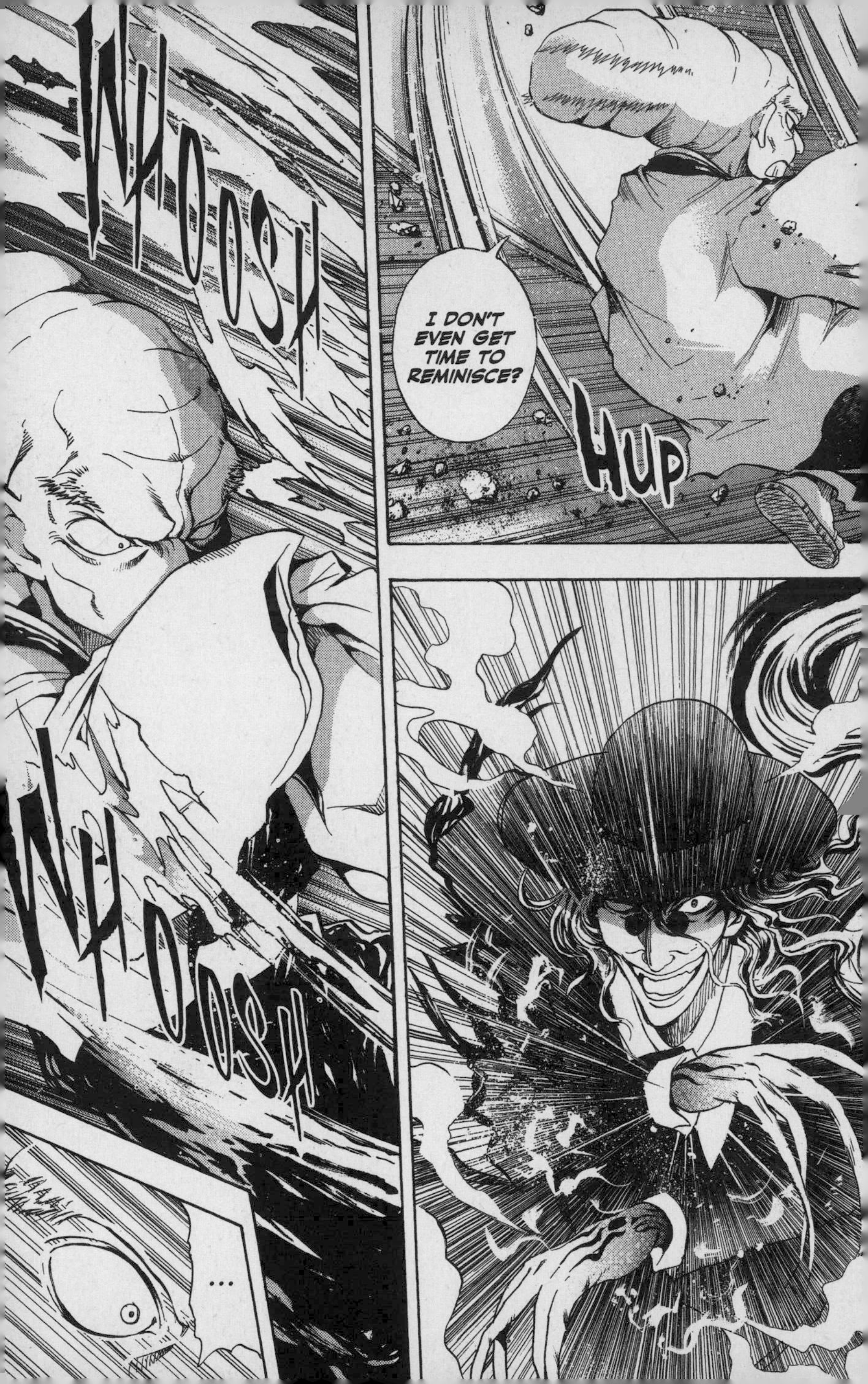
I DON'T EVEN GET TIME TO REMINISCE?
HUP
WHOOSH
WHOOSH
...

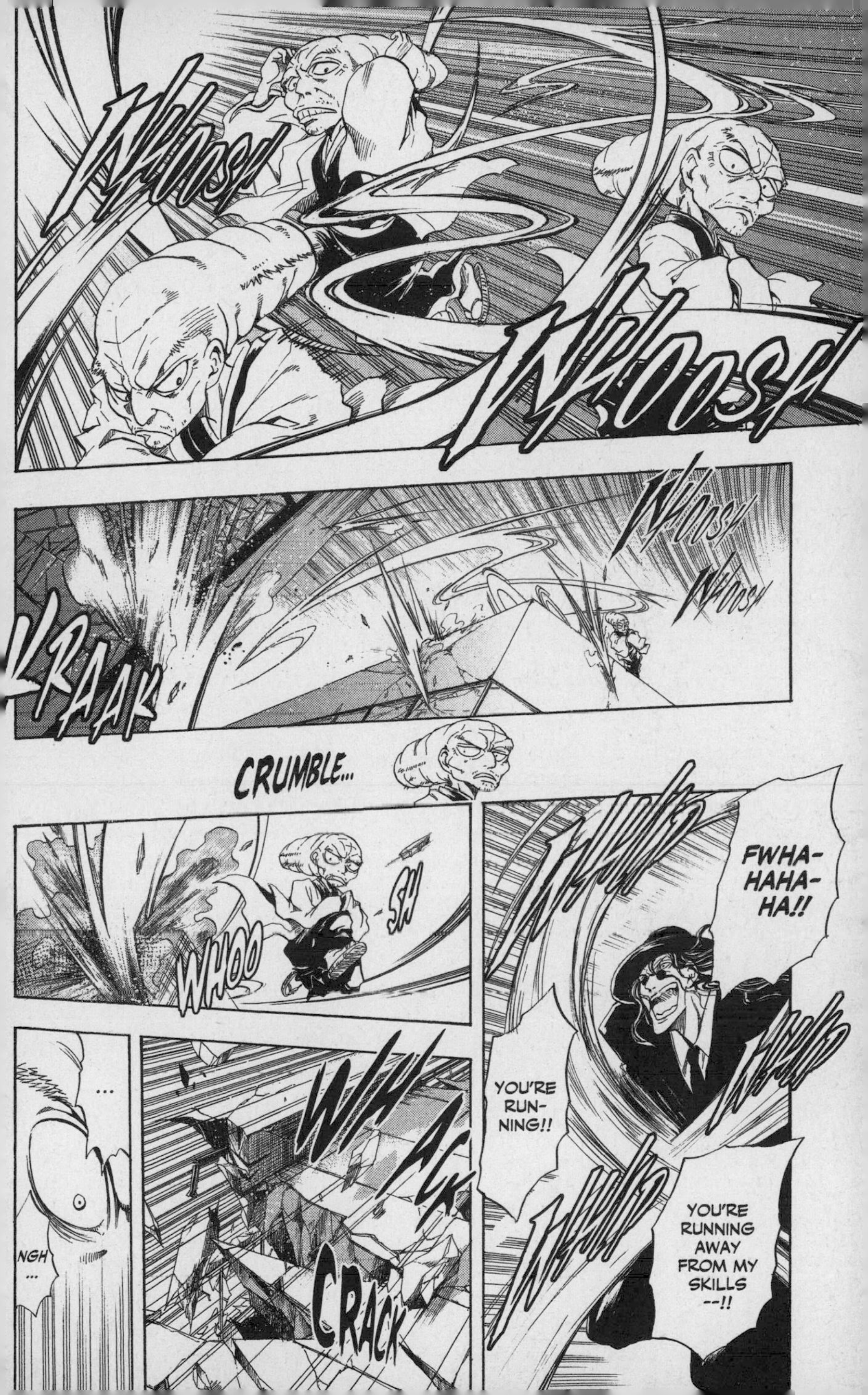
WHOOSH
WHOOSH
WHOSH
WHOSH
KRAAK
CRUMBLE...
FWHA-HAHAHA!!
YOU'RE RUN-NING!!
YOU'RE RUNNING AWAY FROM MY SKILLS--!!
WHOO-SH
WHACK
CRACK
...
NGH...

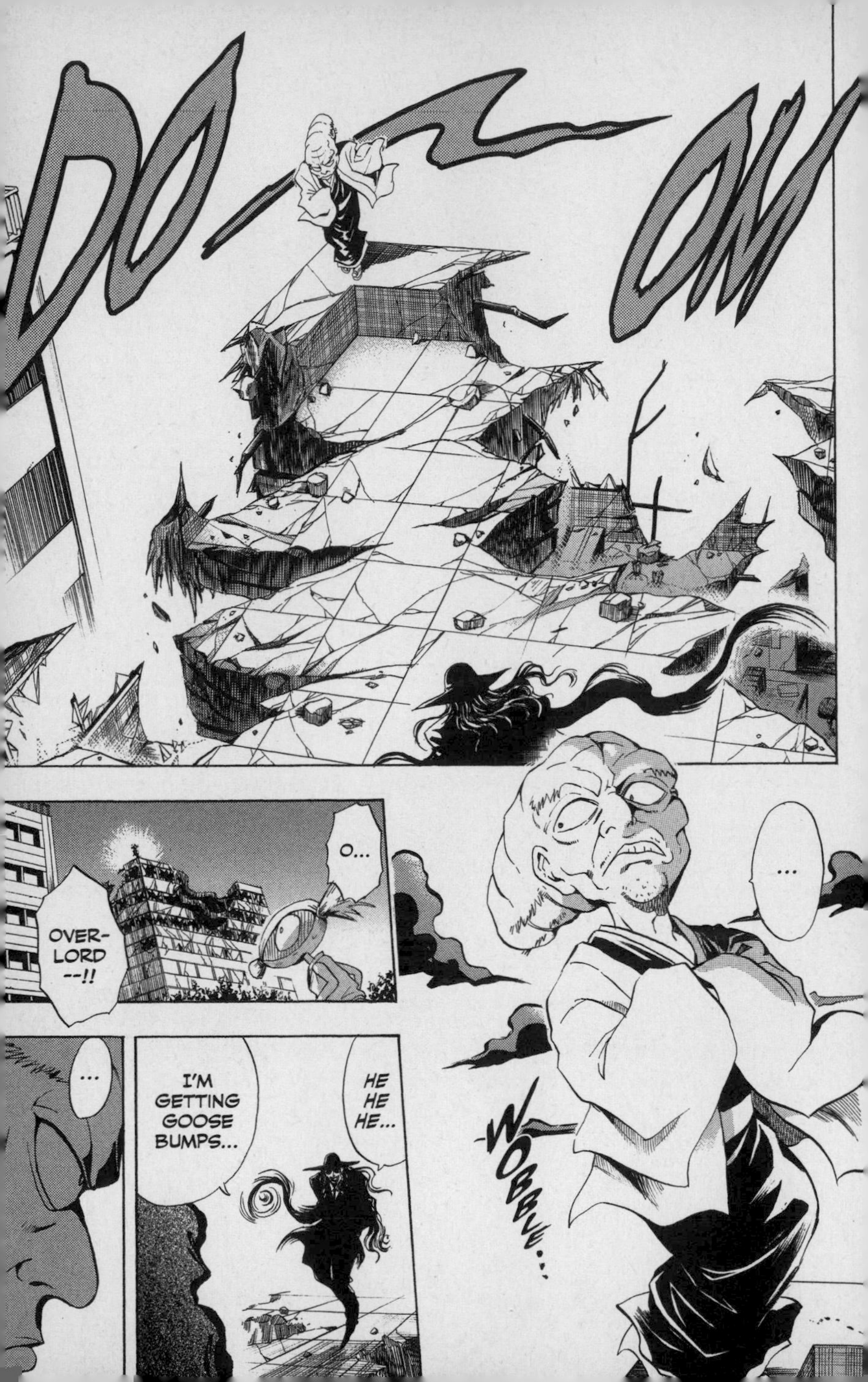
DO~ON
...
WOBBLE...
O...
OVER-LORD --!!
HE HE HE...
I'M GETTING GOOSE BUMPS...
...

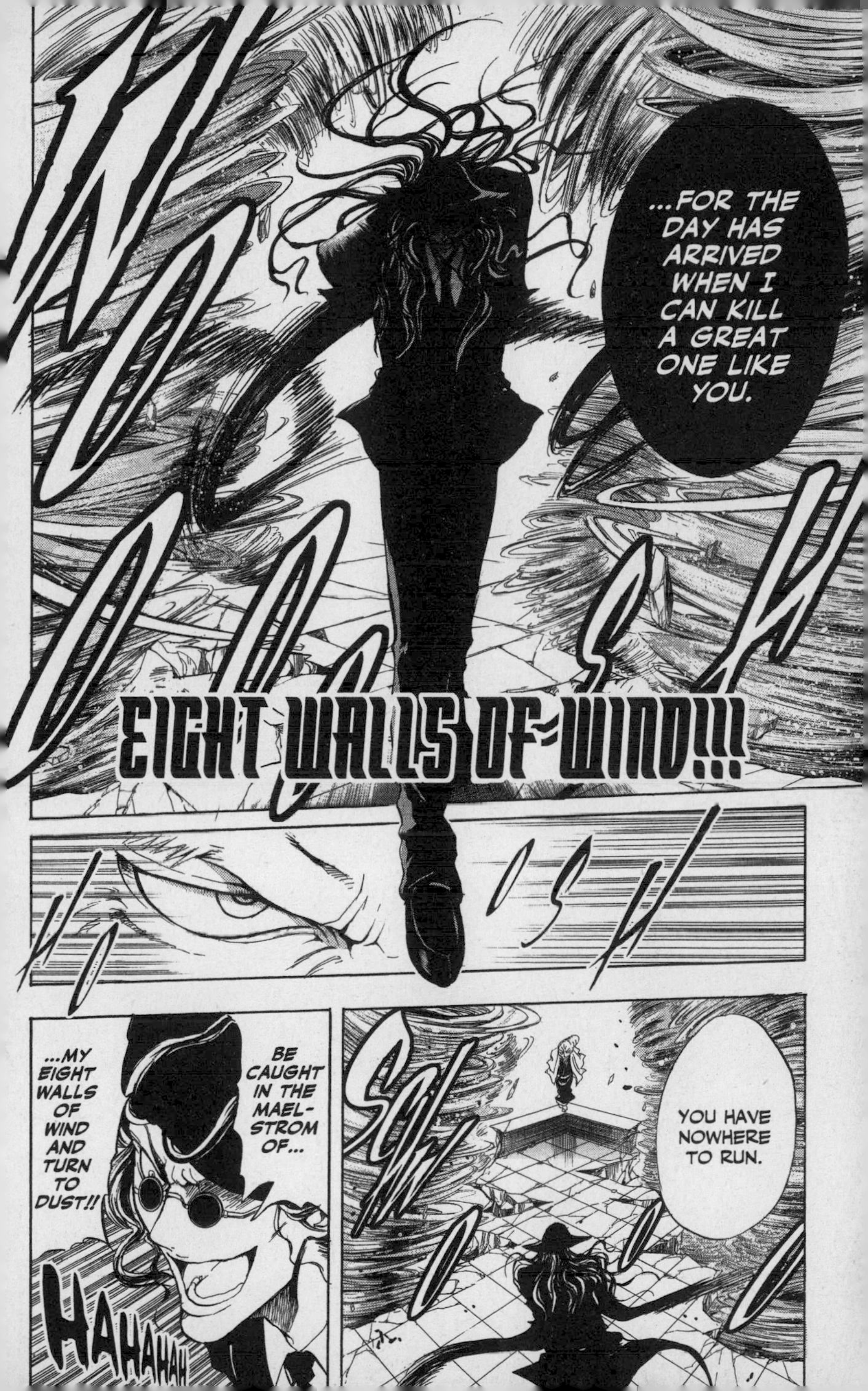
...FOR THE DAY HAS ARRIVED WHEN I CAN KILL A GREAT ONE LIKE YOU.
EIGHT WALLS OF WIND!!!
YOU HAVE NOWHERE TO RUN.
BE CAUGHT IN THE MAEL-STROM OF...
...MY EIGHT WALLS OF WIND AND TURN TO DUST!!
HAHAHAH

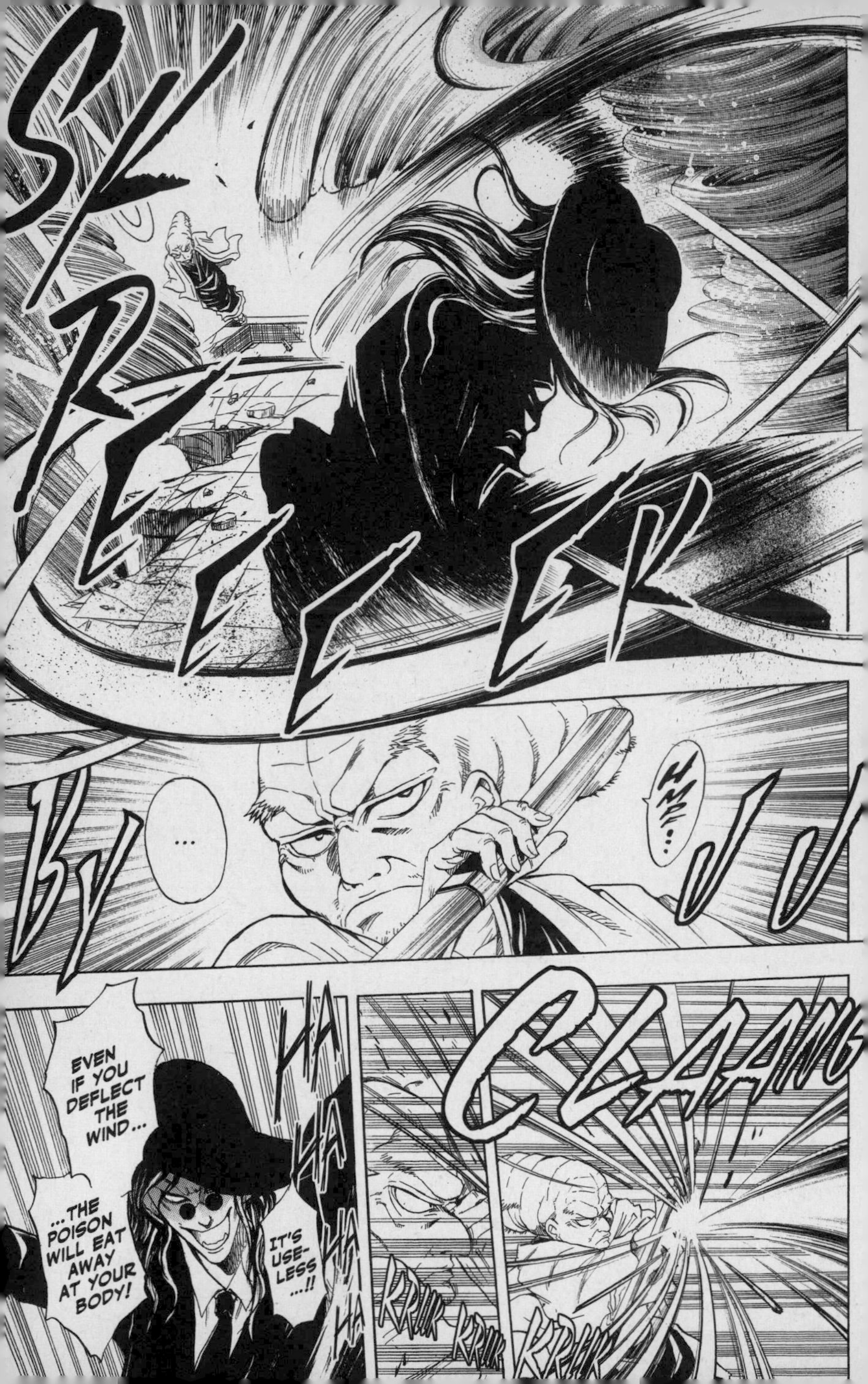
SKREEEEK
HMPH...
...
CLAANG
KRRK KRRK KRRK
HA HA HA HA
IT'S USELESS...!!
EVEN IF YOU DEFLECT THE WIND...
...THE POISON WILL EAT AWAY AT YOUR BODY!

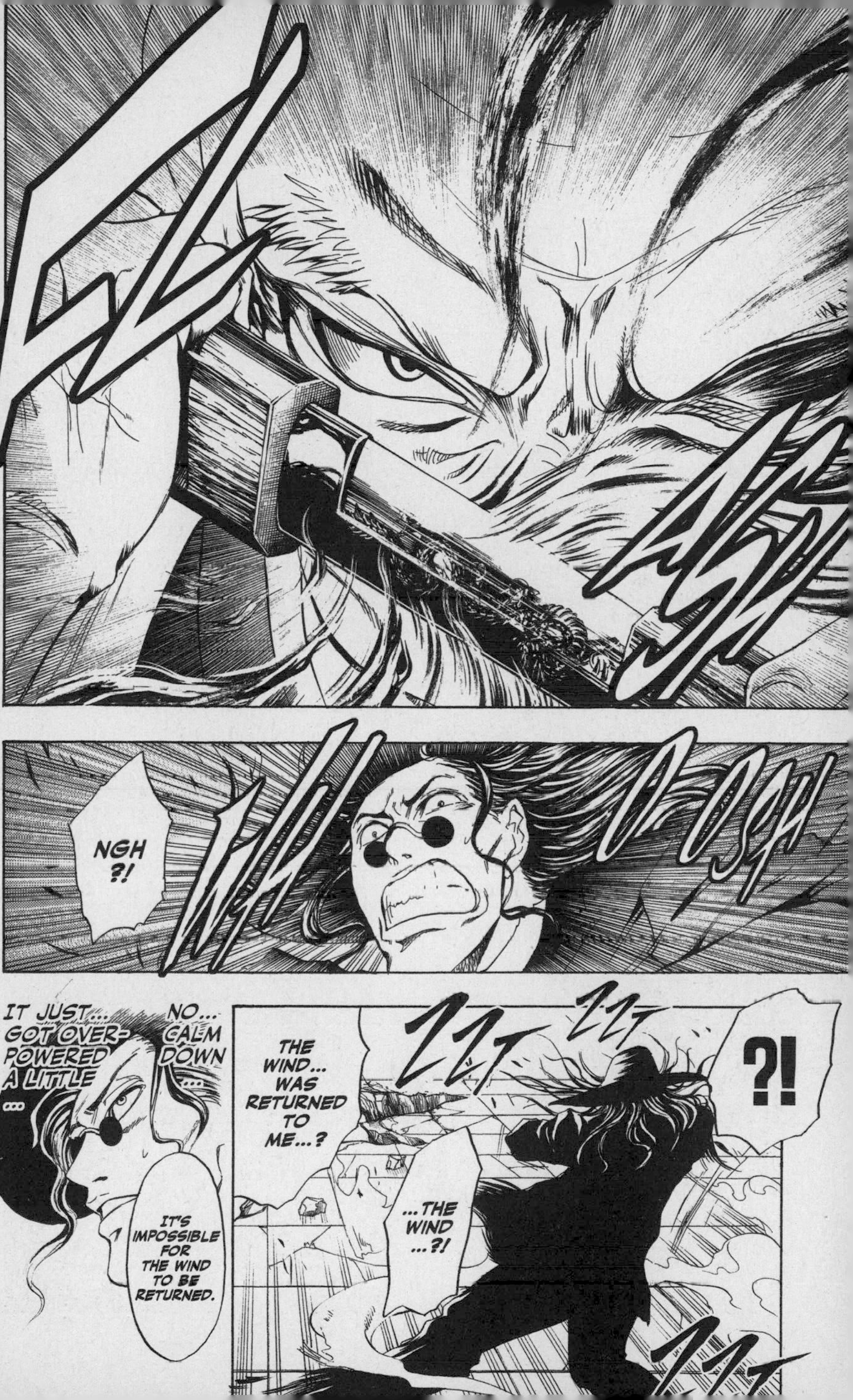
NGH ?!
?!
THE WIND... WAS RETURNED TO ME...?
...THE WIND ...?!
NO... CALM DOWN ...
IT JUST... GOT OVER-POWERED A LITTLE ...
IT'S IMPOSSIBLE FOR THE WIND TO BE RETURNED.

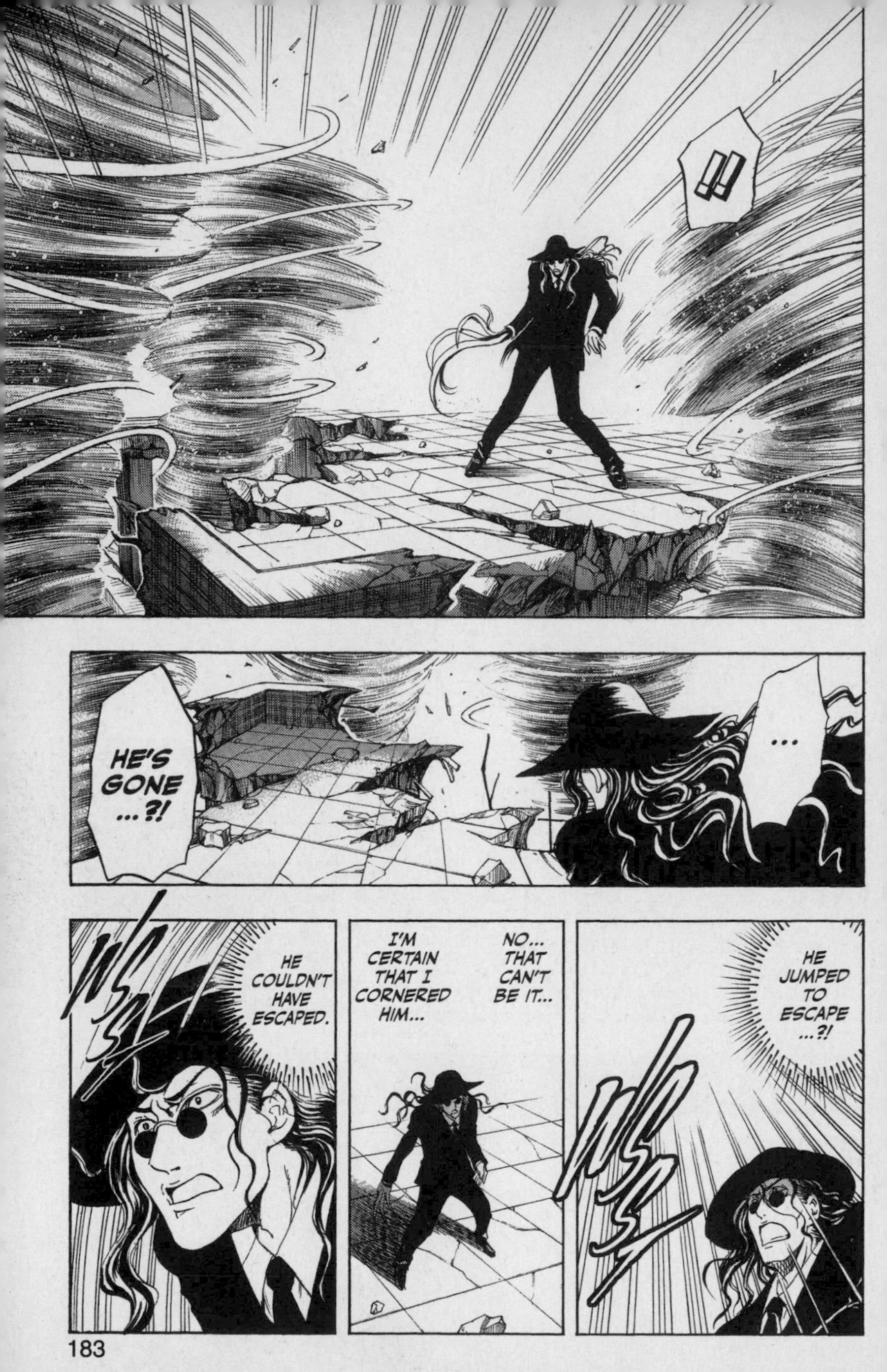
!!
...
HE'S GONE ...?!
HE JUMPED TO ESCAPE ...?!
NO... THAT CAN'T BE IT...
I'M CERTAIN THAT I CORNERED HIM...
HE COULDN'T HAVE ESCAPED.

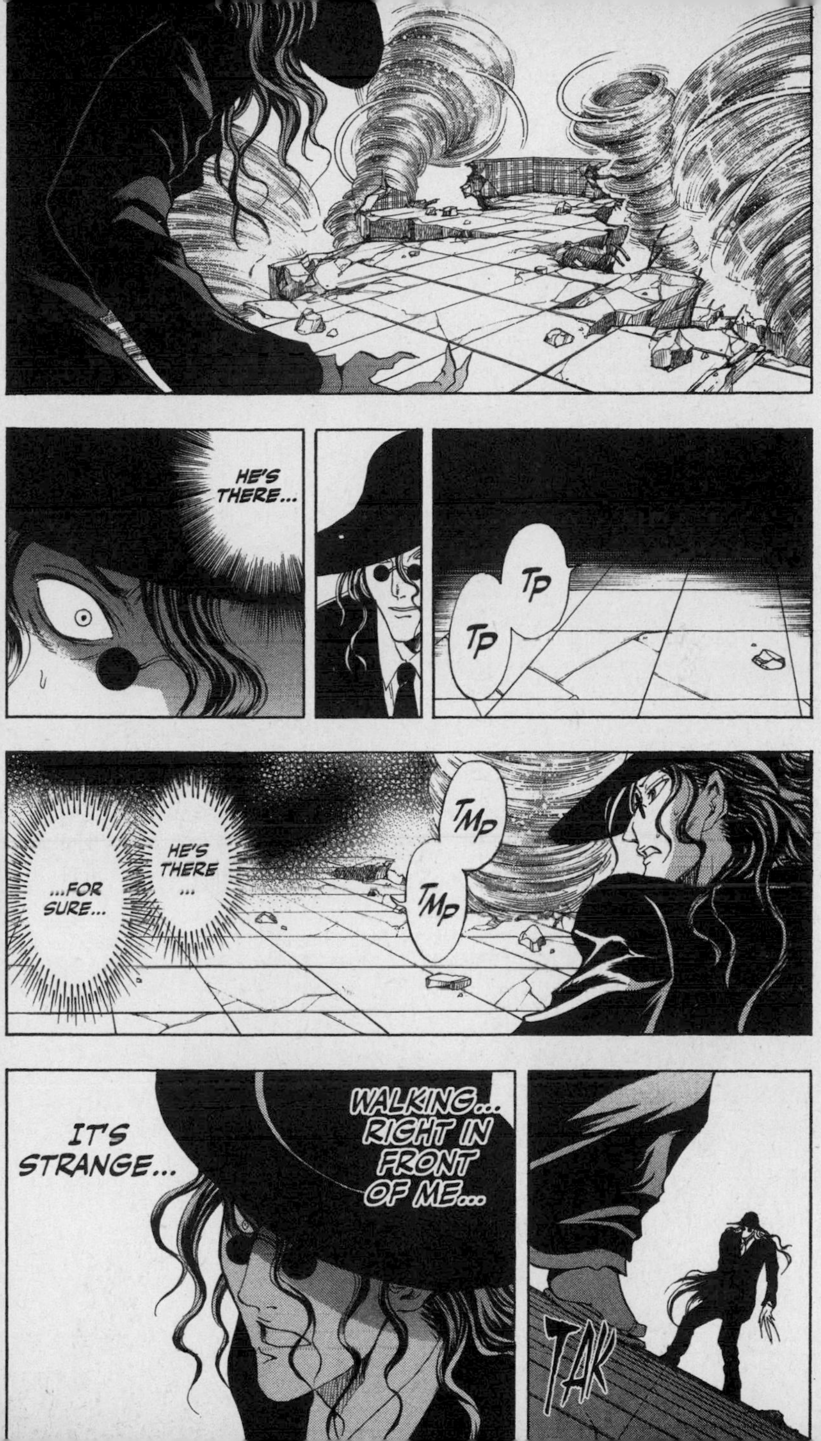
TP
TP
HE'S THERE...
TMP
TMP
HE'S THERE ...
...FOR SURE...
TAK
WALKING... RIGHT IN FRONT OF ME...
IT'S STRANGE...

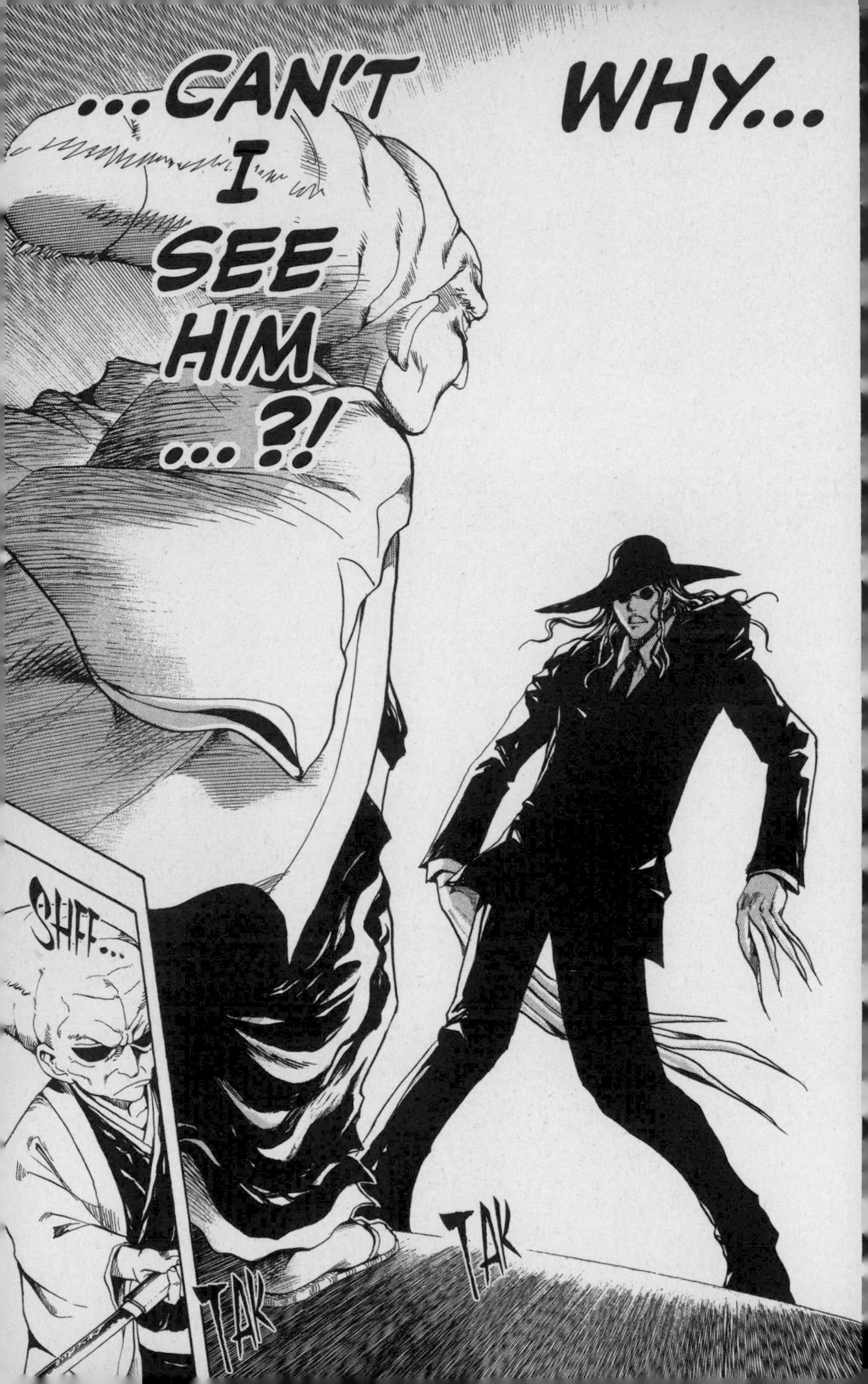
WHY...
...CAN'T I SEE HIM ...?!
SHFF...
TAK
TAK

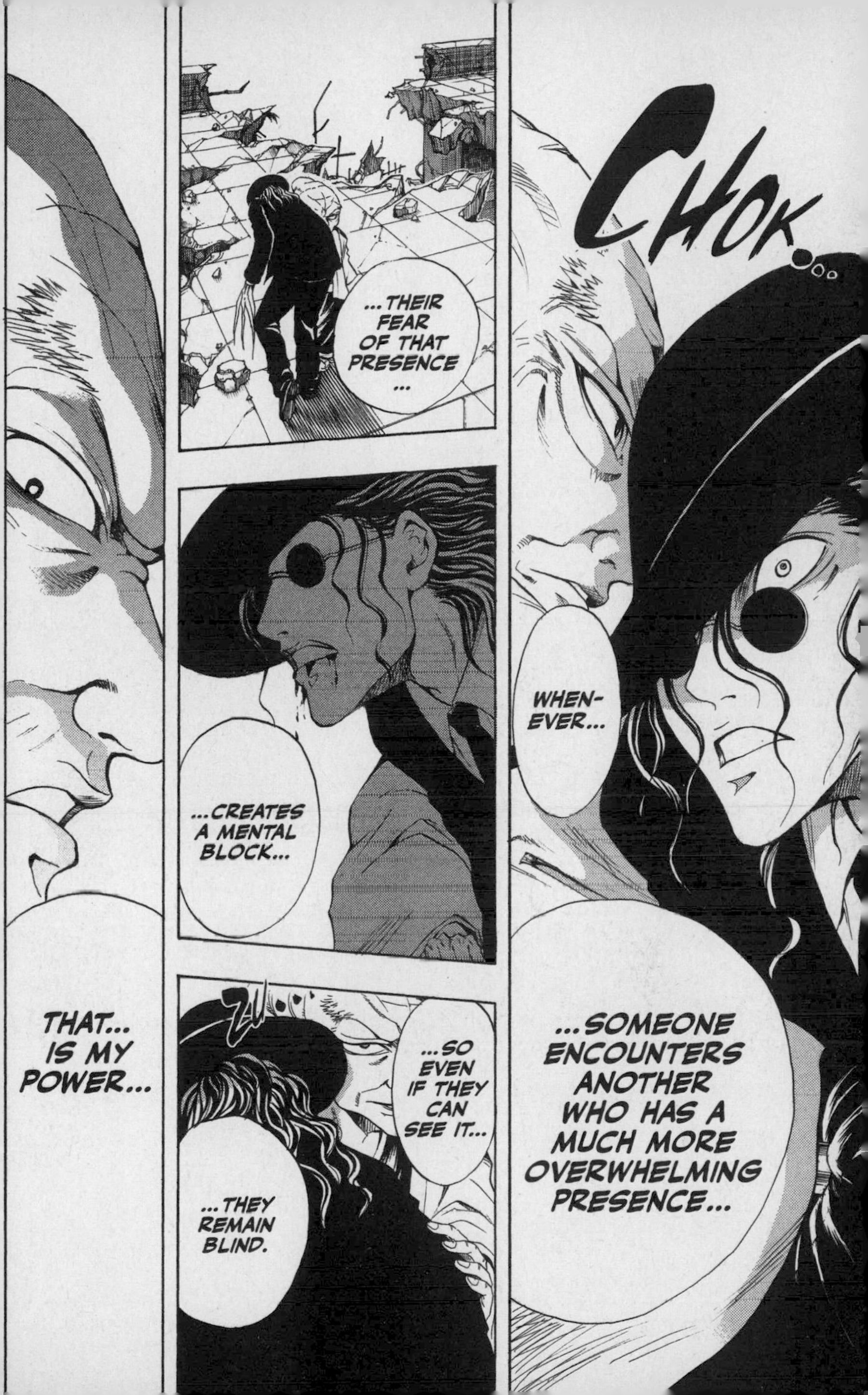
CHOK...
WHEN-EVER...
...SOMEONE ENCOUNTERS ANOTHER WHO HAS A MUCH MORE OVERWHELMING PRESENCE...
...THEIR FEAR OF THAT PRESENCE...
...CREATES A MENTAL BLOCK...
ZU
...SO EVEN IF THEY CAN SEE IT...
...THEY REMAIN BLIND.
THAT... IS MY POWER...

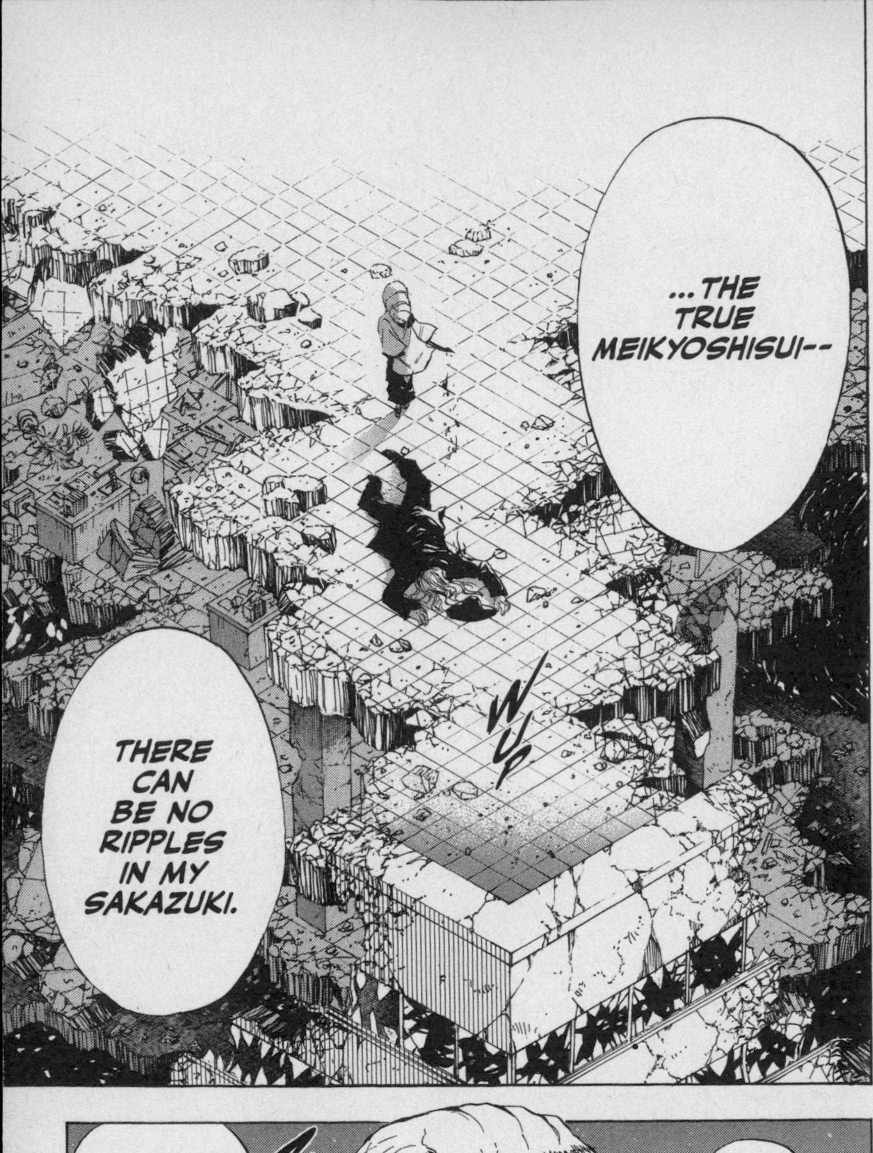
...THE TRUE MEIKYOSHISUI--
WUP
THERE CAN BE NO RIPPLES IN MY SAKAZUKI.

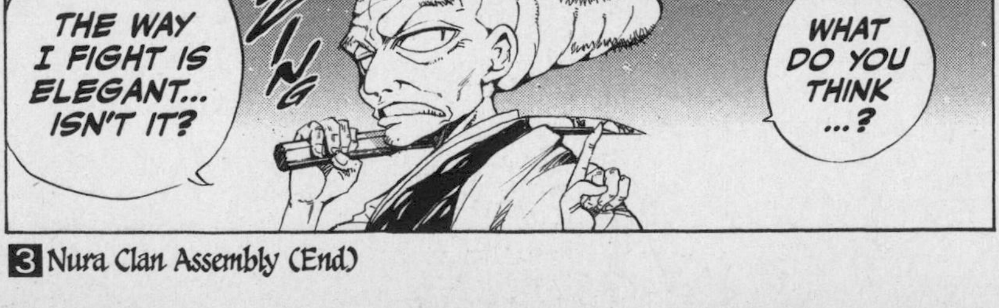
WHAT DO YOU THINK ...?
ZING
THE WAY I FIGHT IS ELEGANT... ISN'T IT?

3 Nura Clan Assembly (End)

Nura: Rise of the Yokai Clan **BONUS STORY**

Kiyojuji Paranormal Patrol Rivalry Episode

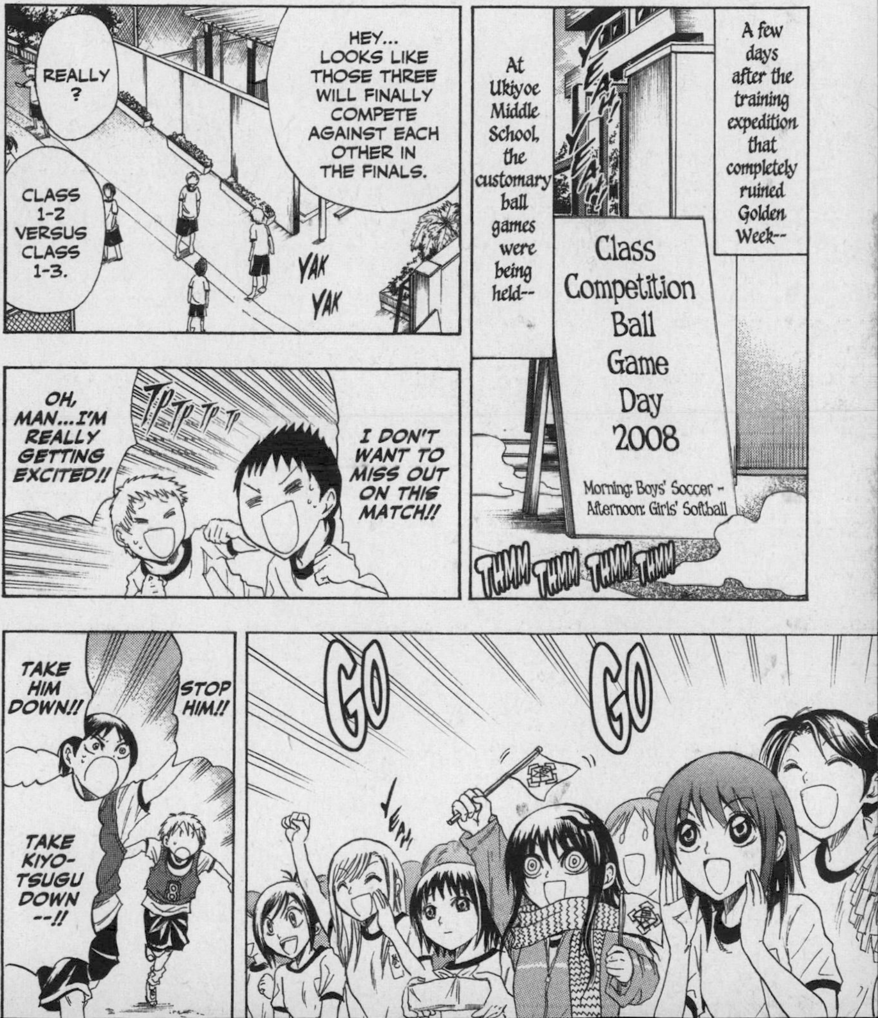
A few days after the training expedition that completely ruined Golden Week--
At Ukiyoe Middle School, the customary ball games were being held--
Class Competition Ball Game Day 2008
Morning: Boys' Soccer -- Afternoon: Girls' Softball
THMM THMM THMM THMM
HEY... LOOKS LIKE THOSE THREE WILL FINALLY COMPETE AGAINST EACH OTHER IN THE FINALS.
REALLY?
CLASS 1-2 VERSUS CLASS 1-3.
YAK YAK
I DON'T WANT TO MISS OUT ON THIS MATCH!!
OH, MAN...I'M REALLY GETTING EXCITED!!
TP TP TP TP
GO GO
STOP HIM!!
TAKE HIM DOWN!!
TAKE KIYOTSUGU DOWN--!!

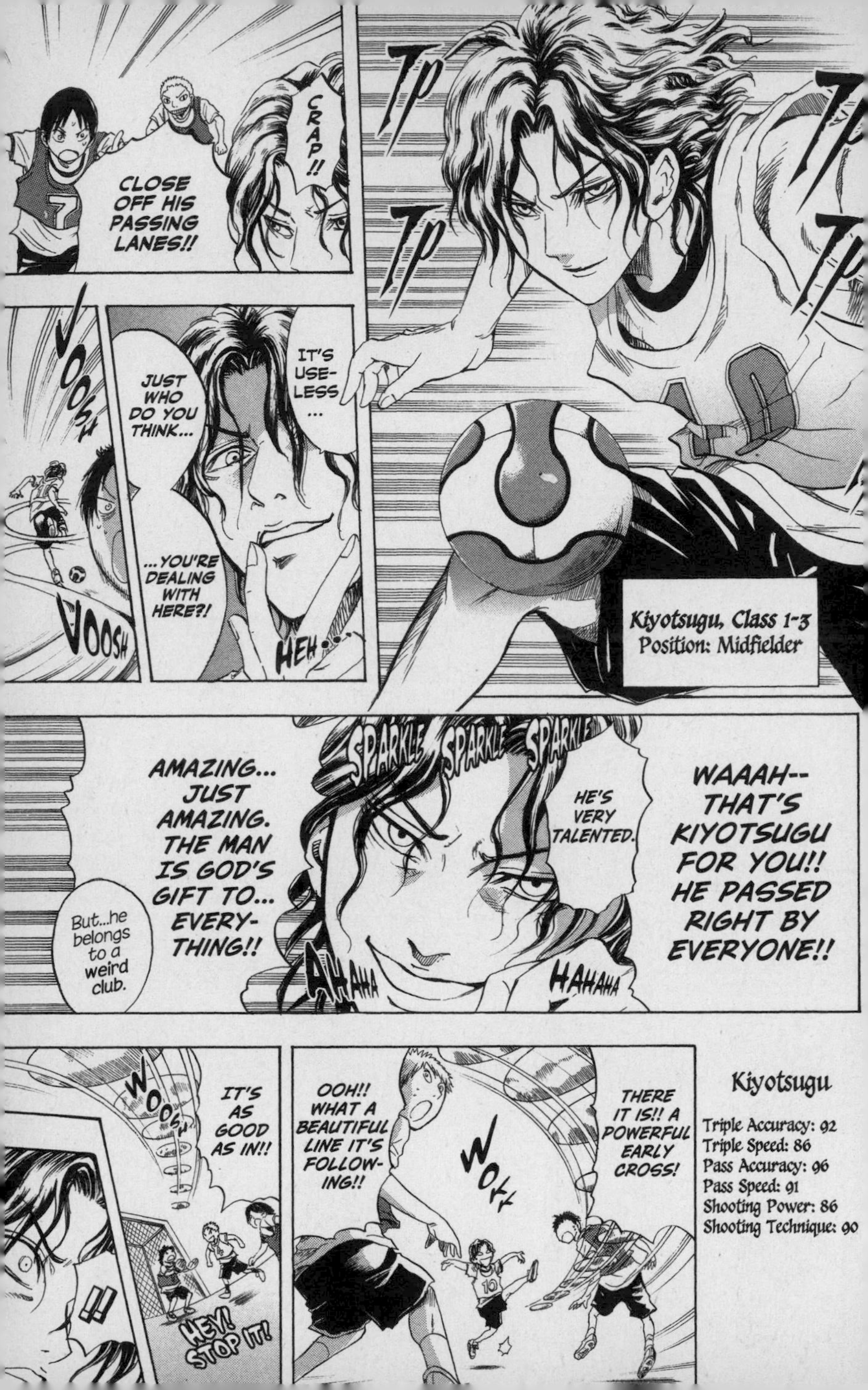
Tp
Tp
Tp
Tp
Kiyotsugu, Class 1-3
Position: Midfielder
CRAP!!
CLOSE OFF HIS PASSING LANES!!
IT'S USELESS...
JUST WHO DO YOU THINK...
...YOU'RE DEALING WITH HERE?!
HEH...
VOOSH
VOOSH
WAAAH-- THAT'S KIYOTSUGU FOR YOU!! HE PASSED RIGHT BY EVERYONE!!
HE'S VERY TALENTED.
SPARKLE SPARKLE SPARKLE
HAHAHA
AHAHA
AMAZING... JUST AMAZING. THE MAN IS GOD'S GIFT TO... EVERYTHING!!
But...he belongs to a weird club.
Kiyotsugu
Triple Accuracy: 92
Triple Speed: 86
Pass Accuracy: 96
Pass Speed: 91
Shooting Power: 86
Shooting Technique: 90
THERE IT IS!! A POWERFUL EARLY CROSS!
WOK
OOH!! WHAT A BEAUTIFUL LINE IT'S FOLLOWING!!
WOOSH
IT'S AS GOOD AS IN!!
!!
HEY! STOP IT!

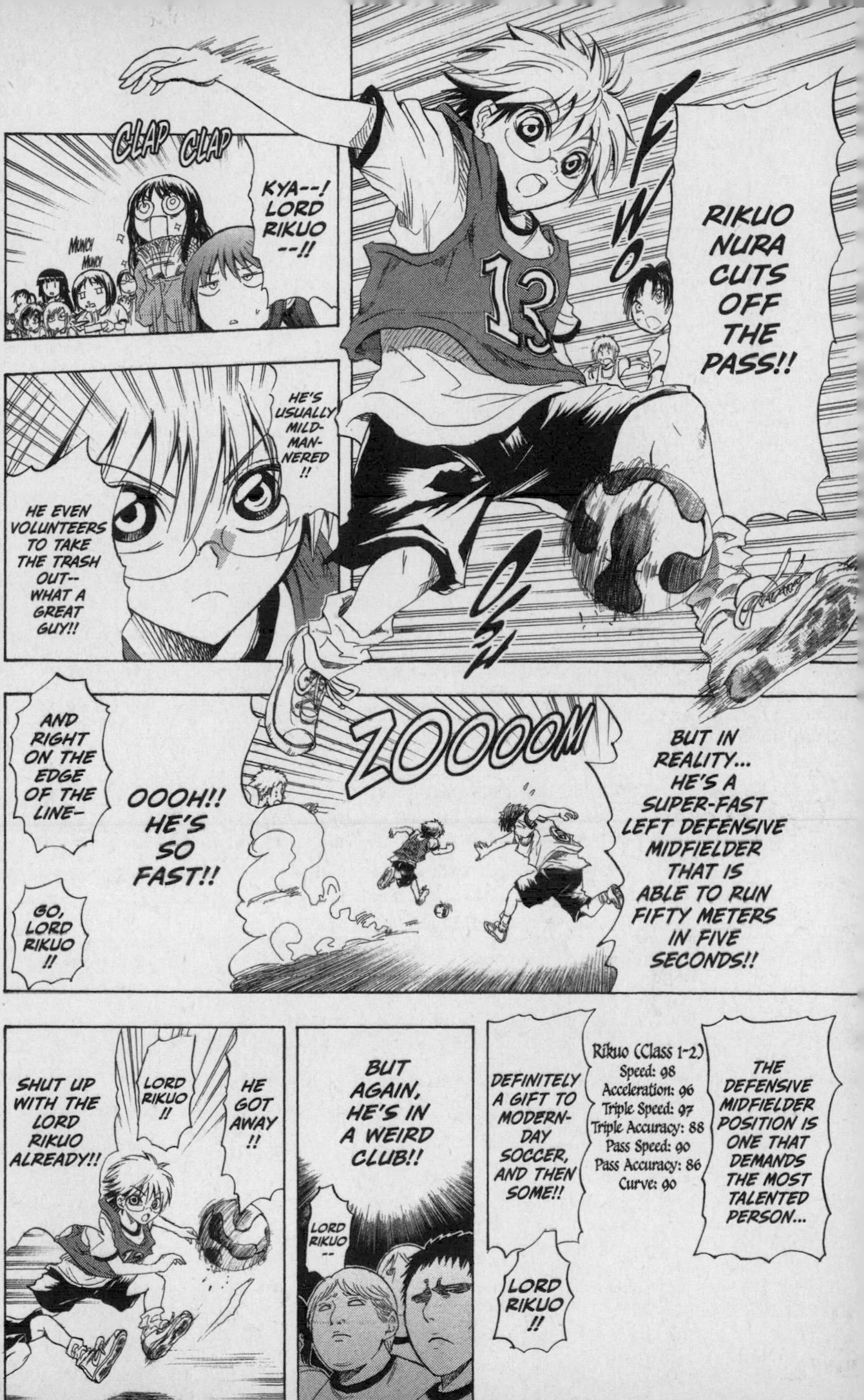
FWOO
RIKUO NURA CUTS OFF THE PASS!!
CLAP CLAP
KYA--! LORD RIKUO--!!
MUNCH MUNCH
HE'S USUALLY MILD-MANNERED!!
HE EVEN VOLUNTEERS TO TAKE THE TRASH OUT-- WHAT A GREAT GUY!!
BUT IN REALITY... HE'S A SUPER-FAST LEFT DEFENSIVE MIDFIELDER THAT IS ABLE TO RUN FIFTY METERS IN FIVE SECONDS!!
ZOOOOM
OOOH!! HE'S SO FAST!!
AND RIGHT ON THE EDGE OF THE LINE-
GO, LORD RIKUO!!
THE DEFENSIVE MIDFIELDER POSITION IS ONE THAT DEMANDS THE MOST TALENTED PERSON...
Rikuo (Class 1-2)
Speed: 98
Acceleration: 96
Triple Speed: 97
Triple Accuracy: 88
Pass Speed: 90
Pass Accuracy: 86
Curve: 90
DEFINITELY A GIFT TO MODERN-DAY SOCCER, AND THEN SOME!!
LORD RIKUO!!
BUT AGAIN, HE'S IN A WEIRD CLUB!!
LORD RIKUO--
HE GOT AWAY!!
LORD RIKUO!!
SHUT UP WITH THE LORD RIKUO ALREADY!!

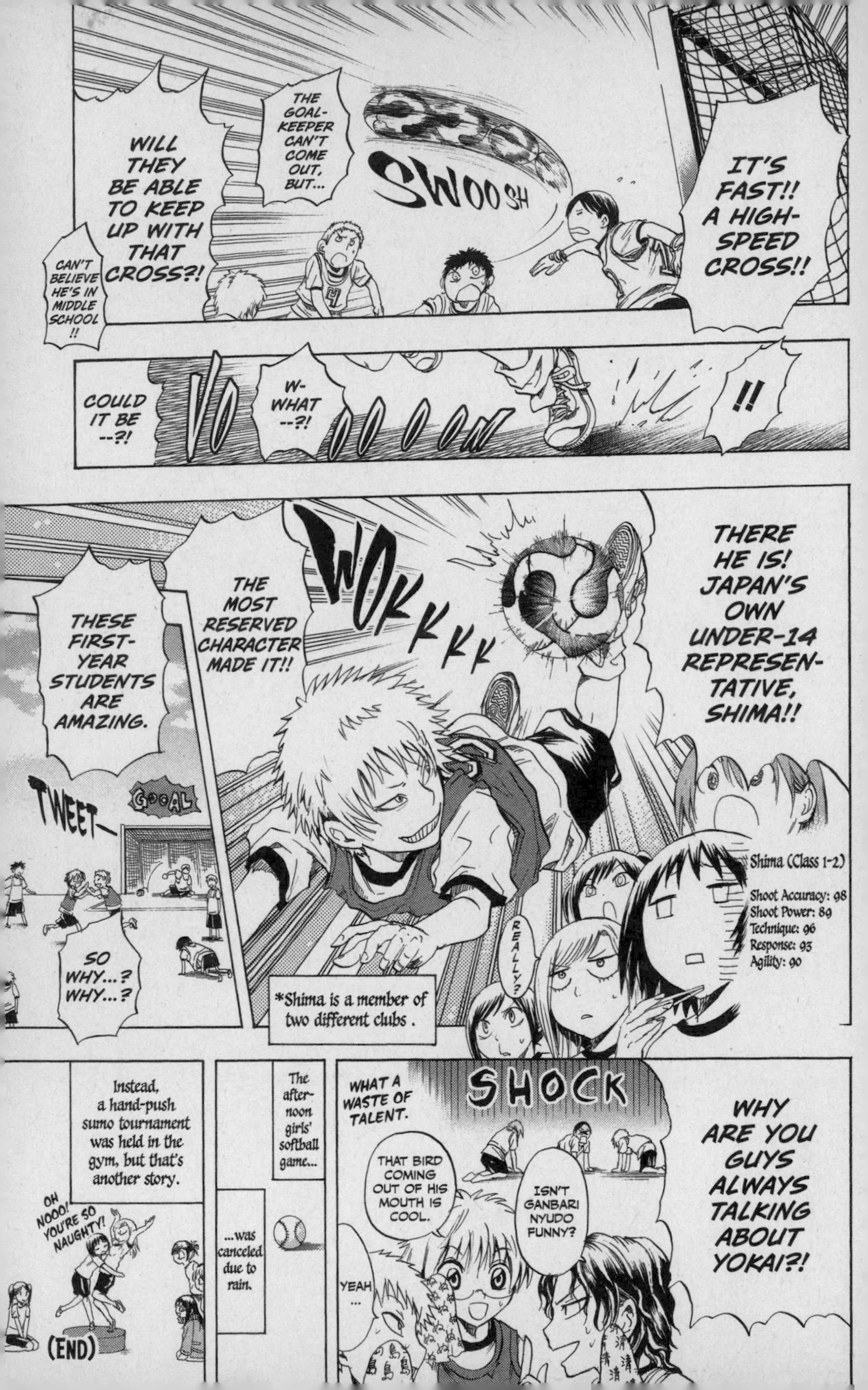
IT'S FAST!! A HIGH-SPEED CROSS!!
SWOOSH
THE GOAL-KEEPER CAN'T COME OUT, BUT...
WILL THEY BE ABLE TO KEEP UP WITH THAT CROSS?!
CAN'T BELIEVE HE'S IN MIDDLE SCHOOL!!
!!
VOOOOOOM
W-WHAT--?!
COULD IT BE--?!
THERE HE IS! JAPAN'S OWN UNDER-14 REPRESENTATIVE, SHIMA!!
Shima (Class 1-2)
Shoot Accuracy: 98
Shoot Power: 89
Technique: 96
Response: 93
Agility: 90
WOKKKK
THE MOST RESERVED CHARACTER MADE IT!!
REALLY?
*Shima is a member of two different clubs.
THESE FIRST-YEAR STUDENTS ARE AMAZING.
TWEET—
GOOAL
SO WHY...? WHY...?
WHY ARE YOU GUYS ALWAYS TALKING ABOUT YOKAI?!
SHOCK
WHAT A WASTE OF TALENT.
ISN'T GANBARI NYUDO FUNNY?
THAT BIRD COMING OUT OF HIS MOUTH IS COOL.
YEAH...
The afternoon girls' softball game...
...was canceled due to rain.
Instead, a hand-push sumo tournament was held in the gym, but that's another story.
OH NOOO! YOU'RE SO NAUGHTY!
(END)

YOU'RE READING THE WRONG WAY!

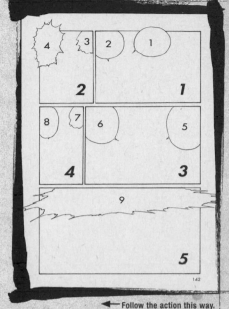

Nura: Rise of the Yokai Clan reads from right to left, starting in the upper-right corner. Japanese is read from right to left, meaning that action, sound effects, and word-balloon order are completely reversed from English order.

← Follow the action this way.

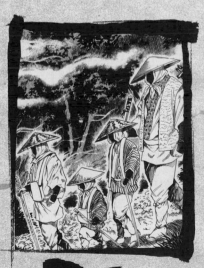

IN THE NEXT VOLUME...
88 DEMONS OF SHIKOKU

The Nura clan's turf has been invaded! A mysterious set of travelers arrives in Ukiyoe Town to wreak havoc and challenge Rikuo in his position as the leader of Japan's most powerful yokai syndicate. They even infiltrate his school! If Rikuo wants to maintain the Nura clan's status and protect his human friends from the rival yokai's malice, he's going to have to call his Hundred Demons to battle and prepare for his biggest fight yet!

AVAILABLE AUGUST 2011!